The End of Lawyers?

The End of Lawyers?

Rethinking the Nature of Legal Services

Richard Susskind

OXFORD
UNIVERSITY PRESS

OXFORD

UNIVERSITY PRESS

Great Clarendon Street, Oxford OX2 6DP

Oxford University Press is a department of the University of Oxford.
It furthers the University's objective of excellence in research, scholarship,
and education by publishing worldwide in

Oxford New York

Auckland Cape Town Dar es Salaam Hong Kong Karachi
Kuala Lumpur Madrid Melbourne Mexico City Nairobi
New Delhi Shanghai Taipei Toronto

With offices in

Argentina Austria Brazil Chile Czech Republic France Greece
Guatemala Hungary Italy Japan Poland Portugal Singapore
South Korea Switzerland Thailand Turkey Ukraine Vietnam
Oxford is a registered trade mark of Oxford University Press
in the UK and in certain other countries
Published in the United States
by Oxford University Press Inc., New York

British Library Cataloguing in Publication Data

Data available

Library of Congress Cataloging in Publication Data

Data available

Typeset by Glyph International, Bangalore, India
Printed in Great Britain
on acid-free paper by
Clays Ltd, St Ives plc

ISBN 978–0–19–954172–0 (Hbk)
978–0–19–959361–3 (Pbk)

1 3 5 7 9 10 8 6 4 2

I dedicate this book to mentors from my younger days

Robin Downie
Emeritus Professor of Moral Philosophy
at the University of Glasgow

and

Colin Tapper
Emeritus Professor of Law
at the University of Oxford

Preface to the Hardback Edition

I already know what many people think of this book.

Consistent with the current spirit of the Internet, extracts of an early draft of the first chapter were placed on *Times Online* in late 2007, alongside some commentary from experts and journalists.[1] Debate from readers was invited. I hoped that those who became involved in online discussion would enjoy having early access to some of my latest work, that the experience of engaging electronically would be fun, and that they would welcome the opportunity to have some input to the book. I am pleased to report that many tens of thousands of people visited the site.

Releasing the extracts early and online allowed me to test some of my ideas. Ordinarily, you write a book; it gets published; and after that, from reviews and feedback, you get a sense of what your readers think, where you have been misguided, and what topics are of greatest interest. And then you write a revised paperback or a second edition. But why not release the ideas and arguments a little earlier, and invite people who are interested to comment and debate? It is surely handy to have advance notice if you have lost the place, or let an error or two slip in, or perhaps neglected some crucial evidence.

It was an interesting experiment. In the event, I found the feedback posted at *Times Online* itself to be quite polarised—there were the sceptics (mainly lawyers) who did not seem to think they should read what I had to say before rejecting it; and there were the enthusiasts, often every bit as biased, who were immediately fond of anyone they thought might be taking a pot-shot at lawyers. Meanwhile, the most remarkable response arrived by conventional postal service and had clearly been prepared on an elderly manual typewriter. It was a three-page letter. And I was sent the carbon copies. There are many (younger) readers of this book who will not know what I am talking about. Suffice it to say that, in the world of law, old habits do indeed die hard.

What fascinated me most was that a great deal of insightful and challenging online discussion on the extracts sprang up elsewhere—on at least 40

---

[1] <http://www.timesonline.co.uk/tol/system/topicRoot/The_End_of_Lawyers>.

other websites and blogs.[2] What helped me most, however, were the considered and balanced responses by e-mail that came directly to me.

In the end, I have to say, none of the feedback led me to make fundamental alterations or to jettison great chunks of manuscript. But it did cause me to refine and tighten arguments, to insert more examples, to address likely objections more fully, and to be braver in some of my predictions.

I am therefore very grateful to Alex Spence, the legal editor of *Times Online* for setting up and managing the project. Frances Gibb, the legal editor at *The Times*, was also very supportive, as she has been of my work for many years, allowing me the space to write over 100 columns for the newspaper. My thanks in that context also go to Clare Hogan, who patiently tolerated many missed deadlines. I have drawn regularly from the case studies in these columns to support many of the claims in this book.

More generally, and from the heart, I thank a group of friends and colleagues who helped me in various ways while I prepared draft after draft. Some offered detailed comments on specific chapters, while others sent me e-mails that helped shape my thinking. The individuals in question are (in alphabetical order) Alex Allan, Ron Barger, David Bone, Simon Carne, Jeff Carr, Mark Chandler, Richard Cohen, Paul DiGiammarino, Matthew di Rienzo, Craig Glidden, David Goldberg, Dick Greener, Chris Harris, Michael Leathes, Michael Mainelli, David Maister, Iain Monaghan, Darryl Mountain, Martin Partington, Anthony Ruane, Mark Saville, and Conrad Young.

I was also very fortunate in having the ongoing moral support of Jeremy Hand, Paul Lippe, Ian Lloyd, Christopher Millard, and Alan Paterson, each of whom, often unknowingly, chivvied me on when the task looked impossibly daunting.

I am sure most authors are more systematic than I am in their working habits. Much of this book was prodded out with two fingers on my faithful Sony VAIO or with two thumbs on my ever-present Blackberry. Some early drafts were created by dictation and Tricia Cato deserves great praise for making sense of my too-speedy Glaswegian stream of consciousness, a series of sounds that no voice recognition system can yet comprehend.

Early versions of two important lines of argument were previously published: the evolutionary model of legal service (Chapter 2) was first laid out in the *Legal Technology Journal*, then under the editorship of Charles Christian;[3] while an initial formulation of my thinking on public legal information

---

[2] See for example <http://www.abajournal.com/news/susskind_are_lawyers_becoming_obselete> and <http://blogs.law.harvard.edu/ethicalesq/2007/10/28/the-end-of-lawyers-or-the-cartels-last-stand>.

[3] R Susskind, 'From bespoke to commodity' (2006) 1 *Legal Technology Journal*, 4.

policy (Section 7.8) was presented in *Intellectual Property*, a book edited by Charlotte Waelde and Hector MacQueen.[4]

Three people read and commented on the entire draft manuscript: Tony Williams, a close friend and collaborator whose ongoing support I value enormously; David Morley, a client over the past few years and an entirely enlightened law firm leader; and Gail Swaffield, whose talents as a legal technologist at the coal face are surpassed by no-one. Pouring over the full text of a book is a very major burden, and I owe these three busy people a huge debt of gratitude for taking on the job with such good humour. Their comments were of very considerable help.

As ever, my publishers, Oxford University Press, have been a pleasure to work with. Although no longer with OUP, Chris Rycroft must be mentioned and thanked – he commissioned the book in the first place and strongly supported its publication. I am also very pleased to express my appreciation to Luke Adams, Kirsty Allen, Andy Redman, Fiona Stables, Christopher Wogan, and Victoria Wright, each of whom contributed substantially to the publication process.

Finally, I have a loving family to thank. My parents, as ever, have always been on hand with a word of encouragement. My brother, Alan, is everything I could want from an older sibling. He is extremely supportive, available whenever I need him, but he is challenging too – his detailed comments on some of the ideas in this book gave me serious pause for thought.

I am blessed with two fine sons, Daniel and Jamie, both now at university. They are more scholarly than ever I was; and I have benefited hugely from their fertile minds. They have helped me more than they know. I am also blessed with a wonderful daughter, Ali, who has been with me in my study during much of the conception of this book – lighting up my workspace with her very special brand of happiness and humour. And Michelle, my wife, has once again (for the seventh time now) exhibited remarkable and uncommon patience during the fraught process of authoring; indeed, since 1981, when I began working on law and technology, she has always shown unwavering confidence in my various writing projects.

To my family, friends, and colleagues, once again I extend the heartiest of thanks.

Richard Susskind
August 2008
Radlett, England

[4] R Susskind, 'The public domain and public sector information', in C Waelde and H MacQueen (eds), *Intellectual Property* (Cheltenham: Edward Elgar, 2007).

Contents

List of Figures

Introduction to the Paperback Edition

The central theme of this book is that lawyers should change the way they work. Better and more efficient techniques for delivering legal services are now emerging and I urge the legal profession to embrace them. Clients—from multi-national corporations to individual citizens—deserve nothing less from their professional advisers.

This theme has also been central to my work over the last 30 years. During this period, my conviction about the need for changes in the legal system has remained fairly steady. In contrast, I think it fair to say that the position of most legal practitioners has shifted. In response to my published views on the future of the legal world, I believe that some lawyers have now progressed through all 'four stages of acceptance' identified by the British biologist, JBS Haldane:

 (i) this is worthless nonsense;

 (ii) this is an interesting, but perverse, point of view;

(iii) this is true, but quite unimportant;

(iv) I always said so.[1]

Haldane was speaking about reactions to new ideas in science and not about the law. But his words resonate in today's legal marketplace.

In November 2008, when this book was first published, many of my claims and arguments were met with the third of Haldane's responses. Lawyers conceded that there was some truth in what I had to say—for example, about new ways of sourcing legal work—but they doubted its relevance for daily legal practice. Nonetheless, I was actually quite pleased. No longer was I interesting but perverse, as seemed to be thought in 2000 when *Transforming the Law*[2] appeared; and, reassuringly, I was now not thought to be the purveyor of worthless nonsense, which generally was the reaction in 1996 to *The Future of Law*[3] and, much earlier, in *1987*, to *Expert Systems in Law*.[4]

---

[1] JBS Haldane, 'The Truth about Death' (1963) 58 *Journal of Genetics* 463–4.
[2] Oxford: Oxford University Press, 2000.
[3] Oxford: Oxford University Press, 1996.
[4] Oxford: Oxford University Press, 1987.

Remarkably, though, in less than two years, we have now migrated into Haldane's fourth stage. Around the world, stirred by the recession, senior lawyers are now sagely proclaiming not simply that the time has come for the profession to modernize and transform itself but that they have been anticipating this for years. In this massive wave of cognitive dissonance, I am rather disconcerted: after decades in the wilderness, it is strange to have become mainstream.

That said, by no means all lawyers concur with what is written in the pages that follow. In fact, some seem to disagree with *all* of it. Often, before I speak at a conference, I am warned, in hushed tones by a friendly organizer, that I should tread warily because some formidable legal dignitary is in the audience and that he or she disagrees with my book. I often quip: the naysayer cannot surely object to *everything* in the text. The index and bibliography, for instance, are entirely unobjectionable.

To oppose the entire book is surely to admit that it has not been read. Some of what is said here is not contentious. The reality is that I present a wide range of analyses, hypotheses, case studies, recommendations, and predictions. I am emphatically not putting forward a single, all-or-nothing argument, or a unified theory-of-everything that can be shot down by a single, well-aimed missile. As I like to say, I am simply laying out a buffet of likely options for the future and am happy for readers to select some of what is on offer and leave the rest to one side. Naturally, I would prefer that most of what I say is accepted, but my mission is to widen horizons and not to force-feed.

Admittedly, I do predict great changes in the legal market that may cause discomfort in the reactionary camp: a movement towards the commoditization of legal services; a shift toward 'decomposing' legal work into its constituent tasks and sourcing each in the most efficient way; a related increase in the outsourcing, off-shoring, and, as I say, the 'multi-sourcing' of legal work; the emergence of new forms of legal businesses underpinned by novel business models and innovative external funding; a rapid increase in the impact of various disruptive information technologies; and much more besides. These changes are being hastened, I claim, by the growing need for most clients (businesses and individuals) to secure 'more for less'—more legal service at less cost. I maintain that there are only two sustainable strategies here.[5] The first is for in-house departments not only to be vastly more

---

[5] For dispute resolution, I have recently become aware of a third possible strategy—third party litigation funding. See S Garber, *Alternative Litigation Financing in the United States* (Santa Monica: Rand Corporation, 2010), AJ Sebok, 'The Inauthentic Claim', forthcoming, (2011) 64 *Vanderbilt Law Review*, and J-F Ng, 'The Role of the Doctrines of Champerty and Maintenance in Arbitration' (2010) 76 *Arbitration* 208–213. I am grateful to Selvyn Seidel for introducing me to this field.

efficient in their deployment of the traditional combination of internal labour and external law firms, but also to ensure that work is undertaken, where appropriate, by less costly suppliers of legal services, such as legal process outsourcers and paralegals. The second strategy is for General Counsel to collaborate with one another and so share the costs of some common legal expenses. In short, the options are either to cut the costs, and I call this the 'efficiency strategy', or to share the costs, which I refer to as the 'collaboration strategy'. These strategies apply not only to large volume, low value work but also, and vitally, to the routine elements of high value work.

For the legal profession, this book suggests numerous radical consequences. For example, it follows from what I say that the market for the traditional legal practitioner will diminish, as will the need for the traditionally trained law graduate; many small firms and sole practitioners will struggle to survive; many medium-sized firms will merge; and some large firms will shrink, while others will fold. Some sceptics will respond by saying that I may be wrong about the future. To them I often say that if there is a reasonable possibility of my predictions coming to pass, then the implications for the profession are so profound that lawyers should surely be preparing in some way.

But I do not wish to concede any ground whatsoever on the central thrust of the book, and I stand by the principal arguments and conclusions. My purpose in this new Introduction, accordingly, is not to revise or revisit them but instead to offer a brief update on my thinking and to provide some new techniques and tools. The update is not comprehensive but it should give a sense of my views on the impact of the recession on the legal market, on some notable recent developments, and on the rise of legal process outsourcing. As for the new techniques, I present a tool for analyzing the legal market and four models for legal businesses of the future. I conclude by suggesting how senior managers in legal businesses might meet some pressing strategic challenges.

Impact of the recession

Although first published in late 2008, I completed the manuscript of this book many months earlier, before anyone had any sense of the depth of the world's economic problems. What, then, is the impact of the recession on my various forecasts? Generally, I believe that the dreadful economic conditions are accelerating the various effects and phenomena I predict in this book.

This is to be expected—many of the changes that I envisage and advocate are driven by the market's need to reduce the cost of legal services. As that need has become more pressing, then the imperative to embrace, say, multi-sourcing, becomes correspondingly stronger.

Some of the consequences of the growing pressures facing the legal profession were identified in late 2009 in a study of the US legal industry, commissioned by LexisNexis.[6] According to this research, clients in the US say that law firms are not doing enough to respond to the economic downturn, while law firms claim that clients are too focused on costs. It was ever thus. Pricing, quite predictably, emerges as the top issue facing the profession, according to 71 per cent of the 150 in-house lawyers surveyed, and to 60 per cent of the 300 practitioners in private practice. Taking the various findings together, US lawyers seem to agree that, in due course, hourly billing will be largely displaced by alternative billing structures; but not in 2010 and never entirely. And clients are keener on this shift than law firms.

This snapshot of the US broadly aligns with similar research conducted in England by Eversheds, the law firm. Their work identifies a shift towards a buyer's legal market, the emergence of clients as major agents of change, downward pressures on fees, new efficiencies being driven by the recession, and the uptake of novel ways of sourcing legal work.[7]

My own research and consulting work suggest that an analogous survey in the City of London today would yield very similar results. Here, many General Counsel tell me that they are under mounting pressure from their boards to cut their legal budgets severely—up to 40 per cent—and so they are naturally turning to their law firms and asking them to rethink their hourly rates and charging models. In turn, in the City and across the UK, law firms have indeed been proposing volume discounts, blended rates, fixed fees, various forms of value billing, and more. However, astute clients say, with justification, that when most firms present alternatives to hourly billing, the underlying modeling is still based on time spent, that firms are not inclined to bid in a way that will reduce their profitability, and so the proposals contain charging models that may superficially seem more palatable but do not substantially reduce the final bill. This, in my view, is a truth that is rarely articulated by commentators.

In the end, the key issue is whether charging differently will, in hard numbers, yield the scale of savings that clients require, or whether firms and

---

[6] See 'State of the Legal Industry Survey' (2009) <http://www.lexisnexis.com>.

[7] See *The Client's Revolution: the impact of the recession on the legal sector* (London: Eversheds, 2010), available at <http://www.eversheds.com>.

clients need to start working differently. Intense recent interest in legal process outsourcing, in leasing lawyers, and in sub-contracting to lower cost
jurisdictions, suggests that some clients are encouraging radical new ways of
working. The business case is clear: with outsourcing, for example, if routine
and repetitive work can be undertaken in India at one tenth of the cost, this
is going to bring savings far in excess of, say, volume discounts from firms
working in the traditional manner.

But what will be the longer term impact of the recession? Given these
changes in billing and working practices, opinion in the US, according to the
LexisNexis survey, is fairly evenly split on the future of the legal industry—
about half of the clients and law firms surveyed believe the recession will
permanently change the way that legal business is undertaken.

Whether the profession is enduring a temporary adjustment or a longer-
term structural upheaval is also a matter of discussion in the UK. Some City
firms are embracing the hunker-down strategy. This involves cutting costs,
winning as much work as possible, keeping morale up, and hanging on in
there until the economy recovers, when, it is assumed, pre-recession working and billing practices will be resumed. Other firms believe that large volume, low margin legal work is being irreversibly changed but that, for their
high end work, clients will be happy in more buoyant times to revert to conventional ways.

There is a growing group of senior lawyers and clients who are less sanguine.
They see that these troubled times are indeed exposing many current working
practices as unjustifiably inefficient, that new ways of working are emerging,
that the costs of routine and repetitive legal work can be cut dramatically, that
boards and CEOs are now aware that lawyering can be conducted differently,
and that irreversible change is likely to extend to some parts of high end work,
such as document review and due diligence. On this view, when the economic
storm passes and the dust settles, there will be no return to past practices.
Even if the economy bounces back with gusto, clients will not suddenly feel
impelled to go back to the old tariff.

I largely agree with those who are saying, essentially, that the genie cannot
be put back into the bottle. But I think there is an exception to this rule of no
return—it seems to me that when, in the future, major clients need external
legal advice on bet-the-ranch deals or disputes, then they will still tend to
turn to one of a handful of top firms (on the 'no-one ever got fired for hiring
IBM' principle) and this kind of work will not be price sensitive (on the 'a million here or there makes no odds in the scheme of things' principle). In other
words, for big-ticket work, the leading firms may indeed be allowed to revert
to unconstrained hourly billing at eye-watering rates.

But I also believe there might be an exception to this exception, one that might change the legal market for ever. Consider the possibility of one of this handful of top firms breaking rank and radically changing the way it works, perhaps through off-shoring, computerization, or sub-contracting. If such a firm were then able to offer the comfort of its brand along with the talents of its finest experts, and yet at a much lower overall cost of service, then it would be hard to imagine, despite the price insensitivity, that major clients would be comfortable going elsewhere. In turn, other leading firms would have to respond and change would cascade across the market.

In discussing economic recovery and future trends in the market with law firms, I am always struck by their attraction to the status quo. Most law firms, I sense, would prefer a return to the working practices and charging models of around 2006; as well they might, because substantial profits were enjoyed at that time. A very few, the most likely market leaders of the future, think differently. They say that, if a reinvigorated economy allows a reversion to past practices, then they will nonetheless press ahead with radical change. They say this because they see great opportunity in working differently— better and less costly service for clients and competitive advantage for the firms themselves. They hope for the return to the mind-set of 2006 because they know this to be the comfort zone of most of their rivals. It is comfortable not just because it is familiar but because it is reassuring to stay with the pack. The deeper truth here, as I say in Chapter 8, is that most firms (other than market leaders) are more concerned about avoiding competitive disadvantage than gaining competitive advantage.

As for in-house lawyers, they betray a puzzling lack of self-confidence when discussing the future. They will often ask me if I think law firms will go back to their old ways when business becomes brisker. I always reply that it is very much up to them as customers to answer that question. If in-house lawyers do not want the reassertion of past habits, they must direct the market accordingly and emphatically.

They must also bear in mind that they will increasingly find themselves subject to greater scrutiny than ever before. As it becomes common knowledge, for example, that legal work can be sourced in different ways, chief executives, chief finance officers, and non-executive members on boards will quite naturally ask their General Counsel whether they are embracing and maximizing the opportunities of these new ways of working. To help shift their mind-set and prepare for this new environment, I suggest that in-house lawyers apply a new test when considering how best to source their legal work. I call this the 'Shareholder Test'—when a costed proposal for the conduct of a deal or dispute is being considered, would a commercially astute shareholder, who was familiar with the growing number of alternative ways of sourcing legal work, consider what is contemplated as representing value for money? If law firms return to pre-recession billing and working practices and in-house lawyers countenance this, they will invariably fail the Shareholder Test.

Recent developments

Much has happened in the legal sector in the two years since I finished writing the first edition of this book. One way of gauging the rapidity of change and progress in the legal sector is by looking at the nature and scale of the published literature on the legal profession. In my view, in the quarter century since I began my doctoral research in law and computers, that is, between 1983 and 2008, only a handful of books (apart from my own, I feel bound to say) could be said to address genuine transformation in the way in which legal services are delivered.[8] Strikingly, in the two years since I submitted the manuscript for this book, I have come across eight new books that contain fundamental challenges to conventional legal service and practice. They represent a variety of genres. Some are more scholarly and better researched; others are more practical and action-oriented. But together they have in common and reflect an unprecedented willingness to question the way that lawyers have worked in the past and to point to a very different future.

Perhaps the boldest and certainly the most prescriptive is *The Smarter Legal Model* by Trevor Faure, who is General Counsel at Ernst & Young.[9] Drawing heavily on management theory, economics, and organizational psychology, and rooted also in his extensive practical experience as an in-house lawyer, Faure offers a set of tools to help reduce costs, increase legal coverage, improve compliance, and increase client satisfaction. More ambitiously, he casts aside the traditional, often fraught, commercial relationship between law firms and their clients and replaces this with a species of partnership arrangement,

---

[8] My short-list of the most important are ME Katsh, *The Electronic Media and the Transformation of Law* (Oxford: Oxford University Press, 1989); ME Katsh, *Law in a Digital World* (Oxford: Oxford University Press, 1995); and M Parsons, *Effective Knowledge Management for Law Firms* (New York: Oxford University Press, 2004).

[9] T Faure, *The Smarter Legal Model: more from less* (London: The Practical Law Company, 2010).

under which the business interests of the in-house lawyers and their external advisers are much better aligned.

Many of Faure's themes are reflected, more anecdotally and in less detail, in *Bright Ideas*,[10] a collection of 26 essays, written by a variety of prominent legal figures in the legal industry; and in *Unbound*,[11] which identifies seven major trends in legal service, based on interviews with a similar troop of leading lawyers. Both of these books exude a sense of unrest and impatience—a group of senior, bold, imaginative lawyers (from firms and in-house) who are suggesting, in a variety of ways, that legal work can and should be undertaken differently.

On the face of it, Philip Howard has an even more radical message, because he is the author of a controversially-titled volume, *Life Without Lawyers*.[12] As I should know better than most, however, we should never judge a book by its title. In the event, Howard's book is a damning indictment not of lawyers, but of the law itself. His focus is on the US legal system. Echoing my theme of 'hyperregulation',[13] Howard laments the excessive legal bureaucracy, the decades of accumulated regulation, and the pervasive litigation, which combine, he says, to restrict citizens' freedoms and to encourage individuals and organizations to behave ever more defensively and litigiously. His mission is to liberate Americans from too much law. Lawyers are largely let off the hook, which is a shortcoming because there can be little doubt that some, if not many, US litigators promote rather than discourage litigation. In common with the other authors mentioned here, however, Howard's is a call for comprehensive change in the law and not mild reform.

According to Julie Macfarlane, substantial change has already occurred in the world of dispute resolution. In *The New Lawyer*,[14] her focus is on Canada and the United States. Based on a decade of extensive empirical research, she charts a move away from lawyers as combative, gladiatorial, adversarial advisers to lawyers as empathetic counsellors who are more inclined to negotiate, mediate, and seek consensus; and to do so with more active participation of clients than accompanies conventional litigation. Macfarlane shows that many stereotypes of legal advisers are outdated and that a new

---

[10] EL Dance, (ed.), *Bright Ideas: Insights from Legal Luminaries Worldwide* (Minneapolis: Mill City Press, 2009).

[11] D Galbenski, *Unbound: How Entrepreneurship Is Dramatically Transforming Legal Services Today* (Royal Oak: Lumen Legal, 2009).

[12] PK Howard, *Life Without Lawyers* (New York: Norton, 2009).

[13] See pp 18–19 of this book, and *The Future of Law*, pp 12–18.

[14] J Macfarlane, *The New Lawyer* (Vancouver: UBC Press, 2008).

breed of lawyer may well be emerging; lawyers who are as skilled at pre-empting disputes as they have traditionally been at escalating them.

Meanwhile, the American Bar Association is to be congratulated for pub-lishing two practical guides for lawyers, one on the use of knowledge tools and the other on technologies that enable collaboration amongst lawyers.[15] These texts are much more than 'how to' aids. If their teachings were imple-mented, lawyers would work very differently. No longer would the legal adviser be an isolated sole practitioner (more or less). Instead lawyers would become consummate team players, who would avoid duplication of effort by capturing and nurturing their knowledge and sharing their experience with their colleagues and clients. More than this, the service on offer from lawyer to client would shift from being a one-to-one consultative advisory service to a one-to-many information service. Full-scale adoption of knowl-edge and collaboration tools would transform the work of lawyers.

Also in a practical vein, and on a subject topic that has profound implica-tions for the practice of law, is Michael Bell's book on legal outsourcing.[16] As I indicate in this Introduction, outsourcing creates enormous opportunities for clients and threats to conventional firms. Bell's manual, complete with case studies, is a useful guide to the key business and management issues, including the benefits, the risks, the importance of quality control, the art of vendor selection, and the regulatory implications of outsourcing.

The publication of the eight books I identify here constitutes a clear signal, I suggest, of an upsurge of interest in alternative ways of delivering legal ser-vice. They reflect fresh, innovative, and entrepreneurial thinking in the legal world; a new open-mindedness amongst some lawyers at least; a willingness to re-invent, to re-think, and to re-design legal businesses. A very few years ago, there was very little appetite for this kind of thinking. Today, in contrast, I am frequently asked by senior lawyers to suggest reading materials on the future of legal service. Not only am I able to point to these books but some more serious and scholarly writings in the field are also appearing.[17]

Aside from the growing literature on the modernization and transforma-tion of legal service, there have been numerous other developments that

---

[15] M Lauritsen, *The Lawyer's Guide to Working Smarter with Knowledge Tools* (Chicago: ABA, 2010), and D Kennedy and T Mighell, *The Lawyer's Guide to Collaboration Tools and Technologies* (Chicago: ABA, 2008).

[16] MD Bell, *Implementing a Successful Legal Outsourcing Engagement* (London: Ark, 2009).

[17] Two of the best examples of new scholarship are M Sako, 'Make-or-Buy Decisions in Legal Services: A Strategic Perspective', Working Paper, Revised (June 2010), available at <http://www.sbs.ox.ac.uk>, and MC Regan Jr and TH Palmer, 'Supply chains and porous boundaries: the disaggregation of legal services' (2010) 78 *Fordham Law Review* 2137–2191.

demonstrate just how rapidly the legal sector is evolving. In the next few paragraphs, I select a few of these to give a flavour of the progress being made.

I start with the systems that are now being introduced in the new Supreme Court of the United Kingdom. When preparing the manuscript for this book, in early 2008, I expressed the hope that these systems would become a flagship for a wide range of case management technologies.[18] In the event, I believe that the Supreme Court, which opened in October 2009, is now equipped to be the UK's most technologically-advanced court. One innovation is that, in each of the three courtrooms, there are four fixed cameras. These record all proceedings which will, in due course, I expect, be available on the Web. These filming arrangements are unique in the courts of England, Wales, and Northern Ireland, where cameras have been forbidden in the past. The courts also have document display systems. When barristers argue their cases, the precise pages under discussion can appear instantaneously on the screens. This should eliminate the need for Justices to search for paper-based folders and documents. Justices can also bring laptops into court. On these, it is possible for them to highlight text within their own electronic copies of the case materials, add comments, and copy and paste relevant words. Later, these annotations and extracts can be gathered together as searchable collections of notes. It is also possible for the Justices to roam around the documents, jumping from one to another using hyperlinks. These features are enabled by another innovation—electronic filing (e-filing). Unless permission is given, all documents and bundles submitted to the court *must* soon be sent both in electronic form and as conventional paper-based files: the core volume of documents will be submitted as a single, bookmarked PDF document. For each case, this will give the Justices a convenient electronic document bundle that behaves like a mini-website. Another advantage of e-filing is that the documents feed easily into the Court's case management systems. These are the back office facilities that support the everyday tasks of document filing, case progression, and listing. The system, in turn, provides officials and Justices with fully electronic virtual case files. Meanwhile, any web user can determine the status of cases before the Court. Details are fed from the case management system onto the Court's website. Citizens can view summary information, while practitioners can peruse in greater detail.[19]

---

[18] See p 206.
[19] See <http://www.supremecourt.gov.uk>.

Staying with the topic of dispute resolution, but in an environment quite unlike that of the Supreme Court, I was amazed recently to learn of the number of disagreements that arise and are settled on eBay. The world's largest online marketplace, eBay has more than 90 million active users. In 2009, around $60 billion worth of goods were sold on eBay. Inevitably disputes arise. What I found remarkable was the number of disputes—about *60 million* disputes each year. As the authors of a paper on this subject note, 'When the tally of disputes runs into the millions, human-powered dispute resolution cannot handle the scale of disputes'.[20] Instead, ODR (online dispute resolution) is used—efficiently and to good effect.[21] Why on earth can we not deploy ODR in resolving other disputes that arise in society? The sceptics will say that ODR only works for hi-tech people and business that is conducted online. But this is misguided—most people who use eBay are not especially hi-tech and the disputes that arise are rarely about online issues. Legal policy-makers and litigators around the world should be investigating ODR in depth. In my view, in years to come, and especially for the Internet generation, ODR will become a mainstream technique for resolving disputes.

Lawyers who find it hard to accept that IT might transform legal work should digest the achievements of LegalZoom, a US-based business that leads the way in providing online legal documents.[22] Since their launch in 2001, their vision has been to help people create their own legal documents and so put the law within the reach of millions of people—reliably and online. They believe it should be easy for non-lawyers to create wills, incorporate businesses, register trade marks, and take care of everyday legal matters without instructing costly lawyers. I have admired LegalZoom from a distance for several years but this year I was impressed to learn the results of recent market research that they undertook. According to this work, LegalZoom is now the best known online legal service in the US, and its brand is better known in the US than that of any law firm. Remarkably too, they have served over 1,000,000 customers. I take this statistic to vindicate the hypothesis I advanced in 1996, in *The Future of Law*, about the realization of what I called the 'latent legal market'. I claimed that non-lawyers who, in the past, had not been able to benefit from legal guidance because it was too

---

[20] C Rule and C Nagarajan, 'Leveraging the Wisdom of Crowds: The eBay Community Court and the Future of Online Dispute Resolution' (2010), p 1, (paper prepared for Dispute Resolution Conference 2010, organized by the Continuing Legal Education Society of British Columbia).

[21] See pp 217–224 of this book.

[22] See <http://www.legalzoom.com>. More generally, for a broader view of the extraordinary progress that has been made in legal technology, see A Paliwala, (ed), *A History of Legal Informatics* (Zaragoza: University of Zaragoza Press, 2010).

costly or impractical, would, in the future, be able to avail themselves of affordable, convenient, online service. That future has now arrived.[23]

Unlike their many users, some lawyers are perhaps deterred by the very name 'LegalZoom' because they feel it lacks the gravitas of, say, 'Messrs. Tulkinghorn & Vholes'. These lawyers no doubt also feel a wheezy exasperation when they hear talk of the social networking and micro-blogging service known as 'Twitter'.[24] Very simply, Twitter enables its users to send short text messages known as 'tweets' to their 'followers' who are friends or other interested parties. And users, in turn, can follow others. Although created in 2006, Twitter was almost unheard of amongst lawyers as this book went to print in 2008. It now has more than 100 million users worldwide. By the end of 2007, approximately 500,000 tweets per quarter were posted; by the end of 2008, this figure had risen to 100 million; by the end of 2009, there was a further rise to 2 billion tweets per quarter; and, in the first quarter of 2010, 4 billion tweets were posted.[25] I find it exhilarating to think that a new tool for communicating can so rapidly take hold in our world. Most lawyers with whom I speak dismiss Twitter as yet another plaything for their children. Of what possible relevance, they inquire, could this possibly be for a senior legal practitioner? I reply that I know quite a few General Counsel and senior in-house lawyers who now use Twitter and regularly send out messages about what they are doing, what they are thinking, and where they are going; and if my clients were sending out regular updates on their news and views, I would want to be on the receiving end, even if the medium has a slightly silly name.

Another technology that I have seen advancing rapidly in the past two years has been e-learning. I was asked in 2009 to undertake a 5-year review of e-learning at the College of Law in England.[26] I was surprised and encouraged to find the extent to which electronic tutorials and online supervision have already changed the learning experience of law students on the College's Legal Practice Course. More than 400 'i-Tutorials' have been developed. These are a type of webcast—online, head-and-shoulders video recordings of legal experts, with slides on the side. Students find these mini-lectures convenient. They can be stopped, started, and replayed; and they are portable too, in that they can be viewed on laptops and handhelds. While many law firms and law schools have dabbled in webcasting, the College has led

[23] *The Future of Law*, p 27, and pp 273–4.

[24] <http://www.twitter.com>.

[25] Compare my cautious reference to Twitter on p 107 of this book, n 9—'If "micro-blogging" takes off ...'.

[26] R Susskind, 'The College of Law E-learning: 5-year Review' (July 2009), available at <http://college-of-law.co.uk>.

the way in industrializing and professionalizing the production process. It is hard to understand why all law schools are not embracing this technology. More controversially, the College has also gone a step further and developed a 'supervised' mode of e-learning. On this mode there is one-to-one supervision by tutors but it is virtual rather than face-to-face, so that the students rarely attend the College. In spirit, this creates what I call an 'electronic Oxbridge'—the strengths of the traditional tutorial system are embraced (the pressure, stimulation, and individual attention of a personal expert tutor) but achieved in an affordable and practical way. Lectures, again, are replaced by i-Tutorials, and tutors keep in touch with students by e-mail. Other tools, such as instant messaging, Skype, and webinars will soon improve the experience. The feedback from students is largely enthusiastic. The online facilities are said to be flexible, re-usable, green, and ideal for part-timers or those who live far from the College. And, on the supervised mode particularly, students welcome the one-to-one attention from tutors. Like the practice of law, the teaching of law is being transformed.

Turning briefly away from lawyers, it is appropriate in this update to revisit the tax compliance work conducted by the major accounting and tax firm, Deloitte. This is the subject of a case study in Chapter 2—I show there, consistent with my model of the evolution of professional service, how their service moved from being a bespoke to a packaged service.[27] In the 1960s, tax compliance work was undertaken manually; in the 1970s, the process was to some extent standardized; at the start of the 1980s, spreadsheets were used, while by the end of that decade, Arthur Andersen in the UK went further and built a tax software package, known as Abacus, for use by tax specialists within the firm. In the 1990s, that system was then licensed directly— 'packaged', in my terminology—to clients. Deloitte purchased the service in 2002 and by 2009 it contained the collective insight and expertise of over 250 tax specialists, and was used by 70 of the top 100 companies in the UK. This, for me, is a definitive illustration of the way in which professional service can evolve—from a heavily manual to a largely computerized service. But the story has moved on. In late 2009, Deloitte in the UK sold its Abacus system to Thomson Reuters, the global information company, whose offerings include many legal services, such as Westlaw. This is a fascinating development. It is not my intention here to discuss the strategic thinking that underpinned Deloitte's sale of Abacus to Thomson Reuters. My interest, rather, is in the lessons here for the legal profession. And I think there are four. The first is that law

---

[27] pp 54–7.

firms may find that they too may be able, at the right time, to sell their online services to the giant online legal publishers. The second lesson, related to the first, is that law firms and publishers may come to compete in the provision of online legal services.[28] Third, law firms should note that Deloitte sold their system before it became 'commoditized' (in the sense I use that term in Chapter 2). At a certain stage in the life cycle of an online service, it is likely that publishers are better resourced (in terms of technology, sales forces, and distribution channels) to provide online services than professional firms. Fourth, lawyers still have much to learn from accountants.

While I am encouraged and excited by progress and innovation in some quarters, old habits are dying hard elsewhere, not least in the Law Society of England and Wales. By way of background, readers might bear in mind that, in 1996, senior figures in this very Law Society said I should not be allowed to speak in public. I had been predicting then that most lawyers and clients would soon communicate by e-mail, and the feeling was that I failed to understand confidentiality and was bringing the profession into disrepute. I was hoping when, in March 2010, I received a copy of their consultation document, 'Access to Justice Review',[29] that we now had a more enlightened Law Society. But I am not clear that we do. Although the title is promising, the report appears to be about finding new ways of funding old-fashioned lawyers. The review is said to set out the Law Society's views. The Society's President calls for a 'radical rethink' and 'a willingness to challenge outdated assumptions'.[30] And the first chapter expands on this encouraging message, speaking of dispute avoidance, public legal education, and the promotion of legal health. Tellingly, none of these three is ever discussed again. Instead, the report is devoted largely to the shortcomings of the legal aid system and to alternative methods of funding and procuring legal services. Government policy and practice are criticized heavily. The 'system' is to blame. And if solicitors cannot earn a sensible living, it is claimed that access to justice will be denied.

The Law Society is right to stimulate debate on the funding of legal services. But it has missed an opportunity in not simultaneously exploring ways that lawyers can change their working practices to help reduce costs. The report tells us that, in 2008, 85.9 per cent of law firms had four or fewer partners, while 44.2 per cent were sole practices. To the business-minded, this looks like a cottage industry, with members who handcraft labour-intensive

---

[28] I anticipated this possibility in 1996, in *The Future of Law*. See p 88.

[29] The Law Society, 2010, available at <http://www.lawsociety.org.uk>.

[30] Ibid, at pp 3–4.

bespoke solutions in delivering face-to-face advisory service. Where in the report, then, in relation to lawyers, is the radical rethink or the willingness to challenge outdated assumptions? Nowhere. There is no discussion, for example, of the scope for project management, workflow tools, outsourcing, wider use of paralegals, knowledge management, economies of scale, or shared services centres. The spotlight is never trained on the inefficiencies of traditional legal practice. It is the same with IT. Three out of four UK homes have computers, and 1.4 billion people use the Internet worldwide, and yet the Law Society devotes just half a page out of 60 to technology and, even then, it simply kicks it into touch. There is no analysis of automated document production, online legal guidance and reporting, video-meetings, or electronic procurement of legal services, each of which can bring significant reductions in legal costs. Instead, in 15 tendentious sentences, lawyers are simplistically discouraged from entering the information age.[31] What legacy is the Law Society leaving the Internet generation?

In England and elsewhere, I now find compelling examples of law firms, small and large, that are introducing new efficiencies—standardizing, systematizing, modernizing, and in turn slashing the costs of legal services. If some firms can do this, all should. Of course our justice system needs attention. As I note in Chapter 7, in 2007, around one million civil problems went unresolved, while over 3000 pieces of legislation were created, each impenetrable for the layman. Our first rate Judiciary is often let down by antiquated court facilities. Public funds are diminishing and, generally, legal action in the courts is open only to the rich or those of low or no income. But the problem is far more complex than the Law Society allows. Improving access to justice involves more than solving a funding conundrum.[32]

The rise of legal process outsourcing

Perhaps the most active area of development in the legal services market in the past two years has been legal process outsourcing (LPO). Indeed, given the upsurge of interest and activity since, it is hard to imagine that there had been no major LPO success stories when I submitted the manuscript of this

---

[31] pp 38–39.

[32] For an authoritative recent affirmation of the importance of accessibility to the law as an integral aspect of the rule of law—see Chapter 3 of T Bingham, *The Rule of Law* (London: Allen Lane, 2010).

book in mid-2008. In all modesty, I did write ambitiously about its great potential, but LPO was doing little more than quietly gestating at the time.[33]

If one single event changed the legal world's attitude towards LPO, it was an announcement by Rio Tinto in June 2009. The international mining group very publicly stated that it was to outsource some of its legal work to India. To that end, they had concluded a deal with CPA Global, a LPO provider. They anticipated savings on their legal costs of up to 20 per cent. This was a ground-breaking arrangement and it sent a ripple of debate across the global legal community. An irreversible trend had been set.

Rio Tinto's intention was to build a team of CPA lawyers in India who would operate, effectively, as an extension to their in-house legal department. This would free Rio Tinto lawyers to focus on more complex tasks. More, on all assignments involving external law firms, their plan was to ask these firms to pass tasks that could be done by lower-cost lawyers to CPA people in India and elsewhere. This approach had already been validated. In less than 48 hours, a team of 50 CPA lawyers had been assembled to operate alongside a conventional US law firm in a document review for the Federal Trade Commission. This single project had yielded savings of $1 million.

At that time, as noted, many of England's leading law firms had already outsourced back-office jobs, such as accounting and word processing, to India. The difference here was that Rio Tinto were retaining CPA to under-take substantive legal work, such as contract review, drafting, legal research, and document review. Different, too, was that the drive to outsource had come not from law firms but directly from the client; and not simply for the occasional piece of work but as a fundamentally new way of working.

It was anticipated at the time of the announcement that law firms might be hesitant to give work to CPA lawyers rather than deploy their own (highly profitable) juniors. But it was clear that they would have little option, because Rio Tinto took a robust stance: if a firm refused to collaborate with CPA, it was told to expect its position as an adviser to be re-considered. Tellingly, Rio Tinto said that the 'magic circle' law firm, Linklaters, one of their leading advisers, had responded positively to the new approach.

The arrangement with CPA was firm evidence of a profound change in the legal world. The context here, to recap, was that in-house lawyers were under great pressure—to reduce their internal headcount and to spend less

---

[33] In contrast, at that time, many firms had outsourced back-office functions to India and other low-cost countries. There has been great progress in this area too—for example, in May 2010, law firm, CMS Cameron McKenna, announced an outsourcing agreement with Integreon to provide back-office and sup-port services valued at more than £500 million over a 10-year period. See <http://www.integreon.com>.

on external law firms, at a time when they had an increasing workload. Clients needed to secure more legal service at less cost. Previously, the main way to meet this challenge had been for external lawyers to charge less. And, in mid-2009, most firms were indeed cutting their hourly rates and offering fixed fee arrangements; while many clients were driving down fees through e-auctioning and other devices. It was clearly a buyer's market.

The Rio Tinto deal suggested, however, that imaginative pricing might not fully fix the 'more for less' dilemma. Lawyers would need to go further and source their work differently, often by engaging less costly labour to carry out routine and repetitive legal tasks. This was not just about out-sourcing. Other techniques were gaining traction as well: off-shoring, sub-contracting, relocating, leasing of lawyers, and more (as discussed in Chapter 2 of this book). And law firms also began to look again at the option of computerization, using tools such as automated document drafting and workflow technology. Some lawyers were following the proposal of this book: creating an optimum blend of these options—task-based, lowest cost, multi-sourcing—when the least costly of the various available techniques are used in combination.

Before June 2009, it had often been assumed that alternative methods of sourcing were applicable only to high volume, low value legal work. The Rio Tinto deal confirmed this to be wrong. Now it was clear that there was no lofty type of legal job whose complexity and value elevated it entirely beyond market forces. The reality was and is that significant parts of even the largest transactions and disputes are repetitive and routine; and many in-house lawyers under cost pressures were and are enthused by the prospect that these parts might be packaged out to manifestly less costly providers.

Although some law firms responded positively, the Rio Tinto approach did present a fundamental assault on their conventional business model—hourly billing in a pyramid-shaped organization. At the top of the pyramid is the partner who passes routine and repetitive work to junior lawyers whose efforts generate more fee income than they are paid; and the more junior lawyers per partner (the wider the base of the pyramid), the more profitable the firm. But if some work can be undertaken at less cost by other means (for example, by LPO), then the base of the pyramid shrinks, the profitability drops, and the firm is left with the high costs of luxurious buildings popu-lated by expensive lawyers who are no longer required. It is this commercial reality over which many highly geared and profitable law firms are currently agonizing today, in the knowledge also of a related threat—that some new-look law firms may soon spring up, streamlined, free of high fixed costs, per-haps externally funded, and designed to work easily with LPO providers.

Other managers in law firms continue to hope that LPO is a temporary phenomenon that will lose appeal when the economy recovers. But the recession has made it clear for all time that traditional law firms are inefficient, that new ways of sourcing legal work are possible, and that legal costs can be cut radically. When these truths become widely recognized, through case studies such as that of Rio Tinto, and not least in boardrooms, it will be hard to justify backtracking to the old tariff.

In September 2009, a few months after Rio Tinto's announcement, I conducted a webcast interview with Leah Cooper, their managing counsel and the architect of the outsourcing deal.[34] In the webcast, we talked about the issues that all lawyers raise when discussing LPO—supervision and quality control, liability and contractual arrangements, the likely benefits and savings, and much more. I was far from alone in finding Leah Cooper to be a persuasive advocate. Numerous General Counsel contacted me after watching the webcast, either to find out more or to tell me that they were moving in the same direction. But partners in law firms were less engaged. Many suggested it was premature to draw firm conclusions and that I should conduct another interview six months later to determine how the scheme had actually worked out in practice.

I followed this suggestion and, in March 2010, Leah Cooper and I re-convened, for a second webcast.[35] Two interesting facts emerged. The first was that Rio Tinto's initial six months of outsourcing had yielded net savings on legal fees paid to external law firms of $14 million. The business case was compelling. Second, Leah Cooper herself had left Rio Tinto and joined CPA Global—she had become so convinced of the potential of LPO that she had decided to become part of this new branch of the legal industry.

Another boost for LPO came that same month, when British Telecom transferred its in-house legal team in India to UnitedLex, an American legal process outsourcer. From its offices in Gurgaon in the north of India, it was announced, UnitedLex would help BT's global legal teams with commercial contracting and antitrust regulation work. In its public statement, British Telecom said that the services provided by UnitedLex would complement its global panel of law firms.

This decision by BT may herald a wider shift in law from off-shoring to outsourcing. On the off-shoring model, an organization relocates a team to an overseas location. In the last few years, several major companies and banks have

---

[34] See <http://www.legalweek.com>.
[35] See <http://www.legalweek.com>.

off-shored routine legal services, piggy-backing on the facilities that they had already set up in low-cost locations for functions such as finance, administration, and technology. It seemed to make sense to move lawyers and legal support staff to work at less costly centres that were already in place. Outsourcing, in contrast, involves transferring teams and their work to third-party suppliers, many of whom operate from India. According to British Telecom, the time had come to move their off-shored legal team out of the company into a specialist outsourcer who could provide industry best practice and global scalability.

If indeed this migration from off-shoring to outsourcing becomes a common trend, then this is further good news for the LPO industry, whose combined turnover in India is already over $400 million. And if further weight were needed, it was reported at around the same time that Microsoft's legal department had also resolved to take the plunge, for contract review and document review work, with another LPO provider, Integreon.

While developments at BT, Rio Tinto, and elsewhere are significant and no doubt offer a glimpse of a transformed legal marketplace, it is instructive to place them in perspective. This was done memorably in Washington DC in March 2010 by Professor Mari Sako of the Saïd Business School in Oxford, at a meeting hosted by Georgetown University Law Center, where leading experts gathered to talk about the future of the law firm. In a sobering aside, Sako pointed out that the global market for legal services has been valued at $460 billion, of which legal process outsourcing accounts currently for a mere 0.1 per cent. She went on to note that, even though some exuberant commentators predict the outsourcing market in law will grow to $4 billion in the next five years, even this will represent less than 1 per cent of the legal market.[36]

More sobering still for outsourcers in India was a writ that was filed in March 2010, in the High Court of Judicature at Madras, submitting ('respectfully') that legal process outsourcing amounts to foreign firms 'practicing the profession of law in India'. In consequence, it was argued that this practice is illegal, impermissible, and that immediate action should be taken against the persons and firms involved. Law firms and legal process outsourcers are in the firing line here, although powerful arguments can be made that the nature of the work undertaken by outsourcers does not meaningfully constitute the practice of law. In India, as elsewhere, legal process outsourcers could anticipate ongoing opposition.

But there are other variations on the outsourcing theme and not all involve India. One of my consulting clients, the City firm Berwin Leighton Paisner (BLP),

---

[36] See M Sako, 'Make-or-Buy Decisions in Legal Services: A Strategic Perspective', Working Paper, Revised (June 2010), p 6 and n 7, available at <http://www.sbs.ox.ac.uk>.

recently announced that it is set to take on all of the legal work of Thames Water, the UK's largest water services company. The utility's General Counsel will remain at Thames Water with a small, retained team, but the rest of the in-house lawyers are transferring to BLP's newly created 'managed legal service' division. Joined by BLP specialists, these lawyers will continue to work on-site. In return for a fixed fee, Thames Water will receive their legal services, at guaranteed levels of performance, from a single provider. Vitally, the fee represents a major reduction in legal expenditure for the utility. The deal is therefore reminiscent of the IT outsourcings that have been popular over the past 20 years—a business transfers a non-core function to an external supplier who is able to provide the service back at a higher quality and lower cost.

Strategically, there are fundamental forces at play here. Consistent with the philosophy of outsourcing in other sectors, BLP intends, on the same basis, to take on the legal work of a series of other clients and so achieve economies of scale that clients cannot secure on their own. Their concept of managed legal service, a break-through if realized, will become a form of cost-saving, shared services arrangement. Importantly, to maximize efficiency, BLP say it will be underpinned by new ways of working, such as heavy use of computerization, sub-contracting to lower cost firms, and use of their own lawyer-leasing service, known as Lawyers on Demand.[37]

A tool for analyzing the legal market

Consistent with the current theme of many newly enlightened lawyers—that substantial change in the legal profession is inevitable and perhaps even imminent—I have sensed recently amongst my clients and audiences an impatience with theory and ideas. It is time, I am told, to take action. Move aside, theoreticians everywhere, while action-oriented lawyers now take the helm.

However, when the legal dynamos do indeed step forward, they often find that they lack tools to help them make progress. They may have the will to effect change and may even be decisive and focused, but they do not have a clear framework within which to plan and act. My purpose in the remainder of this Introduction is to plug this gap, by providing lawyers with some new techniques: in this section, I offer a tool to help them analyze the legal

---

[37] <http://www.blplaw.com>.

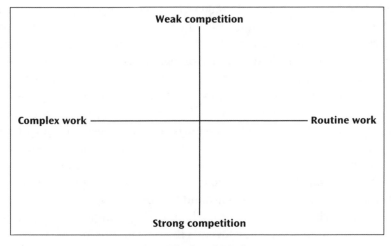

Fig. 1 The Legal Market

market and the work that falls within it; in the penultimate section, I introduce four possible models for legal businesses of the future; and, in the final section, I outline two methods (stress-testing and blank-sheet thinking) that I use with my clients when I work with them on strategic planning.

As with all the tools and techniques that appear in this book, I advance them along with some cautionary words. They are not intended to be intricate and detailed models of reality that will satisfy the purist or the scholar. Rather, they are simplifications of our complex world. They are modest techniques, akin to those used by management consultants, to help lawyers understand and plan.

Turning, then, to the first of these techniques, I propose that one way of understanding the tensions and challenges of the emerging legal marketplace is through the grid presented in Figure 1.[38] The broad aim here is to be able to plot legal work onto this grid and so to improve understanding of issues such as the pricing of legal work and the use of different working methods. The term 'legal work' is used widely here and can include individual matters (for example, deals or disputes), or general categories of legal work (such as IP litigation or domestic conveyancing), or practice areas (for instance, corporate or international arbitration), or, importantly, individual tasks involved in serving clients (including document review and project management).

---

[38] The grid presented here was developed in collaboration with my elder son, Daniel Susskind. I am extremely grateful to him for working with me on this.

Two dimensions of the legal market are reflected on the grid: on the one hand, on the vertical axis, there is a spectrum between weak competition and strong competition; and on the other, the continuum between complex work and work that is routine. Types of legal work can be plotted onto the four quadrants of the grid that are created by the intersection of its axes.

As a starting point, it is helpful to look at the grid from the supply side of the market, that is, from the perspective of law firms providing services to their clients. From this point of view, at the top of the grid, where the competition is weak, there are, accordingly, very few firms who can undertake work that might be plotted here. In contrast, at the bottom of the grid, where the competition is strong, many firms are able to deliver the service in question. Where the work is located towards the left-hand side of the diagram, it is considered to be complex. This work will tend to be handled in a traditional, often bespoke, hand-crafted manner; whereas, towards the right-hand side, the work can be routinized—by standardization and computerization.

Most commercially ambitious law firms of today will want to secure work that is positioned in the top-left of the grid (marked 'x' on Figure 2). These firms will want to say to their clients, first, that the work required is complex (and so to the left) and, second, that they are one of a very few firms that are qualified and capable of taking it on. In contrast, most clients will hope or want to argue that any given piece of legal work can be positioned in the bottom-right quadrant of the grid (marked 'xx' on Figure 2) because here there are many firms that can undertake the work and it is of a highly routine nature. Generally, the work in this area can be undertaken quickly and at low

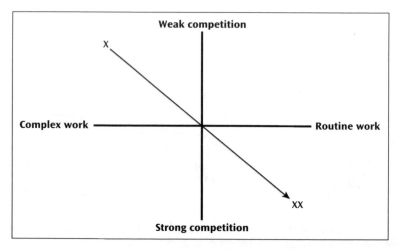

Fig. 2 Firms and Clients

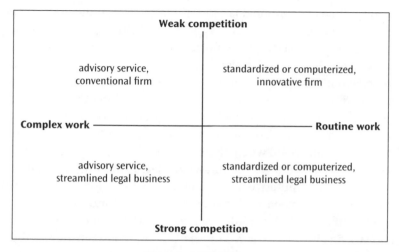

Fig. 3 Legal Providers

cost (because it is routine and there is a plentiful supply of lawyers), whereas, in the top-left, the work will, more likely, take longer and cost clients more (because it is complex and there are far fewer suppliers).

Figure 2 captures the fundamental tension between law firms and clients of today, indicating that the preferred coordinates for each are diametrically opposed. More, this figure depicts the pervasive pull of the marketplace—clients, wherever possible, in these difficult economic times, are encouraging or requiring not only that work be standardized or computerized wherever possible but also that many firms, and not just a few, build the capability to undertake the work.

Broad characterizations of the types of legal providers in the market can be appended as labels to each quadrant of the grid, as is shown in Figure 3. In the top-left, where the work is complex and the competition is weak, we will tend to find the conventional law firm, delivering advisory service in the time-honoured, one-to-one, consultative way. Moving down to the bottom-left quadrant, where the competition becomes stronger, and yet the work still requires relatively bespoke treatment because of its complexity, this service remains advisory in nature but the business that delivers it tends to become more streamlined and tightly managed. As competition intensifies, the prices fall, and so profitability is prejudiced unless the cost (to the provider) of delivering the service is reduced. In this quadrant, we are increasingly finding work being sub-contracted to lower-cost law firms (usually where labour costs are lower) and new entrants to the market, such as Axiom and Voxius, organizations that contract or lease lawyers to clients at rates much lower than conventional law firms charge out their personnel.[39] In the bottom-right quadrant, where the competition is strong and yet the work is routine, again we are seeing the emergence of modernized and streamlined businesses, but here there is also high deployment of standardization or computerization. Typically, then, we see this quadrant being occupied by paralegals who are supported by technology and, more recently, the emergence of legal process outsourcing providers [40] although some of these LPOs also have aspirations to move into the bottom-left as well.

Finally, in the top-right, where there are few competitors and yet the work can be routinized, there will be innovative law firms who have chosen to standardize and computerize. While their competitors still treat this work as complex and so in need of hand-crafting, these innovators create new approaches that render complex activity into (largely) routine process. Beyond law, an illustration of this move from top-left to top-right is the evolution of the tax compliance work of Deloitte in the UK. Complex tax work that once required hand-crafting was in this case computerized and in this Deloitte emerged as a market leader, with little competition in delivering compliance services to clients at relatively low cost.[41]

Figure 4 plots the path of followers in the legal sector. These are firms that cling on to the bespoke hand-crafting ways of working, even when the competition intensifies. On the first part of this trajectory, legal work that was once highly profitable becomes a service that many firms can deliver. Worse, in the second sweep, as the competition intensifies, it is clear that, to have any chance of securing instructions, firms must standardize or computerize and so move from the bottom-left to the bottom-right.

In contrast, Figure 4 also indicates the pattern of leaders in the legal market. These are lawyers who drive their services from the top-left to the top-right quadrant, as Deloitte did with their tax compliance work. Similarly, about a decade ago, when major City law firms in London automated the production of loan documentation, they made precisely this shift. They recognized, through systemization, that they could steal a march on their competitors. In consequence, they disrupted their market and a few competitors followed suit. This transition from left to right resulted in the leaders remaining in a small elite group of a very few lawyers capable of undertaking big-ticket work in the new way. The result was lower fees for clients and more profitable work

---

[39] See p 49.
[40] See pp xxxi–xxxvi of this Introduction.
[41] See pp xxix–xxx of this Introduction and pp 54–57.

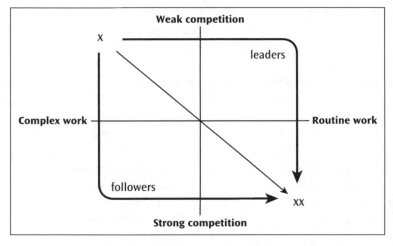

Fig. 4 Followers and Leaders

for the providing firms—fewer hours of effort were required and, although the overall level of fees were reduced, the relative profitability increased.

However, as is the way in competitive markets, other players will recognize, in due course, that they too will need to standardize and computerize and so, as many firms come to work in the new way, the pioneers begin the descent from the top-right of the quadrant into the bottom-right.

The differences between leaders and followers, on this model, is that leaders enjoy a period of greater profitability and market share and seek to remain

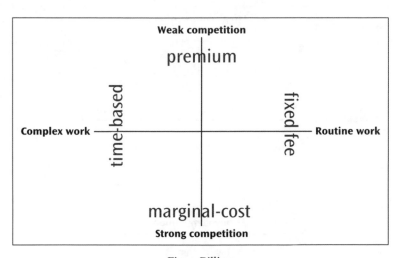

Fig. 5 Billing

in the top-right for as long as possible (by creating sustainable competitive advantage), whereas followers are dragged reluctantly through to the bottom-right having suffered a reduction in profitability (trying all the while to resist competitive disadvantage).

The key point here is that, as Figure 5 shows, legal work at the top of the grid (in either quadrant) can attract premium levels of fees (because the competition is weak) whereas work at the bottom of the grid, again in either quadrant, will tend to sustain little more than marginal cost pricing. It is also interesting to note, as Figure 5 captures, that work to the left of the vertical axis will tend to be charged and priced on a time-based billing basis, where work to the right of this axis will more often be based on some kind of fixed fee.

In practice, however, the picture is more complicated than I have so far suggested. Following my arguments in Chapter 2, deals or disputes should not be considered to be indivisible or monolithic packages of work, the entirety of which must be undertaken and charged in one way only. Instead, and this is fundamental to the thinking in this book, legal work can be decomposed, that is, broken down into its constituent tasks, and, as I argue, the market will increasingly require that each task is undertaken in the most efficient way possible (consistent with the level of quality of service that is required).

With this approach in mind, it transpires that one useful and practical way of plotting particular pieces of legal work (deals or disputes, for example) onto the grid involves decomposing the work into its constituent tasks and allocating each task to its rightful place on the grid, as illustrated in Figure 6.

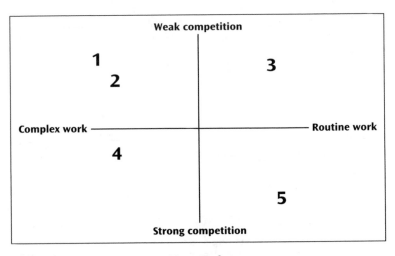

Fig. 6 Tasks

This particular depiction assumes that there are five main tasks involved in the matter in question but it can quickly be seen that these are spread across the grid. The implications of this are immediately obvious—consistent with Figure 3, the work involved here is likely to be undertaken most efficiently when taken on by several different types of legal provider working in collaboration; and, doing so, following Figure 5, under different charging methods. For example, Task 1, in the top-left, is therefore most appropriately undertaken by a conventional firm, charging by the hour, and at premium rates, while Task 5, in the bottom-right, is better suited perhaps to a legal process outsourcing provider on a fixed fee and almost marginal cost basis (noting that the marginal costs for an LPO provider are much lower than those for a law firm).

I accept that, in the past, many law firms would have sought to carry out all the tasks themselves. In the new world, however, it is likely that no single provider will be able to deliver services across the grid at sufficiently competitive prices. This, then, leads us naturally to ask what law firms and in-house legal departments might themselves look like in the future. I turn to this question in the following section.

Four models for legal businesses

I envisage four possible models for legal businesses of the future. Where I speak of legal businesses, I generally have in mind law firms and in-house legal departments, largely run and populated by practising lawyers. I accept, of course, that many other forms of legal concern might also arise in due course, not least because of the impending liberalization of the legal market and the possibility of external investment in legal businesses. However, my focus here is on the next generation of legal organizations that have lawyers at their core.

More specifically, the models I introduce are not only intended as structures for entire law firms or in-house departments. From my consulting work in this area, it has become clear to me that different practices (such as litigation or real estate) face quite different strategic and business challenges, so that the models are often best applied at that operational level. It is conceivable, therefore, that a firm or in-house department might be made up of practices that are based on quite different models.

The four models themselves each present a different structure for legal businesses (or their parts). I call them: the target; the doughnut; the glazed

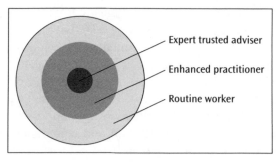

Fig. 7 The Target

doughnut; and the cog. These models are not put forward as directly implementable structures for law firms and departments. Rather, they are intended,
in a rough and ready way, to give a sense of possible approaches for the
future. I deal with each in turn.

The target, as depicted in Figure 7, is the dominant model in law firms and
in-house departments of today. I use the word 'target', partly because it looks
like one and partly because, metaphorically speaking, it is this model that
will be in the firing line in the future as its inherent inefficiencies become
clearer to the market. At the centre of the target is the 'expert trusted adviser'
as discussed more fully in Chapter 8. This is the intelligent, creative lawyer
who is needed in some circumstances to handle matters in a bespoke manner. Generally these individuals have considerable experience of particular
areas of law and deep understanding of their clients and the industries in
which they work. The second component of the target, the middle ring, is the
'enhanced practitioner'. Again as described in Chapter 8, this is a lawyer
whose legal skills and knowledge are needed not to deliver highly bespoke
service but, with the support of various standards (such as standard form
documents and computer systems), to bring to bear legal experience and
know-how for the benefit of clients but not at the depth of the expert trusted
adviser. The outer ring of the target represents the routine legal worker, the
much less experienced lawyer whose work is largely administrative and process-based, such as document review in litigation, due diligence in transaction work, and the production of largely standardized contracts.

Most law firms and in-house departments of today, both large and small,
are organized as targets, populated in the way I suggest. A fundamental
problem here, however, as discussed extensively in this book, is that the
outer ring of routine work is proving too costly. Law firms in particular are

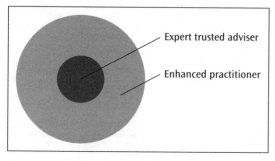

Fig. 8 The Doughnut

criticized in this context—clients rarely complain about the fees charged for the efforts of expert trusted advisers but they frequently say that the rates of junior lawyers, who undertake routine and repetitive work, can no longer be justified. The key challenge here is that, over the past few years, it has become clear that this routine work can be sourced in different ways such as outsourcing, off-shoring, sub-contracting, and even through the leasing of lawyers. This is a central argument of Chapter 2 of this book, in which I explain the way that legal work can be decomposed into constituent tasks and then sourced (multi-sourced) in a variety of ways.

Given the shortcomings of the target, an alternative for lawyers to consider is my second model, which I call 'the doughnut'. This is represented in Figure 8. Essentially, the doughnut is the target with the outer band, of routine legal workers, stripped away. I call it 'the doughnut' simply because, at first glance, it looks like one. I am not suggesting that there is actually some kind of hole or gap in the middle (it could be jam); nor am I intending that any inferences be drawn in relation to the sweetness of their taste. But the doughnut is a model that is intuitively attractive to many managers of legal businesses of today. They recognize that the routine and repetitive work can be undertaken more efficiently by other providers, and so take the view that the business case for junior or less skilled lawyers can no longer be made.

The doughnut is therefore a model that might appeal to a group of senior lawyers, perhaps in their early 50s, who have retired from major law firms and yet wish to continue practising. Rather than set up a new firm along traditional lines (the target) the doughnut model offers a more streamlined structure, with routine legal work (and infrastructure such as accounting and technology) outsourced to others.

For the traditional law firm, adoption of the doughnut model means a considerable reduction in head-count and the need to establish a series of relationships with other providers who are able to undertake this routine and repetitive work, in a reliable and collaborative manner. An important consequence of this new arrangement, however, is a reduction in the leverage or gearing that has traditionally enabled some law firms to be very profitable—if they work great numbers of hours and are charged to clients at high rates, large teams of junior lawyers who are paid modestly can be highly profitable for a firm.

In contrast, for the in-house legal department, the elimination of the outer band of routine legal workers does not give rise to any concerns over profitability, because most legal departments are cost centres and not profit centres. So long as the work that is sourced differently is delivered at lower cost, and at the same (or higher) standard, the model has immediate attractions both for the in-house departments and for the organizations that they serve.

My third model is 'the glazed doughnut', as illustrated in Figure 9. Here, the expert trusted adviser and enhanced practitioner are playing the same roles as in the target and doughnut, but there is an additional ring, or glaze, around the outer edge. This represents the work of what I term the 'legal process manager'. This role itself can be sub-divided into two: the legal process analyst and the legal project manager.

The legal process analyst is the individual who will analyze a legal matter (a deal or dispute), decompose it into its constituent tasks (see Chapter 2), assess the most efficient and appropriate way to carry out each, and identify the best suppliers from whom to source this work. The job of the legal process analyst will, I believe, be crucial in tomorrow's world. If I am correct in this book, in suggesting that we can source legal work in many ways, then a vital responsibility will be that of assessing any given matter and decomposing

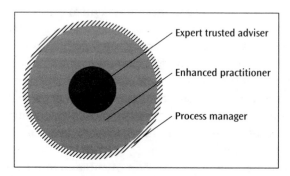

Fig. 9 The Glazed Doughnut

and multi-sourcing accordingly. This assessment will require considerable legal insight and experience, as well as new skills of analysis.

The second role of the legal process manager is what I call the 'legal project manager'. This person's talents will swing into play after the legal process analyst has completed the specification (decomposition and proposed multi-sourcing) of the work. It is likely that the legal process analyst and legal project manager will work together in selecting the team of providers but, once this team is in place, it is the project manager who will ensure that all providers complete their decomposed work packages on time and to budget, and will also be responsible for quality controlling the various packages, supervising their output and delivery, and pulling the packages together into one seamless service for the client. As I say in Chapter 2, this approach is akin to some aspects of production in a manufacturing environment.

The new discipline and activity of legal process management does not need to be invented from scratch. The legal world should be able to draw on the thinking and experience from other management disciplines such as supply chain management and logistics. Indeed, in the future, it is likely that the legal sector itself will develop sophisticated tools and techniques that we might come to call 'legal supply chain management' and 'legal logistics'. These topics will no doubt be covered in courses on 'legal project management'.[42]

Who, in the future, will take on the responsibility for legal process management (process analysis and project management)? This is a fascinating question, upon which the future health of the legal profession may in part depend. The untutored gut reaction of some conventional legal practitioners is that this is not work for lawyers. It is true, certainly, that process analysis and project management were not in the toolkit of the bespoke, consultative legal advisers of yesteryear. In contrast, there are some more enlightened practitioners who see the introduction of legal process management as an opportunity to extend the range of services they offer and the value they bring to their clients. In law firms, these innovators may well find here a new source of profitable legal work. At the same time, some imaginative in-house lawyers immediately recognize legal process management as a job for them. Indeed they anticipate that this is what their boards and shareholders will expect of them—that they take responsibility for identifying the most efficient way of delivering legal service at an appropriate level of quality and of managing the process of delivery itself. In so doing, these in-house departments will serve their own organizations more impressively.

---

[42] Compare SB Levy, *Legal Project Management* (Seattle: DayPack, 2009).

Other in-house lawyers are more cautious and say that legal process management is a service that they would expect to be delivered by progressive law firms and not from within their departments. Either way, those law firms or in-house departments who assume the roles of legal process analyst and legal project manager will be adopting the model that I call the 'glazed doughnut'.

If law firms and legal departments together fail to embrace legal process management, I predict that there will be other new competitors, such as accounting firms, legal publishers, and new-look businesses fuelled by external investment, that will happily recognize and exploit the opportunities here. If these more entrepreneurial organizations step forward, then, ironically, conventional legal businesses may be destined to be sub-contractors on the edge of deals and disputes, rather than trusted advisers and risk managers at the heart of legal work.

Some law firms and legal departments will feel that some of the routine legal work in the outer ring of the target must be kept within their organizations (for example, because of confidentiality) or that they can themselves undertake this work more efficiently than other providers in the marketplace (for instance, by building up an internal paralegal or e-discovery team). Pursuing this line of thinking, these legal businesses might adopt my fourth model which, because of its appearance, I call 'the cog'. As shown in Figure 10, this model incorporates the glazed doughnut and adds some parts of the outer ring from the target. The idea here is that some routine work is retained and undertaken internally and other parts are sourced elsewhere. This model often appeals to lawyers in firms and in-house departments, who are wary of relinquishing direct control over the teams who are doing the routine and

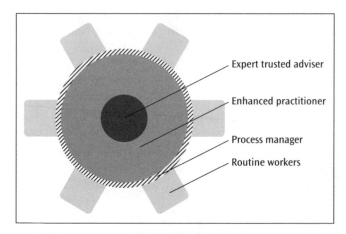

Fig. 10 The Cog

repetitive work. Sometimes this caution is well founded but on many occasions it betrays a fear of losing empire.

In the end, as market forces drive through the legal profession, the interests and preferences of clients and shareholders will determine which models are embraced. For now, however, lawyers who are thinking strategically should carefully assess which models are possible, desirable, or even necessary within their legal businesses.

Meeting strategic challenges

It is never easy to anticipate the likely pace of change in the legal marketplace. In general, though, I have found that the legal world adapts more slowly than most other sectors. And so, although this book often conveys a sense of urgency and imminent revolution, I should acknowledge here what I advise my consulting clients—that the transformations I anticipate will be incremental and will come about not in the next three or six months but, give or take, in the coming three to six years. But this does not mean that work should not begin today.

The world's best managing partners realize that they face two challenges in these difficult times. The first is to steer their businesses through the short-term difficulties of the next one or two years. It may be that the worst of the recession is behind us; or it could be that we will lunge into a second abyss. Either way, in this period of uncertainty, most managerial minds are currently directed at maintaining acceptable levels of profitability. The most notable and common response to the recession has been to reduce head-count, both of support staff and fee earners. Only a few firms, in my view, have succeeded in making cuts strategically, sensitively, and in a manner that will not affect long-term morale and brand. Those that have fired (this is no place for euphemism) high-performing loyal staff because their areas of work have dried up will not for many years, if ever again, command undiluted loyalty amongst their junior people. In contrast, those firms where partners have made serious sacrifices to keep their staff in employment are those whose reputation is now high and will attract and retain the best talent in the future. There are important lessons here for firms as they transform themselves in the coming decade.

As I write, the latest figures are emerging from law firms in England, about their financial performance during 2009/2010. Many are reporting similar turnover to last year and a modest (single figure) increase in profitability. The latter reflects the impact of the cuts they have made, but this level of profitability will be hard to sustain—unless these businesses begin to invest in marketing, talent, technology, and in their clients, they will find it hard to regain real momentum and make the most of the growing economy when it returns. The healthier firms know this and the best of these have already therefore begun to invest in new ways of undertaking their routine and repetitive legal work at much lower cost than today.

However, the second and much bigger challenge for law firms is to ensure their long-term health. This calls for leadership, vision, and strength of purpose, quite different attributes from those management skills that help improve operational efficiency. The main concern here is best articulated by many young partners with whom I speak. They worry about the viability and sustainability of the businesses they are inheriting. They wonder if the glory years are gone and if the old business model is broken. They find themselves as part-owners of firms that are weighed down by heavy fixed costs and that aspire to a pyramidic organizational structure of lawyers that no longer seems appropriate. They cannot see how their firms can reinvent themselves and yet, at the same time, keep the business running. It sounds like changing clothes while riding a bicycle.

In practical terms, then, for those firms that want to prosper in the coming decades, where should law firm leaders begin in bringing about change? I have developed two techniques that I use with my consulting clients. I can introduce them here only in broad outline, but I hope they give a flavour of approaches that might be taken to effect change in a controlled manner. The underlying spirit here is what I call 'incremental revolution'—fundamental reorientation is achieved by progressing in a series of manageable steps, with achievement of each bringing its own benefits. I do not believe it is practicable in law firm partnerships to try to engineer 'big bang' revolutions.

The first technique is 'stress-testing'—I advise that all major business units within firms (practice areas, generally) should subject themselves to formal evaluation of how they will face the pressures the market will bring in the coming three to six years. Using a common framework of analysis, practice area leaders must try to convince firm-wide leaders of the ways that their business units can and will respond to the various threatening trends discussed in this book, such as cost pressures, commoditization, multi-sourcing, external investment, and emerging disruptive technologies. On this approach, and it is fairly aggressive, practice areas must prove to their firm that they have a viable medium to long-term business. The arguments made must, in part, be evidence-based, drawing on research with clients and intelligence about competitors. Some practices may not withstand this scrutiny and may be seen as terminally threatened by new developments. Others may make out a case for survival but not in their current form. They might need, for example, to enter into joint ventures with complementary providers. Still others might seek external capital, perhaps to support technology developments. Some again might find opportunities for exciting new lines of legal business. The prospect of such internal scrutiny is daunting but it is better to carry out this analysis in a systematic and measured way today than to be forced unwillingly and rapidly into radical change in the future.

A second technique, less threatening and generally more productive amongst lawyers than stress-testing, is that of 'blank-sheet thinking'. This involves inviting the partners of practice areas to answer the following question—if you could design your practice area from scratch, using an entirely blank sheet of paper, how would it look? I encourage partners to tackle this question not through group discussion but individually and privately. Each partner is given perhaps a week to reflect and is asked, anonymously, to submit, on one side of A4, his or her blueprint for an ideal practice.

With my clients, I provide some additional questions to prompt their thinking. Here are some, by way of illustration. Where would you be located and in what kind of premises? How many partners would you have and at what levels of seniority? How many other lawyers and at what grades? Who would be your target clients? What kind of administrative support would you require? What support services would you need? What technologies would you use, internally and with clients? What pricing strategies would you prefer? What would be your distinctive capabilities (for what would you want to be famous)? Would you seek to be a thought leader? Would you seek external capital? Would you outsource, off-shore, or sub-contract routine and repetitive work?

These questions are usually sufficient to stimulate the creative reflexes of most partners. Once they have submitted their one-page summaries, the next step is to have an independent adviser or moderator collate and summarize them. Some partners will be more radical than others, but generally, and surprisingly, I tend to find a great deal of common thinking. Strikingly, most partners outline business models that are radically different from the ones they are currently running. This is revealing because it suggests that they can see much better ways of delivering their services than the ones they currently offer. A serious threat follows—if the practice is not prepared to pursue one or more of the alternative models envisaged, then it is surely likely, in these competitive times, that some competitors will.

Radically different, alternative business models cannot be implemented immediately. They take many years to plan and put in place. One way of looking at blank-sheet thinking is that it helps partners to identify their long-term (say three to six year) plans. It encourages partners to create a vision for their future where ordinarily they find this difficult to do.

Stress-testing and blank-sheeting thinking are not conceived as infallible tools that will always provoke partners into rethinking their practices. But it is my experience that they do facilitate structured and systematic contemplation of the long-term health of legal businesses.

With law firms perhaps a little better equipped, my final words of guidance are directed at General Counsel. As I stress in this book, the future of legal services lies very much in their hands. Most law firms are unlikely to change their ways without steady pressure from in-house lawyers. More than this, General Counsel must also be prepared to bring root-and-branch change to the workings of their own departments. Too often, in-house lawyers say to me that they have read this book and that I am absolutely correct in suggesting that law firms have to modernize and work differently. They seem to think my call for transformation is directed only at lawyers in firms. I fear these readers have never reached Chapter 5, which argues that in-house lawyers are also under pressure to rethink the way they work. Commoditization, computerization, decomposing, multi-sourcing, and the many other trends introduced in later chapters are as applicable to the work of in-house departments as they are to law firms. I suggest this not simply as a matter of theory but as a reflection on recent research and conversations with chief executives, chief finance officers, board members, and shareholders. It follows, I suggest, that in-house lawyers too should conduct stress-testing or blank-sheet thinking.

In-house lawyers, the most powerful clients of all, are therefore themselves at a cross-roads, because they must overhaul the way they work internally and the way they source external legal service. In turn, law firms must align themselves with these new working practices and in so doing re-construct their businesses.[43]

Richard Susskind

June 2010

Radlett, England

---

[43] I extend loving thanks to my sons, Daniel and Jamie, who commented on early drafts of this Introduction.

1

Introduction—the Beginning of the End?

The title and theme of this book—the end of lawyers—might appear rather self-destructive. I am a lawyer myself (of sorts). Many of my close friends are lawyers. Most of my clients are major law firms. Socially and commercially, it might seem that I am shooting myself in both feet.

However, as the question mark in the title should at least hint, I write not to bury lawyers but to investigate their future. My aim is to explore the extent to which the role of the traditional lawyer can be sustained in coming years in the face of challenging trends in the legal marketplace and new techniques for the delivery of legal services. The book is neither a lawyer-bashing polemic nor a gratuitous assault on the legal profession. Nor again is it a political rant, presaging the withering away of law and lawyers. Instead, it is a collection of predictions and observations about a generally honourable profession that is, I argue, on the brink of fundamental transformation. More, it is a set of ideas about the law, our main form of social control, and the way its institutions can and should change in our remarkably evolving world.

That said, I do admit, if I may give away the ending, that the book does point to a future in which conventional legal advisers will be much less prominent in society than today and, in some walks of life, will have no visibility at all. This, I believe, is where we will be taken by two forces: by a market pull towards *commoditization* and by pervasive development and uptake of *information technology*. Commoditization and IT will shape and characterize twenty-first century legal service.

Against this backdrop, I should be honest about one issue from the outset. I do not believe lawyers are self-evidently entitled to profit from the law. As I have said before, the law is not there to provide a livelihood for lawyers any more than illness prevails in order to offer a living for doctors. Successful legal business may be a by-product of law in society; but it is not the purpose of law. And, just as numerous other industries and sectors are having to adapt to broader change, so too, when appropriate, should lawyers. This book calls for the growth and the development of a legal profession not by ring-fencing certain categories of work as the exclusive preserve of lawyers; nor by encouraging cartel-like activity which discourages all but lawyers from engaging. Rather, it calls for lawyers, their professional bodies, their policy-makers, and their clients, to think more creatively, imaginatively, and entrepreneurially about the way in which lawyers can and should contribute to our rapidly changing economy and society.

1.1 The challenge for lawyers

More specifically, the challenge I lay down here is for all lawyers to intro-spect, and to ask themselves, with their hands on their hearts, what elements of their current workload could be undertaken differently—more quickly, cheaply, efficiently, or to a higher quality—using alternative methods of working. In other words, the challenge for legal readers is to identify their distinctive skills and talents, the capabilities that they possess that cannot, crudely, be replaced by advanced systems, or by less costly workers sup-ported by technology or standard processes, or by lay people armed with online self-help tools. I argue that the market is increasingly unlikely to toler-ate expensive lawyers for tasks (guiding, advising, drafting, researching, problem-solving, and more) that can equally or better be discharged by less expert people, supported by sophisticated systems and processes. It follows, I say, that the jobs of many traditional lawyers will be substantially eroded and often eliminated. At the same time, I foresee new law jobs emerging which may be highly rewarding, even if very different from those of today.

While I hope this book will be of interest to many general readers, I believe it is relevant for all lawyers, no matter how specialist or expert they perceive themselves to be. I am often amused and bemused when, after presenting to a group of lawyers, I am approached by a small number who purport to be in violent agreement with what I have said. Such lawyers will say that they accept a shake-up in the legal profession is long overdue and that my ideas about the transformation of legal services apply across the board, except for one vital area of legal practice—their own. There follows a stream of rationalizations, clarifying why their corner of the legal universe is and should be immune from change. My scepticism here should be plain. No lawyers should feel exempt from assessing whether at least some of their current workload might be undertaken differently in years to come. And no lawyers should shirk from the challenge of identifying their distinctive capabilities.

Lawyers can learn from the corporate world in this context. At the peak of the dotcom era, Jack Welch, for twenty years the CEO of General Electric (GE), set up a group of teams to analyse whether the Internet could do to businesses within GE what Amazon was achieving in bookselling. In the spirit of the times, they were called 'destroyyourbusiness.com' teams. Before long, however, these were re-designated 'growyourbusiness' teams. They had concluded that the Internet offered more opportunities than threats and so they moved from being defensive to proactive in responding to the new technology.[1] And so it should be with lawyers, or so I argue in this book. The challenge is not to assess how commoditization and IT might threaten the current work of lawyers, so that the traditional ways can be protected and change avoided. It is to find *and embrace* better, quicker, less costly, more convenient, and publicly valued ways of working.

To return to the disconcerting message of this book for much of the legal profession—for those lawyers who cannot identify or develop the distinctive capabilities to which I refer, I certainly do predict that their days are numbered. The market, in ways I discuss, will determine that the legal world is inefficiently resourced (under-resourced in the consumer sector and over-resourced at the high end); it will increasingly drive out excesses and unnecessary friction and, in turn, we will indeed witness the end of outdated legal practice and the end of outdated lawyers.

1.2 Four thoughts

The origins of this book lie in four thoughts and a journey. Let me start with the four thoughts.

---

[1] J Welch, *Jack* (London: Headline, 2001) 346–349.

The first sprung to mind when I sat, in great comfort, in early 2006, in the ancient and splendid surroundings of the dark wood panelled main hall of the Mercers' Company, in Ironmongers Lane in London. Founded in 1394, the Mercers is the longest established instance of a great tradition in the City of London, that of 'livery companies'. With origins in ancient trade guilds and, in the early days, very much focused on regulating their trades, there are now over a hundred of these bodies. Mercers were traders in fine cloths and silks. But the last mercer to become an apprentice with the Mercers did so in 1888; since then, like many other livery companies, the Mercers have supported innumerable charitable causes and educational initiatives. It was probably the fine food and wine that emboldened me and fuelled my imagination. I wondered to myself, in an entirely untutored way, about the fate of mercers. I thought about improvements in transport and communications, the impact of machinery on craftsmen and cottage industries, the emergence of synthetic fibres, the advent of mass-market retailing, and the impact of an ever more influential fashion industry. And I then thought about other ancient trades and craftsmen, now remembered in London largely because of the livery companies that bear their names—for example tallow chandlers (who rendered animal fat as candles), cordwainers (who worked with fine leather), and wheelwrights (makers of wheels). It occurred to me that the fundamental demand for the products of these trades (cloths, candles, wheels) had not diminished; indeed it had often increased. But new technologies, methods of production, and innovations had served to displace most of the associated craftsmen. I reflected upon the legal world and the possible impact of information technology. And I wondered then—and this first thought inspired the title of the book—whether *lawyers might fade from society as other craftsmen have done over the centuries.*

Perhaps a hundred years from now—maybe more or maybe much less—people might sit in fine comfort in some vestige of today's legal world (perhaps an ancient courtroom refurbished as a restaurant, as some of London's banks have been repurposed) and, appropriately nourished, speculate in a leisurely manner about solicitors and barristers and advocates and attorneys, in much the same way as I had been musing about various craftsmen of centuries past. Who exactly were these people, these lawyers? What was their craft? They were involved with the law, of course, but what did they actually *do*? Why did we need them? How did they contribute? And why do we not have them any more? What brought about the end of lawyers? It was just a thought.

The second thought that led to my embarking on this book crystallized after many years of talking with a wide variety of lawyers. Increasingly, I have found that many lawyers seem to have one thing in common—they seem to want to deny that they are lawyers. They downplay the legal content of their jobs.

Private client lawyers (for example those who advise on divorces or draft wills) tell me that their job is not really about the law; rather, they insist, they are experienced counsellors, confidantes, or therapists even, in whom their clients have unwavering faith in relation to their personal problems. In similar vein, litigators say that their primary role in life is that of project manager rather than provider of legal advice, corporate lawyers claim to be deal-makers and negotiators much more than legal draftsmen, in-house lawyers maintain that they are risk managers as opposed to legal counsellors, banking lawyers assert their clients come to them not for legal advice but for their market knowledge, and high street solicitors insist that they rarely undertake legal research. Even judges say that they are becoming case managers.

Where have all the lawyers gone? Why are lawyers not devoting themselves to the rarefied legal work that our law schools led us to expect (and many still do)? My second thought was that *lawyers are denying that they are lawyers because they recognize they need to change and diversify in response to shifts in the market.*

Of course, a variety of reasons might be advanced for lawyers denying they are lawyers. One response might be that being a lawyer is, bluntly, not the coolest of jobs, and perhaps not as prestigious as once it was. There may even be a stigma of sorts attached to being a lawyer (hence the wealth of lawyer jokes). And so, in response, lawyers might be holding themselves out as belonging, at least in part, to another discipline. I do not accept this line of thought. It may be that the ill-informed and the disconnected will trash the legal profession but, in most walks of life, lawyers remain well respected. In any event, I cannot imagine according to what scale it is cooler or more prestigious to be, say, a project manager than a lawyer (with all due respect to project managers).

It may be that lawyers often genuinely forget how much they know about the law and so do not regard themselves as especially lawyerly. Or perhaps they do not feel that it is their legal knowledge that differentiates them in the marketplace and so they point to complementary skills of which they are proud. There is something different here, I believe, from yesteryear's traditional role of the lawyer as the 'man of affairs', the all-purpose rock of an adviser upon whom clients could unfailingly rely. That old boy (and these chaps were invariably male) regarded the law, in contemporary jargon, as their core competence, around which they built more general business acumen.

In contrast, the modern lawyer, who is in denial of being lawyerly, seems to want to argue that they have some different core competence and relegate their legal ability to the background or periphery. I believe this is an indicator of profound forces at play, forces that are lessening the need for the traditional black letter lawyer. When it becomes possible to standardize and computerize the law and legal work, the need for the traditional bespoke handling by the conventional lawyer lessens considerably. Once legal practice is demystified, it becomes feasible to decompose many legal tasks into work parcels that can then be sourced in different ways (for example by outsourcing, off-shoring, and home-sourcing), leaving much less for the traditional lawyer to do. And when legal service is systematized, legal knowledge and legal solutions, in turn, can be shared and embedded in business practices. All of these ideas are explained in this book. For now, I suggest that lawyers' denial of their lawyerliness is an early and yet crucial pointer toward shifts in the legal market—lawyers are adapting to a world in which much conventional legal work is routine and can be handled differently and by others, and in which clients require actionable and practical advice that extends well beyond legal analysis and word-smithing. There is a hint here too of a confession from lawyers—they know that there is room for change and improvement and client satisfaction is not always sky high.

Whether consciously or not, in order to survive, many lawyers are widening their range of skills, broadening their sphere of impact, and are anxious that the world does not pigeon-hole them as detached scribes who sit in ivory towers. Many lawyers, in other words, can no longer eke a living from the law alone.

Lawyers, like the rest of humanity, face the threat of disintermediation (broadly, being cut out of some supply chain) by advanced systems; and, as in other sectors, if they want to survive, their focus should be on re-intermediating, that is, on finding new ways of invaluably inserting themselves in these supply chains. This will lead, I claim, to the emergence of what I call 'legal hybrids', individuals of multi-disciplinary background, whose training in law will have evolved and will dovetail with a formal education in one or more other disciplines. The formality is important. When most lawyers claim today that they are, say, project managers or counsellors, they are nothing of the sort. Too often, they but dabble. They are dilettantes, who have read an article or two and attended a few seminars or intensive courses. We would not dare to call someone a lawyer on the strength of similar schooling. If lawyers want to reinvent themselves and carve out new multi-disciplinary roles that allow them to deliver new value, then their commitment to these neighbouring areas of expertise must be deep and our law schools should be gearing up accordingly. In this way, we will also formally be equipping law-yers of the future with the tools and knowledge to solve business and social problems and not just legal problems.

I am not suggesting that there will be no call for the traditional legal expert. I am saying there will be less call for these individuals, because new ways of satisfying legal demand will evolve and old inefficiencies will be eliminated. On top of this smaller group of genuine legal specialists and this growing cadre of hybrids, I also envisage the emergence of a further grouping of professionals—the legal knowledge engineers. These are the highly skilled individuals who will be engaged in the jobs of standardizing, systematizing, and packaging the law. They will be the analysts who reorganize and restruc-ture legal knowledge in a form that can be embodied in advanced systems, whether for use by lawyers, paralegals, or lay people.

The third thought that urged me to write this book came into focus over the last two years or so, when I have been informally asked to advise the friends of my teenage sons about possible careers in the law. I cannot pre-tend to these enthusiastic youngsters that what they have seen in movies or read in novels or even experienced through work placements will bear any relation to the legal world a generation hence. Can any responsible lawyer sensibly state with confidence that legal work in 2030 will be much the same as today? While major oil companies have plans in place for the next fifty years, very few lawyers look beyond the next five. In fact, when honest law-yers are really pushed, most confess to being clueless about how their pro-fession is likely to unfold in the long run. And yet, in England alone, around 15,000 students each year are now being accepted by our universities to study law as undergraduates. Even if we concede that many never intend to prac-tise, we are nonetheless left with very large numbers (perhaps a quarter of a million in the next generation, at current rates) emerging from undergradu-ate law schools, institutions that, generally, seem to assume and project a model of legal practice that held firm in the mid to late twentieth century but may well bear little relation to lawyering of the twenty-first.

I give lectures regularly at law schools and to legal academics. These talks often provoke interesting discussion but I fear I am regarded by mainstream law professors as an interesting but ultimately misguided sophist, and that trends such as commoditization and IT are looked upon as marginal side-shows. Disconcertingly, undergraduate law students are also sceptical. My ideas on the future of legal services may resonate with many General Counsel in the world's largest financial institutions and companies and I may be asked to advise many of the world's leading law firms on possible futures, but most law schools, by and large, seem much less willing to engage and are comfortable in assuming that it will be legal business as usual for the foreseeable future. It is clear to me that few undergraduate law schools, in the UK at least, are exposing their students even to the possibility that legal service may be radically different in the future and well within the span of their careers.

What, then, are we training our undergraduate law students to become? What should we say to young, aspiring legal eagles about the landscape of the world they are interested in entering? To what reports or publications should we be directing them? In all my travels, I have found only one, and even that is of limited scope, being of interest largely to major US law firms.[2]

For more than fifteen years, I have been a general editor of the International Journal of Law and Information Technology; not once in that period have we received a submission on the subject of the nature of legal practice in the long term. If law schools and legal academics are reluctant to express a long view about the future of law, are others stepping up to the plate? Remarkably, they do not seem to be. For example, professional bodies in England, such as the Law Society and the Bar Council, may currently be discussing or supporting or effecting changes that will substantially affect the future of lawyers but I can find no statement of an underpinning vision for the future of legal service. Similarly, the UK government is unquestionably reforming the legal profession and legal system at a rate of knots but in none of the white papers, consultation documents, or speeches by ministers can I locate a clear articulation of the distant end game, taking account of the phenomena that most long-range strategic planners are wrestling with—such as the impact of outsourcing or of Web 2.0 (two phenomena that are disrupting and reconfiguring most sectors) on legal practice. Nor has the Law Commission focused its lens on the future of legal practice. Even major law firms, which invest substantially in technology, very rarely look beyond the likely terms of office of their senior and managing partners, which tend to be between three and five years.[3] My third thought, then, is that no-one who might be thought to be in the driving seat of the legal system is thinking systematically, rigorously, and in a sustained way about the long-term future of legal service. *No-one seems to be worrying about the fate of the next generation of lawyers.*

[2] J Seidl *et al* (eds), *Legal Transformation Study: Your 2020 Vision of the Future* (Minneapolis: DSI and LRC, 2008).

[3] A recent exception is the law firm, Eversheds, who commissioned and published a study in 2008—*Law firm of the 21st Century.* See <http://www.eversheds.com>.

All that can be discerned in relation to the long term is a common assumption—whether on the part of scholars, professional bodies, government agencies, or leading law firms—that legal service of tomorrow will be quite similar to that of today; perhaps more efficient and more business-like but not fundamentally different in nature. It is assumed, I perceive, that legal guidance will continue to be dispensed by skilled professionals as a one-to-one, consultative advisory service. By and large, no discontinuities, transformations, upheavals, disruptions, or revolutions in the nature of legal service are being contemplated.

One possible exception here is the legal publishing community, a market that has changed markedly in the last decade, in its widespread adoption of online techniques. I have found that many legal publishers, from the large and multi-jurisdictional to the small and entrepreneurial, do have a long-term view, although it is not one they tend to publicize, for fear, perhaps, of agitating the law firms (of swallowing the hand that feeds them).

The fourth and final thought that urged me to write this book came quickly one afternoon, in the autumn of 2006, in a penthouse flat overlooking the River Thames. This was the unlikely venue for a seminar on the possible impact of the controversial Legal Services Bill and the liberalization of the legal marketplace. In the event, the Bill was introduced to Parliament in November 2006 and given Royal Assent in October 2007. The Bill had been inspired in large part by the findings and recommendations of an important independent review by Sir David Clementi, who reported in December 2004.[4] Clementi had been appointed, in July 2003, by the Secretary of State for Constitutional Affairs (referred to by most lawyers as the Lord Chancellor) to review the regulatory framework for legal services in England and Wales. His report covered much ground; and it shaped much of the Bill before Parliament. In the first instance, Clementi proposed a new regime for regulating legal services. And it was this that seemed to capture the attention of most practising lawyers and legal policy-makers. He also recommended much-debated new mechanisms for the handling of complaints against lawyers.

But there was a third major stream of thought—in response to concerns about restrictive practices in the legal marketplace, new legal structures for legal businesses should be permitted. The focal point of the seminar that day was this third and controversial proposed reform, followed by the government

---

[4] 'Report of the Review of the Regulatory Framework for Legal Services in England and Wales' (Final Report, December 2004). See <http://www.legal-services-review.org.uk>.

in its inclusion in the Bill, of 'alternative business structures'. This departure was being mirrored in a few other jurisdictions and anticipated for many more. For the first time in England, there was a strong possibility that, broadly speaking, it would be open to non-lawyers to invest in law firms. During the previous eighteen months, law firms' responses to this particular development had been mixed. Some had seen it as an irrelevance, doubting on a variety of grounds that anyone other than lawyers would want to invest in law firms. Others regarded this development as yet another indicator of a decline from the professionalism of a partnership into the relative amorality of the limited company.[5] Still others were rubbing their hands in glee at the thought of being bought out, serving a couple of transitional years under the new management, and then retiring comfortably.

I listened with growing interest to the debate that afternoon. It was a rare experience to hear legal services being discussed as though they were subject to the normal laws of the marketplace and not some kind of special case, sacred cow, or no-go zone. I learned that the value of the market for consumer-based legal services in England is well over £10 billion. We were told of market research, by *Which?*, that suggested almost two-thirds of adults thought it a good idea to obtain legal services from common high street brands (supermarkets and banks, for example).[6] It was concluded, in a bit of a leap, that at least £6 billion worth of consumer-based legal services was therefore up for grabs. Only a very few of the delegates were lawyers. Most were representatives of these high street behemoths whose remit now seems to know no boundaries. These individuals were not committed to the ways of the past. They were talking about call centres, outsourcing to India, online legal services, the automatic generation of documents, and more. I thought then, with complete conviction, that *the delivery of legal services will be a very different business when financed and managed by non-lawyers.*

I wondered what the legal world would be like if dominated or even strongly influenced by the retail industry, by the management methods and ethos of corporate boards, with the backing of venture capital, private equity, and other forms of external financing? Would this herald a welcome liberalization and demystification of the legal market or a lamentable collapse of its professional underpinnings? I thought how improbable

---

[5] In May 2007, Slater & Gordon, an Australian law firm, became the first to float on a public market. See <http://www.slatergordon.com.au>.

[6] This research was conducted in 2004. See <http://www.which.co.uk>. Also see the various articles in (2006) 16 (6) *Consumer Policy Review*.

(and have since had this confirmed by specialists in the worlds of venture capital and private equity) that investors would choose to put cash into the traditional business model of most law firms—hourly billing, expensive premises, pyramidic organizational structures, and the rest. If it were possible to start afresh and build legal businesses from the ground up, surely the hard-nosed investors would not replicate traditional legal service models. They might buy a firm for its brand but would no doubt bring to bear a more contemporary suite of tools and techniques for managing the delivery of legal services. The new wave of investors and managers will surely find that individual law firms and the legal profession are inefficiently resourced and often over-resourced. They will quickly recognize that, within and beyond law firms, there is enormous duplication of effort and reinvention of the wheel; and, in turn, that there are too many lawyers and too few advanced systems.

And I reflected further that there would be no reason to suppose that investors would restrict themselves to legal services for consumers. I saw it as wrong-headed to think, as so many lawyers do, that the greatest impact would be felt amongst those who undertake high volume, low margin work. Before long, I thought, the entire legal marketplace will be under scrutiny, so that commercial law firms will also be challenged rather than purchased. I know that clients of such firms are increasingly dissatisfied with the level of fees that they pay, that they are under mounting pressure themselves to reduce their legal spend, and that they are pushing for much greater efficiency. Their attention is focused not only on the discrete high volume work. They are also looking at decomposing high value, big ticket deals and disputes and identifying what parts of these legal matters can be carried out more efficiently. And with around $65 billion being spent in 2007 on the top 100 US law firms and about £10 billion on the leading 50 UK firms, there is likely to be some scope for a saving or two. The major firms may feel they are beyond the scope of commoditization and systematization and that, on bet-the-ranch deals and disputes, the legal fees represent but pocket change in the grand scheme. But this is not the attitude I find amongst General Counsel of some of the world's largest organizations. These managers are increasingly expected to function as other business managers do: to find ways to improve productivity and to produce more output with less input. In other words, they are under pressure to reduce their legal budgets and spend. And these clients' loyalty to conventional firms will be limited if new legal businesses emerge that offer quicker, more convenient, lower cost alternatives to low and high value work that seem to be more geared to the interests of clients and are more business-like in their constitution.

1.3 A journey

To recap, the four thoughts that contributed to the writing of this book are as follows: (1) lawyers might fade from society as other craftsmen have done over the centuries; (2) lawyers are denying that they are lawyers because they recognize they need to change and diversify in response to shifts in the market; (3) no-one seems to be worrying about the fate of the next generation of lawyers; and (4) the delivery of legal services will be a very different business when financed and managed by non-lawyers.

As I mentioned earlier, however, this book's origins also lie beyond these relatively recent ruminations. A journey has also been fundamental in the writing of this work. I am referring here to a personal journey—my ongoing activities in the field of legal technology. It is a field that I find endlessly fascinating and one with which I hope to be involved for the duration. Indeed, it is my professional passion to help bring the law and the legal system from the nineteenth into the twenty-first century, in one single technology-fuelled bound.

The journey began in 1981, while I was studying law as an undergraduate at the University of Glasgow. IBM had not yet launched their personal computer and it was over a decade before the Web would be invented. Nonetheless, there was a great undercurrent of excitement about the potential of computers and it seemed to me then, as now, that there was no reason why the law should be unaffected by the great changes that were being anticipated. Indeed, it occurred to me that a good deal of the law, with its piles of documents and its libraries of information, would be particularly well-suited to the technologies that were emerging. In my final year of law school, I elected to write a dissertation in place of one of my final examinations and chose computers and the law as the subject matter. I was especially interested in the extent to which computers might solve legal problems and this led me to the field of artificial intelligence (AI) and law. With the help of a friendly librarian in the law library, I set about finding everything that had been written on this subject in the English language. (An aside—the law library was located on the fifth floor of the university library, a building that was perched on top of a hill; legend has it that the entire building is slipping down the hill at a rate of at least 1 millimetre per year, because someone forgot to factor in the weight of the books when designing the edifice; I remember wondering if computer technology might reduce the number of books and so stop the slippage; I now see that, so far, IT has had no such impact on reducing the amount of print on paper; I presume the library is continuing its journey.)

The research librarian found twenty-six publications in all and I ordered the lot. In retrospect, the research tools we had then were remarkably primitive. There was no question of downloading these articles and being immediately gratified (or not). Instead, I had to use a service known as an 'inter-library loan', the result of which was a delay of about four weeks and then the arrival of smudged photocopies of requested publications. I devoured these and began to formulate my own ideas.

In the end, my dissertation was entitled 'Computers and the Judicial Process'. I have it before me as I write this chapter. The final text, and two 'carbon copies' were produced by my mother using a manual typewriter and transcribed from various long-hand drafts by me. The large fonts on the front cover were created using a kind of sticky transfer known as Letraset. It was a different world. As for the contents of this undergraduate thesis, with the benefit of hindsight, it seems fantastically naive. Nonetheless, at its heart is a conviction that lives with me today—that there are many aspects of our justice system and the way we practise law that can and should be enhanced or even replaced by computer technology.

Having written this mini-thesis, I was hooked. I wanted to work further in the field. The dearth of publications in the area also urged me to investigate further. From my research, I had concluded that the most significant contribution to the field of computers and law had been made by Colin Tapper, of Magdalen College, Oxford. With a collaborator, David Gold, I wrote to Tapper, rather pushily arranged a meeting, and managed to convince him that I might be an interesting doctoral student to supervise. In October of 1983, I began my research as a postgraduate student at Balliol College in what was a joint project involving the Law Faculty and the Programming Research Group at the University of Oxford. Three fascinating years of study followed and I came to submit my doctoral thesis in May 1986. It was entitled 'Expert Systems in Law: A Jurisprudential Inquiry'. At the time, expert systems technology was attracting great interest, both in the academic world and in the popular press. These systems were conceived as computer systems that could solve problems and offer advice to the standard of human experts and sometimes even at a higher level. They operated in various domains, but most notably in medicine where there was great excitement about systems that could be fed a set of symptoms and could deliver an expert diagnosis. I was interested in analogous systems in law. I wanted to study systems that could engage in legal reasoning and solve legal problems. Could expert systems in law, I wondered, match the standard of great lawyers and judges?

In progressing my research into this and related possibilities, I drew heavily on the discipline of jurisprudence which, roughly speaking, is the philosophy of law. Although great thinkers had contributed to jurisprudence for several thousand years, I was particularly interested in work of the twentieth century, much of which had focused on how judges and lawyers go about coming to legal decisions, on the relationship between logic and the law, and on the nature of legal rules. I argued that much of this work was directly relevant for those who sought to build expert systems in law. The fundamental question I asked, and it was a theoretical and philosophical question, was whether there was anything inherent in or special about the nature of law and legal reasoning that prevented the development of computer systems that could hold stores of legal knowledge which they could apply to the facts of particular cases and so draw legal conclusions. My answer was that, from the point of view of legal theory and indeed computation, there were no insurmountable obstacles to building such systems. But I concluded that their scope would be limited. Given the state of AI in the 1980s and the teachings of jurisprudence up to that time, I could not see how computers could at that stage, if ever, be programmed to display the creativity, craftsmanship, individuality, innovation, inspiration, intuition, and common-sense, that lawyers often bring to bear in advising clients and solving legal problems. But I did claim that expert systems in law could hold large stores of complex, interrelated legal rules which they could apply to problems using some variant of deductive logic. I therefore saw expert systems as legal problem-solvers of a particular type—rule processing systems that could identify the literal interpretations of rules as they applied to the facts of particular cases. They could not hope to simulate the subtlety and sophistication, and reason at the level, of the finest judges or lawyers in the hardest of cases but would be of great use, I felt, in solving problems that were straightforward for legal experts and yet hopelessly difficult for non-experts.

I spent about a year revising my thesis for publication as my first book and it appeared the following year, in 1987, as *Expert Systems in Law*.[7] Although it is now out of print, sold relatively few copies, and betrayed in many places its origins as a self-consciously doctoral offering (and so was almost impenetrable), I still look upon it as a fair contribution to computers and law. I like to think that it demonstrated, at length and in a more academic way than my later work, both the potential and the limitations of IT in the law. Some of my fundamental thinking in the field has not really changed that much in the twenty years that have elapsed since its publication and, in many ways, most

---

[7] R Susskind, *Expert Systems in Law* (Oxford: Oxford University Press, 1987; paperback edition, 1989).

of what I have said since, and indeed say in this book, was anticipated in general terms in *Expert Systems in Law*. That said, I was keen at that time to move from theory to practice; out of the research laboratory and into the marketplace.

The following year, I did just that—I took my theoretical analysis and applied my findings in developing, with Phillip Capper, the world's first commercially available expert system in law—the Latent Damage System. The system advised on the law of limitation, by indicating the exact date after which a claimant could not start proceedings in 'latent damage' cases. Research time in this highly complex area of statute and case law was reduced from hours to minutes, as users were taken through a massive decision tree with over two million potential reasoning paths. How did it work? We embodied the legal expertise of Phillip Capper in the system. At the start of the project, he was Chairman of the Oxford University Law Faculty and the author of the first book on the Latent Damage Act 1986—clearly an expert. A user of the system was asked a series of questions about a case, as though in consultation with the expert, and the system identified when an action would be time barred (that is, when it could no longer be raised because time had run out). It also explained how it arrived at its conclusion. Phillip Capper freely admitted that the system frequently out-performed him. We wrote a book on the project that led to the system (*Latent Damage Law—The Expert System*) and we packaged the text together with a complimentary version of the system (2 x 5.25 inch floppy discs).[8]

As the 1980s drew to a close, feeling that I had contributed both theoretically and practically, I left AI and expert systems behind and started to focus instead on less ambitious but more practical systems that were beginning to take hold in technologically sympathetic law firms—litigation support, know-how databases, work product retrieval systems, and even word processing for lawyers. Personal computers were starting to appear on the desktops of lawyers, even if it was not entirely clear of what use they might be. The cynics regarded them as expensive paperweights. They could not see why lawyers should become typists. The enthusiasts waited for the killer application that might transform legal practice in the way that spreadsheets had taken the accounting and tax professions by storm. I do not think any single legal application of technology has ever fulfilled that hope (although automated document assembly, in the long run, may yet do so). But the birth

---

[8] P Capper and R Susskind, *Latent Damage Law—The Expert System* (London: Butterworths, 1988).

of the World Wide Web in 1992 was a turning point, an event as pivotal as the invention of the personal computer.[9]

At first, it was not at all obvious to me how profoundly the Web would affect humanity generally and the law in particular. But I watched its evolution in research centres, and in numerous industries and sectors around the world. I began to see that the Web could provide an entirely new channel for IT-enabled legal problem-solving. Whereas, in relation to expert systems, I had focused on the use of rule-based programming tools into which very formal representations of legislation and case law would be cast, I saw instead the idea of online legal guidance systems. The Web rapidly became my preferred delivery vehicle, carrying much less formal models of the law—practical, punchy, jargon-free renditions of the law as articulated by legal specialists. But whatever the underlying technology and knowledge models, the aim was the same—to spread legal knowledge and expertise using IT.

In this light, I saw that those who were saying at that time that expert systems were dead were, to some extent, missing the point. If we defined expert systems in terms of the underlying technologies, then it was true that comparatively little progress had been made on the commercial exploitation of rule-based systems since the 1980s. However, if we took a wider view, a functional perspective, that expert systems were about making scarce expertise and knowledge more widely available and more easily accessible, then the spirit was alive and well in the mid-1990s, because that is what many contemporary online legal services were all about.

I gathered notes and thoughts on the idea of a Web-based online legal service, read widely in neighbouring fields, visited more research establishments, tested ideas on colleagues and audiences to whom I spoke, and gradually developed a set of thoughts and predictions that I felt were sufficiently coherent to be pulled together into a book—*The Future of Law*, first published in 1996.[10] In retrospect, I can see that the first phase of my journey was complete. The book set out my stall, captured all of my thinking from the previous fifteen years and made a set of predictions about the next twenty.

---

[9] Throughout this book, I use 'the Web' as shorthand for the rather cumbersome 'World Wide Web'. The inimitable novelist, Martin Amis, is amusing in this context—'let's not forget that worldwide fatuity, "www", which cuts three syllables down to nine'—*The Second Plane* (London: Jonathan Cape, 2008) 195.

[10] R Susskind, *The Future of Law* (Oxford: Oxford University Press, 1996, paperback edition, 1998).

1.4 *The Future of Law*

The arguments and predictions in *The Future of Law* were many and varied. Perhaps the most crucial line of thought was that we were witnessing what I called a change in the 'information substructure' in society. I used this term to refer to the dominant means by which information is captured, shared, and disseminated within society. I observed, as some anthropologists have done, that you can see that human beings have travelled through four stages in relation to information substructure: the first was the age of orality, where communication was dominated by speech; thereafter, the era of script; then came print; and now into a world where communication is enabled by information technology. I said in 1996 that we were in a transitional phase between the third and fourth stages.

My next point, and I still strongly believe this, was that the information substructure in society, this dominant means by which information is captured, shared, and communicated, determines to a large extent the quantity of our law, the complexity of our law, the regularity with which our law can change, and those who are able to advise upon it and be knowledgeable about it. If we look at the way the law has evolved throughout history, we can understand this in terms of changes in the information substructure. I argued that there was going to be a shift in legal paradigm; although now the notion of 'paradigm' is rather overused. By this I meant that many of our fundamental assumptions about the nature of legal service and the nature of legal process would be challenged by the coming of information technology and the Internet. In other words, much that we had always taken for granted in the past, about the way that lawyers work and the way non-lawyers receive legal guidance, would change through technology. The paradigm shift I anticipated is reproduced in Figure 1.1.

I also identified a phenomenon that I introduced as the 'Technology Lag'. This was a lag between two forms of technology: data processing and knowledge processing. Data processing is our use of technology to capture, distribute, reproduce, and disseminate information. We have become extremely adept at this. Indeed, everyone who bemoans the information overload that affects all of us will say we have become too good at data processing. But now, knowledge processing is coming to the rescue. This is a set of technologies that helps us to analyse, sift through, and sort out the mountains of data that we have created and helps to make them more manageable. Data processing has advanced well ahead of knowledge processing, but the gap between the two, the Technology Lag, is going to close. When it closes, we will be fully in the information society. I believe now, and I believed then,

TODAY'S LEGAL PARADIGM	TOMORROW'S LEGAL PARADIGM
Legal Service	**Legal Service**
advisory service	information service
one-to-one	one-to-many
reactive service	proactive service
time-based billing	commodity pricing
restrictive	empowering
defensive	pragmatic
legal focus	business focus
Legal Process	**Legal Process**
legal problem solving	legal risk management
dispute resolution	dispute pre-emption
publication of law	promulgation of law
a dedicated legal profession	legal specialists and information engineers
print-based	IT-based legal systems

Fig. 1.1 The Shift in Legal Paradigm

that we are in a transitional phase between the print-based industrial society and the IT-based information society. Only when knowledge-based technologies allow us more effectively to manage these mountains of data that we have created, will we be fully in the information society.

I talked also of the 'latent legal market', and this attracted a lot of interest. This was the notion that many people in their social and in their working lives need legal help and would benefit from legal guidance but lack the resources, or perhaps simply the courage, to secure legal counsel from lawyers. Things have changed since then—on the Internet we now have vast resources available to people who can obtain practical, punchy legal guidance from the government's 2,500 websites or the many sites of the voluntary legal services sector. I contend that there is not just a latent legal market for the ordinary citizen but also for major organizations, when they too find it difficult (largely for reasons of cost) to secure legal guidance on all those occasions when they need it.

All of this led me to speak about access to justice—not in the sense that Lord Woolf, the former Lord Chief Justice, was speaking of access to justice, when he referred to improved access and greater access to dispute resolution; but in a broader sense. I had in mind the notion that as citizens we should be able to find out easily and quickly what our legal entitlements are, and in so doing, we should be able to avoid legal disputes.

I pointed at the same time to a phenomenon I refer to as 'hyper-regulation'. By that I meant we are all governed today by a body of rules and laws that are so complex and so large in extent that no-one can pretend to have mastery of them all. I argued then that hyper-regulation means not that there is too much law by some objective standard, but that there is too much law given our current methods of managing it. Of course I was creeping towards the suggestion that, with the coming of knowledge-based technologies, the volume of the law would be more easily managed with the assistance of our systems.

I also drew attention to innumerable emerging technologies that seemed likely, at the time, to be tremendously important. It is laughable in retrospect, but e-mail was one of them. When I suggested ten years ago that e-mail would become the principal means by which clients and lawyers would communicate, many people suggested I was dangerous, that I was possibly insane, that I should not be allowed to speak in public, and that I certainly did not understand anything about security or confidentiality. But that technology and many other emerging technologies have now firmly taken hold.

A vital and often overlooked point in all of this is that my view, as set out in *The Future of Law*, was a twenty-year view. I was speculating about changes from 1996 to 2016 (give or take). This current book was largely conceived in 2006, that is, at the half-way point of the twenty-year transition. This book is a sequel to *The Future of Law*. As will become apparent, a central theme is that, while much has happened since 1996, much more is yet to unfold. I believe that within the next ten years—it might be a little more, it might be a little less—we will see this Technology Lag, this gap between knowledge and data processing, closing. We will emerge into an era in which we will have at our finger-tips, through the Internet and other facilities, all manner of legal guidance and legal resources, that were barely imaginable ten years ago. And I suspect readers will find some of what I say here as hard to imagine as my readers did in 1996.

1.5 Progress over the last decade

So, what progress have we actually seen over the last decade? In terms of technology, I think it fair to say that the last ten years have witnessed some mind-boggling developments. Let me give a flavour. On some counts, there are now more than 600 billion pages accessible through the Web. Most of these are available to roughly 1.25 billion Internet users (there were fewer than 40 million users when *The Future of Law* was published). In 2006, the world generated 161 exabytes (billion gigabytes) of digital information (about 3 million times the information contained in all the books ever written, apparently). In the fourth quarter of 2007, more than 80 million users sold items worth over $16billion on eBay (the online car boot sale). Around 10 per cent of UK retail spending is now online. Each day, more than 50 billion e-mails are sent, while instant messaging (online, real-time chatting) is enjoyed by more than 300 million users. But it is not just text that is moving around the Internet. With dramatic advances in bandwidth, sound and video files are also downloaded with ease. Meanwhile, many cities have wireless broadband access throughout. Hand-held machines have also proliferated: most notably, iPods; Apple have sold more than 100 million of these units. And around 20 million users, in the US alone, listen to podcasts (broadly, audio recordings that are made available on the Internet).

Podcasts, along with blogs, are examples of the latest wave of Internet innovations. Blogs are personal commentaries that are made available online. More than 100 million people are said to have blogged. The new era to which podcasts and blogs belong is often characterized as that of *Web 2.0*. The idea is simple. As Internet users, we are becoming much more than passive recipients of the content published on websites. We are now able to contribute and participate directly and substantially. That is why *Time* recognized 'You' as its Person of the Year for 2006.[11]

User-generated content is coming in a variety of forms. We are sharing our video clips in the online world: YouTube, sold for £889 million, is a user-compiled collection of video clips that supports over 100 million views each day. We are supplying our own entries and changes to widely used online encyclopaedias: Wikipedia, the best known, free online encyclopaedia, was launched in 2001. It was created by non-paid volunteers in a remarkably short time, and is said to be as good, in most respects, as *Encyclopaedia Britannica* but is many times its size and appears in over 250 languages. We are socializing and networking electronically with kindred spirits: My Space, now owned by News Corp, has over 100 million users. Users are becoming providers. Recipients are now participants. We are finding radically new ways to communicate, to produce information, and to interact with one another. More than 150 million people are said to have online pets, for goodness' sake.

I could go on and on. The reality is that, in a variety of ways, the Internet and IT have already transformed our communication practices, revolutionized

---

[11] *Time*, 25 December 2006/1 January 2007, 28–31.

our information-seeking habits, and, increasingly, are radically changing the ways we collaborate, network, and buy and sell. I therefore join Kevin Kelly, in asking, as he did in his seminal article in *Wired* in 2005—'why are we not more amazed?'[12] Although we are in the middle of a veritable revolution, people are not generally jumping up and down and getting over-excited about it. Humanity is taking the Internet in its stride. Why? Perhaps we are witnessing what psychologists call 'hedonistic adaptation'—the idea that people adapt very quickly to good news. We seem to be taking on board these amazing developments that are changing and enriching our lives without being especially fazed.

Numerous sectors and industries have been radically altered as a result of the various technologies just noted—publishing, financial services, education, health, property, retail, and many more. What about lawyers, though? Have they moved on in the past decade? Hard though it is to conceive, most UK lawyers in 1996 did not have mobile phones or e-mail; they had no access to the Web; very few had laptops; and very few had home computers or hand-held machines. E-business was not even on their horizons. There was no concept then amongst most lawyers of knowledge management and, frankly, very little interest in IT generally. So, have they since advanced apace? On this question, I can flip from positive to negative in a matter of seconds. On the one hand, we can be in no doubt that there are notable pockets of excellence, not least in the English jurisdiction. Some legal pioneers have forged ahead, demonstrating the potential of all manner of exotic applications: from online legal advice systems to Internet-based auctions for procuring legal services; from multi-media knowledge systems to virtual case rooms. Some law firms have embraced document assembly, e-learning, and a whole bundle of other developments that I have written about in a column in *The Times* every three weeks. And it is to some extent revealing that I have comfortably had enough material and case studies to hand to write more than a hundred columns on all manner of fascinating and innovative applications of technology within the legal world. But if I am really honest, and this is where the negativity can creep in, these success stories remain exceptional. In the words of the Canadian science fiction author, William Gibson: 'The future has already arrived. It's just not evenly distributed yet.' The successes and innovations have been relatively rare. IT and the Internet have provided stiff competition for the phone, the ledger, the library, and the filing cabinet, but the substantive work of lawyers has yet to be reconfigured.

---

[12] 'We are the Web' *Wired*, August 1995, 96.

There can be no argument that most lawyers' communication and research habits have been transformed by the Internet. However, many legal practitioners who now have their Blackberry machines and Google as their home page seem to think that they have arrived at their final destination, technologically speaking. The revolution is over. In contrast, I believe that what lawyers have enjoyed so far is little more than improved plumbing. The infrastructure (the global network) is in place now, but the really exciting developments that will penetrate to the very heart of legal service and our legal systems are coming in the next decade. We are just warming up. Lawyers may feel they are through the revolution but, in reality, we have barely started.

How do we figure out what further progress we should expect? While it is tempting (for me, at least) to suppose that most change will be driven very largely by technology itself, to concentrate only on IT would be to let the tail wag the dog. And to leave future thinking and action to technologists would be to let the inmates run the asylum.[13] I now see that it is important also to factor in the disposition of lawyers and, crucially, broader trends in the legal market.

The reality is that most lawyers are relatively late adopters of new technology. Accordingly, we can expect that most law firms will not rush to accept new technologies and may even, in reactionary spirit, resist their introduction. It follows, for me, that listening too attentively to the views of most lawyers on the future is not terribly illuminating. They are not uninterested, objective observers. It is in most lawyers' natures and interests to claim that things tomorrow will be much the same as today but perhaps somewhat streamlined through technology. Lawyers tend to believe, rather conservatively, that the past will offer solid insight into the future. In contrast, I do not find it helpful to be fixated by or driven by what has already happened. There is the danger here, as others have put it, of walking backwards into the future; of being contained and constrained by our current and past ways. I hazard that, at the hands of technology, we are going to experience a number of discontinuities. It may be comforting, but it is naive to hope that we can simply extrapolate from current and recent behaviour and thus identify what is going to be happening in the year 2016 when it comes to legal practice. I suggest that it is a mistake to look for continuity.

If we do want to make informed guesses as to lawyers' likely adoption of emerging systems, I am increasingly convinced that it is most instructive to

---

[13] I borrow the phrase from Alan Cooper, *The Inmates are Running the Asylum* (Indianapolis: SAMS, 1999).

listen to their clients—to determine how their expectations and appetites are changing. It is from clients that we can glean probable trends in the legal market. It is client demand for new working practices and new efficiencies that will ultimately incline law firms to adopt new technologies. A few innovative and entrepreneurial firms will lead the way with some emerging systems. But most will wait to be nudged or dragged by their clients into twenty-first century legal practice.

1.6 The flow of this book

With the scene set, it is time now to offer an overview of the rest of the book.

In Chapter 2, I look at trends in the legal marketplace. I do so by introducing a model that depicts what I call 'the evolution of legal service'. I say that legal service will generally pass through five steps—bespoke, standardized, systematized, packaged, and commoditized. I use this model to explain a variety of phenomena, including the increasing pull by the market towards commoditization, the relative failure (so far) of various legal technologies (such as deal-rooms and auctions for legal services), and the challenges facing lawyers who seek, in a variety of ways, to innovate. I also deploy the evolutionary model as a tool for decomposing legal service into manageable tasks that can be resourced in different ways; for instance outsourcing to lower cost locations such as India. To clarify the arguments of the chapter, I offer two case studies, a personal one about public speaking and the other from the practice of tax.

I turn away from the law in Chapter 3 and focus my lens on what I regard as six vital trends in IT. I make a number of claims: IT is developing at an exponential rate; satisfaction with the performance of a wide range of information systems will steadily increase; online community and collaboration will transform the way we live and work; today's teenagers offer us a glimpse of the future and will come to expect far-reaching change; the distribution of tasks, the division of labour, between machine and man ('clicks and mortals') is currently shifting such that, in the future, much legal work, without raising eyebrows, will be discharged by systems; and that the technologies that will come to shape twenty-first century legal service will be 'disruptive' of conventional law firms.

In Chapter 4, I build on the findings of the earlier chapters and identify nine 'disruptive legal technologies', those that will redefine the legal marketplace and legal businesses. The technologies in question are automated document assembly, relentless connectivity, the electronic marketplace, e-learning, online legal guidance, legal open-sourcing, closed legal communities, workflow and project management, and embedded legal knowledge.

The subject matter of Chapter 5 is often neglected. It is clients. My main object of study here is the in-house legal departments of businesses; that is, lawyers who work as internal legal advisers to organizations (and not lay clients). I begin by pointing to the fundamental asymmetry between the commercial interests of clients and their lawyers. Building on a model that I call 'The Grid'—as introduced in 2000 in my book, *Transforming the Law*[14]—I show how technology, information, and knowledge interrelate: first within a law firm, thereafter within an in-house legal department and then amongst law firms and in-house legal departments. I go on to outline possible approaches to bringing law firms' and clients' data and knowledge systems together and demonstrate the way in which many fundamental challenges facing clients can be tackled through the judicious use of appropriate systems. In-house lawyers are increasingly discerning, knowledgeable, and demanding customers, who are becoming ever more passionate about securing better service at lower costs. I claim that they are destined to play a major role in urging change within law firms and so in the evolution of the legal profession. Their power and responsibility is massive.

I then turn my attention, in Chapter 6, to the resolution of disputes. I start by reviewing several significant, recent reforms and changes, and then show how the litigation work of law firms can be decomposed and sourced in different ways. I revisit the idea and reality of litigation support systems, relating the technologies involved to the emerging phenomenon of electronic disclosure. I suggest that electronic filing (e-filing) is a natural next step in streamlining and enhancing the interaction between court users and the courts. But I argue that e-filing must be introduced alongside improved case management systems, a term that itself, as I go on to suggest, covers a diverse range of systems. I reflect also on courtroom technology and the way in which IT can and should be embraced by judges. I turn also to more controversial matters: the development of online dispute resolution systems; and the challenge of dispute avoidance, a subject that leads to the important topic of legal risk management.

---

[14] R Susskind, *Transforming the Law* (Oxford: Oxford University Press, 2000; paperback edition, 2003) Ch 1.

In Chapter 7, the penultimate chapter, my object of study is the citizen and access to law and justice. I offer a wider definition of 'access to justice' than is normally entertained and suggest that there are six building blocks that will help us achieve greater access: empowered citizens, streamlined law firms, a healthy third sector, entrepreneurial alternative providers, accessible legal information systems, and enlightened public information policy. I anticipate, with some enthusiasm, the day when users will automatically be notified of changes in old law or the coming into force of new law; and we will achieve genuine 'promulgation' of our laws, thus bringing to life a pipe dream of many centuries.

Chapter 8 is the concluding chapter but I do not attempt there to summarize the book. Instead, I pull together various central themes and present a prognosis for lawyers. While the main focus is on those who work in law firms, I do also consider the future for in-house lawyers, barristers, and legal academics. My predictions cover the work of lawyers as well as the future of legal businesses.

What is the provenance, it might well be asked, of my various observations, claims, arguments, findings, predictions, and recommendations? What is the basis of all that follows? The book is rooted in a variety of sources: some academic theory (legal, management, social, information); my experience in practice (some time ago on the management board of an international law firm and, more recently, as an adviser to major law firms, General Counsel, governments and judges); empirical research (some of my own for clients, some of others); some speculation (of my own and versions of ideas expressed by clients and friends); and my own prejudices and preferences (relating to a world I would like to see). Like *The Future of Law*, the book is best regarded as a collection of provisional hypotheses about the future of legal service. If nothing else, I hope it provokes discussion, widens horizons, and encourages further reflection. Although, in my enthusiasm, I might sound as though I am making firm predictions and setting out some inevitabilities, I do not think any particular configuration of the future is predetermined. My purpose is not to predict the future but to lay out what I hope is a buffet of possible options, each of which may be tantalizing and irresistible to someone. I leave it to my readers to select what they fancy and turn my ideas into action. I follow Alan Kay in claiming that 'the best way to predict the future is to invent it'.

In concluding this introductory chapter, and for the sake of completeness, I should note what is beyond the scope of this book. One clear limitation came into focus on a recent trip to Japan, when I was asked by graduate students from Indonesia and Bangladesh about the relevance of my work for their countries. They explained their nations' widespread poverty and the very little impact that the Internet has had on most of their people. I wish I could help but I fear my work is only of relevance to countries whose citizens live above a basic subsistence level, and there is in place a legal system to which general access is provided, albeit poorly. My mission is to improve and transform the operation of existing legal systems; more fundamental economic challenges are beyond the remit of this work.

As a matter of emphasis more than scope, readers will find that I say much less about criminal law (practice, policy, and courts) than other aspects of modern legal systems. For example, I do not squarely confront the ways in which criminal trials might be transformed through technology, although much of my analysis of dispute resolution (in Chapter 6) and of access to law and justice (in Chapter 7) is directly applicable to the criminal arena.[15]

Finally, also beyond the ambit of this work, postponed for another time, is the question of the modernization of our legislature. In an entirely different context, the inimitable Monty Python team has provided me with an appropriate form of words. In the movie, *Monty Python and the Holy Grail*, a peasant by the name of Dennis, played memorably by Michael Palin, declares to King Arthur that: 'Strange women lying in ponds distributing swords is no basis for a system of government.' I think much the same about the House of Commons in the British Parliament. In our current age of pervasive instant communication, multi-media information flows, and real-time online communities, strange people congregating, posturing, and squabbling in an ancient debating chamber is surely no basis for a system of government. We can surely do better when it comes to the serious business of making new laws on behalf of 60 million people. It is tempting to suggest how, but my purpose here is not to contemplate the re-engineering of representative democracy. It is to consider the end of lawyers. And to that task I now turn.

---

[15] I have written elsewhere about the impact of IT on criminal justice—see 'Information technology and the criminal justice system' in P Mirfield and R Smith (eds), *Essays for Colin Tapper* (London: LexisNexis, 2003).

2

The Path to Commoditization

A running theme of this book is that a pair of related forces will fundamentally transform legal service in the coming decade and beyond. The first of the pair will be a market demand for increasing *commoditization* of legal services, while the second will be widespread uptake of *information technology* (IT). I explore the former in this chapter and turn to the latter in Chapters 3 and 4.

A word about terminology is needed at the outset. When most lawyers speak today about 'commoditization', they generally do so reluctantly and frequently do so through gritted teeth. The term 'commoditization' is often used pejoratively to downplay some line of legal service that is no longer worthy of the self-respecting lawyer. If legal work can be commoditized, the conventional wisdom runs, this means it is routine and repetitive and can be standardized or computerized. In turn, for most lawyers, this suggests that it can no longer yield decent fees, for it cannot be undertaken on an hourly billing basis or for a substantial fixed fee. Commoditization, on this view, is the arch-enemy of the legal profession.

I find this line of argument rather limited. First of all, it is unashamedly lawyer-centric and so it invariably neglects the interests of clients. And yet, from the point of view of the recipient of legal services, whether a General Counsel or a citizen-client, if work that needs doing can be standardized and computerized, this is generally good news, because it should mean lower fees. Second, and more significantly, the concept of commoditization is bandied about uncritically, by lawyers and policy-makers alike, with no apparent reflection on what its scope and implications might really be. It is wielded often as a term of derision but rarely as a carefully analysed concept. I think we can and should do better in defining a term that is now so widely relied upon in legal debate. Accordingly, amongst much else, I try to clarify the concept of commoditization in this chapter.

Taking a step to one side, classically speaking, commodities are physical and often raw materials such as coal, silver, or sugar. In business, the term is sometimes extended to include goods or artifacts that are mass produced and are often perceived to be of low value. If we refer to legal services as commodity, this is therefore metaphorical talk, because conventional legal and professional services are not physical materials, or goods, or artifacts. They are information services. But what is a commodity in the realm of information service? That is another key question that I answer in this chapter.

2.1 The evolution of legal service

I also have a broader purpose in this part of the book and that is to introduce a model that might help our understanding of the way in which legal service is evolving. The model, which can be applied to other professional services as well, depicts five steps on a path, as illustrated in Figure 2.1. Using this model, I make two main claims: first, that for the majority of legal services, there is an increasing pull by the market to the right-hand side, that is, towards becoming commodity (in the specific sense that I explain in some detail); and, second, that this move from left to right is being enabled very largely (but not exclusively) by existing and emerging information technologies.

As with all models, it is, of course, a simplification of reality. I am aware, for example, that the boundaries between each step on the path are fuzzy; that not all legal services evolve neatly and in a linear manner through each step; that some legal services might evolve no further than one particular step; and that some legal services may not evolve from the first step in that they may begin life at one of the later steps. Nonetheless, despite these limitations, my experience of introducing this model to numerous law firms and their clients has been positive. I therefore hope it serves as a useful tool for others to explain and predict the evolution of particular legal services and to bring into focus the key strategic options that lawyers face in developing

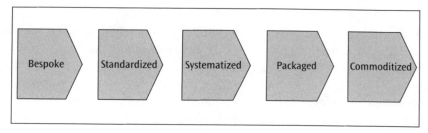

Fig. 2.1 The Evolution of Legal Service

their services for the future. I also hope that it provides a common vocabulary or framework that allows lawyers to compare their approaches to work with those of colleagues within and beyond their firms.

The first of the five steps along the evolutionary path is what I term 'bespoke' legal service. I have in mind traditional, hand-crafted, one-to-one consultative professional service, highly tailored for the specific needs of particular clients. I have come to realize, from addressing American audiences, that 'bespoke' is not a term that is used in the US. I am surprised. In the UK, we speak of bespoke software when we mean software that is specially written for one client or customer. We also talk about bespoke tailoring—a bespoke suit, of a Savile Row variety for example, is tailored for one individual. This contrasts with the off-the-peg suit which is designed to fit (give or take) many people. In short, bespoke service is highly customized service. Advocacy in the courtroom is a good example of bespoke service. The offering here is, in a sense, disposable, in that it cannot really be re-used. Clever arguments are articulated in the hearing room and then substantially lost in the ether, not preserved or bottled for re-use. Another illustration is the lawyer who drafts contracts by starting with a clean sheet of paper, a blank canvas, and not with some pre-existing text or documentation. The bespoke service is ordinarily provided by one lawyer or a very small number of legal practitioners and is delivered in a very personalized manner, usually supported by face-to-face meetings. The bespoke service may or may not be of a high quality. While much will depend on the talent of the lawyer delivering the service, creating a new document afresh, for example, can be an error-prone exercise.

Moving beyond bespoke work, when legal tasks are recurrent, and many are, there is the tendency for lawyers, in one way or another, to 'standardize'. This is the second step of my evolutionary path. Standardization avoids duplication of effort or reinvention of the wheel. If a particular problem or task has been faced in the past, why not draw liberally on previous experience and work product? There are two forms of standardization. The first is standardization of process, where, for example, lawyers rely upon such tools as checklists or procedure manuals that articulate good practice. A proven approach or method for some given legal job is captured and re-used. The second is standardization of substance. This involves lawyers re-using pre-articulated bodies of text such as standard form documents, precedents, and templates, or past work product, such as opinions, advices, or solutions that have been deployed in the past. The standardization that I have in mind in this second step is paper-based. As with bespoke service, standardized service also tends to be delivered in a highly personalized manner, with regular, direct contact between the lawyer and client.

The third step on the evolutionary path is when legal service becomes 'systematized'. Here, systems are developed and used for the conduct of legal work. I am referring to systems that are designed for internal use only within a legal unit, so that within a law firm, for instance, the lawyers will be the users and not the clients. This is not simply the use of IT for the storage of standard procedures and documents. Instead, a variety of enabling technologies automate legal activities. For instance, paper checklists and written procedures can be brought to life using techniques such as interactive checklisting and electronic workflow, while the drafting of documents can be taken beyond the cutting and pasting of standard text into the realm of automatic document assembly, whereby polished contracts can be generated after a user has responded to a series of questions (the system holds standard blocks of text and rules for the use of this text—more is said of this in Section 4.1). In the world of banking and finance, many major law firms have developed document assembly tools to assist in the generation, internally, of large bodies of complex loan documentation, as with Allen & Overy's *newchange* system.[1] At the same time, innumerable smaller practices use these techniques in their conveyancing and personal injury practices. At this step on the evolutionary path, these tools are for internal use only, enabling speedier and more consistent legal work. However, the way in which the service is delivered is frequently less personalized. Electronic deal-rooms and case-rooms can be used—by consulting a website, clients can access their documents on an online basis, and also determine the status and cost of work undertaken for them.

From a technical point of view, the transition from the third to the fourth step of the evolutionary path is often fairly straightforward. Systems that are

---

[1] <http://www.allenovery.com>.

used within a law firm can be made directly accessible to clients, usually across the Internet. One obvious example here is when law firms offer their clients access to their internal knowledge systems. More ambitious illustrations are where document assembly systems are given to clients to use directly, as Eversheds do to enable their clients to generate their own employment contracts.[2] The systems of the law firm and the knowledge embedded within them are thus 'packaged' for the client's convenience as a form (crudely) of DIY legal service. This is the fourth step in the evolution of legal service.

There are various other ways in which packaged legal services can be offered. They are based on IT. One is that a package might be brought directly to the marketplace without having evolved through the other three steps. LRN is a company that produces legal compliance tools which do precisely this.[3] This company deploys multi-media, e-learning technology in support of its offerings. Non-lawyers can easily and rapidly learn about pressing legal issues, such as money laundering, by running through a video-based presentation and then a question-and-answer session. The use of multi-media in this way will be increasingly popular in packaged service, as discussed in Sections 4.4 and 6.7. Some major law firms repackage some of their multi-jurisdictional research as online legal reference services. The first firm to do this in a serious way was Linklaters with some of its *Blue Flag* products.[4] For such law firms, packaged offerings are branded services, linked closely to the providing firms. These are distinctive offerings that seek to differentiate their providers and are ordinarily made available for a fee or on a licence basis. Another approach to packaged legal service is the development of electronic legal modules or products that can be implanted into clients' processes or systems. These packages might settle within clients' Intranets or be embedded more deeply within their systems. They provide a powerful way of injecting legal expertise into the life cycles of clients' business activities. This will prove to be a crucial technique for legal risk management.

The most subtle and potentially controversial transition on the evolutionary path is from the fourth to the fifth and final step, to that of 'commoditized' legal service. The central idea here is that a legal service or offering is very readily available in the market, often from a variety of sources, and certainly at highly competitive prices. A legal commodity, as I define it (and I fully accept that others use this term differently) is an electronic or online

---

[2] <http://www.eversheds.com/hrcontractdemo>.
[3] <http://www.lrn.com>.
[4] <http://www.linklaters.com>.

legal package or offering that is perceived as a commonplace, a raw material that can be sourced from one of various suppliers. Just as barrels of oil or sacks of sugar are regarded as basic and readily available offerings, then so too with legal commodities. As with a package, a commodity is an online solution that is made available for direct use by the end user, often on a DIY basis. Online debt collection services are legal commodities (even though, but two decades ago, debt collection was handled in a bespoke manner). Much of the material found on legal websites consists of legal commodities—more or less similar analyses of new regulations, for example.

Sometimes, lawyers are inclined to speak of some widely used standard form contracts as commodities. For instance, they say that the use of the following has become commodity work—the master agreement of the International Swaps and Derivatives Association (ISDA) and the standard form construction and engineering contract of the International Federation of Consulting Engineers (FIDIC). I used to agree with this but I have changed my mind.[5] These standard form agreements belong in my standardized step. The confusion here is the imprecise use of the term, 'commoditization'. Referring to ISDA and FIDIC work as commodity work is a shorthand way of saying that it is highly routine and that not much cash can be made there any more. I reserve the word 'commodity' in a legal context to IT-based systems and services. This means that some legal services that lawyers already think have been commoditized are often paper-based and manually administered and so are not yet as efficiently delivered as they could be.

In summary, a commoditized legal service is an IT-based offering that is undifferentiated in the marketplace (undifferentiated in the minds of the recipients and not the providers of the service). For any given commodity, there may be very similar competitor products, or the product is so commonplace that it is distributed at low or no cost. My conception of commoditization in law is therefore narrower than that of the many lawyers who seem to use the term to refer to anything from the second to the fifth steps on my evolutionary path. The danger of that use of the word is—once again—that it obscures the commercial reality that high quality service, charged at a reasonable price and subject to regular update and maintenance, can be delivered in standardized, systematized, and packaged form. To reject these as mere commodity is to miss an opportunity to serve clients well and, if delivered cannily, to make a fair profit at the same time.

---

[5] My early thinking was set out in R Susskind, 'From Bespoke to Commodity' (2006) 1 *Legal Technology Journal* 4.

Lawyers fear commoditization (in my sense) for two reasons. First, it seems to devalue the practice of law, reducing it to a mere electronic commonplace. The second is a fear of the economics of information commodity markets. Carl Shapiro and Hal Varian summarize this neatly:

In a free market, once several companies have sunk the costs necessary to create an undifferentiated product, competitive forces will usually move the product's price toward its marginal cost—the cost of manufacturing an additional copy. And because the marginal cost of reproducing information tends to be very low, the price of an information product, if left to the marketplace, will tend to be low as well. What makes information products economically attractive—their low reproduction cost—also makes them economically dangerous.[6]

And so, if more than two firms have made the initial investment in what turns out to be a series of very similar online legal products or services, then competitive forces will tend to drive the price of the commodity down towards the cost of reproducing and distributing the information, that is, to the cost of producing one new copy. Because this cost is negligible, the prices of legal information products, where there is competition, tend rapidly towards zero. Lawyers fear services whose price is zero. On the face of it, lawyers can therefore be expected to resist travelling along the evolutionary path I describe.

2.2 The pull of the market

Even at first glance, a number of distinctions can be plotted along the evolutionary path that I have laid out. For example, in relation to billing, service towards the left tends to be delivered on an hourly billing basis, while service towards the right tends to be offered on a fixed fee basis. The style of service also differs along the path. On the left, there is a stronger emphasis on the service being delivered by a trusted adviser (often even a thought leader), while offerings towards the right may be strongly branded but are essentially shrink-wrapped. Psychologically and emotionally, the comfort zone of law firms is towards the left, while movement towards the right is increasingly uncomfortable.

---

[6] H Varian, 'Versioning: The Smart Way to Sell Information' in JH Gilmore and BJ Pine (eds), *Markets of One* (Boston: Harvard Business School Press, 2000) 134.

From an IT point of view, each step along the evolutionary path requires different forms of enabling technology. Any firm that aspires to providing packaged services, for example, must generally embrace online and document assembly technologies, while those that offer systematization will inevitably need to adopt Intranet, workflow, and (again) document assembly techniques. More generally, the further to the right one goes, the more 'disruptive' the technologies become, in that these systems fairly fundamentally challenge the conventional, bespoke way of working.[7]

The most common initial reaction to the model that I encounter from partners in law firms is as follows—where they have access to a large red pen, they draw a very bold circle around the bespoke box and then utter two assertions: first, that their firms only undertake bespoke work and, second, as a matter of strategy, that is how they wish to stay. The majority of lawyers have little appetite for the journey towards the right. Because commoditization is anathema to many lawyers, any movement in its direction is frequently regarded as generically offensive.

As a matter of fact, however, on careful analysis, very few law firms live by bespoke work alone. As one of innumerable possible examples, look at the leading banking practices of the largest firms in London—most of these firms have standardized long ago, many have systematized and the more innovative have already packaged. More importantly, as a matter of strategy, for reasons I discuss later in this chapter, it may in any event not be sustainable or desirable for firms to resist a move to the right.

I want now to challenge some of these first impressions in some detail. In the first instance, it is helpful to be clear about the nature of legal engagements for clients. Work on an individual matter for a client will seldom map directly onto just one of the five steps on the evolutionary path. Instead, work will tend to be distributed across a number of the steps. Crucially, very few engagements, as just hinted, are purely bespoke. And only a very few firms can live by bespoke work alone; these tend to be smaller, more niche, and genuinely distinctive practices. For most matters, it is hard to disentangle and undertake the bespoke in complete isolation. In any event, it is surely not politic, I would have thought, for a firm to say to its client that it only wishes to be involved in the expensive, bespoke aspects of any particular transaction or dispute and that it washes its hands of the rest (although I do know some very large firms who are sufficiently confident to do this).

---

[7] Disruptive technologies are more fully explained in Section 3.6, and are the sole subject matter of Ch 4.

The key question in relation to any particular matter is this: what is the optimum balance and distribution of tasks and activities across the five steps? Clients should not expect that work will be, for example, entirely standardized. They should expect a spread of approaches for any given matter.

That said, it is clear from my research and discussions with clients over the past few years that they are increasingly encouraging law firms in a rightwards direction. This is partly for financial reasons. On the one hand, as mentioned, work towards the right tends to be offered on a fixed cost basis and clients tend to welcome the certainty that this brings. On the other, they are right to expect efficiency gains as a service becomes standardized, systematized, and more. Clients are attracted to firms with a strong track record in particular areas and this surely entails an ability to draw more rapidly and less expensively on past experience. Why pay for the wheel to be reinvented?

But clients are also attracted to the right because of the promise of better performance by their advisers. With more formal organization of procedures, knowledge, and expertise in place, gathered on a collective basis from across a firm, this should bring greater quality, consistency, and speed of turn-around. This is the essence of the discipline known as knowledge management. More, clients expect a match between the evolution of their offerings and those of their legal advisers. A shrink-wrap software supplier, for example, will require packaged or commoditized software licence agreements to accompany its products. Likewise, financial institutions are happy to instruct lawyers on a bespoke basis for their new products but as their offerings themselves become packages and commodities, it is reasonable for them to expect lawyers' input to be similarly configured. And likewise, as bespoke legal advice becomes more costly, small- to medium-sized businesses will increasingly find this type of advice to be beyond their reach. They will only be able to afford legal service that matches their scale, which will tend to be towards the right of the path. It might be thought, ironically, that only large firms will have the resources to develop these services. However, as examples in this book illustrate, some small and yet highly innovative firms do produce impressive online services.[8]

If the clients' pull away from bespoke service were not sufficient to incline law firms rightwards, then the prospect of competitors driving in that direction should surely give pause for thought. Although direct competitors may

---

[8] eg Fidler & Pepper (see Section 3.3) and Tessa Shepperson (Section 4.5).

also feel most comfortable at the bespoke end, it is realistic to be concerned that one or some may break rank and so attain first mover competitive advantage. Major firms should also be wary of smaller firms who might seek to launch services towards the right, with a view to migrating to the left—the plan here would be to build confidence through efficient routine work and so position these smaller firms for more bespoke, high-end work. A further source of competition is the new player who might jump, as LRN has done, straight into packaged services and seek to dominate that sector. Alternative forms of legal businesses, as permitted under the Legal Services Act 2007, are also likely to start trading some way along the evolutionary path. All of these possible competitors are potentially disruptive and worrying for the law firm. With client pull and competitor thrust in a rightwards direction, it is unlikely that many law firms can prosper by bespoke work alone.

And if none of these arguments convince, then think for a moment about firms which are asked to deliver services on a fixed price basis. Quite naturally they find themselves looking for efficiencies and savings; and so, quite naturally, they will find themselves attracted to the right of the evolutionary path.

2.3 Opportunities for innovative lawyers

While some firms regard any movement to the right as threatening and unsettling, others will see exciting opportunities here. Systematization of service offers the chance to provide clients with a more responsive and competitively priced service and, if the offering is not matched by competitors, then profitability can be maintained and even increased. Firms that deploy automatic document assembly technology internally, for instance, may reduce the unit cost and unit profitability of each document produced for clients, but can radically increase their volume.

Far more contentious is the provision of packaged legal service. The intuition of many lawyers is that bespoke work is the most profitable for them and that venturing along the path that I have laid out is, by steps, increasingly unattractive from a commercial point of view. I accept, for reasons discussed earlier in relation to the tendency towards zero of prices in information commodity markets, that the commoditization of legal services of itself will yield little or no profit. However, I remain of the view, as first fully articulated throughout my book, *The Future of Law*,[9] that packaged online legal services can indeed give rise to substantial income and profit; indeed, on some occasions, much greater profit than is possible when selling one's time on an hourly basis.

I do accept, though, that it is early days and that we have not fully explored the ways in which cash might best be made from providing online legal services. So it has always been with new developments. Consider broadcast radio, which is a well settled service. It was far from clear, at the outset, how to make money from this innovation. Apparently, a magazine called *Wireless World* even sponsored a contest to determine the best business model for radio. The winning idea was 'a tax on vacuum tubes', with radio commercials being one of the more unpopular choices.[10]

At the current time, I believe the most promising commercial opportunity is this: if a chargeable online legal service is developed and is of such value and use to clients that they are prepared to pay serious fees for its use and there are no competitor products, then once the initial investment in the system has been made, all later sales yield funds that are unrelated to the expenditure of time and effort by lawyers. I like to refer to this as 'making money while you sleep'. It will immediately be seen that keeping the competition out of the market is central to success. Providers must lift the metaphorical bar so high that others will shy away from attempting to imitate. This does not mean that the price should be extremely high because this can result either in purchasers not buying or in potential imitators identifying the offering as potentially lucrative and therefore deserving of serious investment. The commercial trick, therefore, is to maintain the offering as a package and not let it slip into becoming a commodity. This distinction, between packaging and commoditizing, has not been recognized by most lawyers in the past. While the latter may indeed be commercially unattractive, I believe the potential for profitable packaged work is considerable. But the economics at play here are quite different from the business models with which most lawyers are familiar. Legal practitioners who want to climb the learning curve rapidly and learn how best to charge for packaged knowledge should draw heavily, as I have done, on the thinking of information economists. I have found *Information Rules*, by Carl Shapiro and Hal Varian, to be an especially

---

[9] R Susskind, *The Future of Law* (Oxford: Oxford University Press, 1996; paperback edition, 1998) especially Ch 8.

[10] See H Varian, 'Competition and market power' in H Varian, J Farrell, and C Shapiro (eds), *Economics of Information Technology* (New York: Cambridge University Press, 2004) 9.

rich source of guidance.[11] From this book, we can learn about techniques such as value-based pricing and versioning (for example when you deliver different versions of the same online offering, according perhaps to the level of experience of the user).

So what can a firm do if another competitor does indeed enter the market, if a package threatens to become a commodity? In summary, several options are open to the law firm. One is to add further value to the package to enhance it in a significant way so that it defies commoditization and once again delivers benefits to the client that are replicated by no other offering in the market. Another tactic is to sell the package to another organization that perhaps sees opportunities for maintaining it as a package and resisting commoditization where the law firm does not. A third option is to build brand awareness, so that users may choose a high profile offering over an unknown, even if the substance of the services is indistinguishable. A final option, when the transition to commoditization seems inevitable, is to give the commodity away to the marketplace at no cost to users. This is clearly a form of marketing. But many firms have unnecessarily adopted this tactic before fully exhausting the income potential of the packages in which they have invested. Some have done so in the mistaken belief that their rightful place is far further to the left and that the rest is a distraction for others to handle.

Although most partners in professional firms say that their firms mainly undertake bespoke work, and that is how they wish to stay, I am suggesting there is a natural flow so that many services will move, more or less quickly, along the evolutionary path. When clients are faced with a legal problem, they will increasingly be attracted to service towards the right and will increasingly call for justification and explanation when firms insist on staying to the left. In contrast, law firms will generally want to stay at the bespoke end and the partners will usually lack enthusiasm when departure from this end is proposed. Here lies the fundamental tension between the needs and wants of clients and their advisers. This is a theme that I reflect upon in more detail in Section 5.1, in my discussion of the asymmetry between lawyers and their clients.

Generally, though, if legal work is (for the provider) routine and repetitive, it is surely reasonable for clients to expect a high degree of systematization, some pre-packaged knowledge services, and even some commoditization,

---

[11] C Shapiro and H Varian, *Information Rules* (Boston: Harvard Business School Press, 1999).

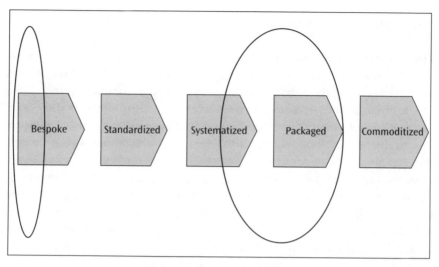

Fig. 2.2 Scope for Innovation

along with highly competitively priced (usually fixed cost) and well distilled collective expertise. If legal work is (for the provider) challenging and complex, it is then reasonable for clients to expect expensive, creative, genuinely expert, and trustworthy professionals, so long as they are supported by first-rate knowledge and research resources, perhaps charging by the hour but, more attractively and better, on the basis of the value brought to the client.

No matter how strong the gravitational pull to the right, I accept therefore that, because of the nature of some legal work, there will always be a place for bespoke work. But I do think that the demand (and justification) for genuinely bespoke work will diminish over time. It is helpful in this context to imagine the series of evolutionary steps as a conveyor belt, always running and bringing about a natural flow of work from left to right. Work that at one time is bespoke will move rightwards, while standardized service in its turn will transition into systematized, and so on. This presents a clear challenge for lawyers who are keen to remain very largely in the bespoke camp—they must continually innovate and so generate new bespoke offerings, because what is bespoke today will not be so in the future. This suggests that the scope for innovation (and so differentiation) in legal services lies as illustrated in Figure 2.2: on the one hand in creating new bespoke work and, on the other, in developing systems and packages ahead of the competition. Lawyers, in other words, can be innovative in the advice that they offer as well as the way in which they deliver their services.

2.4 Some apparent failures explained

The model introduced in this chapter helps to shed light on a number of disappointments that have been endured in the world of legal technology. Take, for example, the apparent failure of online deal-rooms.[12] In 2000, there was a burst of activity amongst a number of leading firms in the City of London as each sought to set the standard for the establishment of what are, essentially, online shared spaces into which all the documents on a transaction can be put. More prosaically, a deal-room is a website set up as a repository for materials generated in the course of a transaction. Some firms thought they could secure competitive advantage by being the first to market with their own deal-rooms. In the event, law firms were disappointed with the take-up of deal-rooms and many no longer offer them to clients; a variety of third party providers and many banks now provide the systems instead. The harsh reality, however, was that many clients in major transactions expressed little interest in these online repositories. Legal luddites cite deal-rooms as typical illustrations of failed legal technology.

But we should look more carefully. It is noticeable that many law firms, understandably, offered their deal-rooms in the early days (circa 2000) in support of very major transactions. In retrospect, in the light of my model, we can perhaps see why deal-rooms of that sort were indeed a disappointment. In terms of the evolutionary path, these deal-rooms were being proposed in support of high-value bespoke work. But it is precisely in relation to such transactions that most clients prefer a personalized, high-touch service and have little interest in logging on to websites to pick up documents or monitor progress.

In contrast, I believe, the real value in deal-rooms, although we may not even end up using that term to describe the systems, will be in their use in more routine and repetitive work, where the associated legal service is being standardized, systematized, and more. When standardization and systematization are in play in support of transactions, there will tend to be an appetite for cost savings, efficiencies, and process improvement. It will be far easier to integrate the use of deal-rooms into that atmosphere and environment than to graft them in a rather contrived way on to conventional bespoke service.

Another technology that was perceived by many doubters to have failed at around the same time as deal-rooms, was the use of auctions for the selection of legal advisers. In Section 4.3, I argue that this technique will yet succeed

---

[12] These are more fully discussed in Section 5.5.

and, more, it will present fundamental challenges for lawyers who receive instructions in the conventional way. For now, though, just as with deal-rooms, with the benefit of hindsight, we can see that most unsuccessful attempts to use online auctions were in the context of selecting law firms for their participation on panels or for their work on large-scale, significant transactions or disputes. However, for such panel work, for heavy duty legal services, the emphasis here is usually at the bespoke, personalized end of the spectrum. For that kind of work, the cost of legal service is rarely of overriding significance. In contrast, the main purpose of using online auction techniques tends to be to help to locate the least costly product or service or firm on offer. Once again, it seems to me, we can see that the attempt to overlay this technology on bespoke work led to apparent failure. However, when work comes to be standardized, systematized, and packaged, the emphasis on bespoke personalized service lessens and the focus instead is on efficiency and value for money. In that context, I anticipate that online auctions will be successfully deployed and increasingly so, as one moves from left to right on the evolutionary path.

Another disappointment in law firms, and indeed in most commercial organizations, has been in the field of knowledge management. It has promised much and delivered a good deal less. Knowledge management is not exclusively a matter of technology, although emerging systems did largely build the hopes of knowledge exponents during the 1990s. The idea is straightforward enough—it is about systematically organizing and exploiting the collective knowledge of a business. And it is clear that a wide range of technologies can help here. One amongst many pitfalls into which lawyers have fallen in the knowledge management area is the trap of trying to develop one single knowledge system for use across a large, diverse business. It is very unlikely that one single knowledge tool (a search engine, for example) will satisfy the needs of different practice areas whose work is spread differently across the five steps. In the world of knowledge management, one size fits none. And we can see this as we look across the evolutionary path. Take, for example, the lawyer whose work is largely bespoke. This lawyer will require quite different knowledge resources from the lawyer whose work is mainly systematized. The former will look for good know-who systems, flexible online research, and stores of work product; while the latter will need intelligent checklists, workflow systems, document assembly, and a well stocked Intranet. Many, if not most, knowledge initiatives in law firms have failed to recognize this distinction and instead have sought to introduce monolithic knowledge systems that, in the event, cannot possibly be flexible enough to support legal work across the evolutionary path.

A final apparent failure of IT that can be explained in terms of the path towards commoditization has arisen in the context of bidding for legal work. In the past decade, it has become fashionable for clients who have been procuring legal service to pose questions in tender documents about law firms' technological capability. This has produced frenzies of confusion. Partners of law firms (whose control freakery reaches new levels when drafting proposals) have tended to ask their IT people to draft some text about their firms' systems. This demand has often been seen by partners as an opportunity to check what they have been spending all their money on. In turn, the IT staff, who have generally been willing but not au fait with the niceties of legal work, have produced some hi-tech gobbledygook which is beyond the ken of the partners in question but looks the part. Everyone is then happy. Except the client. Because clients, or the wise ones at least, are not interested in technology for its own sake. They do not really want to know about systems per se. Instead, they are curious to know if the investment law firms are making in IT means that time or money is saved, that the quality of work is increased, that the firm has become more responsive, or that life will be easier for them. In other words, clients want to know if, how, and why IT is changing the way legal service is delivered. The answer often should have been that the tools that they have developed have reduced the need for inefficient, hand-crafting of routine components of legal work. This can now be demonstrated on the evolutionary path. Indeed, one of my hopes is that the offerings of competing law firms can be compared by indicating, for individual pieces of work, how the respective firms would spread the tasks involved across the spectrum I have provided. This leads directly to the question of identifying the constituent tasks, to which I now turn.

2.5 Decomposing and multi-sourcing

How should a law firm respond to the challenge of moving in a rightwards direction across the evolutionary path? I stress here that responses will tend to vary. Different practice areas may, quite properly, adopt different strategies. Those at the bespoke end, such as corporate lawyers (certainly in England), will view their options rather differently from those who lean towards systematization and even packaging, such as banking lawyers. It is interesting to note, though, that many corporate lawyers overstate the extent to which their work is genuinely bespoke. The potential for systematizing the process of due diligence, for instance, is considerable, if not yet realized.

In any event, I suggest to my clients that there are three basic options open to a law firm and its practice areas. The first is the option to lead the way, that is, to pioneer and play the role of first mover along the path, with all the benefits and potential risks that this entails. The second option is to invest enough to be ready to respond, poised to drive rightwards in the event that a competitor does so or a new entrant jumps in at a later step. The aspiration here might be to avoid being left behind or it might be, more ambitiously, to become a 'fast second', an organization that becomes a market leader not by originating new business ideas but being the best to exploit the ideas of others.[13] The third option is to resist any move to the right. In the medium to long term, this third option, it seems to me, for most areas of legal work, is commercially suicidal. Given that these strategic options are open not simply to law firms as single indivisible units, but are those that individual practice areas should face, I would expect, in any major firm, that some of its practice areas might adopt the first strategy; others would embrace the second; while still others may even adopt the third in a concerted programme, perhaps, of fazing out some particular service lines.

In any event, if it is accepted that a move to the right is desirable or inevitable, law firms must assess how best to resource such a shift.

So, how should lawyers resource legal work in the future? In the few pages that follow, I propose a broad answer to that question and in so doing I provide an outline of what I believe is a more systematic and methodical technique for allocating legal work than has been deployed in the past. I do stress that it is but an outline; management consultants who specialize in legal businesses could no doubt develop what I have to say into a fuller methodology.

I start by recalling an observation that I make earlier in the chapter, that legal engagements or matters, whether they are deals, disputes, or advisory work, should not be regarded as indivisible, monolithic blocks of legal work. Instead, I suggest that any legal job or category of legal work can be decomposed, that is, broken down, into constituent tasks, processes, and activities. From now on, I use the term 'tasks' fairly generically to include processes and activities as well as tasks. In this sense, tasks are identifiable, relatively distinct, and so separable modules or portions of work.

---

[13] For an interesting discussion of why it may be more rewarding for companies to be a 'fast second' rather than pioneers, see C Markides and P Geroski, *Fast Second* (San Francisco: Jossey-Bass, 2004).

If a legal team (a firm or in-house department) is contemplating applying the techniques of decomposition to some area of its business, a prior issue here is the identification of the types of engagement that are best suited to this treatment. I generally advise my law firm clients to choose those types of work that are core to their businesses. While some enthusiasts might step forward and offer their work for this process, these should be rejected if they are, frankly, peripheral to the firm. On analysis, it often transpires that a remarkably small number of categories of work bring in a large proportion of a firm's fee income or consume the lion's share of an in-house department's resource. Here, as elsewhere, the 80/20 rule applies. Focus on the areas of practice that genuinely count.

There is no unique or correct way of decomposing any particular category of work into tasks. Legal work can be diced and spliced in many ways, into all sorts of different chunks. Sometimes, the basic tasks will correspond to fairly obvious phases across the life cycle or timeline of the work involved—it might be thought that the work can be divided into, say, five consecutive phases and that each can be isolated and handled separately. Alternatively, the identification of different tasks may have more to do with the nature of work involved, quite apart from when, in the order of events, it is undertaken; so that tasks such as legal research or document management might be regarded as relatively distinct tasks that need to be undertaken at various stages in the life of the deal or dispute.

Sometimes, by decomposing legal work and viewing it with the eye of a systems analyst, rather than a lawyer, it will become apparent, in the jargon, that some 're-engineering' can occur. This means that some fairly fundamental reconfiguration or reorganization of the tasks can be introduced which of itself might bring greater efficiency. An analyst, looking at some legal work with a fresh mind, might pinpoint, for example, some opportunities for avoiding the duplication of tasks or might identify some tasks as redundant. From a systems and process analysis point of view, the lawyer sometimes cannot see the wood for the trees.

For any particular engagement or category of work, once some collection of constituent tasks has been agreed, the fundamental challenge is to look at each task in turn and honestly assess the optimum way of executing each, bearing in mind the ways in which the tasks relate to one another.

One initial exercise, I suggest, is to assess the legal and commercial risks that flow from each task and its dependent tasks. It may be justifiable, in risk management terms, not to undertake a particular task at all or to perform it in a much reduced way. Given that legal resources are invariably limited, lawyers should always be alive to the possibility of excising tasks or parts of tasks, so long as this does not give rise to serious risks or the loss of important opportunities.

Assuming a given task is still deemed necessary, a next step is to allocate that task to steps along my evolutionary path. In so doing, the analysts involved should be asking 'what is the optimum way of conducting this type of work?' For example, the task may be that of producing a particular document. If the document is genuinely one that needs to be drafted afresh on each occasion, then that task would be allocated to the bespoke step. However, as is so often the case, where document drafting might be to some extent routine and repetitive, it might be judged, depending on factors such as the complexity of the document and the frequency with which it is needed, as suitable for allocation to one or more of the standardized, systematized, packaged, or commoditized steps. It may also be that some tasks will or should draw upon more than one step on the path. In due course, I suspect, as experience is built up, that allocation of tasks to steps will eventually be automated or at least semi-automated.

Once the legal job has been decomposed into tasks and these tasks have been analysed and allocated across the evolutionary path, the next challenge is to select the most efficient of many potential sources of legal service for each task. Conventionally, legal work has either been undertaken by clients themselves (for example through in-house legal departments), by law firms on behalf of their clients, or by clients and law firms working in tandem. However, advances in information technology and the emergence of various low cost service centres in countries such as India, combine with the increasing passion for efficiency that I am anticipating from the market, to suggest to clients there is a richer array of sources of legal services than doing it yourself or giving it to external lawyers.

In the future, I believe, the market will require that—once legal work has been decomposed and the optimal ways of conducting each task have been identified—these tasks themselves will be sourced in a variety of ways. In any one deal or dispute, for example, the end product, as delivered to clients, will have its origins in numerous sources, each chosen for its suitability and efficiency, and combined as a seamless solution. This, I call 'multi-sourcing'.

I admit this is not an entirely novel notion. There are echoes here, for example, of the concept of 'unbundling', although that term, in its early years at least, mainly referred to the division of work as between lawyers and their clients. This was done so that the latter could reduce costs and retain some control.[14] Traditional unbundling has not tended to entail multi-sourcing.

More generally, for many years now, where complex transactions have involved work that could be distributed across the evolutionary path, some firms have isolated and farmed out those parts that they considered were not within their competence or strategy. A law firm might take on a transaction, undertake the bespoke work itself, but manage and parcel out, say, the systematized work to other firms who are better suited to undertaking work at that level. This was the approach underpinning Lovells' Mexican-Wave service when launched—Lovells would carry out the 'higher grade work' while managing the outsourcing of the more routine work to a group of smaller law firms who were supported by various online tools.[15] Another early illustration of decomposing and parcelling out legal work is the legal research service provided by the California-based company, LRN. This innovative legal provider set up a network of legal experts (academics, former judges, and practitioners) and argued that these individuals could undertake legal research more expertly, swiftly, and at a lower cost than law firms who delegate legal research to junior lawyers who take longer and have much less experience. The LRN approach was to encourage in-house departments to take the legal research task from firms and give it to LRN instead.[16]

These and many other examples have hinted over time at the feasibility of decomposing and multi-sourcing but, across the legal world, these techniques have been embraced in a rather patchy and piecemeal fashion. It has been exceptional rather than mainstream to divide and conquer legal work in this way.

If we think about the possibilities in a more systematic way, what sources are now available? I can think of twelve, as laid out in Figure 2.3 and explained more fully below. The categories I have identified, I accept, are not entirely clear-cut and do overlap to some extent. And I am sure others can add to the list. Above all, though, when taken together, they do indicate that a wide variety of options are now available.

The first method of sourcing is *in-sourcing*. Taking law firms as an illustration, on this approach, lawyers undertake legal work themselves, using their own internal resources. A subset of this option, of course, is the delegation of legal work to less experienced lawyers within firms. This might be done

---

[14] The pioneer of unbundling was Forrest Mosten—see <http://www.mostenmediation.com>.

[15] <http://www.lovells.com/Lovells/OnlineServices/MexicanWave>.

[16] <http://www.lrn.com>. For much of the background to LRN, also see D Seidman, *HOW* (New Jersey: Wiley, 2007).

```
1. in-sourcing
2. de-lawyering
3. relocating
4. off-shoring
5. outsourcing
6. subcontracting
7. co-sourcing
8. leasing
9. home-sourcing
10. open-sourcing
11. computerizing
12. no-sourcing
```

Fig 2.3 Sources of Legal Service

because the work does not merit the attention and experience of expert lawyers advising in a bespoke manner. Alternatively, more difficult work can also be delegated to more junior lawyers if there are sufficiently sophisticated standards, procedures, or systems to support them and so to bridge the knowledge gap (between the more and less expert). Delegation is pivotal to the business model of most firms—this provides the leverage or gearing on which profitability tends to be based.

A second possibility is *de-lawyering*, an entirely inelegant neologism that refers to the process by which a legal task can responsibly be handed over to a non-lawyer to discharge; that individual might be a paralegal, legal executive, or perhaps even an intelligent lay person. Again the discharge of the work by the non-lawyers may well be with the support of standards or systems. Many lawyers find it hard to pass along to non-legal staff legal work that historically has required the attention of lawyers. Interestingly, in Japan, reforms to their legal system are moving in the opposite direction—much legal and quasi-legal work that is currently undertaken by paralegals and legal administrators is gradually becoming the exclusive preserve of a rapidly growing legal profession. I think the Japanese should have stayed as they were in this respect.

The third option is *relocating* work to less costly locations in countries in which firms and organizations already have a presence. This is done with a view to providing legal service from lower cost operations, in places where overheads (property and labour) are lower. In England, for example, London-based law firms can reduce their fees by conducting the work from less expensive UK cities.

The fourth is the *off-shoring* of legal work to countries in which the firms or organizations in question have not previously had a presence. One key idea here is to set up a 'captive' unit, wholly owned by the business that is off-shoring but situated in countries, such as India, which are themselves well geared up (with people, technology, and buildings) to support and provide service from afar. The employees of these off-shore functions are largely lawyers from those businesses which are doing the off-shoring; some will have been transferred from the traditional centres, while others will have been recruited locally. Additionally, local support staff will generally be engaged. In-house legal departments have already begun to off-shore in earnest—for example BT has a well established off-shored legal function in New Delhi, while HSBC has set up a team in Kuala Lumpur.

A fifth possibility is the *outsourcing* of legal work to specialist support companies, usually in low cost locations.[17] This is giving rise to a rapidly growing field known as 'legal process outsourcing' (LPO). On this model, law firms pass work packages (such as document review in litigation or due diligence for corporate work) to independent companies that are not themselves, strictly, law firms; even though they may employ legally qualified individuals and paralegals.[18] Generally, these LPO providers keep their overheads low (by operating in places with low incomes and inexpensive property) and rely on well-developed standards, guidelines, methods, tools, and systems which may even be developed in conjunction with the firms outsourcing to them. Most of these companies simultaneously provide their services to a variety of law firms.

My focus in this book is on the outsourcing of legal and quasi-legal work rather than the outsourcing of back-office functions (such as the IT or finance parts of law firms), which is fairly common practice today.[19] In passing, however, it is interesting to observe the progress that has been made with back-office outsourcing. Already it is clear that this is not a static and settled art. For example, many Indian companies to whom back-office services have been outsourced are themselves now outsourcing certain parts of that work to Mexico, Brazil, Chile, Uruguay, and other lower cost centres.

---

[17] Some providers do not operate from low cost areas: eg Novus Law, which undertakes 'routine legal work', is based in the US—<http://www.novuslaw.com>.

[18] The word 'outsourcing' can be very confusing. In-house lawyers often use the term to refer to the passing of work to external law firms. But they will also say they are outsourcing when they themselves send work directly to an LPO provider.

[19] In October 2006, Clifford Chance, the world's largest law firm, announced its intention to outsource much of its back-office to India, in the expectation of making savings of almost £10m on an annual basis. See <http://www.oscesl.com>.

A sixth tack for law firms is *subcontracting* work to other law firms, again with much lower overheads (as in the Mexican-Wave example). In this way, the overall cost of the service is reduced. Where law firms subcontract, they will tend to retain overall responsibility for the work delivered and lend their brand and reputation to the totality of the service.

Co-sourcing is a seventh approach. This involves separate organizations collaborating in the delivery of some legal service. This can be collaboration between law firms and their clients, working together as a team; or may even involve two or many more law firms coming together and delivering a joint service. Under this heading also is the possibility, for example, of a number of law firms and clients setting up a shared services facility, off-shore, to undertake high volume repetitive work as a form of joint venture.

Eighth in my list of possible methods of sourcing legal work is the *leasing* of lawyers on a project basis. This can be done in much the same way as a building or facilities might be leased—for specified periods of time and for particular initiatives. This has become popular in the Netherlands, for instance, where a major recruitment agency has extended its business beyond head hunting and executive search into the provision of suitably qualified individual lawyers who act as a form of contractual fringe on par-ticular deals and disputes.[20] In similar vein, a US-based company known as Axiom was launched in 2000.[21] This business has grown dramatically, leasing lawyers to corporate clients, often to help them meet peaks in demand. This will be particularly useful if in-house departments downsize during difficult times, because they will periodically need to bolster their own capability and Axiom and others are considerably cheaper than law firms. Although leasing in this way is regarded as a facility largely for in-house lawyers, I can also see the service being a key component of a multi-sourced service. Law firms may also come to lease lawyers.

Ninth is *home-sourcing*, which is also becoming increasingly common; and not least as a way of harnessing the very considerable legal talent (often mothers with young children) that is not currently deployed in the main-stream legal workplace and yet that is available, often on a part-time basis. This makes the most of the working potential of lawyers who prefer or must operate from their own homes.

A tenth and more radical option for sourcing legal work is *open-sourcing*. This is rare today but given the impact of open-sourcing in other walks of life

---

[20] <http://www.voxius.com>.
[21] <http://www.axiomlaw.com>.

(software engineering,[22] encyclopaedia compilation,[23] mothers' help groups)[24] it is possible, and, I believe, likely that all sorts of legal materials (standard documents, memoranda of guidance, standard procedures, legal opinions, case studies, personal practical experience, and much more) will soon be gathered together and made available at no charge in public repositories and in private communities.[25]

My eleventh and very wide category of sourcing is *computerizing*. I use this term generically to include systematizing, packaging, and commoditizing of legal work (as introduced and defined earlier in Section 2.1). Accordingly, these systems may be used within law firms, by in-house legal departments, or even directly by non-lawyers.

My final and twelfth category—*no-sourcing*—may look a little facile. This is the option of not doing anything, of not seeking to source some legal work at all. In fact, no-sourcing is often a vital option. If clients and firms are more rigorous in the way they assess legal risk, they will sometimes come to an informed view that given situations are not sufficiently or relatively high risk to consume any of the inevitably limited legal resource that is available to them. Many General Counsel say to me, for instance, that on some deals there is little point, from a legal risk point of view, in conducting a full-scale due diligence exercise.

In summary, then, in years to come, I believe that, for any particular deal, dispute, or other piece of legal work, it will be possible to decompose the matter in question into manageable tasks, to identify for each how most efficiently these tasks might be discharged; and then to pinpoint the best way of sourcing each task (choosing perhaps from the twelve categories above). And so, for any piece of work, it may be that several, if not many, sources contribute to the final product.

There are two additional requirements that will bring this model from theory into practice. The first is that, in the future, one individual organization will, I believe, tend to take overall responsibility for the delivery of the completed and delivered legal service when multi-sourced, even though several organizations and systems may have contributed. This organization may be a form of main contractor, acting as the overall project manager of the service, and so coordinating all the various inputs. This contractor will lend its

---

[22] <http://www.linux.com>.
[23] <http://www.wikipedia.com>.
[24] <http://www.netmums.com>.
[25] Legal open-sourcing is discussed at greater length in Section 4.6. Closed legal communities are the subject of Section 4.7.

brand to the exercise, thus securing the confidence of the purchaser. And, further, this contractor-manager will establish quality systems and procedures to ensure that the work is undertaken to an appropriate standard. This new role will present a fundamental challenge to law firms. Will law firms recognize a clear market opportunity here and step forward to embrace this emerging responsibility, or will they leave this to others (such as accounting firms, legal publishers, or software giants) and be relegated to the function of technical legal subcontractor? Time will tell.

The second requirement will be systems and processes that enable the many legal sources to be managed and brought together as a seamless service. What will be needed is an IT-enabled just-in-time global supply chain, akin in many ways to the logistics systems and assembly lines in the world of manufacturing. In the manufacturing of legal services, as I foresee it, the components are created by the many multi-sourcing suppliers, the goods are transported through workflow systems and electronic transmission, and the assembly is undertaken with the support of project management software under the watchful eye of the main contractor.

Although it may be anathema to many lawyers to liken the compilation of legal service to the creation of a mere artifact, such as a car or personal computer, lawyers have much to learn from the world of manufacturing, a mature market in economic terms, in which efficiencies and cost savings have been systematically and rigorously imposed. And, if we are honest, the dashboard of a car and the motherboard of a personal computer are immensely complex components, often much more so than, say, a tightly drafted contract. The thinking here is not original. Theodore Levett, of Harvard Business School, first saw much of this in a prescient article of 1972, entitled 'Production-line approach to service'.[26] The vision was there more than a quarter of a century ago but it could not become a reality, I submit, until the advent of the Internet as the fundamental infrastructure for the professional service supply chain.

That said, I do not follow any manufacturing or production analogy to the extent that this leads to some kind of mass production model of legal service. I know this is what many lawyers fear—that the computerization (systematization, packaging, and commoditization) of legal work means the imposition of pre-articulated, inflexible solutions on a wide range of circumstances. Clients' circumstances are never identical, so that individual answers (documents or advice) must be crafted for each by human lawyers. I agree broadly

---

[26] *Harvard Business Review*, September–October 1972, 41–52.

with the premise here, about the uniqueness of clients' situations; but I do not accept the conclusion, that it always needs human legal practitioners to deliver service. Instead, I regard the computerization of legal services as leading to what others have called *mass customization*—using processes and systems that meet individuals' particular needs with a level of efficiency akin to that of mass production.[27] Harnessing the power of the various technologies discussed in this book enables us to combine the low production costs of mass production with the tailored effects of individual customization. A document assembly system, for example, does not simply print out a single standard document. Instead, based on the individual circumstances of the situation in question, responses to a series of questions lead to the generation of a document that is often one amongst many millions of possible permutations. The effect is a tailored solution, developed not by the sole craftsman but by the advanced system.[28]

Hal Varian succinctly captures the spirit of the model I advocate. In discussing where we are in relation to our exploitation of the Internet, he says: 'The challenge facing us now is to re-engineer the flow of information through the enterprise. And not only within the enterprise—the entire value chain is up for grabs.'[29]

Despite my enthusiasm for new ways of sourcing legal work, I am alive to some of the potential pitfalls. There are clearly risks in moving from the left to the right on my evolutionary path and sourcing accordingly. Standard documents in the hands of inexperienced lawyers, for example, can lead to fundamentally flawed arrangements which do not protect the interests of clients. And there are other potential stumbling blocks too—it is unclear how the insurance industry will respond to the liability implications of more process-based and systems-driven legal service. And there are, no doubt, conflicts issues and confidentiality questions that have not been fully addressed in relation to the passing of work from law firms to third parties. Nonetheless, the commercial imperatives for change are strong and where there is a will from the market, imaginative solutions will be finessed.[30]

---

[27] See eg JH Gilmore and BJ Pine (eds), *Markets of One* (Boston: Harvard Business School Press, 2000).

[28] Automated document assembly is considered in some detail in Section 4.1.

[29] H Varian, 'Competition and market power' in H Varian, J Farrell, and C Shapiro (eds), *Economics of Information Technology* (New York: Cambridge University Press, 2004) 11.

[30] For an important discussion of changes in the market, see S Mayson, 'Legal Services Reforms: Catalyst, Cataclysm or Catastrophe', Legal Services Policy Institute (21 March 2007).

2.6 Two case studies

To put some flesh on the bones of the theory of this chapter, I thought it might be illuminating to provide two brief case studies that map easily onto the path from bespoke service to commoditization.

The first case study relates to my own work. Not long ago, during a question-and-answer session that followed a presentation I had given on the ideas in this chapter, a humorist in the audience asked whether my own work was also subject to the evolutionary forces I had described. Was I immune from the pull to the right? Although facetiously conceived, the question was actually a good one.

So, let me reflect candidly on my work as a speaker. If I am brutally honest, I regularly give very similar talks on various subjects to different audiences. I use almost identical PowerPoint slides each time. The actual delivery of a live presentation is, I am sure, a largely bespoke offering. That said, although I do not read from a script, I do use similar phrases, sentences, and jokes. The reality is that the content of my presentations is very much standardized and, to the extent that they are supported by PowerPoint, there is an element of systemization too. But the analysis does not end there. When I am invited to make a presentation by video link to some far flung location, there is an added element of systemization there. More radically, however, I have been asked on numerous occasions not to present in person, nor to deliver by video conference, but to pre-record my presentation, either as a simple recording on DVD or videotape, or in the format of a web-cast. Either way, we can see here an opportunity for me to package my offering. One possibility, for example, although I have not pursued this, would be to produce perhaps a subscription based series of web-casts which users could use on a stand-alone basis or perhaps present to groups, preparatory to further discussion. The underpinning business model here would be quite different from the conventional speaking engagement. Ordinarily, I charge a one-off fee. Were I to offer a series of web-casts on a subscription basis, I would no longer be charging an appearance fee; instead, I would be packaging and licensing my knowledge and my delivery of that. So long as there were no competitors to my web-casts, these packages could enable me, as I say, to make money while I sleep. The threat for me, however, would be if a competitor, perish the thought, produced a rival service, of similar content and quality. In that event, we would both be subject to the economics of the information economy, as discussed in this chapter—the market would require that our respective prices reduce and, in the end, they would quite rapidly fall towards zero.

That, in a nutshell, is how my speaking services might be commoditized. My inclination, in that event, would generally be to make the web-casts available at no cost; and to work hard in developing new ones with fresh ideas.

My second case study is more serious and substantive. It is taken, with permission, from the work of my longest standing consulting client, the Tax practice of Deloitte UK. Over the years, I have found it instructive to look at the latest working practices of the so-called Big Four accounting and tax firms. Lawyers can learn much from the ways in which accountants and tax specialists embrace technologies and techniques for improving processes. The particular aspect of tax work that I find most illuminating for the legal profession is the way in which tax compliance work has evolved over the years. Every company has to take data from its accounting systems, analyse the numbers in light of local tax laws, and produce a statement, a return, in a specified form, of their corporation tax liability. In the 1960s, this was a highly bespoke activity, a hand-crafted service supported by all manner of ledgers and manual typewriters. In the 1970s, the process became to some extent standardized, helped along by more powerful electric typewriters and photocopying technologies. This tax compliance process was transformed in the 1980s, however, with the advent of spreadsheet packages running on newly arrived personal computers. Spreadsheets, undoubtedly, were a boon to tax and audit professionals, bringing remarkable flexibility in the storage and manipulation, the dicing and splicing, of figures. Towards the end of the 1980s, some tax firms went further and began to develop tax software tools that automated the main elements of businesses' corporate tax compliance and reporting work. Spreadsheet technology brought early systemization, while more specialist tools were launched in a later period of systematization. At this stage, of course, the emphasis was on tools for use internally within tax practices of major firms. One of the leaders in this field was Arthur Andersen. Widely recognized as an innovator and heavily committed to information technology, the firm developed a tax software package known as Abacus. It enjoyed great success within Andersen's business and became an indispensable tool for tax professionals who were undertaking compliance work for their corporate clients.

The 1990s brought an unprecedented challenge. As so often happens amongst the Big Four, tax experts from within their midst left the firms and joined the in-house tax departments of a wide range of businesses. At that stage, these departments had started, as we would now say, to in-source much of the routine tax work, including compliance. However, ex-Andersen specialists found that they no longer had Abacus at their disposal and greatly missed the system. Rather than revert to more basic spreadsheet technology or indeed develop systems from scratch, a number of these Andersen alumni, and many of them were now clients, approached the firm and inquired whether they might be permitted to use Abacus within their companies. It is said that there were extended and spirited discussions within the firm on this subject. Some enthusiasts argued that this presented a splendid opportunity both to keep clients happy and also to charge some kind of fee, by way of licence, for the use of the system. The doubters, however, worried that the firm would be giving away its crown jewels and unnecessarily losing a handsome source of income and profit. It is a credit to the innovative spirit of the firm that the enthusiasts prevailed and Andersen began, in the 1990s to license Abacus to a wide range of businesses, and to smaller tax and accounting firms as well. Thus, they had reached the stage of what I call 'packaging' their knowledge and expertise. They made their internal systems, with some considerable adaptations, available to their clients.

In the wake of the remarkable and lamentable collapse of Andersen, as part of the transaction, in the UK, which involved the recruitment of a very large number of ex-Andersen professionals, Deloitte also purchased the Abacus system. In the new millennium, the system grew in popularity and is currently licensed by thousands of organizations, and not least to around seventy of the FTSE 100 and to 2000 accounting firms. Despite its great success, however, commoditization does loom as a threat to Deloitte and Abacus. It transpires that Abacus is not the only tax compliance software package available in the UK. The concern for Deloitte is that rival packages are not seen by the market to be significantly different. If indeed the potential licencees came to regard the systems as similar, then, according to the economics of the information world, the prices of Abacus and its indistinguishable competitors would collectively plummet. The challenge for Deloitte, therefore, is continually to enhance Abacus so that the product is demonstrably superior to its competitors; in this way Abacus will remain a differentiated, strongly branded package that commands a respectable licence fee.

In Deloitte and Abacus, we find a case study of the evolution of a professional service from bespoke to packaged service and conceivably (but undesirably for Deloitte at this stage) its emergence as a commodity. Interestingly, if Deloitte found that it could no longer differentiate Abacus from its rivals, it could embrace the phase of commoditization and make the system available on an open source basis, that is to say, at no cost to users and even in a form that these users could enhance themselves. While this would bring reputational benefits for Deloitte, it would also mean that the firm would have to find new sources of income, by developing other aspects of its tax practice— either a new range of bespoke services (that would begin their own journey from left to right on my evolutionary path) or maybe a number of conventional advisory services that would complement the now publicly available Abacus. Whether to encourage or resist this shift from packaged to commoditized service is a key strategic question for Deloitte and, by analogy, will become a similar issue of fundamental significance for the legal profession in years to come.

The story does not end there, however. There is a larger threat and opportunity for Deloitte and its competitors, because the world of tax looks as though it may soon change radically, bringing very great benefits, risks, and technology challenges. The change is perhaps best understood in terms of the single, global financial systems (such as SAP) that most major global companies have now introduced. These systems are intended to be robust and enterprise-wide, operating across and integrating entire businesses. In contrast, the tax systems in most sizaeble organizations, even the world's largest, tend to be fragmented: if systems such as Abatec are being used, they are only deployed in a few countries; many companies in fact use unreliable and out-dated technology; and the systems themselves often run along-side time-consuming and highly manual working practices and processes. Outsourcing and shared services remain largely unexplored. This current approach to tax brings grave inefficiencies and risks. However, many tax professionals are determined that tax systems should no longer be the poorer cousin of financial systems. They have recognized great opportunities for introducing integrated enterprise-wide tax technologies that should work in tandem with overhauled working processes. These new systems and working processes would bring concrete benefits—most tangibly, a substantial reduction in the overall cost of managing a tax and compliance function and, through better insight into the figures and the law, to a reduction in the amount of tax paid (a reduction, that is, in the effective tax rate). Importantly too, there will be increased confidence across the company that regulatory and compliance obligations are being fully met in a more controlled way. At the same time, the automation and outsourcing of routine work will release tax professionals to focus on higher-value work. Broader developments in the market also point towards the conclusion that fundamental change is afoot and that new tax systems and processes are needed. In the first instance, tax laws and related regulations are growing in number, complexity, and global impact, while regulators are becoming more sophisticated, collaborative, and demanding. In large, international businesses, operating in numerous countries, tax compliance is a formidable and high-risk management challenge. Investors are adding further pressure here, by taking a growing interest in tax matters and so needing swifter access than in the past to accurate and up-to-date information. Again, this is especially burdensome for global organizations, where there is reliance on dispersed, local expertise, with varying regional practices. Above all, the prime concern is that there is a worldwide shortage of appropriately qualified and equipped tax professionals, so that many businesses that rely on traditional hand-crafted methods will simply not be able to manage their tax affairs adequately in the future. The risks, in turn, will be considerable—of unpalatably high costs of managing tax, of unnecessarily creeping tax liabilities, of penalties for non-compliance, of costly or embarrassing errors and inconsistencies, and of threats to reputation leading even to adverse effects on share price.

There are very strong analogies here with the challenges facing in-house legal departments of companies: the pressures to reduce costs, the drive to control risks, the mounting challenge of compliance, an increasing work-load; and all of these factors operating against a backdrop of chronic under-investment in the past in modernizing working practices. Lawyers, in-house and in law firms, should monitor the tax world very carefully. It affords some fascinating early insight into what might happen in the legal market. One especially interesting feature of the tax landscape should alert lawyers. My understanding is that, in the highly competitive race to introduce integrated, global tax systems to clients, there is a strong contender in the shape of Accenture, the international consulting business, even though the firm is not known to employ legions of tax experts. They can argue, however, that the implementation of these major tax systems is not predominantly a tax mat-ter; rather, this is about change management, project management, process redesign, and system development; and that the development of tax content and expertise can be subcontracted to tax firms. And I know some company directors who are impressed with this line of argument.

We can see here an analogous threat to the legal profession that flows from my thinking about decomposing and multi-sourcing—major pieces of legal work in the future (disputes, deals, and compliance reviews) could be orches-trated and driven not by lawyers but by business or project or risk managers from beyond the legal profession. They might argue that the major challenge on a particular matter is that of, say, risk management and so risk managers and not lawyers should take a lead. In that event, they may say that the legal content can simply be subcontracted to lawyers. If we can see this phenom-enon already in tax, there is strong reason to take it seriously in law.

As legal service evolves and legal work can be sourced differently, lawyers cannot assume they will always remain the dominant advisers.

3

Trends in Technology

Predicting the future is a hazardous business. Many information technologists nurture a collection of anecdotes about specialists and futurists whose prognostications turned out to be horribly misguided. I also treasure a few tales that I particularly enjoy; and, from my web browsing, I believe them to be true and not apocryphal. I like, perhaps best of all, the quotation attributed to Thomas J Watson, the erstwhile Chairman of IBM who, in 1943, it is said, declared with some confidence that 'I think there is a world market for about five computers'. Similarly misconceived, just six years later, a journal of considerable repute, *Popular Mechanics*, made forecasts about the relentless march of technology in the following terms: 'computers in the future may weigh no more than 1½ tons'. In 1965, Herbert Simon (later a Nobel Laureate in Economics) expressed the view that 'machines will be capable within 20 years of doing any work that a man can do'. And twelve years after that, in 1977, Ken Olson, President, Chairman, and Founder of the then computer giant, Digital Equipment Corporations asserted that 'there is no reason that anyone would want a computer in their home'. I am conscious, then, that there is a long and great tradition of information technologists who have spectacularly missed the mark when projecting ahead. Incidentally, lest it be thought that wayward predictions are the sole province of IT experts, it is instructive to note that HM Warner of Warner Bros, in 1927, asked indignantly, 'who the hell wants to hear actors talk?'

Aside from the pitfalls of getting it wrong, it is often said that information technology (IT) advances so unpredictably that there is little point in seeking to second guess progress. Pursuing this line of thinking, it is pointed out that the personal computer took the world by surprise when it was launched by IBM in 1981; the birth of the Web came as a similar shock in the early 1990s; and, similarly, the widespread uptake, in the last few years, of so-called Web 2.0 systems (discussed below in Section 3.3) was not anticipated by experts, even though they are rapidly coming to be recognized as of immense significance for modern society. Given that we did not predict these major developments and they came to dominate our view of the future, there is no point, it is argued, in attempting to look five to ten years ahead.

I take the view that it remains worthwhile to attempt three kinds of predictions. First, even if there are no shifts in technology in the next few years as seismic as the personal computer and the Web were in their time, if we follow existing and emerging technologies to their likely and much fuller exploitation, this of itself leads us into an entirely different realm of life and experience. The fallacy here is to assume that because we cannot anticipate the revolutionary changes, we should not make predictions within the current framework. If we work within this framework, we are likely to have more of a sense of where we are going than if we ignore the future altogether. We may miss the revolution but at least we will be apace with evolution. Not attempting any kind of horizon scanning is like driving a car at night with no lights. Making guarded predictions of the sort I have in mind is akin to having the headlights on. I accept, though, that there is much that we still cannot see.

Second, I do think it productive in any event to try to identify general *trends* and overall directions in emerging information technologies. We may not be able to pin down precise applications of technology, but if we focus and reflect on likely patterns and trends, both in systems and in human behaviour, then this can provide a useful backdrop when thinking about the future.

The third sort of prediction that is worth making focuses on the impact of some of those technologies that we can imagine taking hold in the legal world. Here, we are not speculating about high falutin and fundamental issues of computation or paradigm-shifting systems; rather, we are looking at systems that are gaining in popularity, perhaps in other sectors or amongst our youth, and suggesting how they could be used in law.

With these kinds of prediction in mind, in this chapter, I identify and discuss six major trends in information technology. Taken together, these trends have shaped my own thinking about the future of our society generally and, more particularly, about the likely development of the legal world. I build on these in Chapter 4, when I discuss how the various existing and emerging technologies will come to challenge the way in which lawyers work.

3.1 Exponential growth

Lawyers, in common with much of humanity, tend to find it difficult to grasp that there is no finishing line when it comes to IT and the Internet. For the tidy mind and the control freak alike, it is hard to accept that there are no clear parameters, limits, or finite pigeon-holes. Perhaps there is some pathological aversion, hardwired into the legal mind, to the inevitability of ongoing advancement in technology, to the notion that no system or innovation can be the last word.

E-mail and web browsing illustrate the point. Most legal practitioners are now comfortable users of e-mail (via personal computers and hand-held devices) and are also at home when browsing the Web, usually courtesy of Google. I often get the sense, however, that lawyers feel that the impact of IT and the Internet has peaked, that the technology has matured, and that, in consequence, legal work can carry on much as before, untainted by any further developments. Whether this is a function of the legal mind-set or wishful thinking or complacency, I am not sure, but I suspect many lawyers would be amazed, if not alarmed, to learn about a law quite different in nature from the sort they handle on a daily basis. I am thinking of Moore's Law, named after Gordon Moore, the co-founder of Intel, the major manufacturer of computer chips. This law, as first articulated in a paper in 1965, predicts an exponential increase in the number of transistors that can be placed on an integrated circuit. There is some debate about the detail here but, in crude terms, Moore's Law, or a common rendition of it, suggests that the processing power of computers doubles every 18 months, while, at the same time, its cost halves in around the same period. [1]

---

[1] For an authoritative statement, see GE Moore 'Cramming more components onto integrated circuits', (1965) 38(8) *Electronics*. For decades, doubters have wrongly predicted that Moore's Law would not hold true for many more years. However, computer chip manufacturers are hugely resourceful in accelerating performance and continually investigate new techniques, such as using hafnium rather than silicon in the making of chips.

A little digging in the world of computer science suggests that exponential growth, in the field of IT, is not confined to transistors and processing power. Perhaps the most alerting analysis of the evolution of technology in exponential terms is provided by Ray Kurzweil in his wholly remarkable and formidable book, *The Singularity is Near*.[2] I have been following Kurzweil's work for over two decades. As a research student involved with artificial intelligence, I started reading his books and predictions in the early 1980s. Outlandish though his many claims have seemed in the past, he is as reliable and prophetic a technology futurist as I have come across. I am not alone in being impressed with his thinking—in 2008, the US National Academy of Engineering appointed Kurzweil as one of a formidable committee of about twenty experts who are addressing fourteen 'grand challenges' for engineering in the twenty-first century.[3] Unusually for a futurist, he has also been a pioneer in the commercial world, in fields as diverse as optical character recognition (OCR), speech recognition, and electronic keyboards (readers in their 40s and 50s may well remember the Kurzweil synthesizer).

The scope of The *Singularity is Near* is life, the universe, and a whole lot more. Kurzweil anticipates 'a future period during which the pace of technological change will be so rapid, its impact so deep, that human life will be irreversibly transformed'. He goes on to say that: 'the pace of change for our human-technology is accelerating and its powers are expanding at an exponential rate. Exponential growth is deceptive. It starts out almost imperceptibly and it explodes with unexpected fury – unexpected, that is, if one does not take care to follow its trajectory'.[4]

The thrust of his book is that, 'within several decades information-based technologies will encompass all human knowledge and proficiency, ultimately including the pattern-recognition powers, problem-solving skills, and emotional and moral intelligence of even the brain itself'. More, he argues that, by the end of this century, 'the non-biological portion of our intelligence will be trillions of trillions times more powerful than unaided human intelligence.'[5]

That the days of 'unenhanced biological humanity' are numbered is due, according to Kurzweil, to the seemingly inevitable, exponential development

---

[2] R Kurzweil, *The Singularity is Near* (New York: Viking, 2005). Also see the superb website <http://www.kurzweilai.net>.

[3] See <http://www.nae.edu>.

[4] Kurzweil (n 2 above) 7–8.

[5] ibid 8–9.

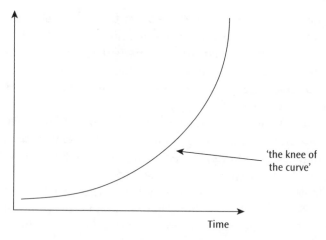

Fig. 3.1 An Exponential Curve

of genetics, robotics, nano-technology, and IT. In this book, I am concerned only with this last category. But I quote from Kurzweil, in passing, in part to encourage readers to delve into his remarkable book; and, in part, to put some of my own, apparently extreme, claims in context. When compared to Kurzweil, my vision of the future is conservative.

Crucial for current purposes is Kurzweil's theory of technology evolution. He identifies a wide range of information technologies and aspects of IT that are progressing at an exponential rate (and sometimes even double exponential, which means that the rate of exponential growth is itself growing exponentially). He shows that this exponential trend extends, for example, to random access memory, average transistor price, the rate of transistor manufacturing, microprocessor clock speed, microprocessor cost, transistors per microprocessor, processor performance, total bits shipped, magnetic data storage capacity, the number of Internet hosts, Internet data traffic, Internet backbone bandwidth, and more. Kurzweil regards this ongoing acceleration of technology and its exponential growth as a form of evolutionary process. In a memorable phrase, though, he suggests that we are currently at the 'knee of the curve'. The shape of the exponential curve is shown in Figure 3.1.[6]

---

[6] In Figure 3.1, if the units of measurement on the x axis and y axis are linear, then the growth depicted is exponential. However, if the y axis is logarithmic, then regular exponential growth would manifest itself as a diagonal, straight line, from bottom left to top right. But, if the y axis is logarithmic, and the familiar curve is shown (as in Figure 3.1), then there is double exponential growth, a remarkable phenomenon that Kurzweil identifies in relation to some developments in technology.

By this he means that, although we seem to have experienced fantastic growth in our information technologies up until now, we have travelled only up the initial and shallow part of the exponential curve. Today, as we are poised at the knee of this curve (at the tipping point, if you like),[7] he anticipates we are about to experience quite unimaginable and explosive future growth in our information technologies.

This dramatic imagery is brought sharply into focus by Kurzweil when he discusses how our machines will come to have the computational capacity of the human brain. Following the exponential curve that depicts hardware computational capacity, he claims that, by 2020, an average desk-top machine (costing US $1,000 or so, in today's terms) will have roughly the same processing power as a single human brain (conservatively, able to undertake 10^{16} calculations per second).[8] More amazing still, he claims that, by 2050, following the same curve, and this is where the exponential effect clicks in, 'one thousand dollars of computing will exceed the processing power of all human brains on Earth'.[9]

Call me radical, but it seems to me that if we can envisage a day when the average desk-top machine has more processing power than all of humanity put together, then it might be time for lawyers to rethink some of their working practices and processes. This is not Google and hand-held e-mail plus a few bells and whistles. This is an unprecedented revolution in the power of the tools available to man.

I acknowledge that Kurzweil's theories are not universally accepted.[10] But many other experts and commentators do come to similar conclusions on the question of the exponential growth of the power of technology.[11] There are also echoes here of related phenomena, such as Metcalfe's law, which states (approximately) that the value of a network to its users is proportional to the square of the number of the users connected to it. Sometimes known as the 'network effect', this means that a network's usefulness increases exponentially with the number of new users who join. The economic effects of this are famously discussed by Professor Michael Spence in his Nobel prize lecture of 2001.[12]

---

[7] See M Gladwell, *The Tipping Point* (London: Abacus, 2000).

[8] Kurzweil (n 2 above) 122–6.

[9] ibid 127.

[10] Debate rages at Kurzweil's website—<http://www.kurzweilai.net>. Also see B Joy, 'Why the Future Doesn't Need Us' *Wired*, April 2000.

[11] See eg J Garreau, *Radical Evolution* (New York: Doubleday, 2004).

[12] AM Spence, 'Signaling in Retrospect and the Informational Structure of Markets', Nobel Prize Lecture, 8 December 2001.

I do accept, however, that exponential growth and development in information technologies do not always and necessarily result in an exponential increase in the rate of uptake of new systems. But, if Kurzweil and likeminded thinkers are even remotely accurate in their extrapolations and predictions, then we are surely at the doorstep of an era of change that is more profound and radical, in terms of technical progress, than humanity has ever seen. My message to lawyers in this context is simple—far from approaching the finishing line, the race has barely begun. Within the lifetime of most readers of this book, our social and economic lives are likely to be radically overhauled as a result of the rapid emergence of a clutch of information and Internet-related technologies of unimaginable power. All aspects of the raw technology with which lawyers are familiar will improve radically in a small number of years and thereafter, at an accelerating rate. Yet further advances can be expected: from the resolution of screen displays to the portability of equipment; from the speed of machines to storage capacity; from the availability of wireless connections to the bandwidth of these links. We have hardly left the start line.

3.2 Information satisfaction

Turning away now from technology itself, my second major trend is an increase in what I call 'information satisfaction'. A definition should help here. In broad terms, I say that we are satisfied, in this sense of information satisfaction, when we receive *all but only* what we want in our quests for information. *All but only.* Many of us, in our information-seeking activities, I think it fair to say, are not satisfied or are only sometimes satisfied. We feel our systems let us down. Users everywhere bemoan the information explosion and suggest that there is 'far too much out there'. I suggest, however, and this is the major trend, that information satisfaction will steadily increase in years to come; we will, in turn, become much more content with the output of our systems as time goes by.

There is a strong link here to the 'Technology Lag' that I mention in the first chapter (in Section 1.4). This is the term that I came up with to describe the gap between data processing and knowledge processing, the gap between our ability to create, reproduce, and disseminate information and the capacity of our systems to help analyse, sift through, and isolate relevant information. By way of brief case study, take the Web, as a general information system.

Before the advent of Google, although there were a range of respectable search engines available, such as Altavista, using these tools felt like a rather hit-and-miss process. That they worked at all, and so swiftly, was truly remarkable; and we should not be blasé. But it was not until Google came along that searching seemed to become a more reliable and mainstream activity. Quite markedly, for the vast bulk of Internet users, Google has shrunk the Technology Lag. Suddenly, the billions of pages of information somehow seemed manageable. That said, it is widely held that, even using Google and similar search tools, we are currently using a tiny fraction of the search capability we will develop in due course. As John Battelle puts it: 'As every engineer in the search field loves to tell you, search is at best 5 percent solved.'[13] Much better search is yet to come.

My hypothesis here, to repeat, is that information satisfaction will steadily increase. To clarify this, it is worth thinking a little more about the ways in which, and the purposes for which, we seek information. There are many ways to divide the information-seeking pie. I like to cut it into five different slices.

First of all, we sometimes search for a document or materials that we know are out there. It is absolutely remarkable, is it not, when we have heard perhaps of a new consultation paper or article, and we know a couple of details about it, that within but a few seconds of making a simple search request on the Web, courtesy invariably of Google, we are downloading our target material? When we search and locate information in this way, I feel we experience just about complete information satisfaction; and we should pause and note just how amazing it is that we now have such ready and reliable access to all manner of *files* (I use the term advisedly, because we search not simply for documents but also for music, photographs, video clips, and animations). Ten years ago, our level of information satisfaction, in searching in this way, was notably lower.

A second type of information-seeking is what can be called the 'fishing expedition'. When we search in this way, we are not really sure what we are after. We are interested in some topic or concept, perhaps; we drop a couple of relevant words into Google and away we go—in an exploratory fashion we glance and click, navigate and jump, browse and link and, in so doing, we come across all sorts of interesting websites of whose existence we generally had no clue just seconds earlier. Within a small number of minutes, when we leave cyberspace we are often newly equipped with a range of fresh and

---

[13] J Battelle, *The Search* (London: Nicholas Brealey, 2005) 252.

fascinating insights, and newly gleaned facts and data. I venture that our information satisfaction from fishing expeditions is often quite high. We may not feel we have isolated or identified 'all but only' the information relevant for our purpose, but for most of our everyday requirements, we are sufficiently edified.

However, information satisfaction is far lower in relation to what I call (and discuss further in Section 4.9) 'personalized alerting'. This is my third subcategory of information-seeking. In 1995, I was inspired in this connection by a punchy book by Nicholas Negroponte, entitled *Being Digital*.[14] In this prescient guide to our electronic future, Negroponte discussed the idea of the *Daily Me*—a newspaper, delivered electronically every morning, made up of news, comments, and reportage but containing only topics of direct interest to each particular reader. Each reader, in other words, receives a personalized newspaper that only contains items of direct interest to him or her. Although today there are all sorts of feeds, services, and alerts that aspire to this level of selectivity and focus, none of these systems yet seems personalized enough. None of these services seems to know quite enough about what we want. To meet this challenge, we will need a variety of improved technologies (including intelligent agents) for profiling, selecting, and editing. More, we will, I suggest, need to rely on systems that can analyse our ongoing online activity (our click-stream) and in so doing capture and articulate our interests, assuming we are happy to expose our information seeking habits in this way. We will achieve information satisfaction in our personalized alerting only if the services that are bringing information to us can know the kinds of materials that interest us; in part, by finding the patterns of our previous searches. Some systems, known as aggregators, already do this, rather relying solely on the profiles we provide.

A practical hurdle here is encouraging usage of available techniques. Existing and rather impressive techniques like RSS can indeed support quite impressive personalized alerting and yet, the uptake of this has been relatively modest, certainly amongst lawyers. RSS, which stands for 'really simple syndication', is a powerful way of publishing and receiving online materials that avoids various hassles of e-mail (filters and spam) and the hit-and-miss experience of web searching. RSS feeds (or web feeds) notify subscribers when new content (an article, blog, or webcast, for example) is available. While this appears to be ideal for lawyers—to keep them and their clients up to date—many have not even heard of RSS. As matters stand, then,

[14] N Negroponte, *Being Digital* (London: Hodder & Stoughton, 1995).

we are quite some distance from achieving information satisfaction with our personalized alerting sources. But, in the coming ten years, I expect that we will enjoy enormous progress in this field.

My fourth and penultimate subcategory of information-seeking might be called 'optimum retrieval'. I use this term to refer to the quest for a search capability that is so impressive that users feel confident their system can immediately isolate, where this is meaningful, the single best document that is available for their purposes. This is not a document of whose existence the user is aware (that situation would fall under my first subcategory) but material that is, almost magically, unearthed and dispensed authoritatively as the most definitive and pertinent source available. Of course, there are considerable conceptual difficulties in characterizing a document as 'optimum' or 'most relevant' but the general thrust is clear. In separating the wheat from the chaff, the aim is to isolate the best that is out there. It will take longer than ten years to achieve optimum retrieval but, within that period, I have little doubt, we will see major advances. Where today we have Google's option, 'I'm Feeling Lucky', which is self-consciously brave and even flippant, in due course such a utility will more confidently deliver prime content. I draw my optimism in this context from a variety of research initiatives around the world, especially work on the development of the 'semantic web',[15] as well from the steady progress that I see being made in artificial intelligence (AI) and natural language processing. Together, these systems and developments give strong reason to believe that our own online searching will become steadily less hit-and-miss. Although our information satisfaction when we try today to achieve optimum retrieval is very low, mind-boggling commercial and research resource is being invested in improving the power of search. One promising line of development here is searching as a collaborative or communal activity (there is some overlap here with what I say in the next section about online community). There are already websites that, in various ways, allow users to see what other people have been finding and ranking as important.[16] Soon it will be commonplace to stand on the shoulders of other searchers.

Finally, in my classification of information-seeking utilities, there is the subcategory of problem-solving. Often, when we use the Web, although we search for documents or other files, in reality we are looking for a solution or answers.

---

[15] On the semantic web, N Shadbolt, W Hall, and T Berners-Lee, 'The Semantic Web Revisited' (May/June 2006) *IEEE Intelligent Systems*, and Y Wilks, 'What is the Semantic Web and what will it do for eScience', Research Report No. 12, Oxford Internet Institute, October 2006. There is huge scope for research into the implications and applications of the semantic web in the legal field.

[16] See eg <http://del.icio.us>, <http://digg.com> (see n 28 below), and <http://www.yoople.net>.

Would it not be wonderful if we could ask a question, in ordinary language, and out would pop an answer, at an appropriate level of detail and with a suitable body of supporting arguments and evidence? This is sometimes called 'perfect search'.[17] Information satisfaction remains very low indeed in the realm of problem-solving; for users who want answers and not documents, who would like problems solved rather than documents to scrutinize. In truth, I fear we are two decades or more away from general (and still quite crude) problem-solving across the Web. Although the techniques already exist (drawing on AI and expert systems) to develop problem-solving systems in small, relatively self-contained areas of knowledge, none of this work is scaleable today. Users should not be deceived by the impressive way in which a question inserted in a search engine in ordinary language may indeed deliver up some relevant documents. Often, this is the power of a successful fishing expedition and, at best, furnishes documents that, in some sense, contain an answer. It is a massive leap from this to a system that can answer questions on a wide range of issues in the manner of highly intelligent human beings.

The general lesson of this section, however, is that information satisfaction will steadily increase in the coming years, even though the bodies of data and information that are stored are increasing at a stunning rate. Our tools and technologies, I predict, will be refined and enhanced, so that the performance of our systems, in their delivery of information to us, will improve over time. For lawyers and clients, these developments will be vital. Vast bodies of legal information will, at last, become manageable.

3.3 Online community

I find it helpful to regard the Internet, not just as a global network of networks, but also as a technology infrastructure that supports three main utilities. The first is electronic mail, an application that has revolutionized the communication habits of hundreds of millions of people on our planet. The second is the Web, the world's largest information resource, which has transformed our information-seeking habits. The third is online community—with human beings connected to one another through the Internet, this gives rise to fundamental new ways for us to interact and collaborate

---

[17] See eg J Battelle (n 13 above) Ch 11.

with one another. I have for long felt and said that this third use of the Internet would be of the greatest significance to mankind. Accordingly, it is the third of the major trends I see in IT—online communities will burgeon over the next decade.

My first glimpse of the possibilities of online community was through a far-sighted book entitled *The Virtual Community*, by Howard Rheingold.[18] In 1993, prior to a night flight from Philadelphia to London, I happened upon this work in a bookstore. I did not sleep a wink on that flight, so absorbed was I by the possibilities. It seemed to me then, as now, that online communities would change the social and economic lives of human beings for ever. However, it was to be many years until online networking and collaboration would become commonplace.

Online community, as I see it, is not of itself a single technology. Rather, it is a blend of systems and techniques that bring over 1 billion people under the one virtual roof. I subdivide online community into four categories: communicating; producing and collaborating; networking and community-building; trading and exchanging. When we are all sitting on the one big network, as one large community, with easy access to one another, each of these four changes radically. Let me give a flavour.

I start with *communicating*. It is unarguable that e-mail, especially when available through handheld machines, has fundamentally changed the way we communicate with one another. Alongside e-mail, however, there now sit a number of other technologies that are bringing further transformations. Mobile telephony is one such technology. The scale of its uptake is mind-boggling—by 2007, worldwide mobile subscription level reached 3.3 billion.

For those who prefer synchronous communication (live, real-time interaction), the mobile phone has become indispensable. Whether secured in a holster like a cowboy's pistol, or nestling, in branded splendour, in a handbag, or in wafer-thin elegance in a briefcase, these devices are surely the world's most popular appliance.

In many ways more remarkable than using these units conventionally for voice calls is the phenomenon of texting to and from mobile phones. This is staggeringly popular, although it is not easy to secure accurate up-to-date statistics about this social revolution. In 2004, as I understand it, there were 1 billion users of text messaging, who together sent over 500 billion texts. In the UK, in November 2006, in that one month alone, 3.8 billion messages

---

[18] H Rheingold, *The Virtual Community* (Reading, Massachusetts: Addison-Wesley, 1993).

were sent. More formally known as SMS (Short Message Service), texting is like a basic e-mail facility—it enables users to send and receive text messages to and from their mobile telephones and pagers. Like e-mail, this is asynchronous—those who are communicating do not need to be available at the same time to interact. Despite the early protestations of bemused parents, texting has become the dominant means of communication amongst many teenagers. The protesting has now diminished, as these same parents themselves have become keen (if less dexterous) users.

This ubiquity of mobile phones has had some impact in law. Upon finding that some of their clients were not web users and so were unlikely to use Internet-based reporting facilities, an innovative six-partner firm in England, Fidler & Pepper, in 2000, launched a free service for all its conveyancing and personal injury clients based on mobile phone technology.[19] On the occurrence of significant events, once these were logged on the firm's case management system, SMS text messages were automatically sent to clients' mobile phones. ('Dear Mr Smith, this is a quick note to confirm we have just received your Local Authority Search.') For other law firms who were keen to adopt a similar approach, a new service known as Client Inform was developed.[20]

A further illustration of online community is instant messaging (IM). To witness this in action, look over the shoulder of any teenage computer user. IM systems, such as MSN Messenger,[21] provide a convenient online way for two or more people to exchange messages in real-time. These live interactions can be supplemented by sound and video; by using web cams, for example. Users compile lists of people with whom they want to chat and the systems will indicate, at any given time, who is online and whether they are available, busy, or away from their computers. This feature is often known as 'presence'. In some ways, this can give rise to something equivalent to the serendipitous meeting of a colleague at the coffee machine—when a user sees a contact is online, they might, by what is really chance, start up a conversation; except that this is more like bumping into a contact in the street because contacts are external as well as internal.

IM dominates communication amongst the Net Generation (see Section 3.4) and is mushrooming in banks and consulting firms, especially in the US. It is quicker than e-mail and more interactive. Experienced users (of, say,

[19] <http://www.fidler.co.uk>.

[20] <http://www.clientinform.net>.

[21] <http://messenger.msn.com>. The social networking system, Facebook, has recently launched its own IM system, so that users can tell when their 'friends' are online and chat to them in real-time— <http://www.facebook.com>.

11 years of age) can conduct many conversations at once, while parents again cluck disapprovingly. So far, lawyers have also been sceptical and very few of the world's 300 million users are from the legal fraternity. Indeed some firms forbid IM. But, in due course, IM will be common in legal practice, encouraging better communication internally and providing a new channel of contact with clients. Some lawyers reject as intrusive any notion that their clients might see when they are online and be able to engage them in chat. Others see this differently: as an opportunity to be more available and responsive.

Video calling, from desktop to desktop, using Skype, is another increasingly popular form of communication.[22] Similar to IM using a webcam, this no-cost service offers a glimpse of a related world that lawyers and clients will find hard to resist. Already, the sharpness of the video is such that a conversation supplemented by seeing the other party is indeed an enhanced experience. As video across the Internet improves in performance, as most certainly it will, speaking while viewing will become commonplace.

And a new generation of video conferencing is indeed now available. It is quite astounding. The first generation was technologically impressive in its time but disappointing in action—people at the other end seemed diminutive and remote, their movements were staccato and puppet-like, and the time delays (latency) in sound were frustrating. These early systems were more effective if participants had met before, but it proved an unsatisfactory medium for a first-time engagement. In short, a meeting by old video link was nothing like a real face-to-face encounter. Using the latest technology—'immersive telepresence', as it is sometimes called—is quite different. It does feel as though you are in the same room as those you are meeting remotely. The images are life-size and almost spooky in their clarity, physical movement is smooth, and there are no perceptible delays in sound. You can successfully meet someone for the first time and look them straight in the eyes. Cisco and HP are IT giants who, amongst others, have invested heavily in the new generation.[23] While their technological infrastructures are different, their offerings are similarly impressive for the end user. The multi-media technology combines with the purpose-built studios to create the impression that you are actually sitting around the same table as your distant colleagues.

The new-look video conferencing, although eye-bulgingly expensive for all but the largest of organisations, will prove invaluable for international legal businesses when the prices start to tumble. Whether for internal

---

[22] <http://www.skype.com>.

[23] <http://www.cisco.com/en/US/products/ps7060> and <http://www.hp.com/halo>.

management meetings or for getting together with clients, the attractions are clear. Telepresence helps to avoid costly and tiresome air travel. It is more convenient than travelling to meet, and it encourages and enables more frequent interaction. And it also helps to reduce users' carbon footprints.

Before long, however, these systems will not be confined to use by prosperous companies and firms. This new emerging technology offers us a glimpse of the quality of video link that the great majority of businesses and homes are set to enjoy from their desktops in a few years' time.

Taken together, mobile telephony, texting, instant messaging, video calling, and immersive telepresence will provide lawyers with a wide range of communication channels that are a far cry from exchanging letters via the postal system, which was the dominant way of communicating not so many years ago.

My second category of online community is *producing and collaborating*. In current jargon, this is a central aspect of what has come to be known as 'Web 2.0'. The idea of Web 2.0, although there is no tight definition with which all experts would be happy, is that we are witnessing the birth and growth of a second generation of uses of the Web; and, as Internet users, in this second wave, we are becoming much more than passive recipients of the content published on websites. We are now able to contribute and participate directly. Users are becoming providers. Readers are also authors. Recipients are now participants. We are finding radically new ways to produce information (in its broadest sense) and to collaborate with one another. To grasp the enormity of this 'user-generated' content, we should dig a little further.

First of all, sharing has become all the rage. With the entire online world, or with restricted groups that we choose, we can now lawfully share (contribute and enjoy) photographs,[24] presentation slides,[25] our diaries,[26] video clips,[27] and even our online experiences.[28] This is not hobbyism amongst a few long-haired doubtfuls—YouTube (the repository for online video clips) currently enjoys over 100 million users per day.

At the same time, another form of communicating has been burgeoning—blogging. A weblog (or blog), is like an online, personal diary, an informal website that records the activities and thoughts of its author (weblogger or blogger).

---

[24] eg <http://www.flickr.com>.

[25] eg <http://www.slideshare.net>.

[26] eg Google Calendar at <http://www.google.com>.

[27] eg <http://www.youtube.com>.

[28] eg Digg, which is an interesting site where people can share and discover content from across the Web—<http://digg.com>. Related techniques here are social tagging and folksonomies, which allow users collaboratively to categorize content—see, eg <http://del.icio.us>.

Over 100 million people have blogged at one time or another. A blog presents a mix of daily log, alongside news, views, commentary, and links. Entries usually offer associated discussion facilities, allowing visitors to contribute their views. Many journalists are especially attracted to blogging, which offers them more space to expound as well as an environment for interacting with their followers. Blogging has become an increasingly popular medium in the legal world for the opinionated, the idiosyncratic, and many others, similarly to edify or simply sound off in a very public manner.[29] Some legal blogs attract very little interest. Others roll along with modest following. Still others are widely digested and genuinely influential—for example that of Stanford University's Professor Lawrence Lessig,[30] and the judicial and academic double-act of Judge Richard Posner of the United States Seventh Circuit Court of Appeals and Professor Gary Becker of the University of Chicago.[31] Legal blogging came of age in 2006, when an entire conference at Harvard Law School was devoted to 'bloggership', on the way in which blogs are transforming legal scholarship.[32] Legal academics, who used to have to wait twelve to eighteen months for their ideas to be published in serious journals, can now ventilate their ideas instantaneously.

Looking forward, some lawyers will come to syndicate their blogs, posting their offerings on many different public blogging areas and on organizational Intranets. Others will come together in a kind of public faculty of bloggers—a small group of thought leaders, perhaps, with overlapping interests and audience, might blog together in the same space. The gravitational pull of this will be stronger than that of one person's blogs (no matter how eminent the blogger). Still others will blog in private communities—for example groups of General Counsel.

Another illustration of a relatively new form of production is the podcast—audio recordings that can be played directly from a website or downloaded in seconds onto mobile devices, such as iPods and mobile phones. Some law firms have been producing podcasts for some time and the growing usage levels suggest that there are clients out there who want to listen.[33] After all, thoughts on the law may well be much easier to digest when delivered orally with expression, perhaps in mellifluous tones, rather than in arid text.

---

[29] For a useful list of legal blogs, see <http://www.venables.co.uk/blogs.htm>.
[30] <http://www.lessig.org/blog>.
[31] <http://www.becker-posner-blog.com>.
[32] <http://cyber.law.harvard.edu/home/bloggership>.
[33] The law firm, Pinsent Masons, at its OUT-LAW website, makes podcasts available on a weekly basis—<http://www.out-law.com>. On average, each episode is downloaded about 1,000 times.

And yet another new technique is the 'wiki'. Named after the Hawaiian word, wikiwiki, meaning quick, these are websites that users can directly alter and add to. The best known wiki, by a long margin, is Wikipedia, 'the free encyclopaedia that anyone can edit'.[34] Since 2001, Wikipedia has been written collaboratively by over 13,000 main contributors, constantly refining and submitting materials, and adding cross-references and citations. This voluntary exercise, a case study in 'mass collaboration'[35] has amassed around 10 million articles in over 250 languages. It is said to attract almost 700 million users annually. While sceptics expect it to be an unruly and untrustworthy resource, Wikipedia is generally a remarkably reliable body of knowledge, built by a self-refereeing community of enthusiasts. Indeed, a highly controversial, peer review investigation led by the prestigious science journal, *Nature*, concluded that 'Wikipedia comes close to Britannica in terms of the accuracy of its science entries'.[36] In any event, corroborating the philosopher Karl Popper, a new form of evolutionary knowledge is emerging here, an online world underpinned by what might be regarded as survival of the smartest.[37]

How will wikis be used in law? In principle, whenever there is an opportunity for lawyers to collaborate with one another or with their clients, wikis can be deployed. Although the legal fraternity is not renowned for collaborating, the clear attractions of legal wikis should help to foster greater cooperative spirit: contributions to wikis can be made easily and quickly; their impact and usefulness is immediate and apparent; they evolve rather than requiring one single act of creation; they provoke stimulating debate and discussion; and they appeal to the ego, in that contributors seem irresistibly enjoined to leave their mark. Wikis may engender a new culture of knowledge sharing for lawyers—on Intranets and the Internet, internally and with clients, bringing the legal community and its beneficiaries under a new virtual roof. As a tool for gathering and sharing insight into clients and markets, wikis stand out as more intuitive and practical than most techniques

[34] <http://wikipedia.org>.

[35] For up-beat treatments of the subject of mass collaboration, see Y Benkler, *The Wealth of Networks* (New Haven: Yale University Press, 2006); D Tapscott and AD Williams, *Wikinomics* (New York: Portfolio, 2006); C Leadbeater, *We-Think* (London: Profile, 2008); and CR Sunstein, *Infotopia* (New York: Oxford University Press, 2006). For a sober critique of the field, see A Keen, *The Cult of the Amateur* (London: Nicholas Brealey, 2007).

[36] See <http://www.nature.com/nature/journal/v438/n7070/full/438900a.html>. This url includes links to *Britannica's* refutation and *Nature's* response.

[37] K Popper, *Objective Knowledge* (Oxford: Oxford University Press, 1972). This series of essays presents a profound theory of the evolution of human knowledge.

of the past. As a method of capturing know-how—about areas of law, types of work, and jurisdictions—wikis seem more natural and convenient than their technological predecessors. And as a way of building up a body of knowledge about live deals or disputes, wikis are ideally suited, providing an accessible shared space for all parties involved and as an ongoing repository of update and insights.

Closely related to much of the progress with wikis is the 'open source' movement. This is a phenomenon that, so far, has attracted little interest from lawyers, other than intellectual property specialists. Open source software illustrates what is going on here and is remarkable in two ways. This is software, first, that is quite unlike conventional code, in that it is made available at no cost to users. Second, like Wikipedia, it is generally created not by a single company or formal consortium or under some strict project management regime but is informally and collaboratively developed by volunteers who cooperate on development projects without compensation. As documented by Steven Weber, in his book, *The Success of Open Source*, many of the systems that lie at the heart of the Internet (most notably Linux, the most commonly used operating system, available at no charge and built by non-paid volunteers) are open source.[38] But the spirit of open source need not be confined to the world of system development. In law, for example, we should expect a build-up of public, or community-based, bodies of legal materials. The radical leap here will be when work undertaken for one client is made available, publicly or to a legal community, for others to re-use. Clients will soon collaborate in sharing the past work product of their advisers. They will soon therefore have a new option beyond in-sourcing or outsourcing legal work—that of open-sourcing (see Section 4.6)

Unlike previous waves of new systems, these new techniques for producing and collaborating (blogs and wikis especially) are comfortably within the purchasing power of modest-sized law firms and cash-strapped in-house legal departments. For example, the latest version of Microsoft's SharePoint, an off-the-shelf package, can provide a solid environment for wikis, blogging, and more.[39] And these systems need not be held on law firms' hardware; once set up, they can be securely hosted by third party providers. This affordability will no doubt encourage widespread experimentation and exploitation of these emerging techniques.

---

[38] S Weber, *The Success of Open Source* (Cambridge, Mass: Harvard University Press, 2004). Also see <http://www.linux.com>.
[39] <http://www.microsoft.com>.

My third category of system under the heading of online community is *networking and community-building*. The basic thrust here is clear—if we are all plugged into the same network, we can easily contact, socialize, and collaborate with colleagues and friends around the world. This is another dimension of Web 2.0. The most striking illustration of its impact is the remarkable recent uptake of 'social networking' systems. In all, there are thought to be well over 300 million users of these systems, most notably Facebook (founded in 2004, with around 70 million users and growing rapidly)[40] and MySpace (over 200 million users, launched in 2003, and bought by the News Corporation in July 2005 for, effectively, US$580 million).[41] This level of usage and the rapidity of adoption, over so few years, is spectacular. This is not analogous to CB radio in the 1970s. This is not the province of geeks. The overwhelming majority of university students in the UK and the US are on one or both of Facebook and MySpace. Nor is this an exclusively Western phenomenon. On a recent visit to Japan, the graduate students that I met there were every bit as enthusiastic about their equivalent, known as Mixi.[42] I know from my clients in the UK that around half the staff in professional firms in the UK are also users, and this number is rising steadily. Very few of these are partners, incidentally, which is telling. The people who own and run the finest professional firms are generally out of touch with the way in which the majority of their people keep in contact. That said, there are signs of tentative adoption by Internet users in their 40s and beyond. This is the beginning. I expect that social networking amongst users of all ages, within five years or so, will become almost as popular as e-mail. Social networking systems, or at least the next generation, in my view, will be the future for all of us.

So what is social networking? What do people actually do on Facebook and MySpace? Broadly, these systems enable users to keep in touch with one another, easily and on a regular basis. Typically, users present information about themselves—photographs, news, videos, updates, views, and more. And they keep in contact with a network of other users (often from all over the world) who similarly provide information on an ongoing basis. Communication and discussion also takes place amongst smaller groups. These can be subsets of users' networks or interest groups made up of people who come together because they share, as the name suggests, an interest

---

[40] <http://www.facebook.com>.
[41] <http://www.myspace.com>.
[42] <http://www.mixi.jp>.

in some topic. A system of alerts keeps users informed about the current and recent activities of their networks of friends.

In the following section, I say more about Facebook, using my teenaged son's experience as a case study. At this stage, I concede that it may not be immediately obvious, from my summary, why it is that social networking is so wildly popular. But it is. I have recently become a user and I was immediately hooked. There is research investigating the attraction and even the addiction here, especially amongst the young.[43] But it is early days for social scientists to come up with anything conclusive. For now, my guess is that a complex mix of motives are at play: a fondness for keeping in touch; curiosity about one's peers; perhaps a penchant for a little bit of voyeurism and its flip side, exhibitionism; and an inclination to flirt, we cannot deny.

What impact has social networking had on the world of professional services and the legal industry? With one exception, social networking, to my knowledge, has rarely been deployed as a business tool for law firms. If the subject has appeared on partnership agendas, it has been because there have been concerns in some firms about alleged time-wasting by junior staff or that the firm's network is groaning because of the additional traffic that social networking has brought. The one exception is the quite common, if often rather intrusive and unsavory, use of Facebook and MySpace by HR departments as a way of gaining insight into the behaviour of actual and potential employees.

Some lawyers, as distinct from law firms, have signed up to Linked-In, which is the nearest we get today to Facebook for grown-ups.[44] While this system has built up a respectable user base of professional and business users, the take-up in the legal world has been low, especially amongst senior partners.

Interestingly, youthful social networkers have not been managing upwards on this one—junior lawyers have not been knocking down senior partners' doors, advocating that Facebook and MySpace have business uses. When I suggest to regular users that they could extend their network to professional contacts, they often looked surprised at the very idea and then, quite quickly, worried about mixing online business with online pleasure. This should not deter us. We have at our disposal a wonderfully powerful tool for keeping in

---

[43] See eg K Withers and R Sheldon, 'Behind the Screen: the hidden life of youth online' (London, Institute for Public Policy Research, 2008).

[44] <http://www.linkedin.com>.

touch with contacts. It is barely conceivable that this will prove to be irrelevant for lawyers.

In projecting ahead in the world of social networking, however, readers should not assume that today's social networking systems will continue to operate as Facebook and MySpace do today. I am reminded of the state of e-mail in 1996, when my book, *The Future of Law*, was published. At that time, many of us used half a dozen or more different e-mail systems and had to endure the laborious chore of logging on to each to pick up the full array of e-mails that had been sent to us. There was little interoperability across these systems and no single mailbox into which all our messages would be delivered. The world moved on, and today most of us operate from a universal mailbox, into which and from which mail from and to many different systems can be sent. Similarly, I expect in the world of social networking that, before too long, we will be able to communicate across the various platforms, enabled, no doubt, by some front-end which will sit on top of the various underlying systems.[45] It will be less important that we have chosen to use Facebook or MySpace for example, than that we are participating in a variety of particular networks. Indeed, I anticipated just this in 2000, in my book, *Transforming the Law*, where I predicted that, in the future, a busy person might belong to fifty or so different networks of contacts. I said then, and I still believe this is helpful, that we should think of every user having a *portfolio of affiliations*—to a range of networks, some devoted to particular projects, others to organizations to which they belong, and still others to bodies of individuals with shared interests.[46] I stand by that prediction.

The key concept here is that of communities. These come in various forms and there is some overlap here with my previous category, producing and collaborating. The community that contributes to Wikipedia is one form and an example of what is often called 'mass collaboration'. I draw a contrast here with closed-community 'peer production'.[47] On this latter approach, there are many fewer users because the community itself is not open to the public (to any users of the Internet), so that a smaller group convenes electronically and works together. LegalOnRamp is the most exciting current example of this kind of closed community. Conceived as a cross between Facebook and

---

[45] One initiative moving in this direction is OpenSocial. For discussion of this, see <http://opensocialapis.blogspot.com>.

[46] R Susskind, *Transforming the Law* (Oxford: Oxford University Press, 2000; paperback edition, 2003), 128–129.

[47] On the concept of peer production, see Y Benkler, *The Wealth of Networks* (New Haven, Conn: Yale University Press, 2006).

Wikipedia but dedicated to the legal profession, this system is being ener-getically championed by Paul Lippe in California, with the support of a cred-itable group of heavy hitting General Counsel and major law firms.[48]

Sometimes online communities are not especially productive, in that their purpose is not so much to create something new (such as a reference book or an operating system) but to exchange news and views. Whether you are fas-cinated by the law on long negative prescription or perhaps by provincial train timetables, there will be others out there who share your passion and will be happy to engage. In law, therefore, in the new global village, across the flat world we are rolling out for ourselves,[49] the sole practitioner need no longer fly solo. All sorts of new legal communities, populated by lawyers and clients alike, will spring up. Some will flourish; others will disband having served their transient purposes.

Beyond straightforward networking, there are all kinds of other communi-ties building up. Under this heading, we should never forget NeoPets, the online virtual pet environment, which has 150 million accounts opened and 220 million virtual pets running around (metaphorically speaking). What is harder to believe—an online pet or an online lawyer?

Finally, under the heading of networking and community-building, I should say a few words about an advanced form of social networking—the virtual world known as Second Life.[50] This is a three-dimensional online area, created by users, referred to as 'residents', of whom there are now over 10 million. In this digital world, engaging with others using online personae called atavars, users can even find land and build businesses, and they can buy, sell, and trade with other residents. Actual commercial concerns have prospered there. A few UK law firms have a presence in Second Life but, once again, it is too early to judge the likely impact.[51]

My fourth and final category under my heading of online community is *trading and exchanging*. I am not referring here simply to online retailing, when businesses sell to citizens across the Internet, a phenomenon that now accounts for almost 10 per cent of retail spending in the UK. Nor am I just alluding to the now widespread phenomenon of searching the Internet for the lowest possible prices for some goods or services; which, in turn, may

---

[48] <http://www.legalonramp.com>. Also see M Chandler and P Lippe, 'Five Ways In-house Counsel Can Talk to Law Firms' *ACC Docket*, No 10 (November/December 2005) 74–89.

[49] On flattening the world, see TL Friedman, *The World is Flat*, updated and expanded edition (London: Penguin, 2006). I have found this book to be extremely helpful and insightful.

[50] <http://www.secondlife.com>.

[51] eg Field Fisher Waterhouse <http://www.ffw.com> and Lovells <http://www.lovells.com>.

lead to an online purchase or perhaps to a more robust negotiation with conventional face-to-face storekeepers. These uses of the Internet apart, I mainly have in mind here the trading and exchanging that now goes on directly amongst citizens, with no wholesalers or retailers or other intermediate channels cluttering the supply chain.[52]

The prime example of trading in this way is eBay, the online auction and shopping website.[53] Founded in 1995, over 100 million people, casual and accomplished users alike, buy and sell in this electronic marketplace. In the fourth quarter of 2007 alone, $16 billion worth of goods were traded on eBay. It is a huge industry in its own right. E-sceptics, who like to suggest that the world reverted to normal after the dotcom era, should reflect on the enormity of this system. Far from fading, eBay has forged ahead, and affected the buying and selling habits of millions of people who would not regard themselves as Internet or IT specialists. More, eBay is a fine example of a service that has liberated what I call a 'latent market'. It is not that the trading that now goes on through eBay was previously being conducted in a pre-Web manner and that eBay spruced and tidied it up a little. On the contrary, eBay created a whole new market. It helped to satisfy a latent demand to trade far more extensively than was previously possible. The online community of buyers and sellers—to repeat, over 100 million of them—did not exist before 1995. The Internet and the Web have played yet another transformational role here.

Another high impact, community-based form of trading and exchanging, but one that has much more controversial roots, is known as file sharing, usually on the basis of a technique known as peer-to-peer (P2P) networking. The technical details here need not detain us, other than to appreciate that, on this model, individual computers on a network share files (documents, music, video clips, and more) directly with one another rather than being connected through some central system. When that network is the Internet and there are millions of users, then exchanging of files becomes possible on an unprecedented scale. The power of this technique first reached the public's consciousness in 1998, when a young student at Northeastern University in Boston, Shawn Fanning, wrote a program called Napster, that allowed users to share music directly across the Internet. A frenzy of music exchange followed, peaking in February 2001 when there were over 26 million users. Someone, somewhere, always had a copy of a track that was wanted. But this

---

[52] <http://www.quidco.com> takes a further step—it earns commission on users' online purchases and passes this back to them.
[53] <http://www.ebay.com>.

did mean that millions of copies of music files were being made and, predictably, a frenzy of copyright activity followed. This was a gargantuan affront to conventional intellectual property protection and the first version of Napster was shut down on legal grounds.

Putting the legalities to one side, though, later versions of Napster were remarkable developments that spawned a wide range of services, some more legitimate than others, using similar techniques. It is mind-boggling to contemplate that we can all be connected to one another and be able to dip into the one single virtual collection of files that we jointly hold in our machines. What if these files were legal resources (letters, advices, reports, opinions, presentations, and so forth)? What if we could exchange legal files on that scale?

In truth, it does not matter what technique is used for the sharing of legal content. My argument here, under the heading of online community, is that we now have at our disposal a fundamentally new tool-kit for communicating, for producing and collaborating, for networking and community-building, and for trading and exchanging. Different users will prefer some techniques over others. But no-one can sensibly complain about a shortage of choice—we now have instant messaging, video calling, immersive telepresence, blogging, wikis, podcasts, social networking, mass collaboration, closed-community peer production, online auctions, peer-to-peer file sharing, and more.

In my travels, I hear four possible views from lawyers in response to the subject of online community and the possibilities I describe. The first is that this will be fundamentally transformational and disruptive for the legal profession. The second is that we cannot be certain of such change but the systems seem too significant to ignore. Third, some lawyers say that this is all very interesting for other professions and industries but it is unlikely to touch the legal world. Finally, there are those who say that all the various techniques and technologies that I have discussed are no more than passing fads. It will come as no shock to readers to learn that I belong to the first camp and work happily alongside affiliates of the second. I despair of the third and fourth, just as I despaired of lawyers over a decade ago who said I was insane to suggest that e-mail would come to dominate the way in which lawyers and clients would communicate. I simply cannot see how major changes in the way we communicate, collaborate, network, and trade are somehow irrelevant for lawyers and their clients. Nor, given the sheer scale of the systems and the levels of their usage, can I conceive that this is a passing fad.[54]

---

[54] I defy anyone to read Yochai Benkler's formidable book, *The Wealth of Networks* (n 47 above), and conclude that online community is a transient phenomenon.

I recognize that the new technologies bring serious concerns (from threats to privacy through to worries about the 'cult of the amateur'),[55] but these should not deter us from facing the future squarely and responsibly assessing their impact for the legal and justice systems.

3.4 The Net Generation

Within the massive and growing population of Internet users (currently around 1.25 billion), I draw a firm distinction between those who can remember a pre-Internet world and those who cannot. The latter group is what I take to be the Internet or Net Generation. If born in or after 1985, give or take, these young adults and children cannot recall a time when it was not possible to communicate by e-mail or instant messaging; nor an existence without the Web and social networking at their fingertips. They cannot conceive of life without mobile phones and text messaging, and find it hard to credit that their parents and their friends, when planning their Saturday nights a generation ago, had to choreograph their activities and all permutations in advance because they were unable to contact one another once they left their homes and so their fixed line telephones.

More recently, and with considerable fervour, this Net Generation, as I say earlier, has embraced social networking systems (Facebook and MySpace, for example) which now lie at the epicentre of their lives. During much of 2006, my younger son, Jamie, allowed me to observe his progress on Facebook; from a tentative novice to an experienced exponent, in a matter of months. Swiftly, he built up a large network of friends, extending to well over 1,000 in number. I contrasted this with my address book in my youth: when I was his age (18) I was probably in regular contact, out of school, with about 12 companions. I was not, I want all readers to understand, an unpopular person; I simply did not have twenty-first century tools for maintaining contact with a large number of friends. For Jamie, Facebook rapidly moved, as he put it, from reflecting his social life, to becoming the core of his social life. In a sense, Facebook became an umbrella under which all his work and social activities were gathered. It was not that he no longer socialized in person. His face-to-face engagements were now facilitated by Facebook

---

[55] See A Keen, *The Cult of the Amateur* (London: Nicholas Brealey, 2007).

(logistically speaking); and when not physically congregated together, it complemented such get-togethers by enabling constant, real-time contact with his network of friends. This was a complementary and not an alternative social option. More, the system introduced him to new people and encouraged a broader, conventional social life.

I also learned from him that Facebook could perform a quasi-management function. At the time, he was Head Boy at his school, which meant he regularly had to organize and consult with around forty prefects. Using Facebook, in one evening, he could arrange lunch and car park duties and debate with his fellow prefects about a variety of issues prior to meeting with teachers the following day. In short, he was using Facebook as a management tool in a way that would put most modern lawyers to shame. Indeed, I believe if most teenagers looked over the shoulders of most contemporary legal practitioners over the age of 30 and witnessed the way they managed themselves and others, they would be horrified by the antiquity of it all.

As he prepared to move from school to university, Facebook eased the transition for Jamie—a group had been set up for all people starting at his particular Oxford college. Using social networking, he was able to make online contact with his fellow students to be, well in advance of the official start date. Today, and now at university, the configuration of his hardware is revealing. He has a laptop machine as well as a separate flat screen. Typically, when he is sitting at his computer, the particular application on which he is working (for example word processing) is on the screen of his laptop, while, to one side, and ever present, on his flat screen, is Facebook. Like financial analysts in the City, who sit before rows of blinking screens devoted to all manner of information feeds, the Net Generation is coming to have dedicated screens for their social information feeds. This also reflects the Net Generation's comfort with multitasking. Younger users of technology seem to find it easier than their parents to engage in various activities in parallel. Where a 14 year-old will find it natural to be on Facebook, while simultaneously instant messaging, downloading music, surfing the Web, and doing homework (perfunctorily, no doubt), the 40 plus person will tend to work sequentially and perhaps a little ponderously, undertaking one task at a time.

I dwell on Facebook because it provides a powerful illustration of a new technology (broadly, social networking) that has taken the Net Generation by storm, overhauling their communication habits and suggesting a way of socializing and working that is quite alien to most lawyers and their clients in 2008. When I speak to lawyers about Facebook, I am greeted by the same scepticism and conservatism that I encountered in the mid-1990s when I discussed the potential of e-mail. Facebook is dismissed as a transient plaything of the youth. It is a nonsense that teenagers have over 1,000 friends. What kind of friendships can these be? None of this is relevant for me, the cynical lawyer goes on, because no-one I know is on Facebook. All of this, I am afraid, is depressingly misguided and characteristically myopic.

Communicating and networking within and beyond their organizations is fundamental to the work of lawyers. Why on earth should lawyers feel they are exempt from using tools that are enabling others to communicate and network with unprecedented ease? We say to our young lawyers that they must nurture their contacts and build their own networks. And yet we do not encourage them to exploit tools that are surely more effective than the clunky systems of yesteryear. Compare the habits of a Facebook user who manages his or her contacts with great ease with the fashion in which most lawyers currently manage their network of contacts, through an unholy confusion of business cards, handhelds, rolodexes, and databases. Why not embrace a powerful and simple way for lawyers to keep in touch with their clients, colleagues, and contacts?

I am more confident today that Facebook-like technology will become indispensable to lawyers in communicating with clients than I was in relation to lawyers and clients embracing e-mail when I wrote and spoke about this twelve years ago.

Aside from social networking, the Net Generation is not satisfied with being confined to the flat world of text. The proliferation of iPods (over 100 million units now sold) although clearly not the sole preserve of the Net Generation, has nonetheless been embraced by teenagers as a way of life. The Net Generation manipulates sound files with consummate and natural ease. Their information units are not restricted to the transport of words. The success of YouTube, the website to which video clips can be sent and at which they can be viewed at no cost, is also indicative of the way in which the Net Generation is embracing multi-media. The majority of the 100 million daily views of YouTube, are by fully-fledged members of the Net Generation. For both entertainment and education, multimedia is embraced and increasingly expected by the Net Generation.

And there is more. Mobile telephony and Internet use are converging for the Net Generation. Unusually, in frenetically embracing Blackberry devices (and the like) the adult population has been one step ahead of youth in the world of handhelds. This is changing, as I write, as we enter the era of 'smart mobs', as Howard Rheingold puts it, heralding what he regards as the 'next social revolution'.[56] These powerful units, with wireless broadband access and daunting multi-media capability, will bring social networking to the palms of the Net Generation. And, with integrated satellite-based global positioning systems, these mobiles will also have location awareness. It is already possible for such systems to alert users when a potential partner (with a promising profile) is nearby.

The Net Generation, then, has moved beyond a world dominated by text and synchronous communications. Their world is a multitasking frenzy, fuelled by multi-media, by portability, and the asynchronicity of e-mails and social networking systems. The natural first port of call *today* for the Net Generation, when seeking information on almost any topic, is the Web. When I suggested this might be the case in the future in my book, *The Future of Law*, I was thought to be an eccentric at best. It was barely imaginable, just ten years ago, that the reference library and especially the encyclopaedia could so quickly fade from prominence as the dominant information source in society.

Pulling together these various strands of thought and observation about the Net Generation, we should acknowledge a significant grouping in society whose communication habits and information seeking habits are under-pinned and dominated by the Internet. One key challenge in thinking about the nature of legal services ten years hence and beyond is to imagine how this Net Generation might provide and receive legal services. Older members of today's Net Generation will be in their early 30s a decade from now and so could themselves be directly involved in the provision of legal services and as recipients of guidance on legal matters. Hard though it may be for many middle-aged lawyers and receivers of legal services of today to accept, pre-dictions about the future of law should take very considerable account of how the Net Generation will want to dispense and obtain legal services. I observe this leap in imagination to be one that many lawyers, who are not far from retirement today, find all but impossible to make. So, the lawyer of 2008, who insists that face-to-face contact is indispensable when legal insight is to be imparted, should pause and wonder whether the Net Generation will think similarly, given that their communication habits today are dominated by social networking, texting, and instant messaging (I say more about this in the previous section). Likewise, while many adults of today cannot imagine turning to the Internet as a source of legal guidance, or for legal documents,

---

[56] H Rheingold, *Smart Mobs* (Cambridge, Mass: Perseus, 2003).

this may be entirely natural for those who need legal help in the future. Leaders and commentators in the legal profession do themselves and the community considerable disservice by assuming work patterns and life patterns in the future will be pretty much the same as those of today. The future of legal services will not be determined by today's partners and law firms, policy-makers in government and in professional bodies, nor by professors in law schools, or General Counsel in substantial organizations. It is our children who will shape the profession, because they are tomorrow's lawyers and clients. And, as enlightened parents, we should facilitate and encourage them to proceed in their own way, and we should do this with an open-minded attitude, rather than impose our own practices in a frequently embarrassing manner. In the world of technology today and in law tomorrow, the child will be father of the man.

3.5 Clicks and mortals

For many years, I intended to write a book entitled *Clicks and Mortals*. It was to be about the impact of the Internet on the professions, government, and education. I wrote a proposal for the publishers, who liked the theme but rejected the title. I was reluctant to let it go, however, and so have smuggled the concept into this book, under the radar, as a section heading if not a book title. This is not mere obstinacy. I believe the fundamental message of 'clicks and mortals' still holds.

I derived the phrase from another phrase, 'clicks and mortar', that was popular during the dotcom era. This sought to emphasize that many organizations would find success in the Internet era by concocting a mix of online offering and physical presence and not simply by exclusive devotion to online commerce. And it has indeed transpired that many leading online retailers also continue to have major physical outlets.

For law firms, this clicks and mortar theme suggested that some thought should be directed to the best ways to exploit, or minimize losses from, their property legacies, whether as long leases or capital assets, in often costly and arguably unnecessary geographical locations. But I suggested that lawyers should think more broadly, with an emphasis also on 'clicks and mortals', on combining online and traditional human service. The biggest challenge here is for lawyers honestly to identify those situations in which personalized, human service is genuinely needed and adds relevant value that Internet and IT-based service cannot simulate or improve upon. As an early intuition, we may conjecture that, in the future, legal service that requires considerable expertise or an ongoing personal touch will still be in demand in the traditional way, but routine and repetitive work will be handled online and by smart systems.

More generally, achieving a balance between clicks and mortals (between machine and human being; between process and personality) will be a central challenge in maintaining a balanced society and an efficient economy. Already, it is clear that the Internet and not human beings is gradually becoming the natural, first port of call for those who need information on most topics and for a variety of services too.

There is a generational point here. Following the distinction of the previous section between those who can remember a world without the Internet and those who cannot, the attitude of the former towards many Internet facilities is and always will be that of amazement—amazement that we can make available and access information so readily across the world. For the Net Generation, there is no amazement. A website or service is useful or not. That the whole phenomenon is in place is of itself unremarkable. That new services and applications emerge so regularly is in the normal order of things for the Net Generation. It has always been thus. Looking forward once again, into a future when today's Net Generation become the opinion-formers and decision-makers, I anticipate a shift in default setting when it comes to obtaining guidance in professional services. Today, when the parents of the Net Generation are involved, and there is a knowledge service to be delivered or received, the natural assumption is that it will be human-based. With the Net Generation, I believe, this default setting will change—their starting point will be that knowledge service comes across the Internet and, if not, they will want to know why. In future, the presumption will be in favour of clicks and not mortals. Mortals will only be justifiably involved if they can add value not deliverable across the Internet. More, human beings will move beyond our current ways of thinking and talking about the Internet (which, after all, is basically a set of technologies and standards—plumbing really). Online life will be natural and human beings (the Net Generation) will give as little thought to its availability as adults do today to the phone or TV (at whose existence we do not generally pause to marvel).

The broad thrust of this discussion of clicks and mortals is supported and extended by Frank Levy and Richard J Murnane in their important book,

The New Division of Labour.[57] As economists, they ask four fundamental questions: 'What kinds of tasks do humans perform better than computers? What kinds of tasks do computers perform better than humans? In an increasingly computerized world, what well-paid work is left for people to do both now and in the future? How can people learn the skills to do this work?'[58] These and related questions are very much the focus of this book too.

Levy and Murnane are always keen to draw a distinction between computers *substituting* the work of human beings, as distinct from computers *complementing* their work. And they make the important observation that substitution by computers and outsourcing are affecting many of the same occupations.[59] This echoes many of my remarks in Chapter 2. At the risk of oversimplification, I think it fair to say that Levy and Murnane argue that, in the workplace, there are two broad sets of activities which are currently beyond the capabilities of computers, and inappropriate too for outsourcing. The first is where there are problems for which there are no routine solutions and so expert contribution is required. For example, if a problem is one that has not been confronted before, they are pessimistic about the ability of computers to respond helpfully. Equally, where the expertise required to resolve some challenge is hard to articulate or represent in the form of rules (or 'representable knowledge'), then we find here another important limitation of computers. (This inability to articulate what is sometimes called 'tacit knowledge' has hindered the knowledge management and expert systems communities for many years).[60]

The other broad categories of task that are the current and foreseeable province of human beings as opposed to computers, according to Levy and Murnane, are what they call 'complex communication'. Where mutual understanding and trust is important or where difficult persuasion or explanation is needed, Levy and Murnane suggest that human beings are still very much required.

To combine their approach with mine, therefore, would be to suggest that mortals are best suited where tasks require expertise or complex communication, while clicks can take care of routine tasks and when solutions can be broadcast rather than discussed. This analysis will come as an immediate

---

[57] F Levy and RJ Murnane, *The New Division of Labour* (New York: Russell Sage Foundation, 2004). A more philosophical book that explores the limitations of computers is HL Dreyfus and SE Dreyfus, *Mind over Machine* (New York: The Free Press, 1986).

[58] Levy and Murnane (n 57 above) 2 and 157.

[59] ibid 21.

[60] On tacit knowledge, see M Polanyi, 'The Logic of Tacit Inference' (1996) 41 *Philosophy* 1.

relief to most lawyers, who will tend to argue that they bring to bear their expertise in most of their daily work, and that complex communications are at the very heart of their interactions with clients. But do not put this book down just yet.

In the first instance, it is instructive to unpack the notion of legal expertise. Uncharitable though this may sound, I do find, and I suspect it is no different in other professions, that many lawyers exaggerate the extent to which their performance depends on deep expertise. Lawyers, like other professions, cloak themselves in a web of mystique, jargon, and apparent complexity, in part to project market value and partly, no doubt, as a matter of bolstering their self-respect. My point here is that simply because lawyers assert that expertise underpins their performance, we should not take this at face value. We should subject it to scrutiny and analysis. Where, consciously or unconsciously, knowledge is being paraded as expertise and yet analysis shows it to be capable of being reduced to routine tasks in whole or part, the journey along the path towards commoditization can begin and, led by the market, will begin. It is also vital to recognize that, in law, legal expertise is not all of the tacit kind. While it may be tempting for legal experts to say that they cannot articulate how they come to their decisions, once again we should not simply concede this uncritically. In the 1980s, an entire discipline in the fields of artificial intelligence and expert systems, known as 'knowledge elicitation' (or 'knowledge acquisition') challenged this assumption; and, with moderate success across a number of disciplines, yielded models of expert knowledge that surprised even the domain experts themselves. They had no idea that the knowledge, upon which their expert performance was based, could be modelled.

Lawyers often overstate the extent to which the content of their work is creative, strategic, and novel. Thomas Edison, best known for his invention of the light bulb, fearlessly noted that 'genius is 1% inspiration, 99% perspiration'. Even the most ambitious artificial intelligence scientist of today would not look to computers for inspiration. However, the perspiration and the drudgery are often especially amenable to computational treatment. If Edison allowed that such a tiny fraction of his work was inspirational, I wonder about the possibility of lawyers' claims that most corporate work (to take an example) involves a higher level of creativity.

In my own doctoral research in the 1980s, I addressed a related issue. I drew the distinction between problems that are routine for experts but hopelessly difficult for non-experts; and problems which are generally acknowledged by all experts to be difficult. The former, I suggested, could to some extent at least be subject to computational treatment; while the latter, given the limits of technology, could not.[61]

A related issue here is that some tasks require some form of expertise, not because the problem has never been confronted before, but because of complexity. A good illustration here is in the area of tax, as I discuss in Section 2.6. Tax rules can be very large in number and complex in their interrelationships such that their application in practice really does seem to require the input of experts. However, on analysis, many tax problems can be reduced, effectively, to a large decision tree or a structured body of rules, so that a computer system would be especially well suited to solving what otherwise might seem to be an insoluble challenge for the non-expert.

If we bring to bear the kinds of techniques I introduce in Section 2.5, where I discuss decomposing and multi-sourcing, I think it can and will be found that many areas of human endeavour that have, in the past, been thought to require human expertise, have significant portions that can be unpacked, standardized, and computerized too.

As for complex communication, the other main activity that Levy and Murnane argue to be beyond the scope of, or at least unsuitable for, handling by computers, again we should not be too ready to accept this without serious reflection. Their observations here do resonate with those of many practising lawyers, who say that high touch, highly personalized, face-to-face, trust-inducing, human interaction is central to the service that they deliver. While this sounds plausible, and may indeed be a salutary charter for first-rate legal service, feedback from clients does not always support the case. For example, as I mention in Section 1.2, research undertaken by *Which?* in 2004, into the preferences of consumer clients of lawyers, suggested almost two-thirds of adults thought it a good idea to obtain legal services from common high street brands (supermarkets and banks, for example).[62] This rather flies in the face of lawyers' claims for the unrivalled attractiveness of their personalized service. Equally, in my own research for major law firms, I have found that the great majority of senior in-house lawyers claim that law firms do not really understand their businesses and are especially poor at listening to their clients and empathizing with their position (also see Section 5.1).

---

[61] See R Susskind, *Expert Systems in Law* (Oxford: Oxford University Press, 1987; paperback edition, 1989) 244.

[62] See <http://www.which.co.uk>.

Further, I am increasingly told by practitioners in the largest of firms that direct client contact at meetings is becoming rarer and rarer, in large financial transactions, for example. Indeed, I was struck recently at a conference with one major firm, where a relatively experienced lawyer who had recently joined a UK firm, said that in her first three months of intensive client work she had yet to meet a client. In banking and finance law, as in other areas, many of the lawyers who today are undertaking the grunt work, do not, as a matter of fact, actually meet with the clients themselves. That engagement is left to relationship or supervising partners; but, overall, on the job, the level of face-to-face contact is diminishing.

There is, moreover and in any event, some interesting evidence to suggest that, in relation to particularly sensitive or embarrassing issues, some people actually prefer to impart their details to a machine rather than a human being. This notion motivated Joseph Weizenbaum, in 1976, to write one of the finest books on the relationship between man and machine. Then a professor of artificial intelligence at MIT, Weizenbaum had written a program, as something of a prank, that simulated a human psychotherapist. He was horrified to discover, when he asked his secretary to test the system, that she then asked him to leave the room so that she could, as it were, confess in private. Weizenbaum worried deeply about the implications of this and wrote a passionate book on the subject—*Computer Power and Human Reason* [63]— warning of the perils of increasingly intelligent machines and their impact on human beings' interaction with one another. Who knows what he would have thought of the burgeoning online communities on the Web?

Leaving to one side a serious question over the extent to which lawyers walk the talk when it comes to communicating with their clients and whether clients actually want to speak directly to their lawyers, we can also link this issue of communication to another trend in this chapter relating to the Net Generation. In short, it cannot and should not be assumed that, because middle-aged lawyers and clients may have a preference for communicating with one another in the time honoured, face-to-face manner, that this will be the preferred mode of contact in perpetuity. Given that social networking, instant messaging, and e-mail currently dominate communication amongst the Net Generation in their social affairs, we should at least be

---

[63] J Weizenbaum, *Computer Power and Human Reason* (Harmondsworth: Penguin, 1984) (edition with new preface).

alive to this pattern extending into their business and legal affairs in later life. So, it may be that some areas of legal practice are not obviously amenable to computerization because the service is irreducibly about personal contact and relationship. But it should not be assumed that the way in which inter-personal contact is made today will not itself be subject to serious change in coming years.

Returning to the major trend, however, my principal observation here is that when non-lawyers need legal help, the default setting will change in the future from a natural inclination towards mortal advice to a preference for guidance by clicks. Whenever legal counsel is required, it will be normal practice, in the first instance, to ask whether there are any online services that might be of help. And although, on the face of it, there may seem to be various aspects of human-based legal service of today that seem beyond the power or appropriateness of IT, I am arguing that this may not be the case in the future.

There is a related and common fallacy, incidentally—that of supposing that for any complex task or process or activity, we must bring to bear *either* clicks *or* mortals but not both. The book contends that for many complex challenges we face it is precisely a judicious blend of clicks and mortals that is often the best course, although the clicks component may be smaller than expected. This blend lies at the core of my thinking about decomposing and multi-sourcing (Section 2.5).

I must stress that for any task or process or activity, there will never be a single optimum division of labour between clicks and mortals, between machines and people. In identical circumstances, different individuals may have quite different preferences. Where one person might be entirely happy to pursue a query online, another might insist on interacting directly with a human being. This is an early call for a new kind of diversity.

3.6 Disruptive technologies

I turn now to my sixth and final major trend in IT. My claim here is that lawyers will be increasingly confronted by what are known as 'disruptive technologies'. I borrow this term from Professor Clayton Christensen of Harvard Business School. His work has been of great help to me in coming to understand the likely long-term impact of technology on law firms.

In particular, I have benefited from reading his outstanding book, *The Innovator's Dilemma*.[64] In the introduction to his book, Christensen sets out his stall as follows:

This book is about the failure of companies to stay atop their industries when they confront certain types of market and technological change. It's not about the failure of simply any company, but of *good* companies—the kinds that many managers have admired and tried to emulate, the companies known for their abilities to innovate and execute. Companies stumble for many reasons, of course, among them bureaucracy, arrogance, tired executive blood, poor planning, short-term investment horizons, inadequate skills and resources, and just plain bad luck. But this book is not about companies with such weaknesses: It is about well-managed companies that have their competitive antennae up, listen astutely to customers, invest aggressively in new technologies, and yet still lose market dominance.[65]

According to Christensen, these companies fail because they are too late in recognizing the impact of what he introduces as 'disruptive technologies'. These are new, innovative technologies that periodically emerge and fundamentally transform companies, industries, and markets. Interestingly, in the early days of these disruptive technologies, they 'result in *worse* product performance, at least in the near-term . . . Generally, disruptive technologies under-perform established products in mainstream markets . . . are typically cheaper, simpler, smaller, and, frequently, more convenient to use'.[66] At the outset, therefore, many impressive companies *and* their impressive customers together reject these new technologies.

Meanwhile, smaller, more nimble, and visionary businesses embrace and exploit them; and by the time their impact is fully recognized by the market-leading incumbents, it is often too late. In powerful case studies in a variety of industries, including retail, automobiles, computers, pharmaceuticals, and steel, Christensen compellingly demonstrates that disruptive technologies have frequently been disregarded or discarded by leading companies (such as Sears, IBM, and Xerox). In so doing, he points to the huge commercial opportunities that were missed and, more significantly, to the ways that more manoeuvrable, often hungrier, and more entrepreneurial competitors have entered marketplaces and often displaced the apparently invincible leaders. In turn, he shows that these newcomers have come to dominate the next phase of evolution of an industry or market sector.

---

[64] C Christensen, *The Innovator's Dilemma* (Boston, Mass: Harvard Business School Press, 1997).
[65] ibid ix (original emphasis).
[66] ibid xv (original emphasis).

It is not that these great companies have failed to listen to their customers. The enduring irony to which Christensen also points us is that it is precisely because leading firms: 'listened to their customers, invested aggressively in new technologies that would provide their customers more and better products of the sort they wanted, and because they carefully studied market trends and systematically allocated investment capital to innovations that promised the best returns, they lost their positions of leadership.'[67] Crucially, these companies did indeed invest heavily in technology. But, Christensen argues convincingly that they injected cash into the wrong types of technology. In a vital distinction, he contrasts disruptive technologies with what he calls 'sustaining technologies'—those that 'improve the performance of established products, along the dimensions of performance that mainstream customers in major markets have historically valued'.[68] In other words, successful companies have tended to put capital and effort into improving and optimizing their current offerings and ways of working rather than into developing new business models.

In relation to the legal marketplace, I anticipate that, in the long run, Christensen's analysis of the failure of great companies will come to apply equally to leading professional services firms and so to legal practices as well. I expect, in the coming decade, that a variety of information technologies will underpin radically new ways of working. Initially, most leading law firms will reject these disruptive legal technologies and the novel approaches to legal business that they bring. And so, firms will instead continue to invest in a range of sustaining technologies that support and enhance the traditional business models.

We can easily recognize and expect in the legal services arena the characteristics that Christensen associates with disruptive technologies—they will not work as well as human lawyers, but they will be less costly and easier to use. Where the under-performance of these systems will constitute a fatal flaw for many lawyers, this of itself is a vital theme for Christensen. He says 'suppliers often "overshoot" their market: They give customers more than they need or ultimately are willing to pay for'. However, and this is absolutely crucial, he goes on to say that 'disruptive technologies that may underperform today, relative to what users in the market demand, may be fully performance-competitive in that same market tomorrow'.[69] In other words,

---

[67] ibid xii.
[68] ibid xv.
[69] ibid xvi.

lawyers who reject disruptive legal technologies (such as document assembly and online legal guidance—see Sections 4.1 and 4.5) for their current level of performance, or dismiss some of the application areas in which they operate (for consumers or small businesses) as indicative of their irrelevance, are missing a vital signal. Today's low-key systems and services, those fuelled by disruptive legal technologies, will grow in strength and sophistication; and indeed are poised, as I suggest in greater detail in Chapter 4, to disrupt the entire legal marketplace.

What makes all of this particularly difficult for the top manager is, as Christensen suggests, that it may appear irrational, for three reasons, for successful organizations to invest in disruptive technology:

First, disruptive products are simpler and cheaper; they generally promise lower margins, not greater profits. Second, disruptive technologies typically are first commercialised in emerging or insignificant markets. Leading firms' most profitable customers generally don't want, and initially can't use, products based on disruptive technologies. By and large, a disruptive technology is initially embraced by the least profitable customers in a market.[70]

And yet, many great companies that have neglected to embrace disruptive technologies have failed for reason of that neglect alone. This is so because: 'Disruptive technologies, though they initially can only be used in small markets remote from the mainstream, are disruptive because they subsequently can become fully performance-competitive within the mainstream market against established products.'[71]

What does this mean for lawyers? I believe it presents a fundamental challenge for the legal profession and that is to assess whether or not various existing and emerging technologies are disruptive in the sense that Christensen identifies. In the following chapter, I introduce a range of 'disruptive legal technologies'. Individually and collectively, these technologies constitute a grave threat to conventional legal businesses. Indeed, disregard of their impact could, I believe, lead to the collapse of complacent law firms.

The response of many firms will be to fall back on investment in sustaining technologies, and to rationalize that it is too early to invest in what will be seen as excessively exotic systems. The business case, it will be said, is not yet proven. Most lawyers will therefore play a waiting game, reluctant to break

---

[70] ibid xvii.
[71] ibid xxii.

rank until adoption of the new systems is unavoidable. It is here that competitive advantage will be won and lost. In Christensen's words:

It is in disruptive innovations, where we know least about the market, that there are such strong, first-mover advantages . . . Companies whose investment processes demand quantification of market sizes and financial turns before they can enter a market get paralyzed or make serious mistakes when faced with disruptive technologies. They demand market data when none exists and make judgments based upon financial projections when neither revenues or costs can, in fact, be known. Using planning and marketing techniques that were developed to manage sustaining technologies in the very different context of disruptive ones is an exercise in flapping wings.[72]

Christensen pinpoints here the grave difficulty I have always had in persuading lawyers of the potential of the 'latent legal market', as discussed in Section 1.4. I have little doubt, for example, that online legal guidance (see Section 4.5) will help to create new demand for legal assistance (and through client work I have had this confirmed), but it is not possible to quantify any latent legal market for the very reasons Christensen notes. Accordingly, firms run by conservative characters will tend not to invest in disruptive technologies; while those managed by innovative, entrepreneurial types or by external investors who are setting up alternative business structures (as permitted by the Legal Services Act 2007) will be more likely to take the plunge.

Before moving on, in Chapter 4, to discussing my collection of disruptive legal technologies, there is one objection to the idea of disruptive technologies that I feel I should address. The heart of the objection is that it is not actually the technology itself that is intrinsically disruptive. Rather, it is either the managers who deploy the technology who are the disruptors or it is the new underlying business models that are brought about by the technology that are disruptive.[73] It is true that technologies do not tend to disrupt spontaneously. For a given technology to give rise to disruption, there must be some human agent who actually puts the systems in place. And, of course, technology of itself is not disruptive unless it has something to disrupt. I know that one underlying concern here is that to focus on technology and not people or businesses models is to be excessively technology-led; it is to let the tail wag the dog. But for the purposes of some of this book, I do want to be technology-led. I feel that IT should sometimes be the starting point for

---

[72] ibid xxi–xxii.

[73] See eg CM Christensen and ME Raynor, *The Innovator's Solution* (Boston, Mass: Harvard Business School Press, 2003) 32. I am grateful to Darryl Mountain for drawing my attention to this point.

discussion and, in turn, the catalyst for change. I am suggesting that there are a variety of existing and emerging technologies that are directly applicable to legal practice and yet will challenge our conventional ways of working. I believe that lawyers should strive to understand the potential of these technologies. IT is now part of the universe of lawyers. It is not a parallel universe. Disruptive legal technologies are too important to be left to technologists.

Returning now to my initial claim of this section, that lawyers will be increasingly confronted by 'disruptive technologies', I come to this view (it is a hypothesis really) on the strength of what I am seeing in law firms, what I am hearing from clients, and what I am observing in other professional sectors (especially tax and medicine). The systems that are increasingly causing a stir and attracting greatest attention among clients are not conventional sustaining uses of IT that bolster the business of law firms; instead, they are applications of technology that challenge the old ways and, in so doing, bring great cost savings and new imaginative ways of managing risk. If we combine this market sentiment with the predicted exponential growth in technology, the steady increase in information satisfaction, the emergence of online community, the expectations of the Net Generation, and the growing preference for clicks over mortals, then the road to disruption seems fairly clear.

4

Disruptive Legal Technologies

I am often asked what technologies, techniques, and applications of information technology (IT) are most significant for lawyers of today. Underlying this question, more often than not, is a grim sense of foreboding rather than a refreshing enthusiasm. Many more lawyers are inclined to set up fortifications to protect themselves from new developments than to rush forward and embrace them. In any event, I respond directly to the query in the discussion that follows, largely in this chapter, concerning those technologies that I call 'disruptive legal technologies'.

In the previous chapter, the notion of disruptive technologies is introduced in some detail (in Section 3.6). By this term, I am referring to those technologies (or systems, techniques, or applications) that do not simply support or sustain the way a business or sector operates; but instead fundamentally challenge or overhaul such a business or sector. In this book, I identify ten such technologies in the legal arena. They are a mixed bunch. Some of them overlap; and most can operate alongside, and even integrate with, one another.[1]

---

[1] I accept that readers may identify other disruptive legal technologies over and above the ten that I have isolated. For example, several colleagues have suggested to me that electronic billing systems are disruptive.

I introduce and explain nine of these in this chapter, while deferring consideration of the tenth (online dispute resolution) until Section 6.6, where that subject sits more comfortably in the flow of the text. Individually, I believe each of these ten technologies will bring very considerable change to the legal market. Collectively, in my view, they will fundamentally change the face of legal service.

Before exploring the intricacies of each technology in turn, it is important to clarify that disruptive technologies do not bring bad news for all players in a market. Indeed, one man's disruption may well be another's salvation. In law, technologies that are disruptive for many firms are frequently a breath of fresh air, if not a revitalizing gust, for the client—a service, for example, that radically improves the efficiency of law firms may be disruptive in the sense of its negative impact on hourly billing and therefore their profitability; but that same reduction in time spent may constitute a very significant cost saving for the client. And indeed that is a chief characteristic of many of the systems described in this chapter. Generally, when I refer to disruption, I am speaking about legal technologies that disrupt the law firm as opposed to the client. Even then, though, some technologies that, on the face of it, appear to disrupt law firms are precisely those that can be embraced by innovative legal businesses; by those who believe that the best way to capture a larger share of future markets is to step forward and deliver solutions or services that no-one else is providing.[2] While these may appear to give rise to less income and profitability than the old ways, the thinking here is that a larger share of the new market, even if the unit charge of services or solutions is less, will in the end be more commercially beneficial than hanging on to an ever smaller slice of the old markets. Moreover, there is anecdotal evidence to suggest that clients will welcome more warmly those firms that seek to innovate and, in turn, they will pass more work along to those bolder firms.

4.1 Automated document assembly

Automated document assembly systems, also known as document generation systems, operate as their names suggest. A user wants a specific type of

---

[2] For an extended discussion of this belief and approach, see WC Kim and R Mauborgne, *Blue Ocean Strategy* (Boston, Mass: Harvard Business School Press, 2005).

document (for example a lease or an employment contract). He or she answers a series of relevant questions and, as if by magic, out pops a relatively polished and customized first draft. A lot of early work in this field was devoted to systems that would generate wills. Users were asked about their financial affairs and their testamentary preferences. Their responses caused various chunks of text to appear in what emerged as a serviceable draft – not as good as might be drafted by the finest of legal practitioners but much better than the document the average layperson would throw together if unassisted.

Inside, these systems have stores of document templates or parts of templates which have previously been set up by legal specialists. The templates are fixed portions of text together with precise instructions as to when given extracts should be used. The body of instructions is like a very large decision tree. Driven by the users' input, the system will automatically generate a document that is based on the system's knowledge of how its standard text should be used.

The potential for automated document assembly is often more readily acknowledged by non-lawyers than by lawyers. When I chat with senior business people, explaining my work, I often use document assembly as an example. In a revealing sense, they are often deeply unimpressed. They quickly accept that the main output of lawyers is documentation of one kind or another. And they see it as self-evident that the legal profession should strive to find ways of streamlining, improving and, where appropriate, overhauling what they take to be a type of production process. Most intelligent lay people assume that lawyers rely on standard bodies of well tested text and do not craft documents from scratch. This is an obvious efficiency to the untutored eye. That we can go further and automate at least part of the drafting process is for most non-lawyers, and especially clients, possible, desirable, and entirely predictable.

The reason that automated document assembly is, in my terms, a disruptive legal technology, is that its use can greatly reduce the time that lawyers expend on the drafting and production of documents. Insofar as lawyers charge by the hour (as many if not most lawyers still do), this automation and the efficiency it brings can reduce the amount a lawyer might be able to charge for a given drafting activity.[3] (A more detailed discussion of hourly

---

[3] See DR Mountain, 'Disrupting Conventional Law Firm Business Models Using Document Assembly', (Summer 2007) 15(2) *International Journal of Law and Information Technology* 170. Also see BC Quinn and KA Adams, 'Transitioning your Contract Process from the Artistic to the Industrial' *ACC Docket* (December 2007) 60–72.

billing is presented in Section 5.1.) While the production mentality underpinning document assembly may be alien to many lawyers, it is second nature for most business people, who are always looking for ways of reducing the cost of the services they provide (perhaps by computerizing or outsourcing).

Interestingly, automated document assembly is not a new legal technology. The first detailed treatment of the subject was by James Sprowl, in 1979, in a seminal article in the *American Bar Foundation Research Journal*.[4] Since then, there have been literally dozens of document assembly tools on the market. Most have withered and died, not because they failed to do the job but, in large part, I believe, because lawyers have been disincentivized by the hourly billing regime from embracing this potentially high-impact technology. I accept there have been other deterrents too, including concerns over liability, maintenance, and the cost of developing these systems in the first place. Nonetheless, some firms do indeed have sufficient demand. One of the best and earliest case studies here is *newchange documents*, an automated document assembly solution, developed by the banking and finance lawyers at Allen & Overy.[5] Launched in 2000, this is an internal productivity tool that enabled the firm to produce and amend certain complex loan documents far more quickly than before and, crucially at the time, much more swiftly than the firm's rivals. In so doing, the firm secured advantage over its competitors for whom, in consequence, this new technology was disruptive. One additional, interesting aspect of *newchange* was that, as part of the project, Allen & Overy re-engineered its standard loan documents so that they would fit together in lego-like modules, ideally suited to the imposition of IT. In the past, many lawyers had attempted (unsuccessfully) to graft this technology onto large bodies of ill-suited templates with countless internal cross-references. It may well be, however, that it is by fundamentally rewriting the underlying materials that very large-scale document assembly can be made to work best.

The issue of scale leads to the question of costs. It is true that many lawyers who have experimented with document assembly have found the cost of developing these systems to be prohibitive and have concluded that very few, if any, document drafting jobs within their firms have been sufficiently high value or high volume to justify the outlay. This often leads lawyers to claim that only the very largest of firms can afford these systems. Insofar as

---

[4] JA Sprowl, 'Automating the Legal Reasoning Process: A Computer that Uses Regulations and Statutes to Draft Legal Documents' (1979) 1 *American Bar Foundation Research Journal*, 1.

[5] <http://www.allenovery.com>.

this is true, here is an area where external investment in law firms (in the form of private equity, for example) may be useful. But, in any event, this line of argument is less compelling today, when these document assembly systems can be packaged and delivered across the Internet for use by many clients. Pre-Internet business thinking saw document assembly systems as internal efficiency tools mainly for law firms; post-Internet, we can see that this technology is a powerful vehicle for making legal know-how widely available on an online basis. In early 2003, Linklaters led the way in this direction, as the first major law firm to offer an online automatic document drafting service for clients. This was Term Sheet Generator, part of the firm's Blue Flag suite of online legal services, developed by the firm's banking practice and launched after the conduct of a successful pilot with clients.[6] It enabled banks, after completing online questionnaires, to generate polished term sheets automatically, speeding up this process, it was said, from hours to minutes. Term sheets are documents that summarize the terms and conditions upon which banks are willing to provide finance. They are generally drafted by banks. Accordingly, the system did not automate a task undertaken by Linklaters. Instead, to adapt the old lager advert, the system enabled the firm to reach parts of its clients that other firms could not. The vital difference in Linklaters' approach was that they were providing the tool to clients and not using it as an internal efficiency tool.

Linklaters were not to be alone in carving out new opportunities in this way. Eversheds, an innovative national law firm in the UK, used a similar approach in setting the pace for the next generation of employment lawyers. The firm's highly regarded employment team developed an online service that automated the process of drafting employment documents.[7] The system was Web-based and was designed for human resource professionals in large organizations. They logged on, filled out simple questionnaires, stroked a key or two and the tool automatically generated reliable service contracts, terms and conditions of employment, compromise agreements, staff handbooks, and other policy documentation. This was not a generic, vanilla flavoured, employment offering but was tailored by the firm so as to contain client-specific materials and standard forms. This 'mass-customized' (see Section 2.5) service had the attraction for clients of being quicker, cheaper and often more reliable than the alternatives, namely, drafting legal documents manually or paying substantial fees to IT-averse law firms.

---

[6] <http://www.blueflag.com>.
[7] <http://www.eversheds.com/hrcontractdemo>.

Document assembly development activity has not been confined to law firms. The potential was even recognized by the Judiciary. In 2004, two retired judges in the UK launched an Internet start-up company. It provided an innovative service for lawyers who wanted to submit documents to court that contained judicially approved wording. The initial service was based on three document generation systems that were already used by many English judges. Instead of creating these directions and orders afresh each time on a blank canvass, these judges entered a modest amount of key information about a case, and the system then automatically generated appropriate documents, filled with standard text that was carefully drafted for regular re-use. The first documents that were automated in this way were civil directions, ancillary relief directions, and orders under the Children Act 1989. Although barristers and solicitors were enthused when they first saw the judicial systems, the potential for such systems, both for judges and court users, remains largely under-exploited (mainly due, I believe, to a lack of government funding).

In-house lawyers have also become interested. In 2004, Microsoft embraced automated document assembly—for its own internal use. After a successful pilot, its legal and corporate affairs department in Redmond in the US settled on document assembly technology for the production of the vast range of the corporation's end user software licence agreements. Master contracts for each product were drafted in Word, converted into templates so that Microsoft lawyers were able to generate appropriate agreements, allowing for variations in language and governing law. Innumerable other companies could similarly use document assembly techniques to automate their standard documentation. Above all, perhaps, here is a vital legal risk management tool—one that controls the content of the documents. However, most in-house legal departments claim that they lack the internal resources to develop such systems. In that event, who is best placed to build them? Law firms may be thought to be the prime candidates here but this possibility separates the staid from the entrepreneurial. The former say that they are lawyers and not publishers, while the latter will recognize a commercial opportunity to package their knowledge and expertise in a novel way and so meet their clients' needs in a new and innovative manner.

Meanwhile, legal publishers did indeed enter the fray. The innovative and widely respected Practical Lawyer Company (PLC), have started to develop off-the-shelf automated document systems for common transactions. These systems confirm, as I note, what many non-lawyers have thought for years— that the production of legal documents in standard, unexceptional circumstances should surely be systematized. The PLC approach is this: they provide most of the system development resource but collaborate with law firms and in-house legal departments, giving these lawyers a cut-price, finished product whose content they have had the chance to influence. A suite of PLC FastDraft modules are now available - finished, off-the-shelf, sets of automated documents in various areas of law, including asset purchases, share purchases, share buybacks, group reorganizations, sale of land, leases, and leasehold management.[8] In the past, the production of such documentation was exclusively the province of lawyers. Today, this work can be undertaken by automated systems, provided by imaginative legal publishers. A clear example, in the language of Section 2.1, of 'packaging' legal service, this is disruptive for most law firms.

4.2 Relentless connectivity

In retrospect, fax technology was a forerunner of a whole rash of systems that are now giving rise to what I call 'relentless connectivity'. By this, I mean that a variety of technologies are conspiring to prevent many professional advisers from ever being able fully to disengage from their clients. While this may bring a rapid and highly responsive service to clients, it can and will impose unflagging pressures on advisers. The enabling technologies that are the culprits here are introduced in Section 3.3. Fax technology is not one of them but, in the 1980s, it did cause considerable agitation within the legal profession and was a harbinger of challenges to come. I remember that the drawbacks and benefits of this radical technology were the subject of many seminars of the Society for Computers & Law in the UK. The advantages of speed and convenience were widely noted, but lawyers tended to dwell on the drawbacks, and especially the expectations that fax systems would engender amongst their clients. If fax technology became popular, it was observed with deep regret, this would mean that lawyers could no longer play for time by uttering the age-old phrase 'our letter to you is in the post'. It was feared that the fax would radically affect expected response times and put unprecedented pressure on lawyers.

---

[8] <http://www.practicallaw.com>. The lease and leasehold management systems are intended to be compatible with PISCES, the standard format for electronically transmitting property-related data— <http://www.pisces.co.uk>.

Clients, on the other hand, were more up-beat. Most liked the idea of their work being turned around more quickly. Lawyers countered that this could encourage a reduction in 'thinking time' which could be to the detriment of clients. In the event, of course, fax technology came, and became a dominant communication tool between lawyers and their clients, although there was an initial shock when it was discovered that the first generation of these systems used rolls of thermal paper whose text seemed to fade and then disappear over time. Later generations overcame this shortcoming, and lawyers had to think and then respond more quickly.

For lawyers, the story continued, rather benignly in the early days, with e-mail which, despite early protestations, was embraced comprehensively by the profession in the late 1990s. The first wave went to and from the desktop machines of lawyers, and so gave rise to no greater pressures or expectations than fax. However, with the advent of hand-held machines, and most notably the Blackberry, lawyers began a love/hate relationship. They were thrilled that these machines were always connected to their organizations' IT networks and that they automatically synchronized with them without the need to log on. They warmly welcomed the ability to keep in touch with the office and clients but—whether because of their diligence, neurosis, or obsessive behaviour—they soon found it difficult to resist having a look at the blessed device every few minutes, to peer into their shiny boxes to see if new e-mail had arrived or if there were updates to their diaries. It was not just lawyers who were hooked. So pervasive were these mobile machines that one US investment bank had a notice above its urinals, as early as 2004, declaring that the costs of repairing a dropped Blackberry would not be reimbursed.

Instant messaging and social networking systems will bring a further dimension of connectivity. With both, it is possible for users to see when their friends and contacts are online, whereas with e-mail it is just possible that the lawyer might be in a meeting and not having a furtive look at the machine. With instant messaging and social networking, our 'presence' online is harder to deny (although it is possible to indicate when we are unavailable). The same is true for video calling on Skype.

Imagine a world, then, where our hand-held devices are much more powerful than today's, with vast, wireless Broadband access, superb video quality display, wonderful processing speed, and more storage capacity than any lawyer could want. When these machines are on, which will be during all our waking hours, our presence will be visible and our network of contacts will have immediate access to us. There will be no place to hide. Clients will know their lawyers are available and will be able to initiate video-calls and conversations using instant messaging, and they will assume that their advisers will take note of the news and information that will be sent out from the social networking systems, the next generation of which I am sure the business community will embrace. A key issue for lawyers in this world of relentless connectivity will be quality control. When inundated with all manner of communications, the temptation to bat back an e-mail, text message or instant message, without adequate consideration or supervision, may for some busy lawyers prove to be overwhelming.

Take but one feature of today's Facebook that pulsates with implications for lawyers—the facility that encourages users to state their 'status', that is, to say what they are currently doing (for example 'I am on holiday in Spain'). Imagine now that a client used this feature to observe, for instance, 'I am visiting our Beijing office'.[9] The lawyer of this client would therefore know the whereabouts of the client and would be able to get in touch if he thought he could be of help. And, as ever, in the world of online community, if he chose not to respond or participate at all, then some of his competitors certainly might.

In practice, I suspect we will stratify our contacts and make our 'presence' known only to those who mean a great deal to us. We will create our own inner circles of contacts. And so, in turn, lawyers will vie to be in the inner circles of their clients.

In any event, the long, leisurely business lunch or relaxing day on the golf course will be interspersed by innumerable intrusions from one's online contacts. We can see this happening already—mobile phones lie unashamedly next to knives and forks, while golfers keep their PDAs holstered and ready for action, the only concession being a switch flicked from full sound to vibrate.

It might be argued that lawyers should be perfectly entitled to switch off and disengage from the network; from the Machine. Of course, it is true that there will be no obligation to remain connected, but if you are not there, there is every chance, as I say, that your competitors will be. The astute lawyer of tomorrow, even if grudgingly, will want to have more or less full-time presence, day and night, on the network, to ensure that any queries from clients will be addressed by their firm rather by than another. Accordingly, law firms will need to put in place practices and processes that ensure 24-hour-a-day availability of some form of client contact. In the future, the winners in the legal world may succeed by dint of survival of the most responsive.

---

[9] If 'micro-blogging' takes off, this will have the same impact. This allows users to send short text-based updates to their contacts—see <http://www.twitter.com>.

Dov Seidman, the chairman and founder of LRN, is surely correct when he says that, 'We will never become *less* connected'.[10] What we see and can foresee today is but a glimpse of the connectivity of tomorrow. Generally, I find myself excited and enthused by emerging technologies and their impact. The relentless connectivity that I describe here, however, sometimes looms as a dystopian shadow over our lives that consumes me with an undeniable sense of apprehension. The pace and pressure may well be oppressive. These communication technologies are disruptive, therefore, not so much in challenging our prevailing business models, but in the way in which they will intrude in our lives as human beings who generally expect and cherish some genuine leisure time. (On the other hand, for the Net Generation, this level of connectedness will be normal; for them, the reverse might seem bizarre.)

4.3 The electronic legal marketplace

The Internet has transformed the way we buy and sell in at least four ways. First, most obviously and commonly, many of us buy goods online, such as books, supermarket provisions, music, airline tickets, and so on. Second, and generally through eBay, many people auction goods online, from small household items through to motor cars and beyond. Third, it is increasingly common practice for purchasers who intend to buy in the conventional way (from physical shops and showrooms) to explore prices online and to determine the lowest, often with the help of price comparison sites. Users electronically window-shop around for good deals on, for example, cars, insurance, and electrical equipment. Fourth, buyers and prospective buyers can benefit from the experience of past purchasers. In growing numbers, buyers leave comments on websites, indicating their level of satisfaction or grading the service they have received; while some sites automatically and helpfully let users know that previous purchasers of given products also bought other specified items ('if you enjoyed S, you may well like Y'). In the past, the application of the legal maxim, *caveat emptor* (let the buyer beware) often seemed rather harsh on the naive customer because information about goods and products was not easy to pin down. Today, there is little excuse for naivety—a trip to the Web invariably unearths insights from like-minded consumers.

---

[10] D Seidman, *HOW* (New Jersey: Wiley, 2007) 39 (original emphasis).

So far, the impact of the Internet on trading and exchanging has been much greater in the world of goods than that of services. However, we are increasingly seeing a shift in consumer behaviour here, so that suitable service providers (doctors, insurance brokers, plumbers, and many more) are frequently being identified, evaluated, and selected via the Internet. This should lead the broad-minded lawyer quite naturally to ponder the eventuality that, in due course, legal services might similarly be secured on an online basis. I am not speaking, for now, about paying for the actual delivery of legal advice or guidance or documents through online services; my focus at this stage is on selecting legal service providers and procuring legal service with the support of various online utilities. Why not conduct *auctions* when selecting lawyers or set up online *price comparison* systems for legal service? And why not build up *reputation* systems—collections of insights from clients about their satisfaction with legal work undertaken for them? In short, why do we not create an electronic legal marketplace, a virtual location, where clients can go to find and select their legal advisers in an informed manner? Soon we will.

We should take a step back and remind ourselves of the ways in which lawyers are selected today.[11] Ordinarily, the seasoned buyer of legal services (an in-house lawyer, for example) is familiar, for many areas of legal work, with a range of law firms which are sufficiently experienced to take on any particular job. Relying on personal experience and that of colleagues, as well as on directories and word of mouth, and through analysis and distillation of reputation and rumour, the client identifies a sensible number of matches between his or her needs and what is available in the market. Sometimes, the in-house lawyer chooses a firm without any tendering process; while, on other occasions, competitive bidding is required, mainly through proposal writing and so-called 'beauty parades'. An emerging trend is for clients to retain the services of their internal procurement specialists, a development that many law firms regard with manifest distrust. Increasingly, large businesses establish one or more 'panels' of appropriately qualified law firms—they pre-select groups of lawyers, creating a pool into which they can dip when particular services are needed.

Taking these various elements together, this is far from being a perfect set-up. Sometimes, admittedly, the system does work quite well—good lawyers are chosen and they provide sound service at a reasonable rate.

---

[11] There is much market research on this. See eg, 'European Study 2006: How mid-sized companies in Europe select and review their legal service providers' (LexisNexis and Martindale-Hubbell, 2006).

But sometimes, we must concede, it disappoints—for example when bad lawyers do a poor job at exorbitant rates. And, in the middle, we find uninspiring work being delivered, with no sense amongst clients of enjoying value for money. This variable performance and the possibility of grave disappointment is inherent in the system. Given that the search process is neither fully comprehensive nor highly systematic, it is possible, if not likely, that the traditional procurer of legal services might miss firms or lawyers, who are better suited (on grounds of experience, cost or convenience, for example) than those advisers who are ultimately selected.

But why should clients settle for less than having great lawyers offering outstanding service at highly competitive rates? The reason is that they invariably lack information: about which firms and lawyers are available, suitably qualified, and well regarded by clients; and about what fee rates are competitive. Economists say that when someone is buying a service without enough information to get a good deal, they suffer from 'consumer detriment'. In law, it is fair to say there is a great deal of client detriment. But not for long, because there is a growing collection of existing and emerging systems that are helping clients to make a more informed choice. For many law firms, this will be highly disruptive. The old system, one that has allowed lawyers to under-perform and overcharge, is to be displaced by a new model, under which all law firms will be subject to far greater scrutiny and competition—on availability, price, performance, and client satisfaction. The free market is coming soon to the world of law.

Many law firms will be swift to point out that their clients have already tried auctioning and it did not work. Most of these sceptics will be thinking of early attempts by various major organizations (including RBS, Barclays, and GE) to select their panels by auction. Anecdotally, most law firms involved found the processes to be cumbersome and the selection methodology to be crude.[12] And, from informal conversations, I know that most of the clients were also disappointed with the experience. With the benefit of hindsight, it is fair to say that these early forays were over-ambitious. The selection of panels is a highly complex process and firms are chosen as much on soft criteria (such as the personalities of the partners) as on more measurable factors (such as hourly rates). More, much of the work that is envisaged falls towards the bespoke end of the spectrum, in terms of the evolutionary path that I introduce in Section 2.1. However, as my analysis in Section 2.4 suggests, auctions are more likely to work in respect of work that

---

[12] P Hodkinson, 'E-auctions: reviewing the review' *Legal Week*, 9 June 2005.

is standardized, systematized, and even packaged rather than for traditional, handcrafted service, where auctioning on price is too blunt an instrument.

Generally, then, if legal services are to be selected via auction, we should expect this to operate better where the work is relatively routine and there is little to choose between providers in terms of the actual service delivered. Auctions will work best where the main source of differentiation is price. Online auctions will help to drive out the lowest prices for routine legal work. On this model, we can imagine auctions being deployed *within* panels. If clients have pre-selected their preferred firms, then they should be comfortable with the credentials of those firms. If the lawyers who are laid out on the buffet have broadly similar capabilities, then the main challenge, for much of the work that will need done, will indeed be to secure the least costly service. Shareholders and stakeholders deserve nothing less. If there is nothing to choose in terms of quality and the element of personalized service is not so important (as is often the case with routine work), then price should be determinative.

Looking beyond the rarefied world of panels, online auctions for legal services hold great potential for helping other clients to secure relatively routine services at highly competitive prices. I emphasize again the routine element because, following my arguments in Sections 2.1 and 3.5, where work is genuinely bespoke and requires complex and highly personalized communication, the selection of lawyers will involve questions of personal chemistry and style that are hard to assess through auctions. But most legal work need not fall into this category and so the market should be keen to find ways of securing best value. A US-based company that was amongst the first to recognize the potential here was eLawForum. [13] The original idea was that clients could lodge requests for proposals for legal services onto the eLawForum website and registered law firms could bid against one another, stating their qualifications, experience, availability, and pricing. eLawForum was an early example of what I termed, in *Transforming the Law*, 'legal infomediaries'—Internet-based services that will help clients to select legal advisers.[14]

Falling short of auctions, online services can also provide a form of legal match-making service. In the UK, for instance, online techniques have been used successfully by another type of legal infomediary, FirstLAW, which helps

---

[13] <http://www.elawforum.com>.
[14] R Susskind, *Transforming the Law* (Oxford: Oxford University Press, 2000; paperback edition, 2003) 50–3.

clients to choose and instruct lawyers, to manage competitive tenders, and to assist with the negotiation of fees.[15] One early client, the General Medical Council, used FirstLAW to select lawyers to advise on the conduct of formal complaints against doctors. Using the online system, fifteen law firms submitted their GMC tenders in a pre-specified, electronic form. This ensured uniformity of presentation and enabled easy comparison amongst the submissions. Glossy brochures, traditionally the hallmark of many so-called beauty parades, were not allowed and paperwork was kept to a minimum.

More recently, and of wider application across society, the original founders of the magazine, *Legal Week*, Mark Wyatt and Mary Heaney, have launched TakeLegalAdvice.com.[16] Users complete a few online pages of forms about their circumstances and their matching system sends the case anonymously to suitable law firms. Law firms are given one to two days to respond, indicating how they would handle the matter and at what estimated cost. Importantly, the responses include ratings from past clients. I expect that this last feature will soon be commonplace. Clients of lawyers will have easy access to repositories of feedback from other clients. Just as with, say, eBay, or Amazon, on which users are able to express their satisfaction or otherwise with their purchases, similar reputation systems will develop in and around legal services.

This feedback will extend beyond the reputation of law firms to feedback about individual lawyers. In the print world, this happened with various directories: at first, they listed and ranked firms; later, they sought to conduct a similar exercise with individuals. As the final manuscript of this book was being prepared, I heard news of a related service—an electronic directory of individual legal advisers (solicitors, barristers, legal executives, and others). The idea here is that these legal advisers are invited, at no cost, to complete their own profiles online, describing their skills and, crucially, insofar as confidentiality allows, indicating the deals and disputes with which they have been involved. Designed to cover advisers from the smallest to the largest of firms, if such a resource assembled a sufficient number of profiles, then users of legal service would have at their disposal a facility whereby they could pinpoint advisers with precisely the experience they require. Clearly, some difficult editorial issues might arise. But the general thrust here is clear— towards greater transparency for users of legal services. [17]

---

[15] <http://www.firstlaw.co.uk>.
[16] <http://www.takelegaladvice.com>.
[17] <http://www.rapoports.co.uk>, cf the US site at <http://www.avvo.com>.

Looking at the various systems just discussed, it is clearly still early days for the electronic legal marketplace. Once again, we find pockets of innovation and excellence but it is all rather piecemeal. We can find an example of an auction here; and some price comparison tools there; and we see some inchoate reputation systems too.

I have little doubt that these systems will come together, in due course, to provide a vibrant electronic legal marketplace, a collective resource that will help clients to identify the lawyers they need at highly competitive prices. These clients will benefit from online auctions that drive prices down, from the power of bulk purchasing, from greater insight into what legal fees to expect, and from the comfort of knowing that the lawyers they choose have given satisfaction to others. For routine work, which is most legal work, this resource will become the first port of call for people who need legal help. For more sophisticated users, this same technique will be used for managing their panels; although I expect that the reputation modules will operate across panels, so that in-house legal departments can share insight with one another into the price and performance of the external firms they instruct. At the heart of these changes will be a far freer flow of information. Client detriment will be a phenomenon of the past.

But the story will not end there. If my arguments and claims about multisourcing, as laid out in Section 2.5, are sound, then online tools and the electronic legal marketplace will be focused not simply on matching clients with single law firms. Instead, these systems will eventually be able to help to identify the optimum blend of sources that a client might best rely upon. An extra layer of assistance will be needed here. Whether IT-based or human, there will be another job here for legal infomediaries. They will supplement the electronic legal marketplace, as described above, by helping clients to understand the nature and scope of their legal problems, and by decomposing the work needing to be done into separate tasks. In turn, these systems will support the identification of the most suitable source for each. On this model, it will be possible for a system or service to advise, for example, that a given client's circumstances might most cost-effectively be handled by, say, a blend of online guidance, outsourced legal research, and conventional law firm input (suggesting perhaps that there is a firm in Birmingham who have two highly-ranked lawyers who are available this week to do the work at a fixed cost of £250).

The electronic legal marketplace will therefore support the multi-sourcing of (mass customized) legal service, characterized by greater choice, increased confidence, tailored (but not bespoke) solutions, better service, and lower costs.

4.4 E-learning

E-learning, in its various shades and forms, will have a cumulatively disruptive effect on the legal profession. I say this because I can see a wide range of uses of e-learning, none of which of itself may be fundamentally disruptive, but in combination, I think, will have an impact that is indeed dramatic and challenging. Sadly, the term 'e-learning' is rather unhelpful.[18] For many lawyers, it suggests a new IT-based tool for training and for training alone. For many training professionals, it refers to the use of web-casting techniques in the provision of training. Both views are too restricted. The techniques normally associated with e-learning—the use of multi-media techniques to deliver presentations via a video-based 'talking head' and accompanying slides—have far broader application than training. For example, these same techniques can also be harnessed by law firms for communication, knowledge sharing, marketing, risk management, and conference presentations—both internally and with clients.

Since 2001, the Law School at the University of Strathclyde has been using multi-media web-casting to convey some of my thinking—essentially, a pre-recorded tutorial or lecture accessible over the Web or via the university's Intranet. The set-up has been quite simple—as a video clip, my head and shoulders appear on the screen together with PowerPoint presentations corresponding to the words I am speaking. We have undertaken some research into the effectiveness of this. The results have been rather depressing for an author—by and large, the students say they prefer watching and listening to a twenty-minute presentation to reading a chapter from one of my books. Perhaps this is not surprising: we like exchanging information with one another, as human beings, in multi-media. Herein lies the power of e-learning: we are able to move from communicating and transferring knowledge through the two-dimensional medium of text to the frequently (but not always) more expressive systems that convey sound, images, and videos to their users. It is often easier and less forbidding to listen and watch than to read. This is borne out in the world of medicine. Users of NHS Online often say that it is so much better to listen to a kind voice explaining a medical condition than reading about it as text on screen. From the voice you can hear intonation and emotion, so often lost in text. [19]

---

[18] For an early and yet useful introduction to e-learning, see RC Schank, *Designing World-Class e-Learning* (New York, McGraw-Hill, 2002).
[19] <http://www.nhsdirect.nhs.uk>.

We are in the early days of exploiting multi-media. And multi-media web-casting represents but the first generation of e-learning techniques. There is much more to come. Multi-media technology itself will improve and systems will become more interactive, collaborative, and adaptive to the preferred learning styles of particular users. The theory and thinking underpinning these systems will also become more sophisticated, as educational psychologists apply their minds to the field. In turn, we will all (or at least most of us) soon find ourselves in simulated, virtual learning environments; not merely the recipients of insight and knowledge, but participants in online systems that resemble the real worlds about which we are seeking to learn more. Further, many e-learning systems will be available to run on our ever more powerful hand-held machines. Instead of reading newspapers on the train in the morning, ambitious, thrusting young lawyers will be able to immerse themselves in simulated learning environments long before breakfast.

As for its disruptive potential, e-learning will, in the first instance and most obviously, come to transform the way in which lawyers, at all levels, are educated and trained. In his recent and erudite book, *Transforming Legal Education*, Professor Paul Maharg demonstrates beyond any sensible discussion that legal education is ripe for digital overhaul. [20]

Let me start by reflecting on the conventional law lecture. The students assemble and in the British way (in contrast with the Socratic method favoured by many prominent US law schools), the audience is 'spoken at' for just under an hour. It is received and unchallenged wisdom that a micro-century is the best length of time for a lecture.[21] I am sure I am not alone in reflecting that many of the hours I spent as a legal undergraduate, listening to some of the less inspiring lecturers, were not hours wisely spent. These lecturers were not trained as orators. Some mumbled and rambled; others simply dictated their notes; while a few were wonderfully articulate and inspirational. I see no reason why the first two categories should not be replaced by online lectures, presented by wonderful and inspirational speakers from other universities who make web-casts of their lectures available. I accept that it would be a shame, of course, if undergraduates were never to experience the enjoyment of assembling amongst friends in a crowded lecture hall and hearing an outstanding live performance. But we should not preserve the old ways in the self-delusion that this is the norm. We should

---

[20] P Maharg, *Transforming Legal Education* (Aldershot: Ashgate, 2007).
[21] A micro-century is one-millionth of a century, which works out at about 52 and a half minutes. I am grateful to Professor John Barrow for telling me this.

identify the best lecturers and encourage them to speak regularly and urge our students to attend. We should also invite these lecturers to create webcasts for the benefit of others. One of the joys of the Internet is that it enables us to drop into world-class lectures when we would otherwise have no opportunity to attend in person. This is complementary and not substitutional and should be one vital benefit of e-learning—having ready access to insight and ideas that cannot be offered through conventional educational channels. In this spirit, world-class edification is but a couple of clicks away. To get a flavour of this, readers need look no further than one of my all-time favorite websites, TED, which provides 'inspired talks by the world's greatest thinkers and doers'.[22] On the site, there is a wide range of webcasts—video clips from some of the world's leading thought leaders in a wide range of disciplines. We should have a TED of world class law lectures.

What, though, is the role for the not-so-great lecturers? Are they rendered redundant by the professorial rock stars, with their oversubscribed live performances and massively downloaded web-casts? Not at all. I believe that the rest should move steadily from being the law lecturer who acts as 'the sage on the stage' to being a teacher or coach, who plays more of a counselling and tutoring role. Much in the way that the Universities of Oxford and Cambridge have conducted small tutorials since the nineteenth century, the emerging role for the law teacher, I suggest, should be that of the 'guide on the side', building on the lectures that students have (generally) attended virtually. As the dominant, face-to-face approach to teaching, educating, lecturing, instructing, and training in the law is called into question by e-lectures, the job specification of the law teacher should change, shifting from a didactic approach to a more facilitative role. And this shift will also have a direct effect on the ongoing education of qualified lawyers. Already, several commercial providers in the UK and US offer stand-alone web-casts, accredited under various continuing education schemes.[23] Busy lawyers do not need to attend training courses and conferences to keep up to date. They can do this from their desktops.

Knee-jerk sceptics should pause and reflect on the success of Strathclyde University's online Masters degree in Information Technology and Telecommunications Law, which has been running since 1995—over 700 students have graduated, while eighty-two more, from eighteen different countries,

---

[22] <http://www.ted.com>.

[23] See, eg, <http://www.spr-law.com>; <http://www.legalpractitioner.co.uk>; <http://www.way2smart.com>; and <http://www.lrn.com>.

are currently taking the course.[24] Physical get-togethers are optional but well attended, perhaps because the study weekends take place at an idyllic spot on Loch Lomond. Interestingly, graduates of the course are very reluctant to sign off for good. They are keen to remain part of the online learning community. Crucially, most of the students are full-time workers who would not otherwise have been able to embark on sustained further study.

However, here as in so many areas of legal technology, we should not fall into the trap of thinking that what we have today is all that will be on offer tomorrow. Paul Maharg's work takes us beyond the world of electronic lectures and web-casts into the universe of simulation-based training and transactional learning. Based on his practical experience of using these methods, he compellingly argues that online simulations will enable students actually to engage in legal transactions, to experience the running of a legal practice, to be assessed reliably, to engage in collaborative learning and, in turn, to change 'quite fundamentally' what and how they learn.[25] He has used these techniques extensively in the Scottish Diploma in Legal Practice and most dramatically he has designed a fictional town, Ardcalloch, in which students play the part of solicitors in virtual law firms and are provided, amongst many other facilities, with characters, institutions, professional networks with whom they can communicate; virtual offices in which they can work; simulations of actual legal transactions; and a remarkable collection of resources that lend authenticity to the environment, including newspaper clippings, photographs, wills, bank books, and advertisements. A full history of Ardcalloch has been written, adding still further to the sense of reality that the designers have been at pains to create. Very crudely, this simulated learning environment is akin to Second Life for law students (although it is not 3-D).

Once again, the potential for e-learning in this broader sense extends well beyond law schools. Using techniques and technologies not unlike Paul Maharg's, I have little doubt that trainee solicitors will serve as much of their apprenticeship by immersing themselves in simulated learning environments as they will by sitting alongside more senior lawyers. In this way, not only will they be exposed to a richer and more stimulating range of training experiences, but they will avoid the drudgery and repetition of traditional trainees' work. It is often rationalized that this groundwork is a vital educational stepping stone for the aspiring lawyer. I wonder. This may justify the same legal work being conducted a few times, but not twenty or thirty.

---

[24] <http://itlaw.law.strath.ac.uk>.
[25] Maharg (n 20 above) 172.

The training of novice lawyers sets me off on a detour that raises much wider issues of concern in this book. One question over which I agonized, in *The Future of Law*, was this—if some legal services and processes are substantially displaced or substituted by smart systems, does this not mean that junior lawyers will lose the traditional way of learning their trade? It is surely true that many trainees learn about areas of legal practice by doing—by drafting routine documents, for example, perhaps by using some standard template or precedent. If that process and many similar routine tasks were automated and so not undertaken by the trainee, how would the young, aspiring lawyer build up experience? Does this mean the end of what remains, essentially, an apprenticeship system? How will lawyers become experts if they have no live work on which to cut their teeth? My answers in *The Future of Law* were not wholly satisfactory.[26] For example, I suggested that law firms might undertake the work using IT-based systems but might, in parallel, have junior lawyers do the work manually, so that they could learn their trade (much as pupils at school learn arithmetic the traditional way as well as using calculators). But I now have a different response. It should soon be possible, using the wide variety of advanced e-learning systems that Paul Maharg and others are working on, to simulate a wide variety of legal scenarios and in so doing provide junior lawyers with a safe, well-bounded environment within which to experiment and from which to learn. They might learn their trade in a virtual, simulated legal environment, which may even offer richer insights into the range of possible challenges than the piecemeal traineeships of the real world.

Shifting emphasis, I turn now to e-learning as a disruptor, I believe, of the traditional distinction in most law firms between training and know-how. I like to refer to legal training as 'just-in-case' knowledge. Lawyers are taken away on courses, often well distanced from the office, and are lectured about important legal issues or are brought up to date on recent developments. The knowledge imparted in this way is 'just-in-case' in the sense that it provides them with insight, just in case they should need this in the future. All too often, however, when that knowledge is actually needed in practice, often many months later, the knowledge that was meant to have been transferred has long since been forgotten; and the relevant conference folders containing the nuggets of expertise have been archived or binned. Contrast this with know-how that is available via lawyers' machines. I like to think of this as

---

[26] R Susskind, *The Future of Law* (Oxford: Oxford University Press, 1996; paperback edition, 1998), 283–5.

'just-in-time' knowledge, legal insight that is at the fingertips of lawyers, delivered electronically, and easy to assimilate and apply.

Rather than hearing an in-house or external expert in full flow in person at the training session, a presentation might instead be captured as a web-cast, and made available at the touch of a button. Most junior lawyers with whom I meet would prefer to watch a short presentation by a leading specialist, along with some PowerPoint slides, than plough through a five-page practice note, when immersing themselves in an area with which they are unfamiliar. Training and know-how are two sides of the same knowledge coin. The content can be very similar but the mechanisms for delivery differ radically. In practical terms, it makes sense, as often as possible, to capture live training presentations and make them available on a firm's Intranet. Training materials thus become a form of know-how. Similarly, some electronically held presentations can also be used when conventional training sessions are convened. Given this likely convergence, in organizational terms, of training and know-how, I always strongly recommend that training and know-how functions are brought together. Fundamental changes follow—much conventional training becomes unnecessary because the content can be delivered in electronic form; while traditional paper-based methods of know-how begin to look rather antiquated.

On balance, e-learning will be disruptive of conventional legal training but it will be beneficial to lawyers' traditional know-how systems. In relation to the latter, e-learning brings a set of new IT-based techniques that can undoubtedly support the transfer of know-how, insight, and expertise. It thus extends beyond distance learning and online training into the topical and yet substantially unfulfilled discipline of knowledge management, which purports to provide techniques for capturing, sharing, and re-using knowledge within organizations. To date, most lawyers have been disappointed with their knowledge systems, which have often been no more than large, inaccessible electronic storerooms of documents. The next generation, underpinned by e-learning techniques, may bring much greater satisfaction.

Returning to training, I know it can be objected that the purpose of many training sessions is not simply to transfer knowledge but also to allow participants to network, engage, and chat with one another. If this is the case, and this is thought to be important, then we might still bring people together at off-sites, but rather than subject them to speeches whose content will be forgotten, there should be systematic, concerted, and professional efforts to encourage networking; but perhaps not purely based on chance encounters but organized so that all delegates meet one another, by so-called 'speed dating' sessions, for example.

A related disruption here is that much of the multi-media content, the e-learning systems, that may soon underpin both training and know-how, may no longer be generated from within law firms. Of course, in some cases, resident partners may be leading specialists and so their words of wisdom should indeed be bottled and shared internally. However, on many occasions the leading experts in particular areas of law and practice will reside in other firms or in barristers' chambers, or perhaps in universities; so that it might make more sense to license these web-casts from these external specialists than to contrive less expert products from within.

Just as law firms might buy in some e-learning offerings, they may also offer their best web-casts to their clients, sometimes as online training services and, on other occasions, as briefings that clients might find useful prior to face-to-face meetings with their advisers. These possibilities also bring disruption. In relation to online training for clients, firms will understandably be nervous that they will lose the opportunity to have the face-to-face contact with clients that training sessions often afford. Traditionally, a prime motivation behind conventional training for clients, whether or not a charge is levied, is not edification for its own sake but to provide an opportunity to demonstrate expertise to clients and to impress upon them their indispensability. The disruptive element of online client briefings is that they displace sessions that formerly were face-to-face and could generate fees. Again, while the client may find it more convenient to be pre-briefed electronically and to save money in so doing, the law firm will lose the opportunity to charge for its services.

There is a final application of e-learning that I consider to be disruptive; but in a more oblique fashion. The context here is that of legal risk management. This is the discipline, more fully discussed in Section 6.7, that most General Counsel say is central to their working lives. Rather than firefighting, they say they are or ought to be in the business of avoiding rather than resolving legal disputes. With this in mind, one challenge that the legal world faces is to inject legal insight and appreciation earlier in the life cycle of clients' affairs. A little legal insight early on can prevent the need for mammoth legal involvement at a later stage. One way of infusing legal insight in an organization is to increase the general level of legal awareness throughout, so that non-lawyers, without lawyers at their shoulders, are able to recognize potential legal pitfalls, when in the past they might have fallen in. One way of providing this training is to use e-learning techniques—complex legal issues can be presented in user-friendly multi-media format, using memorable graphics, case studies, and anecdotes, thus sensitizing employees to crucial legal issues. While a small number of law firms have recognized the potential here and have developed some applications (in areas such as competition law) the majority of e-learning packages to support legal risk management are being developed and delivered by third parties. The best example here is LRN, a company based on the west coast of the US, and now operating across Europe, that offers a wide range of e-learning-based legal risk management tools. They have recorded more than 21 million completions of their online courses and are enjoying considerable success. The disruption here is that a wonderful opportunity for law firms to diversify is being grabbed by leaner, more entrepreneurial providers. Although clients say that legal risk management is fundamental to them, only a handful of law firms have sought to meet their needs. [27]

4.5 Online legal guidance

One of the most obviously disruptive legal technologies is online legal guidance. Some context is needed here. Traditionally, when most non-lawyers needed legal help, the principal way in which this was secured was through direct consultation with lawyers—face-to-face, consultative service, usually delivered on an hourly billing basis. Lawyers, on this model, were the interface between clients and the law. With the emergence of the Web, however, it has been possible for clients to gain access to increasingly advanced online facilities. A wave of websites is now in play, from which legal guidance and legal advice can be obtained. These services belong in the top-right quadrant of the Law Firm Grid that I introduce in Section 5.2. Whether one calls them online legal services, 'virtual lawyers', legal advice systems, or online legal guidance systems, these are Web-based resources that contain knowledge of lawyers that is no longer accessed exclusively by consultation with human advisers.

These systems might provide expert legal diagnoses, generate legal documents, assist in legal audits, or provide legal updates (and here we find some overlap with other disruptive technologies). They might be chargeable but they might not. The disruption and threat here is that clients (whether citizens or multinationals) can obtain legal guidance online, which looks

---

[27] One exception in this context is the Australian practice, Blake Dawson, whose award-winning online legal compliance training should be a wake-up call to law firms everywhere. See <http://www.compliance.blakedawson.com>.

rather threatening for the traditional legal profession which used to have something of a monopoly over the provision of legal help. In the language of Section 3.5, online legal guidance is often substitutional rather than complementary—that is, it replaces some of what the lawyer does. Online legal guidance systems can remove lawyers from the legal supply chain. And there is perhaps nothing much more disruptive than being disintermediated in this way.

I should emphasize that these systems are far from commonplace. Nonetheless, they have a strong pedigree and are growing in impact and relevance. I regard Linklaters as the first law firm to invest seriously in online legal guidance with the launch of its Blue Flag service in 1996.[28] Initially, its systems were designed to deliver detailed information about regulatory compliance to legal and compliance specialists in banks and major corporates. A rich, up-to-date resource, applicable in many jurisdictions, this was the first sustained attempt to provide legal help across the Internet. For a licence fee, clients could assess their compliance without directly consulting lawyers.

Linklaters' pioneering led to something of an arms race amongst leading UK law firms in online legal guidance. In 1998, Clifford Chance launched the first version of its NextLaw service, another compliance system, this one focusing on international data protection compliance.[29] A new version of NextLaw was made available in 2000, extending beyond data protection to advise on online contracts, electronic signatures, encryption, and bank secrecy. Indeed it was held out as an online guide to managing legal and regulatory risk in multi-jurisdictional e-business projects.

Since then, Linklaters and Clifford Chance have extended their online services beyond compliance to e-learning, document automation, and updating services. At the same time, another Magic Circle firm, Allen & Overy, has also been active, if less publicity oriented. Their main investment has been in online systems to support clients working in the world of derivatives—Netalytics and CSAnalytics help to assess risks relating to activities under standard International Swaps and Derivatives Association documentation; while CDS Deliverability offers guidance on the likely deliverability of frequently traded obligations into credit default swaps.[30]

---

[28] <http://www.blueflag.com>.
[29] <http://www.cliffordchance.com/nextlaw>.
[30] <http://www.allenovery.com/onlineservices>.

Investment by UK law firms in online legal guidance has not been confined to the largest international firms based in London. National law firm Mills & Reeve, for example, has created an online legal service relating to healthcare.[31] This 'healthcare resource centre' is targeted at lawyers and managers working in the NHS. Free to the firm's clients, the website provides accessible legal briefings on a wide range of topics, including mental health, judicial review, governance, employment, and patients (including consent). Faced with problems in these areas, clients can read up-to-date summaries of the relevant legal issues and will thus be able to come to their lawyers much better informed. Traditional solicitors may argue that this is giving away the firm's family silver. But the reality is that the Internet has created a new medium for delivering background guidance, so that legal information for which firms were able to charge handsomely in the past has now become an online commodity of sorts. Another reality is that clients who benefit from such services are surely more likely to instruct the law firms that provide them. Yesterday's chargeable information services, formerly packaged as 'advice', are today's online marketing materials.

Many lawyers say to me that these systems can only really be developed by large law firms, that they are beyond the pockets of smaller legal businesses. Defying this conventional wisdom is Tessa Shepperson, a solicitor and sole practitioner who specializes in landlord and tenant law and for many years has maintained an online information service for residential landlords and tenants. She has also developed a subscription service, Landlord-Law Online, that provides a collection of practical information, articles, links, answers to frequently asked questions and some standard documents. For landlords and tenants, this is a useful online resource that is proving popular amongst landlord investors who have bought to let—the service offers them an easy way of determining their legal obligations and keeping abreast of relevant legal developments.[32]

In a similar vein, an American pioneer of online legal self-help, Richard Granat, has single-handedly introduced a suite of Internet-supported services. One of his services is a family law offering that blends conventional and online legal service.[33] In advising clients on divorce matters, the service relies heavily on IT but it does not eliminate lawyers entirely. Granat aims to offer his service at the same price as purely online systems but with the added

---

[31] <http://www.mills-reeve.com>.
[32] <http://www.landlordlaw.co.uk>.
[33] <http://www.mdfamilylawyer.com>.

advantages (in interpersonal and liability terms) of having a qualified lawyer involved. The technology he uses, for streamlining the advisory process and for collaboration with his clients, enables him to keep his costs low. His broader objective is to show that legal technology can be deployed easily and cheaply by small practices. This is a form of complementary rather than substitutional online legal service.

What impact on the world of law has been made by online legal services? Many of the hundred or so columns that I have written for the law pages of *The Times* have been devoted to these services, as devised by a wide range of practices. Delia Venables and Ron Friedmann, in their invaluable websites that provide links to all sorts of legal technology resources in the UK and US, respectively, each list a daunting number of online legal services.[34] So, there are enough of them around. However, even in the major firms that have invested heavily, although we have seen some impressive developments, it would be false to claim that their influence has yet been profound. The truth is that it is early days for online legal services. I stand by my initial thinking in *The Future of Law* that it would take twenty years (from 1996) until a transition to a new paradigm of legal service would be well under way. I remain entirely convinced that, in due course, online legal services will be the dominant source of legal guidance in society. In relation to citizen-clients, this is probably the case already—I suspect that lay people look to the Web for legal help much more than they consult lawyers. The high usage of the UK government's 2,500 plus websites seems to support this view.[35] In time, this will also be true of commercial clients.

In any event, when I discuss online legal guidance, in its various manifestations, with law firms, I often find myself on the receiving end of a barrage of strident objections: we should not give away our crown jewels; we are not publishers; we only work at the high end; no online system could be as good as a good human lawyer; this applies to areas of work that other firms do but not to ours; clients want a professional and not some IT-based service; we do not have the time to develop such systems; knowledge should only be shared internally; online service is only for the huge firms; this is just a fancy tool for marketing; this is contrary to the spirit of professional service; my clients don't want this; it is not yet time for such systems. And so on. In *Transforming*

---

[34] <http://www.venables.co.uk> and <http://prismlegal.com>.

[35] See House of Commons Committee of Public Accounts, *Government on the Internet: Progress in delivering information and services online*, Sixteenth Report of Session 2007–08 (29 April 2008, HC 143) and National Audit Office, *Government on the internet: Progress in delivering information and services online* (13 July 2007, HC 529 Session 2006–2007).

the Law, I have, I believe, offered convincing responses to each of these objections.[36] For now, it suffices to note that the spread of these reactions and the strength of feeling confirm that online legal guidance is indeed disruptive. I am reminded in this connection of a wonderful story about Albert Einstein. When told of the proposed publication of a book, *One Hundred Authors Against Einstein*, he replied, 'Why 100? If I were wrong, one would have been enough.'[37]

Turning away from the doubters to firms that are interested in actually embracing this technology, to those who see this as potentially differentiating rather than disruptive, I have some advice. I have identified three keys to success when it comes to making money from online legal guidance. First, for an online legal service to generate serious revenue, its use must actually add substantive value to clients. Unless clients think extremely highly of the systems and would be near panic stricken at the prospect of their withdrawal, then there is little chance they will actually pay for them. Second, the systems must not be easily replicable or competitors can easily mimic their development and, as explained in Section 2.1, the prices of rival online legal services will tend rapidly towards zero (they will become commoditized in the sense that I explain). Third, for law firms to charge for online legal services, it must not be perceived that these systems are internal systems that are simply being recycled for clients' use. In that event, clients may feel cheated and will argue that such services are a natural (but non-chargeable) extension of the services traditionally being provided. There is a contrast here with non-clients, to whom such recycled applications can indeed plausibly be sold.

4.6 Legal open-sourcing

When discussing online legal service in the previous section, I claim that nothing can perhaps be much more disruptive for a lawyer than being disintermediated. This claim needs to be qualified. In relation to online legal service, users often pay to access and use these systems, so that while lawyers may no longer be directly involved in the dispensing of guidance, they are

---

[36] Susskind (n 14 above) Chs 1, 4, and 6.
[37] <http://www.time.com>.

effectively licensing their expertise and are still, as I like to say, making money while they sleep. I accept that, so far, the revenue generated by such systems has nowhere near matched the amounts garnered through conventional service. But some revenue is better than none at all. What is far more threatening and disruptive is when lawyers are disintermediated *and* what is put in their place is not theirs and is not yielding them any fees. This is what I predict will happen in many areas of law with the advent of 'legal open-sourcing' and of 'closed legal communities'. These topics, respectively, are the subject of this and the following sections.

Let me recap on the open source movement, whose terminology and spirit I broadly rely upon when I speak of 'legal open-sourcing' (also see Section 3.3). The origins of this movement lie in the world of software development. For lawyers who are immediately inclined to skip this section, because programming is nothing like legal practice, I invite you to stay with me. There is, in fact, a fair tradition, in the world of artificial intelligence (AI) and law, of holding that legal drafting and computer programming have much in common, so that lawyers may have something to learn from the experience of software engineers. [38] Even if this is not accepted, the roots of the open source movement in software do not prejudice what I have to say about the potential for legal open-sourcing. Open source software is simply the most powerful example of the open source phenomenon, a phenomenon that I expect will directly affect the law and lawyers. In *The Wealth of Networks*, Yochai Benkler provides us with a useful point of departure: 'Free software, or open source, is an approach to software development that is based on shared effort on a nonproprietary model. It depends on many individuals contributing to a common project.'[39]

So, as I explain in Section 3.3, this is software that is different from conventional code, in that it is generally made available at no cost to users. More, it is not written and organized formally by one company or consortium but is informally and collaboratively developed by volunteers who toil together on development projects without compensation and without asserting ownership. Many of the systems that are at the heart of the Internet (for example Linux, the most commonly used operating system) are available on an open source basis. This is not a peripheral movement. Its output is pervasive. More than this, as Steven Weber puts it, 'the open source software process is

[38] This is a running theme of an important, early collection—B Niblett (ed), *Computer Science and Law* (Cambridge: Cambridge University Press, 1980).

[39] Y Benkler, *The Wealth of Networks* (New Haven, Conn: Yale University Press, 2006) 63.

a real-world, researchable, example of a community and knowledge production process that has been fundamentally changed, or created in significant
ways, by Internet technology'.[40] Crucially, this process, this 'mass collaboration',[41] has been put into service in other domains, most notably in the
creation of the online encyclopaedia, Wikipedia, as I discuss in Section 3.3.
This remarkable online encyclopaedia has been evolved by a very large group
of volunteers whose joint contribution has led to a formidable research
resource.

And so I ask—why should an analogous knowledge production process, in
due course, not be applied to the creation and maintenance of large bodies
of legal materials? What I have in mind here is sustained online mass collaboration in the field of law. In the spirit of wikis, those websites that any
user can amend and add to, I am anticipating an upsurge in user-generated
legal content. If the world's most formidable encyclopaedia can be compiled
on an open source basis, and so too with complex and pervasive computer
systems, then I see no obvious reason why legal content might not be gathered in a similar way. I am expecting a build-up of public, or community-
based, bodies of legal materials.

Of course, huge amounts of legal information and guidance are already
available online. I concede that much of this guidance falls short of direct
implementable legal advice; and, it is also fair to say that much of this content does not compete directly, in any event, with the work of many practising lawyers. These sites are not disruptive for lawyers: while we may be able
to point, for example, to 2,500 government websites in the UK, many of
which provide extremely useful and practical guidance for citizens, little of
this impinges on law firms up and down the country. Indeed, this widespread
provision of information by public sector bodies is an example of 'the latent
legal market' that I mention in Section 1.4. These websites have not displaced
lawyers; rather, they have offered legal insight and help to many people who
otherwise would not generally have sought formal legal help and would have
proceeded in life without guidance. They are clearly of greater relevance and
assistance to the citizen-client as opposed to in-house lawyers.

What about the materials law firms already make available on their websites? Are these instances of the legal open-sourcing that I am anticipating?
I think not. More often than not, when lawyers themselves make information

---

[40] S Weber, *The Success of Open Source* (Cambridge, Mass: Harvard University Press, 2004) 2.
[41] On mass collaboration, see Benkler (n 39 above); D Tapscott and AD Williams, *Wikinomics* (New York: Portfolio, 2006).

and guidance available on their websites, they do so as a taster for potential clients rather than as a collaboratively generated self-help resource. It is a marketing ploy rather than a disruptive legal service.

The legal open-sourcing I am predicting is different from today's government and law firm websites which broadcast legal materials but offer no opportunity for participation on the part of users. Looking forward, and bearing in mind the developments in online community and Web 2.0 that I outline in Chapter 3, we should not be surprised when, in the manner of Wikipedia, legal content and experience is user-generated and gathered on a mass collaboration basis; and online communities of legal interest will emerge, around which formidable legal insight will evolve. I am suggesting that wiki-like legal facilities will spring up and will be available to all Internet users. The key to their success will not simply be the capture of ever-growing mountains of legal documents, but the evolution of large repositories of personal experiences of contributors. These systems will not therefore be built by lawyers but by clients and consumers of legal services; and they might originate in and be built around a core body of legal materials—laws, regulations, commentaries, guidelines, notes, and analysis.

Some clients may have paid lawyers in the traditional way and may want to share the advice and insight they have received with others; doing so, no doubt, in the expectation that other contributors may provide content of help to them in the future.[42] Subject to some interesting intellectual property issues, they might add this legal work product to the core body of materials. User-friendly ways of categorizing and classifying user experiences will evolve, and a large collective wisdom will flourish. On the view that it is unlikely that any individual faces a legal problem that none has confronted before, a natural first port of call for anyone with a legal difficulty will, in due course, be such online, wiki-like, collaborative legal environments. Just as many computer users, when faced with problems today, will in the first instance search the Web for insights that other users may have provided, rather than calling in an IT repair person; then so too, in the future, will many citizens and non-lawyers in relation to their legal problems. Customer support advice is readily and easily accessible at the online resources of major

---

[42] A community called 'docstoc' has already been set up. This is a website where 'you can find and share professional documents'—<http://www.docstoc.com>. A more ambitious initiative might formalize freely available documents—perhaps an international body could certify certain words, phrases, and documents, so that users could more safely assemble their documents.

companies[43] and at innumerable informal forums as well. The knowledge is often most usefully organized around problems and questions that users will regularly confront. FAQs (frequently asked questions) are one commonly used technique. In this way, exceptionally complex technical issues are often rendered soluble. Similarly, in medicine, symptom driven services will offer non-experts straightforward guidance, based on complex medical science that is hidden from the user.

Many lawyers will wince when they think of legal guidance being dispensed as though from an online PC help-desk. But why not? Lawyers and policy-makers alike are now recognizing the potential of call centres as a channel for helping citizens with routine legal challenges and, at the same time, for demystifying the law. Legal wikis are a further, natural development of this.

Another layer of content that might be added into the mix will be derived from publicly available materials that have been submitted to the courts in electronic form. For some time, this has been discussed in the US—the repurposing of the full text of briefs, pleadings, affidavits, correspondence, judgments, and expert witness testimony from trial courts around the country. These materials are publicly available and can be captured directly from state and federal courts. Nestled amongst them are often first-rate tracts of work product from respected law firms. How such second-hand legal documents will be re-fashioned and made useful at no or low cost is, as yet, unclear; commercial providers say it is already invaluable to have sight of the work product of the best and brightest.[44]

All of this could be manifestly disruptive for law firms in that, unlike conventional legal websites, what may soon be made available may compete directly with some of the services ordinarily offered by conventional lawyers. Shockingly for many lawyers, legal open-sourcing provides some form of legal support on an entirely non-chargeable basis. While some of this support might belong in my latent legal market, I have little doubt that, in due course, some will displace legal work that was formerly a source of revenue.

There may, however, still be some roles for conventional lawyers in this world of legal open-sourcing. In the same way that genuine computer specialists, for whatever reason, often contribute today, at no cost, to question-and-answer sessions and make supporting links and materials available to users,

---

[43] eg, Microsoft's Knowledge Base at <http://support.microsoft.com/gp/topkbs> and Dell's Ideastorm at <http://www.dellideastorm.com>.

[44] See the commercial websites at <http://www.briefserve.com> and <http://www.e-law.com>.

then similarly in law, we can expect that some lawyers themselves will participate and contribute to some extent to these new environments, perhaps as a pro bono offering. Or, again, this may be a way of providing early guidance at no cost, in anticipation of receiving instructions if and when work becomes more complex: legal open-sourcing will not always provide the answers that users will want; and the commoditized materials available may well require some refining and tailoring on a bespoke basis. It is also possible that some legal businesses may indeed host such resources and actively help to evolve these communities (in the way that some major computer companies, such as IBM, have publicly embraced open source software).[45] And if legal businesses do not choose to offer such support, we can expect the third sector to engage instead (see Section 7.5).

The social and economic ramifications of legal open-sourcing will be profound. When legal materials come to be widely provided on an open source basis, we will begin to see the accumulated legal knowledge not simply as an online commodity but as what economists refer to as 'a public good'. This means that consumption of the legal resource by one person does not reduce the amount of the resource that is available for consumption by others; and, further, that no-one can be excluded from using that resource. The notion that legal knowledge might be a public good is disruptive in the extreme. It may well be that conventional legal services, involving one-to-one advice from an expert to a client, often on a face-to-face basis, is a luxury that the overwhelming majority of individuals and organizations will no longer be able or wish to afford.

Experience suggests, however, that some clients, especially in-house lawyers rather than citizen-clients, will be uncomfortable with sharing their thoughts and concerns about the law in a very public way. These people are more likely to gravitate towards closed legal communities.

4.7 Closed legal communities

Where mass collaboration harnesses the power of numbers and what has been called 'the wisdom of crowds'[46] in evolving a shared product (for example

---

[45] <http://www.ibm.com/developerworks/opensource>.
[46] J Surowiecki, *The Wisdom of Crowds* (London: Abacus, 2004).

an operating system, an online encyclopaedia, or an open-sourced body of legal guidance), closed communities build up knowledge on the basis of the more focused process of 'peer production'—a restricted group of like-minded individuals or organizations with shared interests come together online, as a club of sorts, to collaborate and collectively build a body of knowledge and experience.[47] In law, although closed community peer production will use techniques (especially Web 2.0 technologies—see Section 3.3) that are common to legal open-sourcing, there is a difference between the two. With closed communities, their content is not widely available to all Internet users; but it is analogously disruptive to legal open-sourcing, because it gives rise to legal materials that can, to some extent, obviate the need for lawyers working in their traditional way.

I ask lawyers to suspend their incredulity for a short while and take a detour into the world of medicine. I recently discovered an online community for doctors that is a fine pointer towards the possibility of closed community peer production in law. The facility is called Sermo and it is a specialized, online community of around 50,000 US medical practitioners.[48] Members of this community, who must be authenticated physicians, can pose questions to other doctors and answer queries themselves. In some ways, the system is a half-way house between a social networking systems such as Facebook and a collaboration environment, such as Wikipedia. Sermo is also described as a 'community based knowledge ecosystem'.[49] A remarkable body of medical expertise and experience is rapidly building there. As is said on their website: 'physicians aggregate observations from their daily practice and then—rapidly and in large numbers—challenge or corroborate each other's opinions, accelerating the emergence of trends and new insights on medications, devices and treatments'. To doctors, the message is clear: 'You can then apply the collective knowledge to achieve better outcomes for your patients.'

I predict that analogous communities will emerge in the legal world and my expectation is that the main users and beneficiaries will be in-house lawyers rather than law firms. It is not obvious, bearing in mind the current business models of law firms and the intense competition between them, that they would be incentivized to collaborate with one another, in a Sermo fashion,

---

[47] See Benkler, (n 39 above).

[48] <http://www.sermo.com>.

[49] See DA Bray *et al*, 'Sermo: A Community-Based, Knowledge Ecosystem', Oxford Internet Institute, Distributed Problem-Solving Networks Conference, (February 2008), available at <http://ssrn.com/abstract=1016483>.

around the world. In contrast, as I argue in Section 5.6, it is very much in the commercial interests of in-house lawyers, who are under considerable pressure to reduce their costs, to share knowledge and experience. So long as this does not pose competitive difficulties, and despite the potential intellectual property and antitrust law implications of doing so, I anticipate that in-house lawyers will persevere and will come to collaborate. This will be very largely enabled and powered by the Internet.

In-house legal departments will coalesce electronically into groups that use their collective purchasing power to secure better legal services at lower cost. These clients will even come to share the advice they receive with fellow members of their communities. Large collections of text-based and multi-media materials will aggregate. They will not be held in arid libraries but will be interleaved with online commentary and discussion, evolved in the wiki and open source spirit. There will be shared bodies of standard form documentation, and opinions from specialists, guidance received from law firms and evaluations of this advice. Again, as with legal open-sourcing, the commoditized materials available may well need some bespoke refining and tailoring.

I say that clients may come to share legal advice. How might this happen? The underlying thinking is that General Counsel consider some of the legal work that they and their opposite numbers undertake to be non-competitive, so that they may well be prepared to pool resources and use their collective buying power. This is one aspect of what I call the 'collaboration strategy' in Section 5.7. By way of example, when a law firm undertakes, say, a multi-jurisdictional review of some particular legal issue, the client of the future might say to the firm that, 'the work product will become our property; and we want to be able to make it available to our own community of General Counsel colleagues'. And so the time-honoured notion, that lawyers perform such reviews, one at a time for each client, will disappear; in the new world of collaboration, such a review, when finished, will probably be plugged into some wiki, relating perhaps to legal risk management in in-house legal departments. It will evolve and be built upon in the open source spirit and, in this way, will be part of a growing corpus of legal documentation, legal briefs and so forth, that will be available freely to given communities—purchased perhaps by one client and then donated to the client community generally. The disruption here is evident. Historically, when a law firm has conducted a valuable and lucrative piece of work for a client, it will often explore the possibility of providing a similar service to other clients. This is a form of knowledge management within a law firm. Rather than treating the work product as disposable, the idea has been that it has been recycled and sold many times to clients other than the original recipient. This has proved to be exceptionally profitable. However, in terms of in-house lawyers, and the market to which they belong, this has been inefficient. I anticipate that, in the future, the recycling of knowledge will not only happen within law firms; it will occur within communities of clients. This is good (although not free of risk) for clients but prejudicial to the conventional business model of law firms.

A related opportunity for closed legal communities of clients is in relation to the widespread challenge of compliance. Across the world, most commercial organizations are troubled by the challenge of ensuring that their organizations and their people comply with ever burgeoning bodies of diverse regulations that are in force in a wide range of jurisdictions. This tends not to be a competitive issue within industries or sectors. It is generally a common burden rather than a place where battles between rivals are fought. In ensuring compliance, there is massive duplication of effort across innumerable, otherwise competing businesses. Shared compliance services, built on the back of online communities, could bring very substantial savings to in-house compliance departments, not least in the banking sector.

In summary, then, the first port of call for in-house lawyers who need some kind of external help may soon be the closed communities to which they belong. They will be in touch with kindred spirits from other organizations who share similar legal challenges, they will have a wealth of common materials and experiences upon which to draw, and they may only refer matters to law firms to fill in any gaps. This gap-filling will be a bespoke contribution from law firms, requiring deep expertise, and will not be the kind of task that can be bundled off to a junior lawyer.

The most promising current attempt to introduce a serious and scalable closed legal community is Legal OnRamp, a start-up based in California and supported by a small group of in-house lawyers and external firms.[50] Like Sermo, this service has a strong flavour of Web 2.0, echoing some of the features of Facebook and Wikipedia. There is a key difference when Legal OnRamp is compared with Sermo, though, and that is the involvement of both sides of the market. With Sermo, there are no patients, so that only one half of the service equation is represented. With Legal OnRamp, the providers and recipients are there (although there are areas from which law firms are excluded). The involvement of law firms is interesting—even though this kind of community is potentially disruptive, their challenge will be to show willing and identify the opportunities for adding value themselves.

---

[50] <http://www.legalonramp.com>.

More than this, I expect that clients will frequently encourage law firms to become involved, not simply as participants in client communities but as active members of law firm communities. This was what happened in London in 2003. In that year, nine major global investment banks in London set up a legal technology group dedicated to the development of IT standards and systems to support their in-house legal departments.[51] These banks then called upon five leading City law firms to work with them.[52] The first initiative of this Banking Legal Technology (BLT) Group, as it came to be known, was to develop an information and knowledge portal—a single point of access for in-house lawyers, through which they intended to enjoy easy and direct access to the combined knowledge and information resources of the participating firms. This made perfect sense. Each of the law firms involved already provided a variety of information and knowledge services to clients. Some of these were chargeable while others were made available at no charge, including newsflashes and updates, practice notes, and even precedent documents. From the clients' perspective, this was to be a major step forward: simply to have all current materials available in one online location.

When it was first mooted that firms might collaborate in developing and stocking an information system for clients, there was much cynicism. The very idea! But the banks persisted, emboldened, no doubt, by their collective annual legal spend (many hundreds of millions). More, their cause—a manageable, single online service—was entirely reasonable. Nonetheless, the order was a tall one. Indeed, when Dr Samuel Johnson said that (second) marriage is the triumph of hope over experience, he could equally have been speaking of the BLT Group. Against considerable odds, in but two years, this redoubtable team of lawyers and information professionals, from law firms and clients, developed a system. Given the level of cooperation required, this initiative bore fruit, in legal technology terms, at warp speed. This, then, was the Internet at its most potent: challenging conventional assumptions, forging new working relationships, aggregating diverse information resources, driving quality improvements, and shifting power from provider to consumer.

I am told there are now eighteen banks in the group. I am not concerned here with the advantages and shortcoming of the BLT portal itself. I offer a

---

[51] The original group of banks was made up of ABN Amro, Barclays Capital, CSFB, Deutsche Bank, Goldman Sachs, HSBC, JP Morgan, Morgan Stanley, and UBS.

[52] The five firms were Allen & Overy, Clifford Chance, Freshfields, Linklaters, and Simmons & Simmons.

critique in Section 5.6, in my discussion of knowledge sharing between law firms and clients. For now, my focus is on BLT as an example of a closed legal community. The significance of BLT lies not in the knowledge portal itself; rather, it is in the community of clients that has been established and the collaboration amongst law firms that it has engendered. BLT shows beyond reasonable doubt that clients can indeed come together in a community spirit and urge law firms to work closely together. That said, the BLT initiative is the first and not the last word in closed legal communities.

A further example of law firms being encouraged to join forces in what may seem to be a counter-intuitive and counter-cultural way, will come about in the context of the groups of law firms that large clients pre-select as their preferred pool of advisers. Today, most major banks and corporates, in the UK at least, select a relatively small number of law firms (normally half-a-dozen or so) as their favoured suppliers and, taken together, these few are referred to as a 'panel' (also see Section 4.3). I expect that individual clients will establish virtual legal functions, made up of the law firms on their panels and their own in-house legal departments; and will also, on occasion, wish to cherry-pick from their panels a 'dream team', constituted of the best from each panel firm. Lawyers from different firms who sit on the same panel will come to work as closely alongside one another, as part of the virtual legal communities serving client organizations, as they do today with their own colleagues. Today, the competition amongst these panel members is often intense. While clients can sometimes be blamed for themselves stirring up this rivalry and playing firms off against one another, more sophisticated users of law firms have recently been calling for panel members to act in a more collegiate manner; indeed, to collaborate and cooperate as though they were one virtual firm. A common website, using methods akin to social networking and wikis, is one tool that might bind these firms rather effect-ively. If clients encourage the use of such a resource, then law firms would be ill advised not to engage. Although there may be a certain amount of inconvenience involved if individual firms have to participate in many such online panel communities, the hassle will surely be outweighed by the goodwill and steady flow of work that will no doubt result.

In terms of competitive strategy for law firms, the creation of online com-munities at once presents grave threats of disruption and great opportunities for differentiation. I believe that there may well soon be a 'land grab' for those communities that are established, hosted, or sponsored by law firms. Bear in mind that these will be rich, interactive online resources devoted to particu-lar legal topics, processes, and sectors. If one firm creates such a facility, and it becomes heavily used by clients, then this could make it unfeasible or unattractive for another competitor to play copycat and inconvenient or undesirable for clients to switch allegiance. Because these systems encourage active client participation and contribution, they can thereby engender significant loyalty amongst their users. In contrast with conventional law firm websites which broadcast materials at their users, with community sites, the users themselves generate content and interact with others. In so doing, this can create a sense of belonging to—even ownership of—the community; and so a reluctance to move from one community to another. It seems, therefore, that there may be clear first mover advantages in this corner of the world of legal technology. The carrot here is the possibility of being a firm that leads a land grab, dominates the market, and excludes competitors.

Lawyers who remain cynical about the possibility or suitability of online communities for the legal profession should reflect on the success of Felix, the conferencing and bulletin board system that was enjoyed by many English judges for over a decade. I believe this to have been one of the UK's most active, early online communities. Crucially, this has never been a replacement for, or a challenge to, conventional face-to-face meetings amongst judges. Instead, Felix offered a type of community interaction where otherwise there may not have been any interaction at all—judges in England are spread around hundreds of court buildings and many, on a daily basis, do not belong to a physical community of fellow judges who can meet regularly. Communicating with Felix may not have been as good as face-to-face socializing and networking amongst judges, but it has been considerably better than nothing at all. It is now being replaced by a Judicial Portal, whose reach and impact in the medium term, I expect, will be even greater. And I have little doubt that judges will in due course be blogging amongst themselves and building up common bodies of knowledge using wiki-like technologies.

4.8 Workflow and project management

For legal businesses whose underpinning business model is charging by the hour (or levying fixed fees which are based on an hourly billing model), a further category of disruptive legal technology is the pairing of workflow and project management. Very crudely, workflow and project management systems inject efficiency and consistency into complex processes and activities.

They are disruptive in that they often break down conventional boundaries within law firms, they discourage the divisive and often redundant management in silos, and introduce administrative efficiencies and savings that may delight clients but fly in the face of time-based charging.

As the name suggests, a workflow system supports the progress of some task or process, from start to finish (from cradle to grave, as we say in the UK; or from soup to nuts, as is said in the US). A workflow system is a little like an automated checklist or procedure manual. In the insurance industry, claims processing is often conducted using workflow systems. Distribution of documents, analysis, authorization, and the generation of reports—these are all standardized and modelled in a system, so that a consistent and efficient process is imposed. Messages and alerts are automatically routed to appropriate people and warnings are generated when deadlines approach. Workflow technology is particularly well suited to high-volume, repetitive work. To a limited extent, this technology has already been embraced in law, in areas such as debt collection, residential conveyancing, and personal injury work. Where the throughput of similar pieces of work is considerable and, generally, when the value of each is relatively low, some firms have sensibly recognized that much of the process of progressing each case or deal can be automated. And, where human intervention or judgment is required, this itself can be accommodated, by providing for facilities that accept human input at appropriate times.

In more complex work, however, where the volumes are low and perhaps the value of each legal matter is higher, it is less obvious that workflow systems are fit for this purpose. In this event, the complementary discipline and software of project management can be deployed. In the worlds of construction and engineering, for example, the use of project management techniques is widespread. The same is true in complex IT development projects. A large project, ahead of its launch, is typically analyzed and divided into a series of manageable phases. Each phase may then be subdivided into a constituent set of tasks and activities, and the resources required for each, as well as the time that each will consume, are identified in advance. Often a large project, subdivided in this way, is graphically represented in what is known as a Gant chart, from which, at a glance, the overall shape of a project can be seen and progress can be gauged by reference to timelines and milestones which are clearly depicted. A central job of project managers, crudely, is to ensure that work progresses according to the pre-articulated plan. Advanced software can support the management of complex projects by, say, automating the allocation of resources, and generating new charts when adjustments to plans are necessary or hypothesized.

Workflow and project management systems can also operate in conjunction with one another. In complex transactions, invariably there will be, as I argue in Section 2.1, significant portions of work that can be standardized or computerized. And so, there may be workflow systems nested within projects that themselves are subject to some overarching control through project management techniques.

There is immense potential for the deployment of project management techniques in the law. Whether in support of major disputes or large transactions, project management can help to impose order on chaos. In large firms, working on major projects, hundreds of lawyers can be involved. Each will have specific responsibilities and all will be generating formidable quantities of documents (e-mails, draft agreements, and so forth). While bright, hardworking individuals can make a fair stab at orchestrating this work using pen and paper, it is to miss a trick, and to waste clients' money, not to take advantage of well developed tools and techniques that can be applied precisely to this kind of task.

Many solicitors who work in litigation already claim that they are project managers. While it is encouraging that they characterize their work in this way, because it is absolutely clear that the organization of the progress of a complex dispute is an ideal application for project management, very few firms that I have seen are in fact sophisticated in their project management. They may generate a Gant chart or two and institute rigorous document management protocols, but these gestures invariably fall short of the more thoroughgoing deployment of case flow management (or case progression) systems that I have in mind.

Beyond litigation, the Practical Law Company, an innovative legal publisher based in London, has developed what is largely a workflow system to support the due diligence process. This is an interesting case study. By way of background—I often find that corporate lawyers (those who advise on deals such as mergers and acquisitions), tend to claim that their work is highly bespoke, because each deal is unique and requires fresh strategic insight and creative activity on every occasion. I always betray some scepticism at this line of talk because, as is the theme of this book, I doubt that all tasks involved in advising in a deal, no matter how large or complex, require bespoke attention. My claim is that some or many tasks can and ought to be standardized or computerized. One such task, and it is a very considerable one, is the process of due diligence; this term refers to the detailed investigations conducted by lawyers to assure their clients, broadly, of the legal robustness of a target company. This is often a long and laborious process, delegated to junior lawyers. When I challenge corporate lawyers and suggest that due diligence is surely not a high-end legal activity that requires the bespoke attention of the finest legal minds, most concede that this is so and many, over the years, indeed go further and say that this is a potential application area for IT. It is fascinating, and perhaps indicative of the future, that it was an innovative legal publisher and not a law firm that was actually the first to develop a polished solution. The resultant system offers progress reporting, structured checklists, integrated know-how, action point generation, report production, interoperability with virtual deal-rooms, and runs on the Web. [53]

Another illustration of workflow comes from the London-based legal software company, best known for its document assembly software—Business Integrity. One version of their DealBuilder system organizes and controls the drafting and generation of particular types of contracts.[54] This takes document assembly (see Section 5.1), to a new level. The system provides a work space in which users can work on agreements throughout their life cycles, from initiation, to execution, and beyond. The system manages the flow and allows for partial completion, submission for approval, exception handling, and so forth. Thus, a salesman out in the field can often generate an agreement for a customer, with no direct contact with lawyers and yet heavily constrained by the rules embodied in the system. The answers entered by such a salesman may be such that the contract can be generated immediately. Alternatively, it may be that the answers suggest problem areas or possible legal risks, so that a document can be automatically routed to a lawyer for review. If the lawyer is comfortable, or has changes to recommend, this feedback is injected back into the standard life cycle.

As a further illustration of the use of workflow and project management systems, consider a UK business called LMS. Founded more than fifteen years ago, this company provides services to the lending and property industries. The company manages around 300,000 transactions each year. On behalf of its clients, it purchases remortgage cases and sale and purchase conveyancing-related cases for a panel of solicitors. Using IT, it has streamlined and computerized much of the conveyancing process. Ten years ago, around eight thousand firms undertook remortgage work. Today this figure has been reduced to around thirty, each earning about £50 for a remortgage case; their profit comes from very large volumes (tens of thousands of cases per year) and extremely low margins. Workflow technology, in particular, has

---

[53] <http://www.practicallaw.com>.
[54] <http://www.business-integrity.com>.

transformed this area of legal practice.[55] Also in the world of conveyancing, an innovative firm, Barnetts Solicitors, has shown what workflow technology can achieve. Striking a chord with most home owners, who have endured the trauma of moving house, the firm launched an award-winning service known as Click Conveyancing.[56] The firm has sought to streamline and computerize the conveyancing process as much as possible, using advanced workflow systems to make transactions quicker and less costly. Communicating electronically with clients is built in, so that text messages are sent at key stages during transactions and clients are able to track progress, at any hour, on the firm's website.

Aside from the use for workflow and project management systems in support of individual deals and disputes, these systems have a further, and potentially far more profound use—in support of the process of multi-sourcing, as introduced in Chapter 2 of this book. I suggest there that, on my assembly line model, complex legal work can be decomposed into tasks that might most efficiently be undertaken in parallel by a collection of quite different organizations spread across the globe. If legal work is multi-sourced in this way, and pulled together in the just-in-time fashion that I advocate, then some advanced tools will be needed to ensure that this happens reliably and seamlessly. I believe that project management techniques will be central to this process, in supporting the allocation, distribution, status checking, and quality control of the work; while workflow systems, operating across the Internet, will provide the basic supply chain through which providers can communicate and deliver their services.

In any event, and to reiterate, whether for use within law firms or in a more ambitious multi-sourcing environment, the reason that workflow and project management systems are disruptive for most law firms is precisely because they support, encourage, and enable much greater efficiency. And efficiency, as I am at pains to point out, is the enemy of the law firm that charges on an hourly billing basis. If one firm can radically streamline and automate the delivery of some legal service through the judicious use of workflow and project management systems, the consequence should be that the market price of the service in question will reduce, perhaps greatly so. The innovator, the first mover, who introduces these systems before competitors, may secure some competitive advantage in so doing. Although the charge for such a service may be less than that delivered conventionally,

---

[55] See <http://www.lms.com>.
[56] <http://www.clickconveyancing.co.uk>.

efficient systems may result in as much, if not more, profit; and in greater throughput as well.

On the other hand, law firms that are required to deliver their services on a fixed fee basis (perhaps because their clients or public legal funding demand this) will naturally be attracted to workflow and project management systems. They will crave process efficiencies. This is in the very nature of the evolution of legal services, as I see it.

4.9 Embedded legal knowledge

Imagine if the wearing of seatbelts in motor vehicles were not only compulsory but it was not possible to start a car unless the belts were actually clicked in place. We could argue at length over whether this would be excessively paternalist, but we would agree that such a car would, in a sense, be designed to be law-abiding. This is one illustration of what I term 'embedded legal knowledge'. Here the legal knowledge—self-knowledge of a sort—would be embedded in the physical design of the vehicle.

Another example of embedded legal knowledge can be found on almost all personal computers. I am referring to the on-screen card game, Solitaire, which, when I was a boy, we enjoyed with playing cards made up of atoms and we called it 'Patience'. Although it rather defeated the point, when playing conventionally in the physical world it was possible to cheat. For example, in the appropriate place, a red 4 might surreptitiously be placed beneath a red 5 (even though this might cause later problems). In contrast, with the PC-based game, it is simply not possible to break the rules in this way. Any attempt to put a red 4 under the 5, in the way suggested, will lead to an unceremonious and automatic return of the card to its starting place. The rules are embedded in the system; that is the game. In the world of bits and bytes, non-compliance is not an option. The legal knowledge is embedded in the design of the computer program itself.

Traditionally, in our social and working lives, we have tended to view the law as a set of obligations, prohibitions, and permissions that, in a sense, overlay our activities. More, when some law or regulation applies to our circumstances, our normal expectation is that it is a human task, and often the job of a qualified lawyer, to recognize that some legal provision is applicable or in play. In some aspects of its execution, then, the law is a rather passive phenomenon. In theory, it obliges, protects, empowers, and guides us all but, in practice, given the quantity and complexity of the law, few people, even lawyers themselves, recognize all the circumstances in which the law might benefit them or impose a constraint. This is the essence of the problem that I call 'hyper-regulation' (see Section 1.4).

The idea of 'embedded legal knowledge' is that the law is injected into our machines, systems, processes, and working practices, in such a way that it is no longer a passive resource but instead it is brought to life and integrated with our lives by being embedded in, amongst other places, our infrastructure. Thus, the car that 'knows' that wearing seatbelts is compulsory, or the computer-based card game that 'appreciates' the rules, automatically impose and enforce the rules without the need for the driver, passenger, or player to be fully conversant themselves with them. These, of course, are trivial illustrations. A more obvious example, as I consider earlier in this chapter, is the idea of automatic document assembly. A user of such a system need only answer the questions posed (preferably in ordinary language) and need have no knowledge, for example, of the law of contract, even though the documents that are generated are legally robust from a contractual point of view. The legal knowledge, the legal content, is actually embedded in the document assembly system and is largely hidden from the end user.

The same principle can also be extended to workflow systems, as I discuss in Section 4.8. In designing these systems, it would be sensible and even strategic to build in compliance with the relevant regulations and laws, so that, for example, if an action needed to be undertaken, in law, within a particular timeframe, then this would automatically be required by the system; or if a document has to be submitted in a prescribed form, then the system should constrain users so that only this format can be produced.

There is a deeper philosophical issue lurking here and that is our tendency to assume that the application, invocation, and imposition of the law is invariably a human interpretative process; that there needs to be some interface, as it were, between events, actions, activities, and behaviour in the real world, and the assessment of their implications from the legal point of view. I am suggesting that we should aspire, on many occasions, to remove this interface. For example, in relation to citizens and their interactions with the State, given that large bodies of personal information are now held by various government agencies, if a particular citizen were entitled, under some legislation, to a particular benefit, then this should be recognized automatically by the agency in question and automatic payment should also follow. Public bodies should not be waiting for citizens to apply. More commonly, in business, if we can build compliance with, say, Health and Safety regulations into our buildings and working environments, so that various forms of non-compliance are simply not possible, then this would be greatly preferable to imposing the ongoing burden on human beings of understanding applicable regulations and monitoring their activities relative to these. We should design our systems to comply with the myriad laws and regulations that fetter us all, rather than needing to enlighten the people or engage the lawyers.

A hybrid technique that to some extent embeds legal content in organizations is 'personalized alerting'. Imagine that clients had at their disposal a first rate team of professional support lawyers and legal research specialists, whose sole purpose was to scour the Web to identify all materials that might be of interest to their boss, to gather them together, subject them to analysis, and distil them into punchy summaries that can easily be consumed. Perhaps a short, crisp report containing these summaries would be lying on the desktop of this lucky client every morning on their arrival at the office. In years to come, such a service will be deliverable to lawyers and non-lawyers alike,[57] and yet the work product will not be the result of a human team but the output of a combination of technologies (including intelligent agents, intelligent searching, RSS (really simple syndication) feeds, and natural language processing). According to research being conducted by the Oxford Internet Institute, such research might be even conducted by our own personal, electronic assistants, known as 'companions', who will interact with tomorrow's Internet on our behalf.[58] In any event, we can anticipate that legal updates, briefings, and alerts will automatically and proactively be delivered to non-lawyers across organizations (and this is disruptive to the extent that law firms seek to provide such a service today).

Under the heading of embedded legal content also comes the phenomenon of real-time contract management. Many contracts are, essentially, sets of conditions—they stipulate that under condition x, y, and z, certain consequences follow. Some organizations that might have five, ten, or even twenty thousand contracts in place are currently looking at the idea of building databases of all the conditions and having regular feeds into these systems, so that when specific conditions are satisfied, these are flagged. In this way,

---

[57] Various alerters have been provided for some time, eg by Clifford Chance at <http://www.clifford-chance.com>; the Law-Now service from CMS Cameron McKenna at <http://www.law-now.com>; and the EU Tracker from LexisNexis at <http://www1.lexisnexis.co.uk/abouteutracker >.

[58] See M Peltu and Y Wilks, 'Close Engagements with Artificial Companions: Key Social, Psychological, Ethical and Design Issues', OII/e-Horizons Discussion Paper No 14 (Oxford Internet Institute, January 2008). Also see <http://www.companions-project.org>. These companions sound like a cross between a Tamagotchi (<http://www.tamagotchi.com>) and a 'dæmon', from Philip Pullman's superb trilogy, *His Dark Materials* (London: Scholastic Press, 2001).

we can automate the management of contracts in real-time. The best time at which to build in this automation would, of course, be when the document is first assembled.

Yet another illustration of embedded legal content can be found in the controversial field of Digital Rights Management (DRM). This refers to the use of certain techniques and technologies, largely by copyright holders, to restrict the ways in which their content can be used. For example, if a feature film on a DVD is encrypted, then most consumers (who are unable to decode the film) will be able to watch the film but not copy or distribute it. Controversy rages here between copyright holders who believe they should be able to use advanced technologies to prevent the unauthorized replication of their work, as against those who argue that DRM technologies can be anti-competitive. In any event, all such technologies illustrate a further way in which the law can be imposed—not by the actions or inactions of human beings, but by encoding the rules in the systems themselves.

The most extended analysis of the law being embedded in and imposed by code is found in the work of Professor Lawrence Lessig of Stanford University. He argues that code can be systemically used in this way either to protect or erode our fundamental values.[59]

Looking further ahead, using AI and expert system techniques, it will be possible before too long to develop diagnostic systems that will operate alongside project management, document management, and even with process control systems. Such diagnostic systems will be able constantly to monitor the activities of these other systems and will in turn be able to recognize combinations of circumstances which raise legal questions or which require legal precautions. Thus computer systems, nuclear power plants, air traffic control systems, office workflow systems, will all in due course themselves be able to reason about the legal implications of their own activities—by identifying the legal impact of the tasks they are performing and even by recommending or taking remedial action.

Such invocation and application of legal rules, along with many of the other disruptive legal technologies of this chapter, are very different from the traditional, one-to-one consultative, advisory service that has characterized the legal profession for centuries until now. In fact, these technologies will to some extent displace conventional lawyers. With embedded legal knowledge, we see an illustration of a wider phenomenon that applies also to many of the other disruptive legal technologies—these technologies are usually,

---

[59] L Lessig, *Code: Version 2.0* (New York: Basic Books, 2006).

but not always, examples of what I called, in *The Future of Law*, innovation rather than automation.[60] Automation, as I define it, refers to the computerization of pre-existing tasks, activities, processes, organizations, and so forth. Innovation, on my terms at least, is the use of technology to enable users to do things that previously were not possible, or perhaps even imaginable. Generally, disruptive legal technologies extend far beyond simple automation (the streamlining, optimizing, or motorizing) of current and past legal activities, into the realms of innovation, often with radically new possibilities for the delivery and receipt of legal services.

It is my contention that these disruptive legal technologies will present fundamental, unavoidable, and pressing challenges for most legal businesses. Each technology on its own would be worrying enough; in combination, they will irreversibly and emphatically change the face of legal service. These are not merely systems of some possible future. As some examples in this chapter show, a very few law firms, most notably in London, have recognized the threats and the opportunities here and have been innovating accordingly. The game is afoot. It is in this sense that I borrow the words of the Canadian science fiction writer, William Gibson, who said in another context: 'The future has already arrived. It's just not evenly distributed yet.'

---

[60] Susskind (n 26 above) 49–51.

5

The Future for In-house Lawyers

It is tempting to believe that law firms live at the centre of the legal universe: in most jurisdictions, the great majority of lawyers are indeed in private practice; many of the best known brands in the legal profession do belong to law firms; the largest of the firms undoubtedly receive considerable media attention; and it is law firms that tend to be the first port of call when serious legal advice is needed. But where do clients sit in the legal pecking order?

Last year, in 2007, I spoke at around twenty-five events (conferences, seminars, and workshops) for clients or, more precisely, for in-house lawyers. I was struck then by how seldom these corporate counsel spoke about law firms. Instead and understandably, they were pre-occupied with themselves—with the broader performance of the businesses in which they sat, and with issues such as compliance, risk management, and dispute resolution. In these meetings, the law firms that serve them were not discussed very much at all, and certainly not as central players. They were spoken of, respectfully as a general rule, but as a pool of service providers at the edge rather than as key players at the core. There is a salutary reminder here for law firms. Lawyering in private practice is a second order activity—without organizations and individuals going about their daily activities and facing legal issues, there is nothing or no-one for lawyers to counsel; there is no business to be done. While this may seem self-evident and hardly worth observing, many partners speak and behave as though the work of their law firms is of prime significance in and of itself.

There is good reason to argue, therefore, as in all sophisticated sectors where the customer is king, that it is clients who sit at the centre of the legal universe. One specialist subset of the client community is the in-house legal department of businesses and public sector bodies. Here we generally find the most knowledgeable and discerning of all legal clients; these clients are lawyers themselves. Surprisingly, despite their pivotal role and special insight, relatively little scholarship, empirical research, or academic commentary have been devoted to in-house lawyers; on how they work, how they are managed, and how they integrate within the organizations in which they sit. In this chapter, I want to patch that gap in a modest way, by considering in some detail the relevance of information technology (IT) for in-house lawyers and how their systems should interact with those of law firms. Before delving into that subject, however, I must raise a more fundamental and perhaps rather unsavoury issue, one that is a potential obstruction at the heart of the lawyer/client relationship.

5.1 The asymmetry between lawyers and clients

It is seldom acknowledged explicitly that there is a fundamental asymmetry between the commercial interests of law firms and those of their clients. In the ordinary course of events, when a client (whether an individual or a major organization) instructs a lawyer, it will generally be the hope of the client that the involvement of the lawyers and the resultant fees can be kept to a bare minimum. While the engagement of lawyers is not always a necessary evil or a distress purchase, it is fair to say that most clients would prefer to avoid or minimize legal expenses, whether for the resolution of disputes, assistance with transactions, or for some more general or particular advice. Those who hold the purse strings (whether of the lofty boardroom budget or of the weekly household kitty) want to avoid overspending on legal matters.

Contrast this cost consciousness of clients with the very different cost consciousness of most lawyers when a client or potential client walks into their offices with new work. It is hard for lawyers in this situation to suppress the hope that the circumstances that have precipitated the visit are those that require extended and detailed attention by a serious team of legal advisers.

A law firm, after all, is a business and its fee income and profitability depends on clients needing legal help. The more clients and the bigger the legal challenges, the larger the income and profitability might be. And then there are the expenses. When, some years ago, I heard a litigator friend outline a potential case and then add, with some relish, 'I smell first class travel', this chap did not reveal a passion for controlling the costs and disbursements incurred on his client's behalf. The client would have been horrified, of course—lawyers should remember that, for most clients, legal expenses are an overhead, to be monitored, managed, and trimmed.

Here, then, is the fundamental tension. The client will generally hope their legal requirements are routine and can be disposed of quickly and painlessly, while the law firm will generally hanker after more challenging instructions that will occupy them for some time. The law firm is not improper in harbouring such aspirations and is no different here from most professionals, including architects, management consultants, tax advisers, investment bankers, and many more. But another approach and ethos is imaginable. I think of the legal advice that my brother gives me when I need guidance on a point of law. If I say to him that I think I have a legal problem, he does not hope that it is a gargantuan can of worms that will keep his firm occupied for weeks. He hopes, almost as much as I do, that he can dispose of my issue quickly and painlessly. He does not write me a long letter. We do not have long formal meetings. Instead, and usually by phone, he gives me punchy, practical, jargon-free, and actionable help. Imagine, then, if all lawyers served their clients as though they were advising their close friends or family. A very few do. Most do not.

On the strength of extended involvement with General Counsel and other in-house lawyers over the past twenty years or so, I have come to the view that the ideal law firm is one that not only exhibits and brings to bear technical excellence but is one that also strives to align its commercial interests with those of its clients. A firm that, in the spirit of the lawyer advising a friend or family, has a shared hope of keeping clients' legal difficulties and expenses to a minimum, is a legal business that could create enormous, even unprecedented, levels of confidence and would deserve the often misplaced honorific of 'trusted adviser'. While it might seem, at first glance, that this would be commercially naive and self-destructive for the law firm, the technically excellent firm that shared its clients' enthusiasm for minimizing the involvement and cost of lawyers, would, in the medium or longer term, be precisely the legal practice that would attract the genuinely complex and high value work that inevitably faces most businesses, at least at some stage.

There are two fundamental obstacles facing most firms attracted to this approach. The first is that many, if not most, lawyers who work in law firms turn out to be poor empathizers. This is not speculation on my part. It is a finding of a series of research projects that I have conducted for my law firm clients over the years and has been confirmed on innumerable occasions when I have held workshops with in-house lawyers. Remarkably, most in-house counsel say that law firms generally do not understand the client organizations that they advise. It is not that they lack a broad understanding of the nature and structure of the businesses and the sectors in which they operate, but that firms do not strive to find out what it is actually like to work as an in-house lawyer within any given client organization. Law firms, the claim continues, are generally not alive to the culture of client organizations, the ways in which lawyers are regarded, the appetite for risk, the extent of the internal bureaucracies, the nature of the internal communication mechanisms, and, importantly, the *realpolitik* and broader business context of disputes and deals that are being advised upon. In part, this does indeed betray an inability to empathize. Too often, partners from law firms are reported to pontificate at meetings without pausing for breath, rather than focusing their energy on what is actually on the minds of their clients. In the language of popular psychology, I say that law firms are from Mars while clients are from Venus[1]—where law firms are determined to supply definitive answers, clients are often wanting no more than for their advisers to appreciate what it is like to be in their position and to get a sense of the bigger picture. If this diagnosis is accurate, and law firms really do fail to put themselves in their clients' shoes and look at business issues through their eyes and from their perspective, then how can they genuinely align their interests with those of their clients, and, in turn, justifiably secure the position of trusted adviser?

The second obstacle is an old chestnut. It is the curse of hourly billing. More printer cartridges have been consumed in discussion of this topic than most others in the field of law firm management. Like many other commentators, I have been anticipating the demise of hourly billing for many years now: most forcefully, since I read a convincing anthology of articles published by the American Bar Association in 1989, which presented a possible array of alternative billing methods.[2] And yet, this method of charging has

---

[1] J Gray, *Men are from Mars, Women are from Venus* (London: Thorsons, 1992).
[2] RC Reed (ed), *Beyond the Billable Hour: An Anthology of Alternative Billing Methods* (Chicago: American Bar Association, 1989).

proven to be remarkably resilient and still dominates the mind-set as well as the daily invoicing of law firms. Today, even when hourly billing is not directly in play, often the ways in which alternative methods are conceived, for example on a fixed fee basis, are underpinned by a model of value rooted in time spent. However, the fact that alternative methods are being adopted with growing enthusiasm across the legal sector does suggest that the tide is turning.

Until the late 1950s, the standard way of billing in the legal profession, in England and the US at least, was through some kind of fixed fee arrangement, ordinarily regulated by minimum fee schedules, as recommended by local State Bar Associations or Law Societies. However, after a decision by the US Supreme Court in 1975 had declared such schedules to be in violation of antitrust laws, hourly billing emerged as the standard method of charging, certainly amongst commercial law firms. In a masterful article on the subject, Professor Huseyin Leblebici, of the University of Illinois, provides a detailed historical account of law firm billing practices and concludes that law firms are undergoing fundamental transformations in their billing practices and pricing strategies. Here is further evidence to suggest that hourly billing may be reaching the end of its natural life.[3]

And so it must, if law firms are genuinely to align their commercial interests with those of their clients. So long as the focal point of law firms' profitability is premised on the number of hours spent advising clients, their motivation will always tend to be to spend more rather than less time on the work, where clients will prefer precisely the contrary. Only when the fees rendered reflect the value of the work to the client will law firms and their clients share the same commercial perspective.

I can see that hourly billing is a model with which some General Counsel are quite comfortable, in part because they themselves have often been recruited from law firms that prospered under this charging regime. But this should not deter us from the reality. At worst, hourly billing can tempt lawyers to dishonesty. At best, it is an institutional disincentive to efficiency. To put it more crudely, hourly billing often rewards the inefficient practice that milks the work given to it and it penalizes the well run legal business whose systems and processes enable it to conclude matters rapidly. This simple truth was brought into focus recently for me when undertaking a project with my then 12-year-old daughter, Ali. We had agreed that she would help

[3] H Leblebici, 'Your Income' in L Empson (ed), *Managing the Modern Law Firm* (Oxford: Oxford University Press, 2007).

me, as a summer job, to build my database of contacts. Once we had settled upon the matter of data input, we turned to the question of payment. I suggested to Ali that I would pay her a certain amount per hour. She thought about this only very briefly, smiled and said 'I'll take my time then'. If a 12-year-old girl can immediately recognize the intrinsic commercial weakness of hourly billing, it is remarkable that the world's most venerable profession cannot do similarly and overhaul its practices. Failure to do so will perpetuate the mismatch between the commercial interests of lawyers and those of their clients.[4]

The most powerful case study of which I am aware in this context is that of the in-house legal department of Cisco. Their General Counsel, Mark Chandler, is one of the world's most innovative in-house lawyers. He has publicly stated his aversion to hourly billing on numerous occasions and indeed 75 per cent of his annual spend on legal matters (US$125 million) is now on a fixed fee basis. Strikingly, one law firm undertakes almost all of Cisco's commercial litigation for an annual fixed fee. This shocks most litigators, because the conventional wisdom is that litigation, by its very nature, is an open-ended process; at the outset of many disputes, this conventional wisdom maintains, no-one can anticipate the likely time or resources required to bring the conflict to an end. Clients are therefore asked to pay for the number of hours spent. Cisco takes a different approach and so, in turn, does the firm that it instructs. Other than for exceptional disputes, the company expects one law firm to look after all its litigation for a fixed fee. What is fascinating is that the law firm in question, after finding its profitability impacted after two years of the arrangement, only agreed to continue at the same price on the understanding that they could be far more heavily involved in advising at an early stage on the high risk areas of Cisco's business. They asked to be able to attend certain meetings, review particular documents, and be allowed a level of access and involvement that litigators would not normally enjoy prior to problems arising. In addition, they decided to deploy contract attorneys rather than their associates to undertake routine work for

---

[4] Underlying this mismatch is a related phenomenon—an 'asymmetry of information'. This comes about when one party to an arrangement has more information than the other. When serving clients on an hourly billing basis, law firms have more information than their clients about the resources needed and being deployed. One outcome of this asymmetry, after a contract has been agreed upon, is known as 'moral hazard'—this comes about when a party (in our case, a law firm) with more information may be tempted or is incentivized to behave inappropriately in relation to the party with less information (the client). These are issues that occupy professional economists, who have developed a range of solutions, although for other sectors, such as insurance and finance. The legal profession would benefit from some of this insight. I am grateful to my son, Daniel, for drawing my attention to this.

Cisco, such as processing subpoenas and some document review. This was because of the heavy costs incurred in employing associates (the starting salaries in the US for new associates in large law firms, immediately after graduation from law school, are now in excess of US$160,000).

And this surely, in a most convincing way, illustrates my point about the alignment of law firms' and clients' interests. In the case of Cisco, because it is directly in the law firm's interest to minimize the expense and effort expended on litigation, the nature of their involvement and participation in their clients' affairs has changed radically. They have as strong an interest as Cisco in avoiding disputes and, accordingly, are offering what amounts to a range of legal risk management services as well as conventional help with dispute resolution; and some subcontracting too. Cisco's handling of its litigation is a case study in the future of legal services.[5]

Other case studies are coming through as I write—we have recently seen a few in-house legal departments (for example that of Tyco International) retaining single firms to undertake all or most of their work. These arrangements are underpinned by complex schemes of incentives and safeguards, all of which are intended to lead to better commercial alignment between firms and clients than has been possible in the past.[6]

5.2 The Law Firm Grid

Unsurprisingly, given the company's dominance in the provision of Internet services, part of Cisco's success lies in its commitment to finding ways of using IT to improve the delivery of legal services. However, very few in-house legal departments have Cisco's technological expertise or Mark Chandler's insight. My challenge in the remainder of this chapter is to help the late adopters. I do so by introducing another model. This one clarifies the scope and relevance of IT for the in-house legal department. But before I do this, there is some groundwork to be done. To understand IT for the legal department, I believe we need to start with a clear understanding of the ways in which law firms have exploited IT over the past few decades, because they have led the way.

---

[5] For the transcript of a much cited lecture by Mark Chandler, entitled 'State of Technology in the Law', delivered at Northwestern University in January 2007, see <http://blogs.cisco.com/news/comments/cisco_general_counsel_on_state_of_technology_in_the_law>.

[6] R Lloyd, 'In-house Lawyer: The Power of One' *Legal Week*, 29 May 2008.

In 2000, in a collection of essays entitled *Transforming the Law*, I introduced a new model that I called the 'Grid'.[7] This is a shorthand, uniform way of analysing the impact and interrelationships of IT, knowledge management, e-business, and various other related concepts. I had developed the Grid to respond to an ongoing challenge that I faced at that time. At meetings with senior partners from law firms, I was finding, even in the heady days of the dotcom euphoria, that unless I could capture the imagination of a senior partner within ten minutes or so (assuming they had no special interest in IT) then I had lost them. And so, based largely on my experience of providing consulting services to major law firms, I set about developing a model that I hoped would, at once, clarify some of the jargon in the world of legal technology, highlight the broad areas of potential investment, and even generate some enthusiasm. Like all models, as I always stress, it is an oversimplification of the reality that it seeks to capture and explain. Nonetheless, I have found that senior lawyers with little interest in technology do seem to find it helpful.

As depicted in Figure 5.1, the Grid is made up of a horizontal axis, with 'technology' at the extreme left-hand side, and 'knowledge' at the extreme right. In between, sits 'information'. I am suggesting here that there is a spectrum in the world of IT, so that when people speak of IT they can mean anything from their raw technology (perhaps the cabling or the hardware) at one end, through to very advanced systems for capturing and sharing knowledge, at the other. And in the middle, admittedly rather vaguely, is the idea of information systems. Running vertically, the second axis is labelled 'internal' at the bottom and 'client' at the top. This draws the distinction between uses of IT within a law firm and applications that are accessible by clients. On the Grid that is created by the intersection of these two axes, the space below the line is intended to refer to internal systems, and the space above the line denotes systems for use by clients.

The Grid comprises four quadrants: in the bottom-left is what I call 'back-office technology'. In this category fall systems such as word processing, electronic mail, instant messaging, social networking, video conferencing, document management systems, accounting and finance systems, marketing databases, human resource systems, project management systems, workflow tools, client relationship management systems, diarying applications, as well as the hardware, networks, and various operating systems that underpin these applications. Back-office technologies in law firms are little different

---

[7] R Susskind, *Transforming the Law* (Oxford: Oxford University Press, 2000; paperback, 2003) Ch 1.

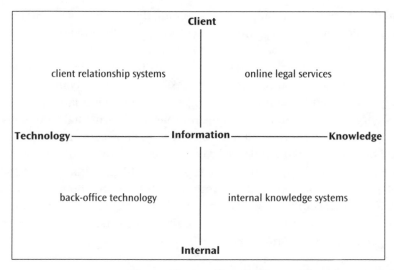

Fig. 5.1 The Law Firm Grid

from back-office systems in any other businesses. Although many of these systems are rather unglamorous, not least because they are hidden from clients, they generally attract the great bulk of law firms' investment in IT. They provide the basic infrastructure for the running of much of the law firm, and the extent to which law firms rely on them cannot be overstated. If the average law firm were simultaneously denied access to its word processing, electronic mail, and financial systems, I would hazard that the business would collapse in a modest number of days.

In the bottom-right quadrant of the Grid are 'internal knowledge systems'. These are the various systems that help to capture and share a firm's collective knowledge and experience. Examples of these are know-how and work product databases, searchable repositories of selected e-mails, libraries of standard form documents (templates and precedents), procedure manuals and practice notes, know-who systems (those that help members of the firm to find out who knows most on a particular subject), and more ambitious applications such as document assembly, e-learning, wikis, podcasts, and blogs as discussed in Chapters 3 and 4 of this book. These knowledge systems are often accessible through a firm's Intranet. It is in this bottom-right quadrant that the discipline of knowledge management should flourish. I define knowledge management as the systematic organization and exploitation of the collective knowledge of a firm, as an identifiable activity and responsibility, intended to maximize the firm's return on the combined experience of its lawyers. In more prosaic terms, the purpose of knowledge management is to help firms to avoid duplicating effort and resist reinventing the wheel. It is about increasing efficiency, productivity, consistency, and the quality of work undertaken for clients. The focus is on leveraging knowledge rather than (or as well as) leveraging human beings. Generally, law firms have invested far less in this quadrant than in the bottom left. This lack of investment, coupled with the widely acknowledged cultural challenges of encouraging lawyers to share knowledge with one another, has meant that many firms have been disappointed with their efforts in this area. I return to knowledge management in the following section to underline its centrality to the future of legal services.

Moving diagonally upwards to the top-left, in this quadrant we find what I call 'client relationship systems'. To explain the nature and scope of these systems, I find it helpful to think of the way that we can now track the progress of parcels that we send by major couriers. We simply enter a reference number at the relevant website and we are able to find out where that parcel might be. We do the same when tracing an eagerly awaited book from Amazon. So too, in the world of law, it should surely be possible for clients to be able to follow the progress that has been made on work undertaken on their behalf, not by playing telephone tag or by waiting for updates in letters, but by logging on to some secure service that can bring the client up to date. Typical facilities here are status reporting (being able to check what progress has been made), financial reporting (the ability to monitor how much time and money has been spent on particular pieces of work), and work-rooms (where documents relating to particular deals and disputes can be accessed easily). In other words, websites are set up for particular deals and disputes. Through these sites—variously called online work-rooms, client sites, or deal-rooms—clients who wish to monitor the progress of their lawyers can review the latest documents, identify who is actually doing their work, and keep a sharp eye on the amount being charged. And all of this without needing to pin down lawyers at meetings or on the telephone. English-based law firms led the world in this area, by developing specifically branded client sites. In 2000, for example, Allen & Overy was first to this market with newchange,[8] Andersen Legal (as then was) announced its Dealsight, and Linklaters launched Clients@Linklaters.[9]

In a sense, what is happening here is that clients are being offered access to information, directly or indirectly, that is held within the law firms' systems; for example in securing information about time and money spent on work, the client is, actually or metaphorically, dipping into a law firm's

---

[8] <http://www.newchange.com>.
[9] <http://www.linklaters.com>.

financial systems. Some firms do indeed provide, under secure conditions, direct access into parts of their systems, while others make information available in a more sanitized form. I regard these systems as client relationship systems, alongside newer techniques such as social networking, instant messaging, and video conferencing, because they can deepen and strengthen the communication channels between client and firm. They do not fundamentally change the nature of legal service; rather, they can provide new and improved ways of delivering traditional service. The transparency that they bring often makes lawyers a little nervous. I liken this reaction to that of the owner of a restaurant when asked by a diner if they might see into the kitchen. The owner may feel rather apprehensive and indeed may engage in some frantic tidying up, but it would be inappropriate, if not suspicious, if he denied them entry. The same goes for law firms—to deny access to such information may well prejudice the trust between law firm and client.

The fourth and final quadrant of the Grid holds systems that I refer to as 'online legal services'. These are generally regarded as the most controversial applications of legal technology on the Grid. Often, but not always, these are illustrations of 'disruptive legal technologies' as I explain in Chapter 4. The broad idea here is that legal knowledge and expertise is made available online rather than being secured in the time-honoured manner of one-to-one consultative advisory service. One approach here is to provide clients with direct access to law firms' knowledge systems. This sometimes happens unintentionally—when law firms promote the power, depth and richness of their internal knowledge systems, some clients quite naturally ask whether, as long-standing recipients of conventional advice, they could perhaps enjoy access to some of these resources. Unwittingly, law firms find themselves offering online services in this way. Aside from client access to firms' knowledge systems, a variety of other techniques and technologies belong in this category. When firms issue newsflashes, personalized alerts, and updates in electronic form, they are providing modest online legal services. More ambitiously, online systems can help clients automatically to assemble documents, they can provide broad legal guidance and, using expert systems techniques, can even provide legal advice or diagnoses. Also in this quadrant is online dispute resolution (see Section 6.6). In this corner of the Grid, we find significant and often radically new service opportunities for the legal world, underpinned by new business models. If firms seek to charge for such services, they cannot sensibly do so on an hourly billing basis. Instead, a fixed licence fee is more appropriate. But, crucially, the test of whether or not a service is an online legal service is not whether a charge is levied; nor is the test whether what is on offer can be called 'advice'. Online legal service simply involves the provision across the Internet of structured professional content—information, news, guidance, processes, methodology, knowledge, expertise, or advice in a way that adds value to clients.

I am often asked which parts of the Grid are more strategically significant than others. In *Transforming the Law*, I discussed this at some length and also identified eight possible strategies for law firms.[10] For now, however, taking a helicopter view, it is worth drawing a firm distinction between applications to the left of the vertical (client/internal) line, and systems to the right. Generally, I believe that there is little competitive advantage to be gained from being first to the legal market with systems to the left of this vertical line. True, firms can find themselves at a competitive disadvantage by not investing in such systems but, by and large, a promising application on this left-hand side of the Grid can usually be replicated with ease by potential imitators. Even in the top-left quadrant, where innovative new ways of working with clients might be identified, it is hard to imagine such an application that cannot swiftly be copied. Clients will often expect a wide range of facilities to the left of the vertical line, and will rarely be overwhelmed for long by a system in either quadrant. In contrast, I believe that competitive advantage *can* be secured by law firms in the two quadrants to the right of the line. This must be correct—a law firm should be superior to another not by dint of its plumbing towards the left-hand side, but because of the way it captures and shares knowledge internally (bottom-right) and imaginatively and creatively makes that available to clients externally (top-right). Law firms are in the knowledge business and not the technology business. While the technology provides vital infrastructure, it is knowledge systems that can and will differentiate law firms.

5.3 The importance of knowledge systems

It is worth taking a quick detour to drive home the importance of knowledge systems for lawyers.[11] I begin by repeating myself—in the Introduction to *The Future of Law*, I related one of my favorite stories, one that is worth rehearsing here, as follows. One of the world's leading manufacturers of electric power tools is said to take its new executives on an induction course, at

---

[10] Susskind (n 7 above) 30–40.
[11] For a clear and detailed analysis of knowledge management in law firms, see M Parsons, *Effective Knowledge Management for Law Firms* (New York: Oxford University Press, 2004).

the opening session of which they are asked to consider a slide which depicts an image of a gleaming power drill. 'Is this what the company sells?' they are asked. The executives are rather hesitant but collectively pluck up the courage to concede that, yes, this is indeed what their new employer sells. It seems rather obvious. However, the trainers, with a flourish, immediately confront the executives with another slide, that of a photograph of a hole, neatly drilled in a wall. 'That is what we actually sell', it is claimed with ill-concealed pleasure. 'Very few of our customers are passionately committed to the presence of electric power tools in their homes. They want holes. And it is your job, as new executives, to provide ever more competitive, efficient, and imaginative ways of giving our customers what they want, of putting holes in their walls.' Since writing about that story in 1996, I have told it again, at innumerable seminars and conferences, and each time have asked, 'what is the hole in the wall in the context of legal services?' The power drill in the legal world, it might be said, is traditional, one-to-one consultative advisory service, often delivered on an hourly billing basis. But is that actually what clients of law firms want? Is it to this that they are passionately committed? To think so, I argue, is to confuse the medium with the message.

When I ask lawyers about holes in walls, I am really asking, 'what value is it that lawyers bring to the markets they serve?' Over the years, only two responses to that question have struck me as satisfactory. I deal with one here and defer the other (relating to risk management) until later in the book (see Section 6.7). The first answer came to me, in fact, not as a direct response to one of my queries but in the course, one day, of surfing the Web. I came across a website of KPMG, the global audit and tax firm. Their mission statement, or at least part of it, I discovered, ran as follows: 'We exist to turn our knowledge into value for the benefit of our clients.'[12] Is this not a wonderful way to capture the essence of professional service? In a wide variety of disciplines, professional advisers have knowledge, expertise, experience, insight, and know-how that they apply in the particular circumstances of given clients. The hole in the wall, on this account, is the knowledge to which clients want access; or, more precisely, the application of that knowledge in their specific circumstances. Notice that the KPMG rendition does not flow along the following lines: 'we exist to provide one-to-one consultative advisory service, delivered in long reports or at extended meetings, on an hourly billing basis'. On the contrary, the mission statement is silent as to the way in which the professionals' knowledge is turned into value. It follows, I believe,

---

[12] <http://www.kpmg.com>.

that if advisers can find less expensive, quicker, less forbidding, more convenient, higher quality means of turning their knowledge into value, then clients will readily welcome this.

To turn knowledge into value often requires the support of knowledge systems. It has generally been said that UK firms more readily embrace these systems than their counterparts in the US. This was confirmed in 2006, when an interesting study concluded that US law firms invest less in knowledge management than European practices.[13] Knowledge management is about capturing, nurturing, and recycling the collective expertise of a business. In a law firm, this means building up readily accessible bodies of standard documents, procedures, checklists, and advice, so that duplication of effort is avoided and clients benefit from the combined experience of many lawyers. The study investigated seventy-one major law firms around the world, 40 per cent of which were expected to spend more than US$1million on knowledge management in 2006. The apparent parsimony here of US legal businesses sits significantly alongside the fact that US firms are generally more profitable than their counterparts in Europe. Of course, this is not just because they save cash on knowledge management. It is, at least in part, because they often handle legal work, in the terminology of Chapter 2, in a bespoke fashion where UK firms will standardize and systematize. Bespoke work takes longer and, because lawyers still bill by the hour, more work means more income. The efficiencies brought by knowledge management often mean fewer hours which means less cash. As long as it prevails, as I say in Section 5.1, hourly billing provides a systemic disincentive for investment in knowledge management. Note, again, that when law firms charge on a fixed fee basis, there is frequently much greater interest in knowledge management because time saved is of more direct value to them.

5.4 The Client Grid

In *Transforming the Law*, I confined the Grid to the analysis of law firms. I have since found that a similar Grid can usefully be applied to in-house legal departments. I have now formalized this and it is presented in Figure 5.2. The horizontal axis of the original grid remains unchanged. The vertical axis,

---

[13] <http://www.almresearchonline.com>.

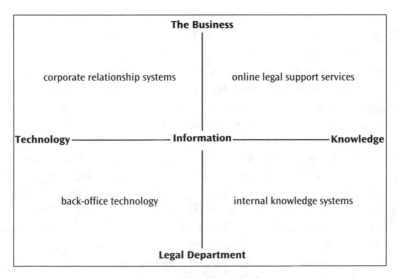

Fig. 5.2 The Client Grid

however, has been relabelled. At the bottom is 'legal department' while at the top is 'the business'. In other words, systems below the line are those that are used within the in-house legal department, whereas those above the line are directly accessible by non-lawyers within the organization. I am using the term 'the business' to refer here, generically, to the 'clients' of the in-house legal department itself. Wandering around the Grid once more, the category of back-office systems on the Client Grid is broadly similar to that within law firms. Here again we find word processing, electronic mail, instant messaging, document management, hardware, networks, and so forth. They serve the same broad functions as they do in law firms, and similar benefits will accrue. The crucial distinction here, however, is that most legal departments have very little say in what particular systems are available for their use. An in-house legal department tends to be one (relatively small) user of a broader range of systems being deployed across the organization. In-house legal departments very rarely have their own technology functions. Instead, they are internal customers of some central IT department or provider.

As for the bottom-right, the same types of systems fall into this category as in law firms, including know-how databases, precedent libraries, intranet services, document assembly systems, wikis, archives, and opinions. In principle, these internal knowledge systems should be more attractive to in-house legal departments than to most law firms. The latter, insofar as they are providing services on an hourly billing basis, will always tend to be wary about knowledge systems if they bring excessive efficiencies that the market

does not yet seem to be demanding. In contrast, the in-house legal department has a direct interest in managing its knowledge resources as efficiently
as possible. It is surprising, therefore, that many General Counsel say that
they have insufficient budget available to invest either in professional support lawyers or know-how specialists, or indeed in systems (such as document assembly, advanced Intranets, e-learning, or suites of standard form
documents). At some stage, they may need to spend to save.

In the top-left, we have what I call 'corporate relationship systems'. These
are the applications that are designed to enhance the communication channels and the relationships between an in-house department and the rest of
the organization in which it sits. Given that the in-house departments and
their clients are all under the one virtual roof, there should be all manner of
opportunities for harnessing the power of technology in the delivery of legal
services. This can extend beyond status reporting and work rooms, for
example, into workflow applications so that the input of in-house lawyers
can easily be integrated within the wider business practices and process of
the business. In-house legal departments are often, rather unfairly, regarded
as a hindrance rather than facilitators. On several occasions, I have heard
senior business people refer to their in-house lawyers as 'the business
obstruction unit'. Sophisticated clients, however, realize that the activities
and operations of their organizations often do raise significant legal risks.
If in-house lawyers are to be consulted in the traditional way, and offer their
services as consultative advisers, to avoid any impression of obstruction,
they should take advantage of new and emerging techniques for streamlining the process by which they communicate with their clients. This could
mean instant messaging, social networking, wikis, or perhaps websites into
which clients can easily dip to determine progress and retrieve documents
and advice. Better still, these tools should make it easier for in-house lawyers
to provide input earlier in the life cycle of their clients' affairs.

The fourth quadrant of the Client Grid, the top-right, I call 'online legal
support services'. The same sorts of technologies can be used here as by law
firms, but, once again, I can see a far stronger imperative for in-house lawyers to embrace these systems. Given that it is simply not possible for in-
house lawyers to guide and counsel each and every individual in the
organizations in which they work, it is surely attractive to find different ways
of making their legal expertise available to non-lawyers. Whether these
online facilities provide practical, business-focused guidance, or the ability
to generate standard and safe documents, or legal risk analysis tools, or perhaps personalized legal updates and awareness raising through e-learning,
the common theme is the same—that legal knowledge and expertise is
spread across the organization with the support of IT. Radically new models

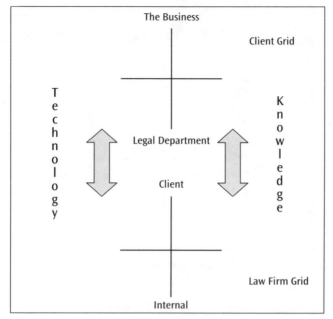

Fig. 5.3 Aligning the Grids

for legal service can be conceived here, with legal assistance being delivered by knowledge-based online services as a complement to the traditional offering by the in-house lawyers themselves. In-house lawyers can multi-source too.

In proposing this Grid for in-house legal departments, I hope that it is found to be as useful as it seems to have been in some law firms—as a way of understanding potential uses of technology, as a tool for analysing the current and future spread of systems, and as a method to help to prioritize amongst available options.

We should be clear that the Client Grid and the Law Firm Grid are not distinct from one another. On closer examination, I have found that they are coming together in a telling way. I find it helpful to imagine, as depicted in Figure 5.3, a Client Grid sitting above a Law Firm Grid and the two drawing towards one another.

When we align the grids in this way, we create, as shown in Figure 5.4, a common area for the systems of legal departments and law firms. Take, for example, the back-office systems available to in-house lawyers. These are substantially extended when the Grids come together because much of the data that in-house counsel will require for management information purposes are precisely those that law firms make available in what I call client relationship systems. In other words, much of the data that in-house

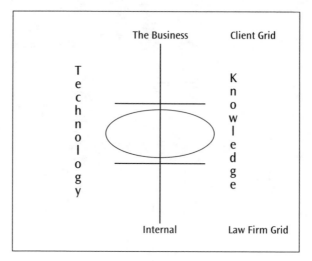

Fig. 5.4 Common Systems

counsel, ideally, would like to process—data about law firms and the work being undertaken for them—are held in law firms' systems which, in turn, are made available through client relationship systems. This data then slots neatly, as it were, into the back-office systems of legal departments.

The same goes for the internal knowledge systems of a legal department. When the Grids come together, the systems of the law department sit alongside the online legal and knowledge services provided by law firms. From the enlightened client's point of view, they should become integrated. This effectively extends the internal knowledge systems of a legal department to embrace the externalized knowledge systems and the online legal services of law firms. In other words, the knowledge systems at the disposal of in-house lawyers are not simply their own internal systems (which, as I observe, tend to be insufficiently resourced) but also include the online legal and knowledge services provided by a variety of law firms. If law firms are either providing access to their know-how systems or providing dedicated online legal services, then these become part of the knowledge armory available to in-house counsel. And it is IT that enables this extension to the knowledge facilities at the disposal of clients.

This coming together of the Grids is a conceptual representation of law firms and legal departments working much more closely with one another and sharing data and knowledge more freely. The net result for the client is that they have readier and easier access to many of the data, information, and knowledge resources that they need.

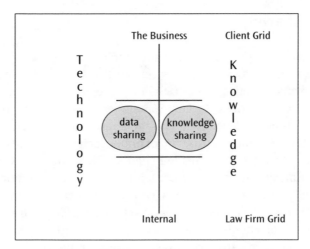

Fig. 5.5 Data and Knowledge Sharing

In practice, however, the world is considerably more complicated than pulling two diagrams together, not least because very few in-house legal departments, if any, work with one firm alone. And to muddy the water still further, there is not a law firm in the world (that I have heard of) that has only one client. This means that the one-to-one mapping of Law Firm Grid to Client Grid is an oversimplification of what happens in the actual legal marketplace. The conjoining of Grids may be a useful way of highlighting the attraction for legal departments in having greater connectivity with law firms, because the model shows the way in which their facilities are considerably enhanced; but we need a richer model, on paper and in practice, if we are to reflect the fact that in-house legal departments tend to instruct more than one law firm (some instruct many hundreds) and that law firms are engaged by numerous, and often very many, clients. From a systems point of view, and here is the crux, the in-house legal department should want ready and easy access to the systems and services of all the law firms they instruct; while the law firm should want a simple and convenient way of making appropriate information and systems available to the many clients that it serves. So, how do we make this happen? How do we establish the many-to-many relationships that I am envisaging here? It helps, for this purpose, to distinguish between the way in which law firms' client relationship systems and clients' back-office systems might come together (I call this 'data sharing', as depicted in Figure 5.5); and the techniques for conjoining law firms' online legal services and clients' internal knowledge systems ('knowledge sharing', as shown in Figure 5.5).

5.5 Data sharing

During the dotcom period, we saw the rapid emergence of a law-firm-centric approach to data sharing between law firms and their clients. On this model, law firms, effectively, set up their own separate websites and clients were invited to visit them. In late September 2000, within hours of one another, two of the world's largest and most respected law firms, Linklaters and Allen & Overy, launched this kind of online facility for clients. Linklaters' service, Clients@Linklaters, provided clients with secure access to a single website (technically, an extranet) containing customized contact information, financial reports, updates, and access to documents relating to particular deals.[14] Allen & Overy's service was newchange caseroom. It was designed to provide litigation clients with access to secure websites containing the key documents relating to particular cases, including witness statements, expert reports, summaries of progress, and timetables.[15] Clients@Linklaters and newchange caseroom were examples of the first wave of data sharing systems—tools that sought to enhance the working relationship between lawyers and their clients. Soon after, Clifford Chance, now the world's largest law firm, announced a similar online facility,[16] while a much smaller (six-partner) firm, Fidler & Pepper, showed that this technology was not just for the multinational giants.[17]

These virtual deal-rooms, as they often came to be known, captured the imagination of many lawyers, although many more understandably confessed to being confused by the terminology—legal technologists also talked variously of shared legal websites, digital workspaces, and online reporting. But the central idea was straightforward and important—that a type of website could be set up to enable clients to monitor progress on work being undertaken for them, to look at documents, to offer their own input, and generally to keep in touch.

A problem quickly became apparent to clients who were keen on these systems—those who instructed many law firms (and some of the organizations involved engaged hundreds), found it unacceptable to have to log onto the many different systems. An in-house counsel who worked with, say, ten law firms had to visit each of the ten facilities to gather up the data it required and to avail itself of the services on offer. Plainly, this was deeply unattractive

---

[14] <http://www.linklaters.com>.
[15] <http://www.allenovery.com>.
[16] <http://www.cliffordchance.com>.
[17] <http://www.fidler.co.uk>.

and far from practical. Instead of visiting many different sites, clients began to say that they wanted to monitor their entire matter load from one single, online location. They wanted the sum total of law firms' client relationship systems to be integrated and made available to them, either as one dedicated master site, or perhaps sitting on their own Intranets. In either event, rather than visiting many different sites, clients were keen to be able to monitor their entire matter load, as well as their panel of external lawyers, from one single online location. Thus, if a particular client had three deals and four disputes being conducted for it by seven different firms, it would not need to visit seven different sites, but would have the information about all seven, distilled and available to it on one site. This would be more convenient than consulting a series of different sites, especially when supplemented by facilities to enable clients to undertake comparative analysis of their lawyers, assessing, for example, the relative productivity and efficiency of the various firms currently acting for them.

In contrast, in the early days of online deal-rooms and status reporting, a number of major firms around the world genuinely thought that if their systems were demonstrably superior to those of competitors, then clients might abandon these less technically able firms in favour of the hi-tech first mover. This was naive. For reasons that extend well beyond IT, clients prefer to spread their legal work across a variety of providers and this preference was not affected in the least by the advent of any online systems, no matter how attractive. Nonetheless, for a while, the various firms with these first law-firm-centric data sharing systems jostled at some putative starting line, each arguing to clients that their tool should become the standard. This initial skirmish was rather melodramatically (but transiently) termed 'the battle of the deal-rooms'. It hardly moved clients.

There were strong analogies then with e-mail systems of five years previously, when clients rightly bemoaned the need to log on every morning to the numerous different systems of different law firms. This had been entirely inconvenient and the answer had been the universal mail-box, into which all e-mails generally came, irrespective of the systems from which they had been sent. Client sites, it was being asserted by some informed in-house lawyers, would soon need to be as integrated as contemporary e-mail.

Meanwhile, other in-house counsel took a different and much more adventurous tack. They opted for electronically linking many law firms to many clients on the basis of what can be termed a client-centric model. On this approach, the client makes available some Internet-based service and requires its external law firms to post the data in a specified format, one that clearly suits the client. From the client's point of view, the many contributions of their various outside advisers can thereby be brought together into one single body of data. In 2002, British American Tobacco (BAT) and Ford Motor Company launched such a system. It was called Anaqua and it was conceived by BAT and Ford as the focal point for the conduct of work undertaken for them; as a kind of electronic master file containing all sorts of relevant documentation derived from many law firms, and as a communication centre, linking these companies to their professional providers.[18] For any given deal or dispute, Anaqua enabled BAT and Ford to retrieve relevant documents, monitor costs and invoices, generate and file tailored reports, and send and receive messages that themselves would be automatically attached to appropriate online files. The driving force behind Anaqua was a passion for closer and more effective collaboration between BAT and Ford and those with whom they worked, including their lawyers, domain name managers, patent agents, and inventors. The system brought all diverse strands of work and advisers under the one virtual roof. This, then, was a tool, and a powerful one at that, that enabled BAT and Ford to manage external law firms as one coherent body. A number of other major organizations, such as BP,[19] followed suit and developed Anaqua-like systems for themselves.

Interestingly, BAT added an extra edge with Anaqua by making it unambiguously clear on launch that its use by their professional providers was not optional. If you wanted to continue advising BAT's intellectual property function in the future, you had to use Anaqua. Full stop. Rarely in this field, if ever, had an injunction been so starkly formulated. And no exception was therefore made for partners in law firms who were not sure if the Internet was a good thing or if it would last.

From the client's point of view, the client-centric approach to data sharing, as pioneered in Anaqua, was extremely powerful. Clients who had found it unsatisfactory to have to visit the many different sites of their many advisers now had a one-stop shop. More, they were able to monitor their entire matter load from one single, online location. The centre of gravity became the work—and convenience—of the client; and not that of the lawyer or other professional. However, just as clients found the law-firm-centric approach to be unworkable, the same became the case for the client-centric system. Law firms understandably baulked at the idea of having to feed information into the systems of numerous different clients, each no doubt requiring the

---

[18] <http://www.anaqua.com>. In 2004, Anaqua Inc was formed to provide a wider range of businesses with intellectual asset management solutions.
[19] BP is one of the few clients which has published its experience of using its own tool. See K Sinniger, 'Low Cost of Going High-tech' *ACC Docket* (October 2003).

postings to be in different formats. For major clients, of course, law firms were willing to suffer the inconvenience. But most seasoned legal technologists saw this as a temporary solution that was bound to be superseded in due course by a more flexible set-up. To this day, there are client-centric systems in place but, from the point of view of the legal market generally, they are piecemeal and inefficient. There may be one exception to this rather sweeping rejection; and here I am projecting ahead. I anticipate that a rash of websites will be created for particular clients which will act, effectively, as online communities for 'panels' of law firms. This idea is introduced in Section 4.7.

Given the shortcomings of and the tensions between the law-firm-centric and the client-centric approaches, what other options are there? One was created in Australia, in 2002, when a group of commercial lawyers collaborated in developing Secure Document eXchange—a website for the management of legal transactions.[20] The service provided an independent virtual deal-room facility, enabling all documents and communications on a deal to be stored electronically in one online location. Law firms who used the facility could communicate and share drafts with one another and with their clients; and they could also use the tool internally. The service, independent of any single firm, contrasted sharply with the initial approach in England, where several leading practices had launched their own branded services. Secure Document eXchange was made available worldwide. It is still operational but it has not been adopted as a de facto standard across the global legal profession. Interestingly, a later and analogous attempt, in 2000, by several top London-based firms to collaborate in developing a similar system never became airborne.

There were also intriguing opportunities here for third parties to offer data sharing services: neutral territory, owned, developed, and controlled by intermediaries. Initially, the most prominent provider of such a service was IntraLinks, an American company that had been specializing in digital workspaces since the late 1990s.[21] Leading US law firms quickly favoured IntraLinks, again in contrast with the major UK-based practices, with their proprietory law-firm-centric services.

There was always going to be competition, however. Some senior in-house lawyers still felt they should be setting the standards; various investment

---

[20] <http://www.securedocx.com>.
[21] <http://www.intralinks.com>.

banks[22] and accountants also had strong views and vested interests; while an array of technologists were keen to promote dedicated private networks. Proposed standards for the interoperability of deal-rooms began to ooze into the marketplace from all directions, bringing to mind the old, ironic IT quip that the great thing about standards is that there are so many to choose from.

Today, there are still many players jockeying for position. Some of the systems did not fulfil their early promise, largely, as I argue in Section 2.4, because many attempts to use these systems were in support of bespoke, large-scale transactions, whereas they are better suited to more routine deals, where clients are keen to keep the costs low. In the long term, I have little doubt that online deal-rooms and data sharing environments will be commonplace. The great unanswered question is—who will emerge as the leading providers? If we are keen to introduce a generic facility that will benefit all conceivable clients (from citizen-clients through to multinational corporations) and all law firms (from sole practitioners to global firms) then we need some kind of open legal exchange. I borrow the term 'exchange' from the dotcom era, when we heard much about B2B (business-to-business) exchanges, which were electronic marketplaces that, in effect, easily linked buyers and sellers as well as intermediaries who were participating in the same commercial space. I have been advocating this tack for some years now—for example in the preface to the paperback edition of my book *Transforming the Law*.[23] I still believe that the obvious answer is the development of a 'hub', a business-to-business exchange, which becomes a one-stop shop for clients and simultaneously a single pot into which law firms are able to load all sorts of material. Whether this hub is a single system underpinned by a very clear set of standards, or a virtual system, defined by a settled suite of protocols and standards, is an issue I am happy to leave open. What matters most, it seems to me, as shown in Figure 5.6, is that clients can easily access in one place all the information that has been provided by their various external firms, while these firms themselves are required to transfer their data to one place in a uniform format.

I have hoped for some years that one of the well-resourced global legal publishers might see the opportunity here, because I have feared such an exchange would never come about if it were left to a group of law firms to agree the standards by themselves. So far, the publishers have not yet committed,

---

[22] Many banks still run and operate their own data rooms, a type of virtual deal-room used in the due diligence process, in merger and acquisition work. Fairly recent research, by ACG and the Merrill Corporation, into the practices of US-based deal-makers, found that around two-thirds of deals in 2006 used this kind of virtual deal-room. This was up from about one-third in 2004. See <http://www.cfoasia.com>.

[23] Susskind (n 7 above) xxii–xxiii.

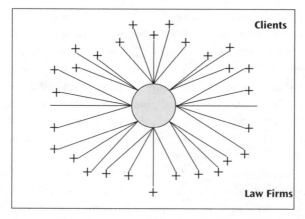

Fig. 5.6 A Hub or B2B Legal Exchange

although I do know they are interested in principle. Perhaps an entrepreneur will step in here. Only time will tell. But, in due course, I have no doubt such an exchange will be in place. This will be the platform that brings together the top-left of the Law Firm Grid and the bottom-left of the Client Grid.

Where does this leave law firms that have already invested in their own client relationship systems? In all likelihood, in due course, their own systems will be rendered largely redundant. That said, the firms that have been providing access through their own services should find it easiest—technically and culturally—to feed the relevant files into any new exchange. In strategic terms, though, the opportunities for law firms to gain competitive advantage simply by offering online data sharing facilities are rapidly diminishing.

One last thought on data sharing—it may be that the hub idea is superseded or swallowed up by some social networking system, as discussed in Sections 3.3 and 4.7. The next generation of social networking systems, developed for business, may indeed integrate with the more traditional online exchange. The hub might be delivered online via a social network, as adapted for business use.

5.6 Knowledge sharing

Turning now from the sharing of data between law firms and clients to the sharing of knowledge, here we have seen the law-firm-centric model in operation much more than the client-centric approach. Innumerable law firms over the last decade have enjoined their clients to visit their websites or extranets where rich repositories of know-how and insight are said to await them. Once again, though, as with client-centric data sharing systems, clients quickly tired of navigating through the many different sites of the numerous firms that advised them. More, these websites often became yet another contributor to the information overload from which most in-house lawyers suffer. On top of the myriad glossy newsletters, bulletins, updates, magazines, reports, and kindred bumph that were already assailing them, they were now being offered the chance to surf a whole host of law firm websites.

In response to this onslaught of information and in large part as a corrective to inconvenience of the law-firm-centric approach to knowledge sharing, a fascinating initiative was launched in London in 2003—the Banking Legal Technology (BLT) Group. Nine large investment banks, most of them household names, asked and then cajoled five leading law firms in London to set up a single knowledge portal—a website, really—into which these firms were encouraged to place, at no charge, their formidable combined collections of updates and newsflashes, analyses of legal developments, practice notes, even some precedent documents, and so on. Previously, all of these materials had been sent by the firms to these clients in a variety of formats (from glossy publications to e-mail alerts) but the clients found they were inundated and thought it wise to have all such documents pulled together into one easily accessible online facility. From the point of view of these clients, as I say in Section 4.7 where I discuss BLT in greater detail, this project made perfect sense. In the event, it has worked better than the cynics, within and beyond law firms, had expected. The community of participating banks has grown.

I have always been a strong admirer of this initiative. Indeed, I regularly use it as a case study in collaboration amongst clients. Yet, as a generic approach to knowledge sharing amongst lawyers in firms and in-house counsel, I think it is open to three criticisms. The first is that, for practising lawyers in in-house legal departments, the types of materials that are generally held in the BLT portal do not directly offer help; they do not tend to offer practical suggestions about what to do; there is not so much actual know-how. Instead, BLT offers a large repository of possibly relevant source materials. They are generally well researched, thorough, and accurate, but an in-house lawyer still has to plough through these sources in search of an answer. It assists rather than replaces research. Often, however, the busy in-house lawyer will not have time to undertake research and would prefer online guidance that is more practical, punchy, and action-oriented. This is why some sceptics claim that the BLT service is more of a tool for information specialists and professional support lawyers than for in-house lawyers at the coal face. This objection is not a fatal blow for BLT. Instead, it can be looked upon as a call for the next generation of systems. With the collaboration and technical infrastructure in place, the current information service should surely evolve into a central repository of more powerful online services for in-house lawyers, including, for instance, document assembly, intelligent checklists, compliance audits, and e-learning.

There is, however, a second and more profound difficulty with the BLT system—that there is excessive overlap and duplication of content. This reflects the way in which the materials are entered into the system. In a form of blind bidding, the five participating firms do not actually see what the others are contributing and so, on any given topic, are likely to load similar materials. The original conception, I think, was that this blind bidding would stimulate frantic competition. According to some speculative game theory, it was anticipated this would ensure that all firms would always strive to provide the finest and most extensive of materials, in the fear that if they did not then the others most certainly would. In the event, firms do not behave in this way and, although they contribute handsomely, most do so a little grudgingly. This blind bidding model, I am afraid, rather reflects the unhelpful way that some in-house lawyers, more generally, play law firms off against one another. Far more productive in building up such a common store of materials, I believe, would be to adopt a wiki approach (see Section 3.3). This would mean that the law firms would have full access to the system, would be able to see one another's contributions, would be encouraged not to duplicate material, but instead would be asked to build, in an evolutionary manner, on the materials that they find there. An evolutionary wiki-based model of collective knowledge would, I suggest, be much more useful and easier to manage, than a rather hit-and-miss, blind bidding approach.

The third and most fundamental problem with BLT as a generic model for knowledge sharing amongst firms and clients is that membership of the club is restricted. As it stands, access is limited to a very modest number of firms and banks. It is an early example of what I describe in Sections 3.3 and 4.7 as closed community peer production. For the clients who are beneficiaries, if new tools and a wiki approach were embraced, then it could evolve into a wonderful resource. But for law firms and clients who are not involved, that is, for most of the legal world, it has not provided protocols or de facto standards upon which other systems could build. Accordingly, this is not an all-purpose solution for the legal profession. It is a useful fix for a select few, and is driven by clients who are fortunate enough to have massive collective purchasing power. If similar such services were developed by other communities, then the old problems of law-firm-centric and client-centric systems would arise—firms would be feeding their knowledge into diverse systems while clients would have different services to consult.

I believe, again, that the best long-term solution to the challenge of knowledge sharing between firms and clients, one that could support closed communities and mass collaboration, would be some kind of hub or exchange (see Figure 5.7). This would be a one-stop shop for clients and a single pot into which law firms would be able to inject their knowledge resources for all their clients. And, once again, I also advocate that this hub should be provided by a third party. Even more so than with data sharing systems, the strongest candidates for establishing standard knowledge sharing hubs would be those legal publishers with experience of implementing major systems, with expertise in security of systems (a pivotal issue), and the added advantage of having their own content (for example databases of legislation and case law) to add into the mix. Involvement of such an intermediary could also lead to a more rapid adoption of the hub across the legal community: by law firms and clients, both large and small; by the courts; by third party know-how and knowledge providers; and even by other professional service providers. It would be here that closed communities of in-house lawyers might also share their resources. Ideally, there should be one hub only—internationally. This vision could be achieved through one major system, a legal Wikipedia perhaps. Alternatively, the solution could be a more basic platform—agreed standards and protocols, supporting, in effect, a virtual hub for knowledge sharing and one that, ideally, dovetailed with the analogous systems for data sharing.

5.7 The challenge for clients

What is the motivation here for clients? Why should they be interested in embracing IT and data and knowledge sharing solutions in the manner I suggest? In responding to these questions, I feel increasingly sure-footed. Through my own research into in-house legal departments and at countless workshops and conferences with General Counsel during the past few years, I have been able to gain a very strong sense of the commercial pressures now facing in-house legal departments. My particular focus in this chapter is in-house lawyers in commerce and industry but my thinking is also applicable to lawyers who work within the public and voluntary sectors.

In one way or another, the great majority of General Counsel with whom I speak, share a common dilemma. Most are under considerable pressure from their Boards to reduce their internal head count. By natural wastage or harsher means, legal departments are being asked to cut their numbers. On top of this, there is generally an even greater pressure to reduce substantially the amount that is spent on external law firms. The fees paid to many law firms are regarded by many executive and non-executive Board members alike, as spiralling out of control. And, to be clear, from my discussions at Board level, it seems that many in-house departments are not regarded from above as sufficiently tough on fees when dealing with large, experienced firms. On top of these pressures on head count and external spend, there is a third factor—legal and compliance departments (and they are often rolled together as one) are expected, year on year, to take on what seems like an ever increasing workload. Worse still, I am told that this work is higher risk than in the past. In short, when it comes to legal and compliance services, many major corporations and financial institutions have in-house legal functions that are being compelled to provide much more for much less.

If we also fold into this mix the undeniable propensity of law firms to want to increase their hourly rates each year as well as their overall profitability and fee income, then we must surely see some remarkable tensions are being created. Something has to give. This is absolutely pivotal and I wish that all solicitors in private practice would think more deeply about this. If the pressures just noted continue, and the recent credit crunch crisis gives us cause to believe that they are likely to increase, then some fundamental changes are needed.

I submit that there are only two sustainable strategies here. The first is for in-house departments to continue working in the traditional and time honoured way, with the usual combination of in-house work and external service, but to be radically more efficient in so doing. The second strategy is for General Counsel to collaborate in one way or another and so share the costs of some common legal expenses. In short, the options are either to cut the costs, and I call this the 'efficiency strategy'; or to share the costs, which I refer to as the 'collaboration strategy'. (A third strategy, the 'elimination strategy', involves stopping doing certain kinds of legal work, but I regard this as a subset of the efficiency strategy.)

The good news for clients, brought by this book, is that both the efficiency strategy and the collaboration strategy are more achievable today than ever before. In relation to new efficiencies, there are clearly many opportunities for lawyers to run tighter ships. For example, many back-office and administrative functions can be systematized, relocated, or outsourced. More, if in-house lawyers use online status and financial reporting tools to manage their external firms collectively, further efficiencies are likely to result. More fundamental, though, is bringing new efficiencies to the actual delivery of legal services. My aim throughout these pages is to show that novel ways of working in law are rapidly emerging, for in-house teams and law firms. For example, there is the promise of engaging less costly labour to carry out routine and repetitive legal work. As Chapter 2 shows, this is the era of offshoring, subcontracting, home-sourcing, and more. Further, there is also the possibility of ever greater computerization (systemization, packaging, and commoditization), using increasingly mainstream tools such as automatic document drafting systems and e-learning applications. These new tools and new efficiencies are relevant not just for streamlining and taking the cost out of current work. These are the tools that will enable in-house lawyers to grapple with broader and potentially graver challenges, most notably in legal risk management. Every General Counsel with whom I speak suggests that their primary function is the management of legal risk; but they are ready to acknowledge that conventional one-to-one consultative advisory service cannot be extended across their organizations to help manage all legal risks. It simply is not possible to have a lawyer on the shoulder of all non-lawyers, and so different tools and methods are needed.

Similarly, we have never been better equipped to encourage and introduce collaboration, fuelled by various emerging technologies. In a world where social networking systems such as Facebook, and knowledge sharing tools such as Wikipedia, are taking humanity by storm, it is a short leap for General Counsel, by analogy, as suggested in Section 4.7, to share and syndicate legal advice and documents, and to club together to tackle problems that they collectively endure, such as regulatory compliance.

Are General Counsel rushing forward with gusto to embrace either or both the efficiency and collaboration strategies?[24] By and large, they are not. When I speak to them, they agree that, in theory, they need to pursue either or both of the efficiency or collaboration strategies. Indeed, at every meeting I attend on the subject, violent agreement breaks out and it is acclaimed that this must be the way ahead. So what is the problem?

In fact, there are at least two problems. The first is that General Counsel, especially in the UK, seem to have little appetite for investing their own time,

---

[24] For an indication of the relatively modest level of take-up of advanced IT by UK in-house legal departments, see 'Technology: a ten-year view', a special report: (October–December) 3(4) *PLC Law Department Quarterly*. See <http://www.practicallaw.com/lawdepartment>.

energy, or money in actually developing efficiency or collaboration solutions. They are busy people; and technology planning and implementation is rarely their core competency. Asking them to pause to reinvent their services and the way they work is like urging them to change the wheel on a moving car. Ideally, they would prefer pre-packed, off-the-shelf solutions that save cash, developed by law firms, and delivered to them with the minimum of hassle. I exaggerate a little, but not much.

This problem relates to the second one—there is little incentive for law firms themselves to support the efficiency or collaboration strategies. Most leading firms have been enjoying unprecedented prosperity.[25] Why should they destabilize their businesses with potentially disruptive innovations when clients seem indifferent and competitors themselves are inactive? This is a version of 'the innovator's dilemma' as introduced in Section 2.6.

The textbook response that most strategy consultants and commentators would venture is quite simple—a law firm should innovate, and try to anticipate its clients' needs ahead of competitors, so that it creates competitive advantage. However, I find that many successful law firms are more anxious to avoid competitive disadvantage than to secure a lead. Even the finest firms are happy to be part of an elite grouping rather than to lead the pack.

For quite different reasons, then, most General Counsel *and* leaders in law firms of today are not sufficiently incentivized or innovative to pursue the efficiency and collaboration strategies. So, what might break this mould? A genuinely innovative law firm could; one that went out on a limb and launched ground breaking solutions. So might new legal service providers, entrepreneurs, or businesses backed by external finance (as permitted under the Legal Services Act perhaps), who challenged the very sustainability of the business model underlying traditional in-house departments and conventional law firms. A third option is that General Counsel, in the not too distant future, will find the cost pressures on them to be truly intolerable and will have little choice but to overhaul the way they work internally and how they source external legal service. But in-house lawyers should not be waiting for meltdown. They should be preparing for the challenge. In so doing, they should bear in mind, although some do not seem to grasp this, that they have very considerable purchasing power. Today and for years to come, I suspect, for major clients certainly, it will be a buyers' market. I simply cannot

---

[25] At the time of writing, however, the fall-out of the credit crunch and the rather uncertain economic conditions cast serious doubt over whether leading law firms will be able to maintain their high levels of profitability in the next few years without taking radical cost-cutting measures.

understand why General Counsel do not push external law firms far harder than they do today. The world's top 100 law firms are sustained, in large part, by the top 1,000 businesses. By becoming more demanding and discerning, these businesses have it within their grasp to redefine legal service.

With regard to technology, I do appreciate that legal departments' internal IT strategies are inhibited, and not least by a lack of cash (ironically, while the budget for a monster piece of litigation may be almost unlimited, funds are rarely available for IT or knowledge systems that might prevent legal problems from arising in the first place). Another barrier is that, generally, the technology that in-house lawyers would like to use does not align with the mainstream technology and technologists within organizations. Other than in the bottom-left of the Client Grid, the IT that is central, for example, to the running of manufacturing, retail, or insurance companies bears little relation to the systems discussed in this chapter. It is also not unreasonable to say that many in-house lawyers lack insight into what is actually possible now and likely to be possible soon in the world of legal technology. This is not true of all legal departments. But it is of most.

Vitally, though, General Counsel should bear in mind that they do not need to become specialists in IT-enabled efficiency or collaboration. They should expect this of the law firms that serve them, because these private legal businesses have far greater technical know-how and resources; and, in many cases, they are charging enormous fees, so that some innovation from them can reasonably be expected. In-house counsel seem generally unaware of the influence they can and should have on law firms' IT strategy. On average, for example, UK law firms spend about 7 per cent of their fee income on technology. Yet only a very small proportion of this investment is ever directed to systems for clients. In terms of the Law Firm Grid, most of the expenditure is below the horizontal line. This is partly due to law firms' conservatism and aversion to innovation but, much more significantly, it is because most clients are not sufficiently demanding. If clients asked more resolutely and regularly, for instance, for online knowledge resources, or collaborative work spaces, or e-learning, or document assembly tools, or litigation support systems, then law firms would have little choice but to respond; and respond positively. Again, if clients demanded that law firms decompose their work into separate tasks and were urged to multi-source, in the manner I suggest in Chapter 2, then they would generally toe the line, especially in tougher market conditions, for fear of losing business. This may be unfortunate news for law firms, but one important way for legal departments to overcome their lack of funds is by sharing the systems and innovations with their external advisers in the spirit of the converging Grids, as sketched out in Section 5.4.

The main long-term IT challenge for in-house lawyers is to harness the power of technology in tackling their common concerns—compliance, legal risk management, e-mail and document management, and the effective management of law firms. IT, knowledge systems, and e-business can be deployed to good effect in each of these areas and will, in due course, come to fortify what should be a highly professional legal risk function. Few legal departments have recognized this although some have started the journey with very impressive early results.

I must add that it is not at all clear that in-house lawyers are monitoring the latest technological developments and are poised to exploit them. Phenomena such as wikis, open-sourcing, online dispute resolution, social networking, and instant messaging may look like passing fads or techno-babble to many, but, as this book claims, they are likely to transform the way we live and work, the way we commune and collaborate. Are these new systems being factored into the strategic planning of most legal departments? Are in-house Counsel encouraging law firms to think strategically here? Not quite yet, I fear.

In managing external law firms and embracing either or both efficiency and collaboration strategies, I am suggesting that in-house legal departments need to be much more strategic and businesslike. More than this, though, in-house lawyers should not think that they are immune from the disintermediation that I suggest hovers as a threat over lawyers in firms. Just as I advocate that law firms must decompose their work into constituent tasks and identify the most efficient ways of sourcing each, then precisely the same approach should be taken by in-house lawyers. The same difficult questions must be asked. Just as it may not be commercially justifiable to have expensive solicitors operating out of expensive city centre offices when they rarely, if ever, see clients, then so too with in-house functions. The various options of out-sourcing, off-shoring, home-sourcing, and the rest, are as relevant for in-house legal departments as they are for law firms.

In-house lawyers will only survive if they can add relevant value over and above alternative sources of legal service. On the face of it, there is a strong case for highly specialist in-house lawyers or wise and experienced generalists who have an intimate understanding of the business of which they are a part, and the industry in which they sit. These internal trusted, expert advisers should play a pivotal role in managing legal risk, resolving and avoiding legal difficulties, overseeing and enabling transactions, directing multi-sourced projects, perhaps even in designing online legal support services, and certainly monitoring and ensuring compliance. It is not obvious, however, that less skilled in-house lawyers of the traditional variety, whose

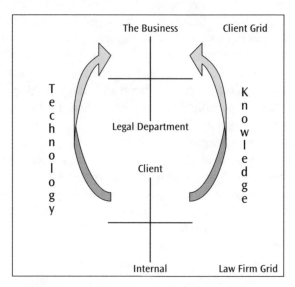

Fig. 5.7 Disintermediation of In-house Lawyers

work is largely routine, will make the cut in the long term. And as the Law Firm and Client Grids come together, client relationship systems and online legal services of law firms will no doubt insinuate their way directly into the top-left and top-right quadrants of the business, missing out the in-house counsel, as illustrated in Figure 5.7.

Does this mean we are shortly to witness the end of in-house lawyers? I think it unlikely, though not unimaginable, that in-house lawyers will fade entirely. As I say, the genuinely expert trusted adviser, who lives and breathes the business, should always be invaluable. But unless the rest are prepared to drive efficiency and collaboration strategies within their own departments and in the law firms that serve them, their future is far from clear.

6

Resolving and Avoiding Disputes

One morning in early January 2008, as I sat at my laptop writing this book, I received an unsolicited phone call from a man employed by a claims company. He wondered if I had recently been involved in any accidents. I paused for a short while before answering and, in that hiatus, I thought I could hear him salivating; he was hoping to hear that some calamitous event had recently left me severely disadvantaged. Knowing perfectly well why he was calling, I asked him why he was calling. He explained that his company might be able to secure compensation for me. I explained, with no regret, that I had suffered no relevant injuries.

Yet I was troubled by that call. On the one hand, I do think that many of the new-look claims companies serve a serious social purpose—if a citizen has endured significant loss and may be hesitant about approaching a conventional law firm or embarking upon legal proceedings, then these organizations may well provide a route to recompense that was formerly not available. This rather benign view focuses, of course, on the needs of the consumer rather than the motives of the provider. However, and on the other hand, a more cynical interpretation might suggest that these companies are encouraging people to contrive claims where no real loss or genuine inconvenience has been endured; and it is a short hop from there to a society where legal action is regarded as a source of income rather than a form of restitution. I share the nervousness of many who worry that the work and marketing of claims companies will give rise to a more litigious society in the UK. And this nervousness, I am quick to add, also extends to lawyers who are 'ambulance chasers', as it does, in more subtle ways, to contingency fee arrangements (under which lawyers can enjoy a percentage of the damages awarded to their clients) and to the external funding of litigation (whereby third parties can fund legal actions and receive substantial payback in the event of success).

I welcome greater access to dispute resolution but condemn people (lawyers and citizens alike) who play the system. I find it depressing, for example, that otherwise law-abiding citizens stretch the truth to support suspicious whiplash claims when there are car accidents, or exaggerate the losses suffered when formulating their claims for damages or insurance. These are no less dishonest than the often fraudulent claims of those who sue local authorities, maintaining that they have been injured by tripping over uneven slabs on pavements.[1] I salute attempts to streamline and speed up dispute resolution processes but am concerned that the improved system might make it easier for the dishonest, vexatious, and the avaricious to pursue their own dubious ends. I want citizens and organizations to be able to assert their legal rights but I will work to resist the emergence of a culture that is compensation-obsessed, and excessively adversarial, combative, litigious, and claims-conscious.

I know that red-blooded litigators will dismiss the last few paragraphs as armchair idealism. Many court lawyers will say that the name of the dispute game is gladiatorial combat, and any thoughts of greater cooperation amongst warring parties are naive and misplaced. At the risk of getting sued, I generally regard this as rhetorical posturing on the part of senior lawyers that is more often self-serving than client-facing. Of course, in disputes where the very life of an organization may be at stake, a wholly robust stance is likely to be taken and a fight to the bitter end, using the full force of the law and lawyers, may well seem inevitable and even understandable. But we should not claim in the grand landscape of dispute resolution that such conflicts litter the terrain. And we should also be alive to the possibility that head-on conflict, even in the weightiest of disagreements, may not, ultimately, be in the interests of any parties involved (aside from the lawyers).

I accept that human beings and organizations will tend to have disagreements. Even in peaceful communities and in civilized times, we will find overlapping interests, direct rivalry, and fierce competition, all of which can

---

[1] For a brief but interesting discussion of 'tripping and slipping' cases, see 'Alternative Dispute Resolution: an English Viewpoint', a speech by Lord Phillips, the Lord Chief Justice of England and Wales, 29 March 2008, India, at <http://www.judiciary.gov.uk>.

bring parties into some kind of conflict, from mild to extreme. Given that human beings are limited in their generosity, their natural resources, and their will power, disputes are bound to arise.[2] It would be an exceptional society whose inhabitants were never in dispute and, in turn, would have no need for the law. This would require a level of inter-personal accord and coherence that is scarcely imaginable. Aristotle says it all when he notes, 'when people are friends, they have no need of justice'.[3] In contrast, when men are acquaintances, strangers, and competitors, we should surely accept that disagreements are all but inevitable. It does not follow, though, that we should uncritically accept the current mechanisms that our legal systems provide for the handling of disputes—today's lawyers, courts, systems, and processes, underpinned by our prevailing culture, expectations, and even our art and literature (on stage and in novels, for instance, we generally find a stereotypical portrayal of combative litigators in fierce opposition to one another).

In the spirit of this book, I challenge the status quo. As elsewhere in the law, I have no doubt that our current ways of resolving disputes can be decomposed into constituent tasks that could be sourced in different and more efficient ways. I see no reason why the pressures that are leading clients to urge their advisers along the path towards commoditization should not also extend to litigators. Equally, I can find no sensible objection to investigating the greater use of information technology (IT) in the dispute resolution process, both to automate and streamline current working practices and also to introduce radically new and even disruptive technologies. The introduction of new efficiencies and technologies is long overdue. Too often, the expense of litigating in our courts is absurd. Often the cost of litigating exceeds the amount at issue. Much of this expense is down to the intermediaries who sit between those in dispute—solicitors, barristers, technologists, experts, and the court system itself. This traditional legal apparatus, an industry that has been built on human conflict, is frequently unwieldy and often unfit for purpose. The heavy-handed involvement of lawyers and courts can distort the process of resolving disputes, diverting focus from the parties to their advisers, driving an often unnecessary wedge between the clients themselves, and incurring disproportionate costs. As elsewhere in this book, where we find intermediaries, I entertain the possibility of

---

[2] For a more detailed and broader discussion of the consequences in law of various 'truisms' about 'human nature', see HLA Hart, *The Concept of Law* (Oxford: Oxford University Press, 2nd edn, 1994) 192–200.

[3] Aristotle, *Nicomachean Ethics* (trans, T Irwin) (Indianapolis: Hackett, 2nd edn, 1999) Book VIII, Ch 1, 120.

disintermediation—removing the middle men from the process. And where there are gross inefficiencies, I suggest that fundamental overhaul should be considered. I go further: if we can find ways of avoiding disputes altogether, then we should not shirk from examining these as well. And when we cannot prevent or pre-empt disputes, we should be looking hard for ways to contain disagreements amicably and to avoid unnecessary escalation. These are all avenues that I explore in this chapter.

6.1 Reforms and changes

As a springboard for my discussion about the resolution and avoidance of disputes, I begin by considering three relatively recent attempts to bring about improvements to our justice system—the reforms of Lord Woolf, the adoption of alternative dispute resolution (ADR), and a government initiative launched at the peak of the dotcom era.

Turning first to Lord Woolf, in March 1994, Lord Mackay, the then Lord Chancellor, announced there was to be a review of the rules and procedures in the civil courts in England and Wales. He invited Lord Woolf to lead this inquiry. At that time, Lord Woolf was a Lord of Appeal in Ordinary in the House of Lords (a Law Lord); later, from 1996 to 2000, he would be Master of the Rolls; and, in mid-2000, would be appointed the Lord Chief Justice of England and Wales, a position he held until 2005. During that decade, he became a towering influence on reforms of the courts and the Judiciary; both constitutional reforms and changes to the working practices of judges and the legal profession. I was delighted to be appointed as IT Consultant to Lord Woolf in early 1995. It seemed to me then that the very appointment of someone who specialized in legal technology was of itself significant. I did not know of any other prior law reform initiative in the UK that had taken IT particularly seriously.

The aims of Lord Woolf's review were, in summary: to improve access to justice; to reduce the cost of litigation; and to reduce the complexity of the rules and terminology. A tall order. The review itself became known as the *Access to Justice* inquiry. In June 1995, Lord Woolf produced an interim report.[4]

---

[4] *Access to Justice—Interim Report* (Woolf Inquiry Team, June 2005), available at <http://www.justice.gov.uk>.

And, in July 1996, he published his final report,[5] together with a set of draft rules, proposing a unified body of rules to replace the Rules of the Supreme Court and County Court Rules.

Lord Woolf recommended a new landscape for civil litigation. In the new world he advocated, he suggested that civil litigation should be: avoided wherever possible; less adversarial and more cooperative; less complex; more certain with shorter timescales; and more affordable, predictable, and proportionate. He recommended that parties should be placed on more equal footing (financially); that there should be a clearer division of judicial and administrative responsibilities; that the courts and judges should be more litigant-oriented; that there should be a more effective deployment of judges; and that the civil justice system should be more responsive to litigants' needs.

When the Labour party came to power in England in May 1997, after reviewing Lord Woolf's recommendations alongside various proposals for the reform of the Legal Aid system, they published a White Paper in December 1998, entitled *Modernising Justice*.[6] This led, in April 1999, to the start of the first phase of the implementation of a major suite of civil justice reforms, largely as envisaged by Lord Woolf.

There is some dispute amongst litigators and commentators as to the lasting impact of Lord Woolf's reforms. For my part, I believe that his articulation of the shortcomings of the civil justice system was definitive and that his recommendations themselves have had enormous practical impact, not simply in changing the rules, procedures, and practices, but also in shifting the culture of dispute resolution in England and Wales. The system that has emerged still suffers from many imperfections but, for the purposes of this book, I am drawing attention to the broad thrust—a government-backed set of reforms that have moved some way to reducing the costs, complexity, and inaccessibility of the English justice system.

Lord Woolf's proposed reforms in the mid-1990s also dovetailed with the growing interest in and success of ADR. The result today is that far fewer cases are pursued through the courts than in March 1994; and many litigators no longer operate as conventional court lawyers.

It is worth dwelling on the ADR movement—this phenomenon that pre-dated and then ran in parallel with Lord Woolf's Inquiry and the later

---

[5] *Access to Justice—Final Report* (Woolf Inquiry Team, July 2006), available at <http://www.justice.gov.uk>.
[6] *Modernising Justice: The Government's Plans for Reforming Legal Services and the Courts* (December 1998, Cm 4155), available at <http://www.justice.gov.uk>.

implementation of his proposals. I first encountered ADR in the early 1990s, when I was working at the international law firm, Masons (now Pinsent Masons). I was asked to edit an explanatory and promotional booklet on ADR for the UK firm. It had been drafted by Tony Bunch (later to be Managing Partner of the firm), who had just returned from many years in our Hong Kong office and was re-establishing his practice in London. In Asia, we learned, there had been many positive experiences of using methods of resolving disputes that were quite different from conventional litigation. Tony brought news of mediation, conciliation, adjudication, mini-trials by neutrals, and several more techniques that enabled disputes to be resolved away from traditional judges and the shadow of the courts. At the time, Masons was the leading global practice in construction law and its particular focus was large-scale litigation. The firm was in the middle of advising on the Channel Tunnel dispute, then one of the largest cases in European legal history, both in terms of the size of the claim and the very large number of documents involved. Admittedly, this case was far from typical. But there always was a wide range of significant construction disputes on the books of the firm—and conventional, mainstream litigation was taken, almost without question, as the definitive route to resolving these conflicts. In short, large-scale litigation was the lifeblood of the firm, and so suggestions of ADR seemed exotic if not outlandish.

Eighteen years on, in Pinsent Masons as in many major law firms, ADR (in its various manifestations) has become a mainstream tool. Litigation is no longer seen as the single dominant means of settling differences. Across the English legal system, the most commonly used form of ADR is mediation. Where parties (itself, sadly, a term that smacks of the courts) do not manage to settle their differences by negotiating on their own, the services of a mediator can be retained—as an impartial catalyst who helps to identify an outcome with which the parties are comfortable. The mediator does not judge or determine issues; nor can the mediator impose a decision. Without needing to resort to courts or formal proceedings, the mediator often helps parties to reach a pragmatic and voluntary settlement in a manner that is invariably less public, formal, confrontational, and debilitating than litigation; and in a way that is often more likely than through legal action to preserve good relationships.[7]

---

[7] For an extremely helpful analysis of ADR, see 'Alternative Dispute Resolution: an English Viewpoint', a speech by Lord Phillips, the Lord Chief Justice of England and Wales, 29 March 2008, India, at <http://www.judiciary.gov.uk>.

Nonetheless, it is still strongly argued by many in the litigation fraternity that in disputes where the survival of the parties may be at stake (so-called 'bet the ranch' disputes) all concerned are more likely, or so it is argued, to engage in highly combative, gladiatorial combat. Others counter that this excessively confrontational approach is in the interests of neither party and that a more conciliatory settlement of conflict is more rational for all concerned. Experts in 'game theory' should be let loose here, pondering and weighing the various incentives and motivations for escalating disputes as against handling them in a more measured and mellow manner.[8]

In any event, Lord Woolf's reforms and the ADR movement have, in combination, given rise to a shift of emphasis in the much changed world of dispute resolution, away from court-based litigation as the natural first port of call when a serious dispute arises. Can more fundamental change be envisioned? With one exception, I have found, amongst policy-makers and litigators alike, an apparent reluctance to think about more radical transformation of courts and litigation. The exception was *civil.justice*, a consultation paper issued by the Lord Chancellor's Department in September 1998.[9] This was the result of an exciting initiative led by Geoff Hoon MP, then the Minister of State at the Department. Perhaps best known, some years later, as the Secretary of State for Defence during the invasion of Iraq, Geoff Hoon at that time was preoccupied with the civil justice system and how it might be improved and even overhauled. Hoon led the *civil.justice* initiative with great enthusiasm and considerable integrity. The title of the paper, which may not have withstood the harsh test of time, reflected the excitement in 1998 over the dotcom movement. Hoon wondered about the impact of the Internet on the legal system and set up what was known as the Civil Justice IT Strategy Development Group, of which I was an active member. In the second chapter of the consultation paper, some fundamental assumptions about the civil justice system were challenged, under sixteen headings. For example, we questioned whether or not the work of the civil courts needs to be conducted in physical courtrooms with parties appearing in person; whether the resolution of disputes is best conducted on an adversarial basis; whether presentation of legal arguments orally is central to the administration of justice; whether the legal profession is well or best organized as a two-tier

---

[8] Game theory seeks to provide mathematical models for decision-making, where the success or otherwise of choices made by individuals are dependent on the choices of others. See J Kay, *The Truth About Markets* (London: Penguin, 2003) 195–6, 209–10, and 242–5.

[9] *civil.justice: resolving and avoiding disputes in the information age*, a consultation paper issued by the Lord Chancellor's Department (September 1998).

profession; and whether the civil justice system concerns the resolution and not the avoidance of disputes. These were issues that I and other members of the group felt had been skirted around in previous reviews of civil justice, including Lord Woolf's. We further felt that the advent of the Internet presented an opportunity to rethink civil justice and to take no institutions or practices for granted.

Around sixty responses to the consultation paper were received, from a wide cross-section of interested parties, including lawyers, consumer groups, court users, and judges. And in June 2000, the Lord Chancellor's Department responded by publishing a strategy paper, *civil.justice.2000*.[10] By this time, Geoff Hoon had left the Department. His successor, as champion of the initiative, was the Parliamentary Secretary, David Lock MP, who brought fresh energy and support. Indeed, in my view, that strategy paper represents the most promising and ambitious statement of government reform of the court system, advocating, for example, virtual hearings, electronic case files, and video conferencing.

Alas, when David Lock lost his seat in Parliament and was no longer driving the programme ahead, the boldness of the strategy paper was not embraced by his successors, and the government simply did not follow through. In the background, and this is a running theme, HM Treasury was reluctant to make funds available for radical improvements to the court system. In short and tragically, the impetus was lost. A few relatively minor investments were made but, to this day, the fundamental questions we asked remain substantially unanswered and the proposed reforms remain unimplemented.

Nor have practising lawyers been inclined to challenge the status quo. Indeed I sometimes hear senior lawyers and judges discussing some of the assumptions identified in *civil.justice* but in tones of uncritical acclamation rather than reasoned reflection. I hear, for example, that the adversarial system, oral pleading, and the split profession are golden threads or jewels in the crown of our justice system. This may well be right but rarely is supporting evidence adduced. We cannot assume these claims to be true *a priori* (as philosophers would say). If we are serious about the future of our court and justice systems, we should not be afraid to ask bold questions and to challenge conventional assumptions. Intellectual honesty and sound policy-making

---

[10] *civil.justice.2000: a vision of the civil justice system in the information age*, a strategy paper issued by the Lord Chancellor's Department (June 2000).

demand that there should be no sacred cows. To some extent, then, my purpose here is to reignite some of the debate we started in 1998, even though I am just scratching the surface of some profound issues. I do not, in fact, address the three issues just mentioned; but I encourage others to do so. However, I do explore two of the major themes of *civil.justice*—the need for congregating in physical courtrooms to settle disputes (Section 6.6) and for dispute avoidance as well as dispute resolution as a responsibility for the legal profession (Section 6.7). Further, I call once again, throughout the chapter, for the more widespread adoption of a range of information technologies that would help to bring our justice system from the nineteenth into the twenty-first century.

6.2 Decomposing dispute resolution

As elsewhere in this book, I start by looking at law firms. The intuition of many battle-hardened litigators in private practice is that the relative uniqueness of the cases they handle means that the heart of their work will be largely untouched by advanced technology and other modern efficiencies. They can see that their deal-making colleagues should be wary of future developments in IT and trends such as outsourcing, but many in the world of dispute resolution anticipate no IT-based alternative to their basic conventional craftsmanship. This, I feel, is short-sighted. I take the view that solicitors involved with dispute resolution, especially in litigation and arbitration, should be considering where their work fits along the evolutionary path that I chart out in Section 2.1 and should be assessing the possibilities of decomposing and multi-sourcing (see Section 2.5) as carefully as their non-contentious colleagues.

Today, many law firms treat the handling of a dispute as a single, monolithic, indivisible job that is given to them to handle in its entirety. However, even at a glance, it can be seen that the dispute resolution work that they undertake can be decomposed into a variety of constituent tasks. For example, one component task is legal research. Much of the analysis and exploration of the law, as it applies to any particular case, is often undertaken by fairly junior lawyers whose output, although well intentioned, is not always especially expert; and often consumes considerable time because the novices in question are not entirely familiar with the field. In a sense, this was the premise or mischief that led to the establishment in 1992 of the US based company, LRN.[11] Dov Seidman, a Harvard law graduate with a passion for delivering legal services differently, set up LRN to build a network of legal academics, retired judges and practitioners, and other specialists who, when appropriately briefed, could produce first-rate legal research in very short order. Seidman argued to General Counsel that, in major disputes, in-house legal departments should handle legal research separately, diverting it away from junior lawyers in external law firms towards LRN's dedicated legal research business. In the language of Section 2.5, this often became a form of subcontracting or local outsourcing. Some major international corporations even came to insist that all legal research, for which their external law firms would charge in excess of a given sum, instead be passed to LRN.

Another component task of litigation is document management. In any dispute, there are documents to identify, gather, organize, index, and review. While, again, this task is often passed to junior lawyers, there are growing bodies of specialist companies which have teams of paralegals who have greater experience in document management and are supported by more advanced systems and processes. While some paralegals remain within law firms, increasingly their services are being delivered by third parties — in the terminology of Section 2.5, this might be a species of de-lawyering or, on other occasions, a type of outsourcing.

When the documents involved have been originated and are stored electronically, this raises the formidable challenge, discussed in more detail in Section 6.3, of electronic disclosure. A few firms have built their own internal resource to cope with this challenge but many more accept that this highly technical job is best left to third party specialists. Equally, once documents are identified and organized, they may be stored for consultation, manipulation and search, by litigation support systems (see Section 6.3). And, once again, while some firms have their own litigation support capability, external third party providers are often more experienced and expert.

Decomposition of dispute resolution work will also identify a further task, that of project management. In large disputes especially, the organization, progression, and control of all related resources (people, parties, advisers, documents) in accordance with strict timetables, is essentially a project management task (see Section 4.8). Although, as I say on other occasions in this book, many solicitors in English law firms will say that their central task as litigators is that of project management, I challenge the extent to which

---

[11] <http://www.lrn.com>.

many lawyers are genuinely trained and skilled in this complex area. Yet again, this is another task that can be de-lawyered and subcontracted to external specialists.

And so, in dispute resolution, we can already see that legal research, document management, electronic disclosure, litigation support, and project management can all be parcelled out from law firms that traditionally would have been responsible for all these tasks from start to finish. It might well be asked what is left for law firms to do, once these various component tasks have indeed been distributed elsewhere. Certainly, we should expect law firms to formulate and advise upon the strategy and tactics for a dispute, and perhaps to be involved in ongoing negotiations (though this is an area of expertise in which full-time professional negotiators could instead be involved). It is also possible that firms can take on any advocacy but, in England at least, although there are solicitor advocates, this key job still tends to be sourced through expert barristers. Interestingly, barristers withstand decomposition rather well. These skilled, deeply knowledgeable lawyers have not strayed beyond their core competence of delivering legal expertise through opinions and through advocacy in court. There is little there to be sourced in alternative ways. In contrast, the dispute resolution or litigation functions of many law firms are surely threatened by decomposition and multi-sourcing. The underlying imperative here is, as discussed in Section 5.7, clients' growing need to reduce their expenditure on legal matters. If other methods of sourcing can reduce the cost and indeed increase the quality of some constituent tasks of the dispute resolution process, then, as clients come under increasing financial pressure, they will direct their law firms to decompose and multi-source accordingly. Some major law firms will be able to resist this by setting up their own internal capabilities (for example in electronic disclosure and project management) but whether these will be able to compete with leaner, dedicated, often more businesslike third party contractors, remains to be seen.

Perhaps the greatest opportunity here for law firms is for them to take on an oversight and project management function over and above their roles as strategists and tacticians. This would involve firms in: initial analysis of the best ways of multi-sourcing a dispute; allocation and subcontracting of tasks to providers; supervision and quality control of these multi-sourced providers; and branding of the final product. Law firms, in this way, would remain the first and main ongoing point of contact for clients. However, they may face stiff competition here—others, such as in-house lawyers and management consultants, may also see the attraction of overseeing and managing work in this way.

6.3 From litigation support to electronic disclosure

One of my bolder predictions in *The Future of Law* ran as follows: 'The stage is set for major change in the world of litigation. Even by 2000, large-scale or complex litigation without IT will be virtually unimaginable.'[12] At the time, I had in mind the impending impact of litigation support systems. Whatever the worth of my original prediction, I believe, in 2008, that heavy duty litigation without technology is now even harder to conceive—largely because of a phenomenon closely related to litigation support, that of electronic disclosure.

A little history is in order. One of the first applications of IT in the metaphorical front-office of lawyers (as opposed to back-office uses such as word processing and accounting) was litigation support. First introduced in the US in the mid-1960s and embraced more extensively there since then, litigation support systems convinced many practitioners in England and Wales in the early 1990s that IT could directly affect legal practice and the actual delivery of legal service. The attraction of this technology was simple. In large disputes especially, lawyers had to organize and pore through piles of documents. Surely IT could help. Instead of having teams of paralegals and junior lawyers thumbing and fumbling through mountains of files, litigation support technologies promised to streamline the manual processes. Once documents were loaded onto a computer, searching, retrieval, cross-referencing, and annotating could all be supported through IT. Lawyers could locate relevant papers more quickly than using hand-crafted methods.

Three techniques have dominated litigation support over the past twenty years. One approach has been to compile electronic indexes of documents relating to cases. Each document in a case can be represented in a database as a collection of 'objective' features (for example the date of document, author, recipient) as well as subjective features, requiring lawyers' classifications (such as whether a document is privileged or prejudicial to the client's case or raises a particular point of law). Once set up, such a system can sort all documents, for example in date order or by authors' name.

A second and complementary approach to litigation support has used document image processing technology. This relies on a scanning process which can be likened to taking and storing photographs of individual documents, so that this technology can cope well with materials that are neither printed nor typed, such as drawings or documents with handwriting, signatures, marginal annotations, date stamps, and so forth. Users of systems that hold

---

[12] R Susskind, *The Future of Law* (Oxford: Oxford University Press, 1996; paperback edition, 1998) 174.

images cannot search for individual words within the imaged documents, because the text is not held in machine-readable form.

The third technique has been to build a retrieval system that holds not an index but the full text of a collection of papers. This has enabled lawyers to search quickly and easily within the entire text of documents for the occurrence of single words (for example names of individuals, companies, places, or terms such as 'warranty' or 'delay') or for words in combination (for instance the name of a company within a specified number of words or the name of an individual or a phrase such as 'defective software').

Advanced users have found that the greatest benefits of litigation support come with a judicious combination of these three techniques. There is some considerable expertise needed in selecting, for any case at hand, which one or more of the three appropriate technologies should be deployed. This is a decision over which lawyers often agonize.

Some firms have gone further by hyper-linking the documents held in litigation support systems with the opinions and advice being generated by the lawyers, thereby creating a work product management system of sorts.[13]

It should be recognized that none of these litigation support technologies detracts from the need to read documents in the first place. In the absence of what are known as 'natural language processing' technologies, it is hard to see how computers can undertake an initial review of documents. This means that any competent lawyer or paralegal has to look through case documents once, for it is only during this first pass that the relevance or otherwise of the documents can be assessed. One aim of litigation support, it might therefore be said, is to ensure that full sets of documents should not need to be read more than once.

What other advantages does litigation support bring? Some lawyers hanker after strategic benefits: in complex cases, such as large-scale commercial, construction, or computer disputes, it is often said that the party who has mastery of the documents will enjoy a clear advantage over others; and so, well conceived systems can provide this edge. More prosaically, the overriding aim for other lawyers who use these systems is to handle the documentation more efficiently and so control the costs of disputes. Whether litigation support in fact reduces the cost of litigation is not clear, however. One view I hear from seasoned users is that these systems enable lawyers to do far more for their clients (more thorough and comprehensive work) in the available time but for the same (but not lower) fees.

[13] On work product management, see Susskind (n 12 above) 198–9.

I should also mention reluctant users—some lawyers, of Luddite inclination, only use litigation support defensively. They would prefer not to be users at all but are sometimes motivated into deploying the technology by a fear of being left behind; when, for example, opposing parties have indicated they are using IT (or it is suspected that they are).

How widely have litigation support systems been adopted? Was I hopelessly misguided in predicting that, by 2000, large-scale or complex litigation without IT would be virtually unimaginable? On balance, I was misguided but not perhaps hopelessly so. In the US, the take-up over the last decade has been far greater than in the UK. There is, and has been since 2000 or so, a strong expectation amongst American firms and clients that serious disputes involving large numbers of documents are best handled with the support of technology. This is not to say that there are no advanced users and sophisticated suppliers in England. On the contrary, some are as leading-edge as can be found anywhere. However, the technology is far from pervasive; in my experience (mainly from my consulting work), a comparatively small number of English practices use the technologies as a matter of course and only a similar proportion of clients insist on their usage. I find this remarkable. Certainly, if I had to instruct lawyers on a document-intensive, high value dispute, I would not countenance the use of manual methods alone. A well designed litigation database is immeasurably more useful and efficient than, say, card files and yellow sticky notes.

Why, then, has the uptake of litigation support been relatively modest, in England at least? Once again, echoing my observation in Section 5.7 about incentives, I suspect that conservative law firms would prefer to stay in their comfort zones, hang on to the old ways of working, and perpetuate a system (hourly billing) that rewards cumbersome manual methods rather than streamlined electronic techniques of document management. In short, if the main impetus for litigation support is to come from law firms alone, progress in many corners of the profession is likely to be slow. Solicitors and barristers need to be driven harder. This is a sad indictment of clients. I simply cannot understand why commercially savvy clients, whether in-house lawyers or lay people, do not demand that large piles of documents are organized electronically. Why pay for systemic inefficiency? Clients (in-house lawyers and top managers) should be more knowledgeable and demanding. Judges should also shoulder some of the responsibility and be more insistent. In their expanding role as case managers and applying their conventional powers to award costs or not (depending, for example, on whether a party's expenses have been reasonable), judges could help to modernize the practices of law firms. If disputes can be resolved more quickly and at lower cost by using IT, then they surely should be, whether or not this is in the financial interests of law firms.

In fairness, there are two credible counter-claims to this line of argument. The first is that litigation support is wonderful or at least beneficial but only suitable for the largest of disputes, those that involve vast quantities of documents. Where the document load is smaller, it can be suggested, there is no point in using litigation support. A sledge-hammer to miss a nut, I have heard it called. Although superficially plausible, this trajectory of thinking is wrong-headed. Accomplished users (in stark contrast to non-users who speculate) invariably report that litigation systems are invaluable whatever the size of case—in all disputes, there are documents to administer, and IT is invariably more efficient at this than manual systems. The argument-from-size is not supported by experience.

A second defence focuses on cost. The common concern here is that litigation support systems are prohibitively expensive; a position caricatured by the no-doubt apocryphal tale of the international corporation whose in-house lawyers, in defending a massive claim, 'exceeded the unlimited budget' that had been allocated to them for litigation support.

Understandably, the prospect of large up-front expenditure on litigation databases horrifies many clients. More than this, early investment in IT is also inconsistent with the post-Woolf landscape for dispute management, which urges early resolution and not strategic preparation for a long-term wrangle. Be in no doubt—the euphoria of a negotiated settlement can be diluted dramatically by the appearance of a titanic bill for litigation support. A sophisticated response to this argument-from-cost holds that the speedy set-up of powerful litigation systems can of itself bring about earlier and more favourable settlement. This was always the view of one of the doyens of litigation support in the US, Deanne Siemer.[14] One of her tactics as a trial attorney was to load documents into a database at a very early stage in the dispute, run some standard queries (she maintained a library of these), and freak the other side by showing an early and apparently uncanny mastery of the evidence.

The argument-from-cost is also weakened by changing patterns in the use of IT. Remember that in the early days of litigation support, most of the documents that were being loaded into these systems had been originated on

---

[14] In my early days of working on litigation support technology, I found one of her (co-authored) books to be very useful—DC Siemer and DS Land, *Wilmer, Cutler & Pickering Manual on Litigation Support Databases* (New York: John Wiley, 2nd edn, 1989).

manual or electronic typewriters. The master file on any given project (all the relevant documentation) was invariably a set of papers, often held in a collection of lever arch files. To transfer the master file into a litigation support system of the imaged or full text variety involved scanning these papers or converting them (using optical or intelligent character recognition) into the system. This scanning and converting was costly; hence the up-front expense. Fast forward a decade or so and documents were increasingly being created by word processing and so were in some kind of machine readable form from the outset. It was for this reason that I suggested, in *The Future of Law*, that document management systems were nascent litigation support systems.[15] At the flip of a switch, I said in my book and to clients of law firms, if you set up your electronic filing systems (broadly, document management systems) in a sensible way, then they could easily be re-purposed as litigation systems in the unfortunate event that a dispute arises. The cost implication was clear—if you organized your systems with half an eye to managing the risks of disputes, then the cost of setting up a litigation support system would be modest; it would simply be a document management system used in a different way.

It might be thought today, given the fact that documents (now word processed materials and e-mails) are almost exclusively originated in electronic form, that all organizations, as a matter of course, develop document management systems that can double as litigation systems. Instead, this electronic origination has brought a whole new challenge—that of electronic disclosure (or e-disclosure, also known as e-discovery). I anticipated this phenomenon in the late 1990s while advising senior English judges on likely future trends. But, in the event, the scale and criticality of the issue has extended well beyond my expectations.

Disclosure involves parties to a dispute letting one another know about the existence of relevant documents. It helps them to prepare for trial, by indicating what evidence the other side has. Historically, disclosed documents were hand-written or typed and parties then exchanged bundles of paper. Today, the overwhelming majority of documents are created electronically (using word processing or e-mail), generated in far greater quantity than in the past, many are never printed, most are backed-up while new versions are created, some are deleted (but can be recovered), while information about documents (meta-data) is now also captured (for example dates of creation and amendment). In short, disclosure is no longer about

---

[15] Susskind (n 12 above) 206–7.

piles of paper. Electronic disclosure involves a potentially boundless, high-tech digital trawl through innumerable systems and files for explicit and hidden information and meta-information. For banks especially, the requirement to disclose extends beyond conventional litigation to regulatory investigations where similar demands to make documents available can be made. It is more than a challenge. It is a logistical, technical, and legal minefield.

Logistically, electronic disclosure is particularly daunting for most large organizations, whose electronic filing systems tend to be, frankly, vast, and chaotic.[16] One way of looking at the problem is to think again of master files. While they used to be paper-based, they often no longer exist—the documents relating to a given project, for example, might include e-mails, spreadsheets, databases, presentations, graphics, and video files, as well as conventional word processed documents. Some are printed out and put on file but there is seldom a systematic attempt to bring them all together in one single location, whether paper-based or electronic. The master file has largely disappeared. The problem here is that, when a dispute arises, organizations and their advisers need to isolate all relevant documents. But if they are not collocated in well organized files, this task becomes a search for a digital needle in an electronic haystack.

I have now heard about half a dozen stories of large financial institutions that have settled disputes prematurely and expensively, in anticipation of not being able to cope with the demands of e-disclosure. In the language of Section 3.2, their filing systems could not yield *all but only* the documents they needed. When I speak about IT to General Counsel, especially of global banks with substantial business in the US, I am increasingly finding that electronic disclosure is the only show in town. Anxiety levels are high because they know that their systems for managing documents and e-mails are crude and that the isolation of a complete body of relevant materials is a near impossible task. Even when organizations do have document management systems in place, it is still no trivial task to extract and organize all but only the materials that are relevant for disclosure for the purposes of disclosure. To be sure, this is less of a job than scanning and converting from paper into electronic form, as in days gone by, but unless the document management systems were designed with a view to electronic disclosure (now a vital sign of litigation readiness), the work involved is still daunting.

---

[16] Research conducted by Deloitte in October 2007 (Information Risk Benchmarking Survey) into the preparedness of UK companies for a regulatory request found that, in relation to the possibility of a request by a regulator, only 29 per cent of corporate counsel said they were fully aware of where their company's corporate data were held. See <http://www.deloitte.co.uk>.

Fears about not being able to isolate and disclose e-mails were greatly fuelled by a case in the US, in May 2005, when the financial institution, Morgan Stanley, was ordered to pay US$850 million in punitive damages because of its inability to disclose relevant e-mail documentation. In March 2007, this decision was thrown out on appeal, although the panel did not rule directly on the e-discovery issue.[17]

For the technologist, electronic disclosure constitutes a veritable e-fest. E-disclosure technologists draw on a variety of tools and techniques, including intelligent searching, data mining, and document management systems. Specialist e-disclosure software is also available, with powerful features, including de-duplication ('de-duping') which is especially helpful in trimming down messages that appear numerous times in e-mail chains.[18] When a dispute arises, an organization's preparedness now depends, in part, on its ability to extract data rapidly from its document management systems for disclosure purposes. There are analogies here with the work of auditors in the 1980s. They had to become adept at extracting information from clients' increasingly computerized accounting systems; and so the discipline of computer audit emerged. Perhaps a similar speciality will materialize in law. E-disclosure may also lead to greater use of online case-rooms, which are dedicated, secure websites to which all materials are sent and from which they can be retrieved in manageable quantities. The alternative, the exchange of vast bodies of electronic documents by e-mail, could bring most firms' networks to their knees.

And the volumes are undoubtedly mind-boggling. I recall that about ten years ago, I was asked to advise on a dispute that involved approximately 100 million documents. The client wanted to know how on earth they might manage such a quantity of documents. At the time, I wondered with colleagues whether the case might in fact be impossible to take to trial, precisely because of the vast quantities of materials involved. In the end, they muddled through but today such volumes look modest—on one back-up tape, about the size of a paperback book, it is now possible to store over 100 million pages. And many large organizations have cupboards full of these.

From a legal point of view, uncertainties abound. How much electronic material must be disclosed? Should this extend to meta-data (information about documents, such as dates of amendment)? Who should pay for the

---

[17] <http://www.reuters.com/article/businessNews/idUSN2128294020070321>.

[18] A first rate resource for readers interested in most aspects of e-disclosure can be found at <http://www.chrisdalelawyersupport.co.uk>.

process of recovering data from archives and back-ups? Above all, how can the cost of e-disclosure be rendered proportionate to the value of a claim? So far, the English legal profession's response to these and related questions has been measured. In October 2003, the first sustained piece of analysis appeared in draft. It came from the Commercial Litigators' Forum, an influential group of litigators. Their report on e-disclosure emphasized the scale of the problem and showed that England's Civil Procedure Rules offered insufficient guidance to those who were already beginning to struggle with the proliferation of electronic documents.[19] In October of the following year (2004), another influential report emerged, this time from a working party of the Commercial Court Users' Committee, chaired by a High Court judge, Mr Justice Cresswell.[20] That document concluded, rather optimistically, that current English law was sufficiently flexible to cope with the demands of e-disclosure, largely because of the reasonableness and proportionality tests governing the search for documents under existing Civil Procedure Rules. Nonetheless, it recommended various modest amendments to these rules and to the Commercial Court Guide. In parallel, and more pragmatically, the Litigation Support Technology Group (LiST), a group of experienced litigation technologists, has produced succeeding drafts of a Practice Direction for the use of IT in civil proceedings, which directly address some of the challenges of e-disclosure.[21]

What we have not yet seen in England, however, is a major case before the courts in which the nature, scope, and impact of electronic disclosure have been the subject of dispute between parties. When this happens, and only then, I suspect, will we know the extent to which the English legal system is actually equipped to handle the logistical and technical challenges. I am particularly keen to observe how the principle of proportionality is invoked, so that, on individual cases, the costs of e-disclosure are commensurate with the value of the disputes. I am less sanguine than many litigators and commentators about the ease with which e-disclosure can be accommodated without upheaval into large-scale litigation in England. Further, while the various published reports in England are invaluable, they leave a nagging doubt. They tend to place undue emphasis on where information is physically stored, on what electronic medium it is stored, in what format it is stored, and for what purpose it is stored. The result is that whether or not a

---

[19] <http://www.commerciallitigatorsforum.com>.
[20] Available at <http://www.scl.org>.
[21] <http://www.listgroup.org>.

document might, in law, be disclosable, could turn in the future on some rather arbitrary criteria (for example where a document is stored and in what format) rather than on sound principles of reasonableness or relevance. In any event, clients need help here—not just conventional advice when a dispute arises but legal risk management service in readiness for litigation, so that when trouble looms, the state of their document retention and filing systems enhances rather than hinders their negotiating position. In turn, I anticipate that litigators will be able to differentiate themselves in this area—those familiar with the pitfalls, able to offer early guidance, and equipped with powerful technology (both for isolating data and for searching), will be superior in capability to those who are not yet ready for the avalanche.

We should learn here from other jurisdictions and particularly from the US, where e-disclosure has been the focal point of numerous cases; most notably in the landmark series of decisions by Judge Shira Scheindlin in the Zubulake cases.[22] There is much that English lawyers can learn from these judgments; and from other sources too, such as the work of the Sedona Conference, whose Sedona Principles have been influential in US juristic thinking.[23]

Looking forward, I anticipate that e-disclosure will cast a shadow across much civil litigation (and regulatory investigation work) in the UK. This is why I now say, with even greater conviction, that within a very small number of years, any form of litigation without IT will be scarcely conceivable.

At the same time, and looping back to the earlier discussion about litigation support, the challenge for conventional litigation support systems is far from over. When I wrote about these technologies just over a decade ago, we were grappling with methods for storing and searching through text. Since then, with the increasing capture of voice recordings (for example many financial institutions record dealers' telephone conversations) and the pervasive introduction of CCTV technology, the much more formidable challenge that emerges is that of using search technology to operate across voice and multi-media files as well. We have much to learn here, as we have done in litigation support since the 1970s, from the intelligence services, who have been labouring for years now to perfect systems that can search across sound and video files for important data.

[22] For Zubulake I-V, see <http://www.krollontrack.co.uk/legalresources/zubulake.aspx>.
[23] <http://www.thesedonaconference.com>.

6.4 Case management and electronic filing

It is time now to look at our courts.[24] I have advised on the computerization of the courts in England, in various capacities over the past fifteen years and, since 1998, as IT Adviser to the Lord Chief Justice. Looking back, it is hard not be disappointed at the progress that has been made. The reality in 2008, in England and Wales at least, is that many of our courts remain, in administrative and organizational terms, shamefully antiquated and, in many areas, are in a parlous state. The running of a large system of courts is a massive, document-intensive, information-intensive, and labour-intensive operation. Most of the administrative and management systems that are in use today were developed at a time when the throughput and workload of the courts and lawyers were much lower than they are today. Many of the systems are crude, paper-based, oriented more towards the process of administration than to the community of court users, and increasingly are unable to cope with growing demands placed upon them. Often, this brings unjustifiably high running costs, inefficiencies, errors, delay, poor reputation, and dissatisfaction.

Although few lawyers, judges and officials would put it in these terms, the court system can be regarded, in large part, as a huge information system—an entity that receives, processes, stores, creates, monitors, and disseminates large quantities of documents and information. The current set-up employs large numbers of clerical staff who maintain and run a very large document management capability, which is partly computerized but is very much paper-based too. Experience from other industries and other jurisdictions strongly suggests that the systematic and widespread introduction of better systems would bring great efficiencies and major cost savings. Anyone who doubts the scope for an organizational step change should pay a visit to the back-offices of the Royal Courts of Justice in London and marvel at the piles of papers, files, and ledgers. Well implemented information technologies, displacing papers with systems, would blow away the dust and give rise to more productive, responsive, and effective courts, with swifter and cheaper disposal of individual cases. Improved methods of filing, diarying, communicating, document production, and the management of cases, would bring reduction of delays. There is a vital message here, however, for those who

---

[24] In this and the following sections, my main focus is on the courts of England and Wales. I say very little about the tribunal system. While IT is unevenly spread across our tribunals, some have first rate systems, eg the Traffic Penalty Tribunal—see <http://www.trafficpenaltytribunal.gov.uk>—which should be of direct interest to those who work in the courts.

hold the public purse strings—the productivity gains would not necessarily lead to cost savings to the State. Instead, for the same expenditure, the system could process a larger number of cases more quickly. This, of course, rather diminishes the dreaded 'business case' that so many policy-makers demand; because, in civil justice at least, investments that save expenditure are generally preferred to those that enhance public service.

This is not mere cynicism. It captures the reality of post-Woolf investment in IT. In the two or three years following Lord Woolf's recommendations in his *Access to Justice* inquiry (see Section 6.1), there was little enthusiasm, from either politicians or senior officials, for the technology that he was advocating. However, towards the end of the 1990s, a new wave of ministers and top civil servants at the then Lord Chancellor's Department embraced the idea of an IT-fuelled courts system with some enthusiasm. Sadly, their proposals for the investment of £200 to 300 million in the civil justice system were not accepted by HM Treasury. As I was told, the business case was not compelling. I wondered then about another scenario—closing our courts altogether. Think of the public money that would be saved. Now, that would be compelling! We need a much richer model of business thinking in relation to the courts. Obsessing about reducing short-term costs and failing to account for increases in accessibility combine into a dangerous cocktail that threatens the very future of our justice system.

In the event, a modest fraction of the requisite funds was eventually made available to civil justice. In practice, this allowed the government to put in place a robust technological infrastructure for the court system. This was undertaken in the hope that there might be later investment in systems that could build on this infrastructure. However, very little such funding was ever made available and so we had put in place, crudely, a set-up akin to a sophisticated road system but without any cars.

In summary, since the early 1990s, when I began to advise on the computerization of the courts, the Tory and Labour governments have lamentably under-invested in our courts and the result is an embarrassingly old-fashioned system. I visit and am in contact with courts around the world. Sadly, many seem to be higher-tech than ours. Judges and court users in England have to endure interaction with a public body, many of whose systems and processes have not changed substantially for decades.

I join many lawyers and commentators who advocate reform to formal litigation and the court system in suggesting that one key to a better future would be the introduction of 'case management' technology. In the first instance, of course, case management systems can be deployed well before a case reaches the courts. Within the litigation practice of a law firm, for example, case management systems operate in at least two quite different ways. On the one hand, especially in relation to large, complex, and high-value cases, one category of these systems are, in effect, no more than project management systems, as discussed in some detail in Section 4.8. On the other hand, and more commonly, a different kind of case management system within legal practice supports the organization and flow of high-volume, relatively low-value disputes. The incentive here is simple and maps neatly onto the second and third stages of the evolution of legal service, as I explain these in Section 2.1. If law firms seek to deal with routine and repetitive cases (for example debt collection and low-value personal injury claims) in a bespoke and hand-crafted manner, then it is unlikely that they can do so to a high standard and at the same time turn a reasonable profit. To inject greater efficiency, firms seek to standardize and systematize much of the process of handling and progressing these common claims. Similarly, lawyers who undertake work that is funded by Legal Aid also find that the limited fees available mean that they need to set up case management systems to secure appropriate efficiencies and so make the service viable. However, there is no reason why these case management techniques should not be deployed more widely—whenever there are high volumes, even if the cases are high value, there is considerable scope for standardization, document automation, and the workflow benefits that case management technology can bring.

We can learn much about case management from a system and website of BERR (the Department for Business Enterprise and Regulatory Reform) that streamlines the process of claiming compensation.[25] The Coal Health Claims Unit of BERR has been running two personal injury compensation schemes, paying out at one stage around £1.75 million each day in respect of respiratory and vibration-related illnesses. In 2002, over 300,000 claimants had registered for the schemes, and a further 1,200 new claims were being lodged weekly, in expectation of a final government payout in excess of £6 billion. This has been the biggest personal injury scheme in British legal history and is well suited to systematization. (Note that I am leaving to one side some other controversies that have arisen in relation to these schemes—for example the fees earned by some law firms.)

While their early website originally offered no more than online form-filling, later versions provided a start-to-finish e-claims process. Using the online service, solicitors have been able to register new claims, complete and

---

[25] <https://coalclaims.com/Home.do>.

submit claims forms, monitor the progress of individual claims, update personal details, agree employment histories, and manage their entire caseloads. This service shows the power of case management for solicitors and the potential of such technology for managing cases with the court system.

Unfortunately, discussions of 'case management' in relation to the courts are often fettered by terminological confusions, because the term is used in many different ways. At a high level, I like to distinguish between case *flow* management systems and case *load* management systems. The former help progress individual cases through the courts, while the latter assist with the management of the resources needed for given groups of cases. At a lower level, as listed in Figure 6.1, I identify at least seven categories of case management system for the courts.

This does not make easy reading but I can find no more elegant way to analyse the possibilities. The first type are management information systems, which help politicians, officials, judges, and others to monitor the throughput, costs, and performance of courts. Then, second, are case administration systems: these support and automate the formidable back-office, administrative, and clerical work of running courts. Third are judicial case management systems. These are intended for direct use by judges, to support their work in managing the flow of particular cases for which they have responsibility. The fourth are judicial case management support systems, being the systems used by court staff who assist judges who are involved with case management. The fifth category is non-judicial case management systems, those that help court staff to progress those many cases which are not disposed of judicially. Penultimately, there are case tracking systems that allow court users and other participants who are outside the court system to monitor progress on cases in which they have an interest. [26] Finally, there are document management systems, which—so the thinking runs—store and organize all records and documents relating to cases as 'electronic case files': these files should be able, effectively, to flow quickly and cheaply through the court system and be available, under strict access controls, in electronic form, to authorized users—as an accurate, complete, and up-to-date record.

Each of the seven categories might be better regarded a sub-system of the next generation of court systems. But they are of historical significance too. Fundamental to the Woolf reforms, for example, were two quite different

---

[26] XHIBIT is an example of a case tracking system. It provides online hearing information about cases in the Crown Court in England to police, victims, witnesses, prosecutors, and others. See <http://www.hmcourts-service.gov.uk>.

> management information systems
> case administration systems
> judicial case management systems
> judicial case management support systems
> non-judicial case management systems
> case tracking systems
> document management systems

Fig. 6.1 Categories of Case Management System

categories of case management system. For example, for the 'fast-track' (very broadly, for claims of up to £15,000 in value, other than small claims), Lord Woolf argued that it was vital that the Court Service had efficient, reliable, and effective ways of monitoring and administering all those cases that were following fixed timetables. In terms of the classification above, this required first rate case administration systems. Such systems continue to be evolved in England at a snail's pace. In addition, it was central to Lord Woolf's new landscape that judges became more proactive in the management and progression of cases on the 'multi-track' (also broadly, cases then worth more than £15,000). In this respect, looking to the medium to long term, Lord Woolf envisaged a range of technologies for direct use by judges in support of their new case management responsibilities, largely on the multi-track. In the language used above, what were needed here were judicial case management systems. This was a rather radical new departure and he recommended four categories of case management system: *case tracking systems*, producing daily reminders, progress reports, lists of outstanding tasks, and notices of who has responsibilities for further actions, thus supporting judges in supervising, monitoring, and controlling their cases from start to finish; *case planning systems*, simple, PC-based, project management software to enable judges to generate their own plans and charts for cases, depicting time scales, key events and activities; *telephone and video conferencing*, as important tools for judges in maintaining the progress of cases and keeping in direct contact with parties where formal meetings would be impractical; and *document retrieval systems*, to allow judges to gain access to documents relating to the individual cases on which they are working: including full case histories, pleadings, affidavits, orders, and document bundles for example; and to be able to retrieve these, either as images or as searchable text, from some central location. In the event, other than a very modest deployment of telephone and video conferencing, none of the four has been delivered in earnest. If we are ever disappointed that judges have not fully embraced their new case management responsibilities, perhaps we should not be surprised. They have not been given the tools for the job.

Lord Woolf's recommendations on judicial case management technology did, however, raise a clutch of further issues. For example, it must always be borne in mind that the different kinds of case management systems are *interrelated*, such that judicial case management systems are not entirely separate systems. A key objective for the future is to move towards unified court systems that support all seven case management applications noted above. Case management systems for judges will not, therefore, be separate and distinct applications. Instead, they will draw on much of the same information that is needed for judicial case management support systems and for non-judicial case management systems. It is perhaps best to anticipate court systems of the future as single systems, serving a range of different users; and judges will be one category of user with their own specific requirements. A version of this vision is sometimes referred to as the 'electronic case file'—for each case running through the courts, there should be a single electronic repository, containing both information about the case and documents relating to the case (from skeleton arguments through formal source materials to evidential documents).[27]

This broad thinking—in terms of electronic case files, although not using this terminology—is behind the design of the systems for the new Supreme Court of the UK, which is scheduled to open in 2009. Refreshingly, this is one of the most promising court-related projects with which I have been involved—it is relatively self-contained, the number of users will be small, the quantity of data and throughput of cases will be manageable, and there seem (in early 2008) to be funds sufficient to deliver the systems as specified. I am hoping the Supreme Court systems will be a flagship project for case management (in all senses).

Interestingly, during the course of the Supreme Court project, the need for sound case management systems (of the administrative and document management flavour) has come from another direction—the call for 'electronic filing'. Known in the trade as 'e-filing', this involves, in rough terms, the submission of documents to court in electronic form. For several years now, a number of progressive judges and law firms have been calling for greater use of e-filing in England. In some jurisdictions—for example Singapore—it

---

[27] The electronic case file is also referred to as the 'electronic case record'. A comprehensive discussion of this concept appears in a report prepared in 2001 by a Judicial Working Group led by Mr Justice Cresswell: 'Modernising the Civil Courts—The Judges' Requirements', available at <http://www.court-service.gov.uk>.

is becoming commonplace. At least one major supplier is now offering an e-filing service that can be implemented at no cost to the State and only modest cost to the parties.[28] Accordingly, the Ministry of Justice is taking this whole area very seriously. In so doing, it has opened something of a Pandora's Box, because the officials progressing the initiative quickly and rightly recognized that e-filing cannot be introduced in isolation from a group of related technologies. At first sight, e-filing appears to entail little more than introducing a system that enables lawyers, parties, and others to send documents, securely, reliably, and electronically into the courts. Quite aside from this being mightily less trivial than might be thought (putting in place a robust system to support all the civil courts in the land is not a small undertaking), the success of e-filing also depends on whether there are systems in place to organize the documents upon arrival. For e-filing to work, the courts into which the electronic submissions are being made must have case administration systems and document management systems into which the submitted materials are lodged in an orderly and systematic way. Otherwise, it would be chaotic, with clerks and administrative staff manually filing the innumerable electronic submissions. I liken this to aiming a fire hose into a garden bucket. More than this, though, if the documents so sent are to be useful to judges and officials, then they need to be accessible to them—in the form (in my terms) of judicial case management systems, judicial case management support systems, and non-judicial case management systems. In other words, for e-filing to have any chance of functioning reliably and smoothly, the submissions must slot neatly into electronic case files, to which judges and officials will then have easy access from their desktops. This is not straightforward but it seems to have become the aim of the now very ambitious electronic filing and document management (EFDM) project at the Ministry of Justice. From an early aspiration of some forward-lookers to be able to e-mail documents directly into the courts, we have swung round full circle to trying to develop most of the systems that Lord Woolf recommended but which were not implemented because they did not make the cut at HM Treasury.

While I will continue to support the EFDM project, I am realistic about the prospects of it being delivered on time. It is a reasonable prediction that e-filing will be used in some courts over the next few years. Officials are expecting a start date of 2010 for a national solution, as I understand it. I would hazard an optimistic guess of 2013 as the date by which full roll-out

---

[28] <http://www.lexisnexis.com>.

across the system might therefore have taken place. Even this would require a good following wind, as they say in golfing circles, as well as some heavy duty investment. However, if EFDM goes the way of most public sector projects, we can expect the roll-out date of 2013 to look naive.

Given, in any event, that 2013 is some time away, I have urged the government to consider interim deliverables, perhaps operational pilot systems that might be introduced into a limited number of courts. I always worry about what are known as 'big bang' projects—when the entire solution is introduced in one step and prior to this there are no benefits to be seen. In the meantime—that is to say, before 2013—I think there is an alternative course. I have been encouraged here by the work of a group of specialist solicitors who have developed a system that could turn out to be useful for judges. The lawyers are from the Technology and Construction Solicitors' Association (TeCSA),[29] and their latest in a series of innovations is an online case file facility. This provides participants in a dispute with a dedicated, secure website that can hold a range of relevant documents.[30] Surely judges could also use such a service. Indeed TeCSA's work points to a practical and affordable way in which a basic type of electronic case file could be made available to the Judiciary much earlier than expected. The TeCSA system is similar in concept to the Internet-based, online case-rooms that many law firms now provide to their clients. The document sets available on these sites vary but often include letters of advice and reports prepared by firms; correspondence between parties; expert witness reports; skeleton arguments; databases of evidential materials; case plans and progress reports; financial summaries of fees charged; links to source materials; and collaborative work spaces where firms and clients can work together.

If judges cannot, in the medium term at least, be given their own electronic filing system by the government, why not therefore make online case-rooms available to them too? They could be given access to law firms' sites, although it may be more appropriate if instead they used more neutral online case-rooms provided and hosted by communities of court users, such as TeCSA. These could become the definitive, standardized repositories for given cases, to which, for example, lawyers would send statements of case, defences, and other submissions, while judges could similarly post directions, case plans, and decisions. These would not, of course, be sites containing advice from lawyer to client but would be online stores of the

---

[29] <http://www.tecsa.org.uk>.
[30] <http://www.tecsacase.co.uk>.

documentation that is generally shared amongst parties to a dispute, including the judge. Such a service would not be part of, or automatically linked to, any court systems. If court documents were made available in these online case-rooms, they would need to be transferred there by a process not unlike sending an e-mail. Nor would these sites be integrated with court diaries or listing systems. Instead, they would be stand-alone, online collections of papers. I would not advocate this approach if substantial funds were clearly available and no-one was worried about delay. In its favour is that it would offer a workable solution now for the judges and the courts and would also be a major step forward towards full-scale, electronic case files.

Whatever solution is preferred, one issue that remains unresolved in relation to e-filing in the English courts or lodging documents in case-rooms is the format in which electronic documents should be submitted. There are strong arguments and emerging technologies in support of the view that electronic documents should be organized not as separate items but as an interlinked body of documents, so that when judges come to browse, it will be akin to roaming around the Web rather than opening a series of distinct Word documents.

Take a side-step for a moment from the intricacies of e-filing to the visionary words of MIT professor, Marvin Minsky, who once said, I understand, that people of the future will be amazed that there used to be libraries with books that did not talk to one another (or words to that effect). A pioneer of artificial intelligence, Minsky was anticipating no fewer than two developments—that texts of the future would be directly linked to one another and that they would automatically update and revise one another. We might need to wait a while for the second possibility but lawyers are already comfortable with the first; with navigating through 'hyper-linked' materials. They do so when surfing the Web, browsing their Intranets, and when using online services that allow users to jump easily from, say, a case report to a section of a statute. However, lawyers have been notably less enthusiastic in providing their own work in linked form. Today, when a lawyer submits bundles of documents to court, even if they are delivered in electronic form, they rarely have a rich body of internal links. This is a missed opportunity because judges would often find it helpful to navigate around an electronic web-like set of documents. And lawyers unfamiliar with the process of creating an inter-linked suite of documents should be reassured that tools are readily available to help with this job.[31]

---

[31] eg Affinitext—see <http://www.affinitext.com>.

All of this is not simply the indulgence of futurists. In Lord Saville's Bloody Sunday Inquiry (see Section 6.5), the use of electronic filing was standard practice: any documents submitted to his inquiry had to be sent in electronic form. But Lord Saville himself went further and strongly encouraged lawyers not just to submit documents as discrete files. He indeed argued that they should be hyper-linked, joined together so that what came to his Inquiry office and swiftly thereafter into his machine was—effectively—an information system, allowing him to roam amongst arguments, transcripts, formal sources, and evidential material. On this model, the burden on the lawyers is not only to prepare and transmit material electronically but also to insert hypertext links, so that the submissions coalesce into a workable information system. Here we see yet another glimpse of the future of law.

In the light of the historic lack of funding, am I entirely off piste in giving contemplation time to all these developments in case management, electronic case files, and e-filing? I often sense, when discussing such systems, that they are regarded by the mainstream as interesting optional extras akin to sun-roofs, metallic paints, and alloy wheels on cars. I strongly contest this. Case management systems, all seven in combination, should constitute the engine of tomorrow's court system. My hope is that, within a decade and possibly much less, they will indeed come to be widely regarded as central to any modern court system in a civilized twenty-first century society.

6.5 Courtroom technology and judges

Many courtrooms of today are equipped no differently from those of the mid-twentieth century, when modern computers were invented and first used. The actual dispensing of justice, it might be inferred, is a manual, hand-crafted art upon which IT can have little impact. This would be too sweeping an inference. In the spirit of this book, much of what goes on in the court-room can be handled differently and supported by technology. It is true, I am sorry to say, that the systemic under-investment in the modernization of the English courts extends from the back-offices of the courts into the courtrooms themselves. Nonetheless, there have been numerous instances of advanced technology use in English hearing rooms; and over the past decade, the English Judiciary has come to embrace IT with some enthusiasm. These uses of technology offer a clear picture of what is possible today and, with sufficient political will, could be implemented within a modest number of years.

The story of courtroom technology in England is that of a patchwork quilt. There is no elegant way of discussing the various techniques; nor any possibility of synthesizing them together in practice into a single system. If what follows is rather piecemeal, it reflects the object of study. I start in the early 1990s, with a technology known as computer-assisted transcription (CAT). Through CAT, the words spoken in the courtroom as captured by the keystrokes of stenographers are converted into text that appears almost instantaneously on the judge's monitor. There is also a facility to annotate text as it appears. Under the auspices of the Society for Computers and Law, a short research project was commissioned in 1992, that sought to explore the impact of this technology. The study suggested that the use of this technology could reduce the length of hearings,[32] a finding supported by later projects and by the widespread anecdotal evidence of judges who used these systems. Most judges still say that using CAT in their courts cuts time taken by around one-third. CAT is an interesting case study—although I have not heard anyone challenge the proposition that this technology saves time and money (even after deducting the cost of the CAT service), its widespread adoption has not been funded by the government. Its usage today, more than fifteen years on, is largely confined to large disputes (litigation and arbitration), when the parties themselves agree to use and fund the technology.

In the future, perhaps in another fifteen years, with the advent (if you will forgive the jargon) of speaker-independent, continuous speech, multiple-speaker, large vocabulary, voice recognition systems, today's techniques for recording and transcribing—including shorthand writing, tape-recording, and even CAT—may no longer be needed. Thus, proceedings in court may instantaneously, and in real-time, be captured in electronic form, thereby revolutionizing court reporting. (So too with meetings and, for example, the taking of witness statements.) Voice recognition technology will, in due course, immediately deliver polished transcripts, in printed or electronic form. Until then, though, we are left with traditional court reporting and occasional uses of CAT.

Two other courtroom technologies that date to a similar period in the history of the English courts are document display systems and electronic presentation of evidence (EPE). The former ensure that everyone in the courtroom is, literally, on the same page—rather than making a reference to a particular file or folder, then perhaps a tab, and thereafter a page number, and waiting

---

[32] J Plotnikoff and R Woolfson, 'Replacing the Judge's Pen? Evaluation of a Real-time Transcription System' (1993) 1 *International Journal of Law and Information Technology* 90.

for all parties and judges to locate the page manually (a process that can take many seconds), the court's attention can be brought to a particular page by inviting everyone to look at their monitors, upon which the document in question appears for all to see. This undoubtedly saves time, although some judges say that they miss the chance to mark up documents that are presented in this way.

The second set of technologies, known as EPE, reflects the old cliché that a picture is worth a thousand words. Rather than relying exclusively on oral advocacy, court lawyers can present evidence in the courtroom using a wide range of non-verbal tools, including charts, graphs, time lines, maps, diagrams, drawings, sketches, models, animations, reconstructions, and simulations.[33] These can be displayed in the courtroom on individual monitors or projected onto very large displays. A package as common as Microsoft PowerPoint can be used,[34] although for moving images and video and for 3-dimensional work or even holographs, more advanced systems will be deployed. Whatever the techniques, the effects can be striking and memorable. I am still haunted by a simulation that I saw in the early 1990s—this recreated the view in the cockpit of a plane that was crashing, linking the horrendous downward plunge with the recording, as retrieved from the black box, of the voices of the pilots in the final seconds of their lives. Much less dramatically, the extent of a delayed project can be demonstrated powerfully by an animation that compares actual with projected time taken. Or complex movements of funds can be captured in a simple graphic rather than by convoluted verbal summary. In all, this 'tangible' or 'demonstrative' evidence has been more widely adopted in the US and other jurisdictions, where civil juries are more commonplace than in England, where interest in this kind of technology has been confined mainly to criminal cases. Even in criminal cases, however, it is interesting to note that many senior advocates and judges in England harbour reservations about the lack of relevant court procedures to control this use of IT and are alive to the possibility of technology being misused in misleading jurors and judges. At a Society for Computers and Law litigation support conference in 1990, this hesitation was captured by the then Law Lord, Lord Griffiths—in paraphrasing one of Disraeli's aphorisms—by suggesting that 'there are lies, damn lies and graphics'.

---

[33] See eg DC Siemer, *Tangible Evidence* (Notre Dame, Indiana: National Institute for Trial Advocacy, 1996).

[34] See eg DC Siemer, FD Rothschild, ER Stein, and SH Solomon, *PowerPoint for Litigators* (Notre Dame, Indiana: National Institute for Trial Advocacy, 2000).

Yet another technology that has shown potential over the years but has not yet been introduced with fervour across the justice system is participation in court proceedings via video conferencing. Again, the uptake has been greater in criminal work: for bail and remand hearings, conducted through links between prisons and courts; and to enable child witnesses, vulnerable and intimidated witnesses, or witnesses outside the UK, to give evidence remotely.

The incidence of adoption of video conferencing in civil cases has been notably lower. Generally, parties have preferred to gather together for civil combat, despite some authoritative calls for its take-up: by Lord Woolf, in 1996, in his final *Access to Justice* report[35]; by Sir Jefferey Bowman in 1997, in his review of the Civil Division of the Court of Appeal;[36] and, in June 2000, in the *civil.justice.2000* strategy paper issued by the Lord Chancellor's Department.[37] Not long after, in late July 2002, for the first time, video conferencing was used for an application for permission to appeal in a civil case to the Court of Appeal. It was significant that the technology was being used in the upper reaches of the court system. The video hearing, conducted by Lord Justice Nourse, was part of a pilot scheme, linking the Royal Courts of Justice, Cardiff Civil Justice Centre, and Leeds Combined Court. It was realistically expected then, as now, that this technology would help to render the civil justice system quicker, more accessible, and less costly. Crucially, though, its potential goes well beyond civil appeals, and would be especially useful for interlocutory hearings, case management meetings, and all manner of other interactions with the courts.

Looking forward, the latest generation of video-conferencing systems offers the promise of far more reliable and life-like, virtual attendance in court. These systems, as I discuss in Section 3.3, use technology sometimes called 'immersive telepresence', which creates the feeling that users are indeed gathered in the same room as one another. So, a party, witness, or lawyer could 'appear' in court (or in an arbitration or mediation for that matter) and the gravity of proceedings, as well as the gravitas of the judge, could to a large extent be conveyed and maintained in the new environment.

Taken together, CAT, document display, EPE, and video conferencing are good illustrations of technologies that have been shown to work well in

---

[35] *Access to Justice—Final Report*, Woolf Inquiry Team (July 2006), available at <http://www.justice.gov.uk>.

[36] *Review of the Court of Appeal (Civil Division)* (September 1997), available at <http://www.justice.gov.uk>.

[37] *civil.justice.2000: a vision of the civil justice system in the information age*, A Strategy Paper Issued by the Lord Chancellor's Department (June 2000).

occasional practice but have not been embraced extensively in the courts. In contrast, they have been widely taken up in various major public inquiries. The most technologically advanced of these has been the Bloody Sunday Inquiry, currently being concluded by Lord Saville.[38] Fittingly, as President of the Society for Computers and Law and for many years the leading advocate of IT amongst English judges, Lord Saville used a wide range of systems, setting up what I regard as the world's most technologically advanced hearing. Over and above all of the systems discussed in this section, Lord Saville also developed an award-winning, 360-degree virtual reality model of Londonderry in 1972, based on historical plans and photographs. Using touch-screen technology, witnesses (and others) were able to walk through the streets as they appeared at the time. In this way, the technology proved to be a powerful tool to help the Inquiry understand as accurately as possible the events of over thirty-five years ago.[39]

Building to a large extent on the experience gained during Lord Saville's Inquiry, IT was also a success at the Hutton Inquiry, supporting a hearing that was swift and notably accessible to the public. CAT increased the pace of the proceedings, and the full collection of transcripts generated were converted into a searchable database of over 2,000 pages. All evidence put before the hearings (around 10,000 pages) was put before the Inquiry using document image technology. Lord Hutton and the eight legal teams had continuous access to these transcripts and images of evidence in a courtroom that was reminiscent of a NASA control room, complete with forty-four desktop flat screens and four large plasma displays (of the sort coveted by home cinema aspirants). The entire set-up sat on the network of the Royal Courts of Justice, facilitating links to an adjacent court for the public and a marquee for the media. These locations housed a further twelve plasma screens, which also displayed live broadcast of the actual courtroom proceedings. The public had open access to the transcripts and evidence through the Inquiry's website,[40] which enjoyed, on average, over 10,000 visitors each day. Video and audio conferencing were also used, enabling certain witnesses to give evidence without appearing in the courtroom itself. This was an option for the bereaved and certain intelligence officers.

---

[38] <http://www.bloody-sunday-inquiry.org.uk>.
[39] See Lord Saville, 'Information and a public inquiry', in M Saville and R Susskind (eds), *Essays in Honour of Sir Brian Neill: The Quintessential Judge* (London: LexisNexis, 2003) 33, and R Susskind (ed), *The Susskind Interviews: Legal Experts in Changing Times* (London: Thomson, 2005) 223–8.
[40] <http://www.the-hutton-inquiry.org.uk>.

It is striking that all the technologies used by Lord Hutton and most of those used by Lord Saville were recommended for the civil courts by Lord Woolf in his *Access to Justice* Inquiry in the mid-1990s. Why, then, is it still a relatively rare civil case that exploits these systems? The main stumbling block, as I keep saying, has been funding. For public inquiries, it appears much easier to secure the investment needed. It is perhaps relevant that the Hutton Inquiry did not produce a detailed business case for IT deployment. Common sense prevailed. Past users of transcription and display technology agreed that these systems reduce the length of hearings by around one-third. You do not need to be Fermat to calculate that savings in lawyers' fees alone would comfortably meet the entire cost of the technology. And so it should also be in civil cases.

In some large commercial cases, this is fully appreciated. Take, for example, the claim against the Bank of England by the liquidators of BCCI. Courtroom 73, the venue for the Hutton Inquiry, was once again awash with IT. This time, the use of IT was introduced and driven largely by the major law firm, Lovells, the lawyers acting for the claimants. The use of the technology was also supported by the judge, Mr Justice Tomlinson. The case demonstrated how effective IT can be in the Commercial Court—with twenty-two desktop monitors and four large plasma screens displaying either the live transcript of the hearing or showing the documents under consideration (taken from a bundle of some 150 lever arch files). Nonetheless, as I say, this scale of IT usage remains unusual and its widespread adoption across the court system is not envisaged by the government.

What about judges and their use of IT in the courtroom? Aside from the technologies I discuss earlier in this section, some judges also take laptops into court, largely to take notes. Others dismiss this as a fiddle or a distraction. There is no right answer here—we must be able to accommodate in our courts (and elsewhere in the justice system) groups of users of varying abilities and preferences. It is noteworthy, despite my general lamentations about funding, that any full-time judge in England and Wales will now be issued with a laptop if he or she so chooses. Although there is some judicial consternation over the limited range of applications available on their laptops, it was barely imaginable in the early 1990s that judges would ever be given machines at all.

Aside from the use of machines in the courtroom and for case management (see Section 6.4), judges' use of IT does not differ greatly from that of most practising lawyers. They have word processors, e-mail, access to online legal information systems, some e-learning and training tools, and an Intranet for shared judicial materials such as bench books. The last facility is now delivered through what is known as 'the Judicial Portal', whose birth was a fraught delivery indeed. This portal also replaces Felix, the now legendary conferencing and bulletin board system that has served as an exemplary online community for many years (see Section 4.7).

Where English judges are poorly supported today, in my view, is on the document management front. I speak here not of electronic files for the courts but of standard tools to help judges name, index, file, archive, retrieve, and share the documents that they create. Judges are not trained to organize their documents on their machines. This is a critical gap; and I believe judges are exposed here to unnecessary risk. For example, they should not, on a daily basis, be taking the chance that they might lose documents (for example by overwriting) or send out old drafts in error (due to lack of sound version control). An industry standard document management system is needed.

More generally, though, to what extent are some of the broader challenges of this book applicable to judges? Can their work be decomposed and multi-sourced, in accordance with the thinking of Section 2.5? Will judicial work be unsettled by the disruptive technologies introduced in Chapter 4? As to the first question, I can see no reason why judicial work cannot be analysed, divided into separable tasks, and, where appropriate, alternative means of discharging these tasks be found. I can see no reason, in other words, why the routine and repetitive work of judges cannot be sourced in different ways. I regularly hear judges say that they are bogged down by administrative matters that others could handle on their behalf. Closer to the heart of their work, there is considerable scope for standardization of parts of the documents they create (directions, orders, and so forth). They could clearly benefit from the use of document assembly technology (see Section 4.1) if much of what appears in final documents is standard wording with minor variations. Even preliminary legal research could be conducted differently, as is demonstrated by the use of Judicial Assistants in the Court of Appeal and the House of Lords. Clearly, they could not be employed across the court system, but other ways of sharing know-how and experience could be introduced. At the very least, I submit that the idea of decomposing and multi-sourcing judicial work deserves further study.

In relation to my second question, about the impact of disruptive technologies, I generally regard their impact on judges much in the same way as I see their effect on clients—they are more likely to support rather than eliminate the traditional ways of working. In summary, following the classification of Chapter 4, I expect that, for judges: document assembly, relentless connectivity, e-learning, closed legal communities (for judges), and workflow and project management will bring greater efficiencies; while the electronic legal marketplace, online legal service, legal open-sourcing, and embedded legal knowledge will have little direct impact. One category of system that might challenge the judicial role, however, is my tenth disruptive legal technology—online dispute resolution (ODR). I explore this subject in the next section.

Before moving on to ODR, I must return, by way of conclusion to my trip across the uneven terrain of courtroom and judicial technology, to the question of funding. Around £15 billion is spent in the UK each year on government computing. Given that the Judiciary is one of the three branches of government, is one-third of that gargantuan sum allocated to the courts and judges? Not even nearly. According to my calculations, they receive more like one-thirtieth of the pot and the result is administrative and management systems that are often unacceptably dated and inefficient. While the court system has no doubt had its share of problem projects, the major stumbling block to progress has been HM Treasury's unwillingness to pay directly for the technology that is needed to impel the civil courts into the modern world. This cannot be funded by court fees. To put in place court systems that would befit the English legal system will require a decade of substantial investment.

6.6 Online dispute resolution

In Chapter 4, I claim that I have identified ten 'disruptive legal technologies' that together will fundamentally change the face of legal service. I introduce nine of these technologies in that chapter, but I defer discussion of the tenth—online dispute resolution (ODR)—until this section, where it fits more comfortably in the flow of the arguments of the chapter.

I first gave serious thought to ODR in the mid-1980s, when I theorized as a doctoral student about the possibility of computers replacing judges.[41] I concluded then that it was neither possible nor desirable for computers fully to assume the judicial function. My position has not changed. Judicial decision-making in hard cases—when judges handle complex issues of principle, policy, and morality—is well beyond the power of current and foreseeable computing. I expand upon this in describing my doctoral work in Section 1.3.

---

[41] R Susskind, *Expert Systems in Law* (Oxford: Oxford University Press, 1987; paperback edition, 1989) 249–51.

I returned to a closely related topic, but in a more practical vein, in 1998, while working as a member of The Civil Justice IT Strategy Development Group on the consultation paper, *civil.justice* (see Section 6.1). At that time, I posed a question to my fellow members—'is court a service or a place?' I thought our team should be giving sustained consideration to whether parties and their advisers needed to congregate together in one physical spot, in order to present arguments to a judge.

At that stage I was thinking particularly of video conferencing. With Lord Saville, I had recently visited British Telecom's research laboratories at Martlesham and had been impressed by their ten-year predictions and demonstrators of video conferencing (which turned out to be remarkably accurate and similar to the latest generation of systems—see Section 3.3). With the prospect of such technology coming into play, I wanted to challenge some conventional assumptions about courts. Specifically, I wondered about the extent to which courtrooms would actually be needed in the future for judicial work.

Reflecting and building on these early forays, I now distinguish between two different ways in which IT and the Internet can impact on the resolution of disputes. The first is where elements of conventional dispute resolution processes are replaced by technology. Examples of this include the use of telephone conferencing rather than physical meetings to conduct case management meetings or pre-trial reviews with a judge; or where witnesses or parties appear before a judge via video conferencing; or where judges use a sentencing system to help them to work out what prison term a convicted criminal should serve.[42] I do not consider these to be ODR. Rather, these are illustrations of the use of IT to substitute or support an inconvenient or inefficient part of traditional proceedings. In the language of Section 2.5, these are illustrations of using IT to source decomposed tasks of the judicial process.

This is different from a second set of circumstances—when the dispute resolution process, and especially the formulation of the solution itself, is wholly or in large part conducted by or through Internet-based systems. This is ODR. A decision that emanates from or is enabled by an online system without human intervention is certainly ODR; as, in my view, is an alternative dispute resolution process that is conducted across the Internet without

---

[42] A special issue of the *International Journal of Law and Information Technology* ((1998) 6(2)) was devoted entirely to judicial sentencing support systems. Although much has happened since, this remains a solid introduction to the topic.

the participants meeting in person. In terms of the evolutionary path that I lay out in Section 2.1, ODR sits towards the right-hand of the spectrum.

I accept that the above distinction, between IT-enabled convention dispute resolution and ODR, may not be a watertight dichotomy. Others cut the ODR cake in quite different ways. Ethan Katsh and Janet Rifkin, for instance, in the first book on ODR, develop the interesting argument that, in ODR, technology becomes the fourth party at the table, working in support of the third party mediator or arbitrator.[43] I like their work but, for current purposes, I prefer to stick to my simpler model. To repeat in shorthand— when the process of resolving a dispute, especially the formulation of the solution, is entirely or largely conducted by or through the Internet, then we have ODR.

With this broad definition to hand, the best way to understand ODR, I have found, is through examples. A starting point is the application of ODR to disputes that have arisen amongst Internet users. Predictably, the use and growth of the Internet has itself spawned legal disagreements and indeed it is here that we find some of the most widely used and best known ODR systems. One class of cyber-squabble arises amongst disgruntled online traders. In this context, an ODR solution that is often cited is SquareTrade. This service was founded in 2000 and has helped to settle hundreds of thousands of conflicts over transactions between traders on eBay, the online auction site.[44] SquareTrade is eBay's preferred dispute resolution provider and offers two services. The first is a free negotiation process—a web-based forum that enables users to try to sort out their differences on their own. Many disputes are said to be resolved at this stage. However, if agreement is not reached, SquareTrade also provides an online mediation process with a human mediator. This costs US$15; eBay subsidizes the balance of the expense. The mediator seeks to understand both points of view and to encourage reasonable settlement. If a resolution cannot be reached, the mediator recommends a solution based on principles of 'fairness and good conduct'. It is said that this process generally takes ten days.[45]

Another type of Internet-related altercation is the domain name dispute. It is not unusual for dubious attempts to be made to use or sell an Internet

---

[43] E Katsh and J Rifkin, *Online Dispute Resolution* (San Francisco: Jossey-Bass, 2001). This is a practical and clear introduction to the field, offering history, introductory analysis, and explanation, alongside numerous helpful case studies, mainly from the US. The literature on ODR is expanding rapidly. See <http://www.odr.info> and <http://www.mediate.com/odr>.

[44] <http://www.squaretrade.com>.

[45] <http://pages.ebay.com/services/buyandsell/disputeres.html>.

address which carries a brand that arguably belongs to another. Since 1998, the management of the domain name system has been the province of the Internet Corporation for Assigned Names and Numbers (ICANN). Consistent with ICANN's policy for the settlement of such disputes, various ODR systems have been developed, each designed to be quicker and cheaper than conventional mechanisms for settlement. On one model, submissions have been made to neutrals selected from a strong panel, experts mainly on intellectual property and Internet matters; and this process has been conducted entirely electronically rather than on a face-to-face basis.[46]

Beyond disputes that arise from online matters, ODR has enjoyed much wider usage. Perhaps the greatest success story of all is the US company, Cybersettle.[47] Launched as a web-based system in 1998, it is claimed that Cybersettle has handled over 200,000 claims and settled more than US$1.5 billion worth. Most of the cases have been insurance or personal injury claims. How does it work? Using a patented process referred to as 'double-blind bidding', a claimant and defendant each submit the highest and lowest settlement figures that are acceptable to them. These figures are not actually disclosed to the other side. If the two ranges overlap, a settlement is achieved, the final figure usually being a split down the middle. If there is no overlap, the process can be repeated. The system is used mainly by claims professionals, lawyers, and insurance companies.

Consider this case study. The City of New York, under budget pressures, was looking for a way to cope with a backlog of 40,000 personal injury claims and to speed their settlement process. Cybersettle was introduced. More than 1,200 claims were submitted. It is claimed that there was a 66 per cent settlement rate within thirty days of submission, savings in litigation costs to the tune of US$11.6 million, and an average reduction in settlement time of 85 per cent. It is hard not to take this approach seriously.

Another kind of ODR that merits attention is mediation across the Web. When a face-to-face mediation is too costly relative to the amount in dispute or logistically not possible because of the locations of the parties, then an online mediation can be undertaken. Through a blend of web-based tools and human mediators using e-mail exchanges and online discussion areas, conflicts can be resolved (or dissolved) electronically. Parties to a dispute can therefore settle their differences across the Internet without convening in a meeting room or discussing their cases orally. In 2002, alternative dispute

---

[46] See Katsh and Rifkin (n 43 above) 64–5 and 108–12. Also see <http://www.icann.org/dndr/udrp>.
[47] <http://www.cybersettle.com>.

resolution specialists, the ADR Group, were the first to launch such a service in Europe. Imaginatively, they also offer an e-learning-based training course in online mediation to accredited mediators.[48]

Looking beyond commercial and personal injury disputes, ODR has even crept into family law. A system to help divorcing couples to resolve some of their differences has been under development at Victoria University in Melbourne. The objective of The Family Winner system is the more rational settlement of the disagreements afflicting the 43 per cent of Australian marriages that end in divorce. Described in an important article in the *Harvard Negotiation Law Review*,[49] this ODR system is also said to deploy game theory techniques originally formulated by Nobel Laureate John Nash and popularized in the film, 'A Beautiful Mind'. Through a series of trade-offs and compensation strategies, the system distributes items in a dispute to those who most desire them. It is claimed that disputants can often achieve 70 to 80 per cent of what they require, rather than the traditional 50-50 approach to dispute resolution. The system encourages disputants to focus upon their interests rather than using the negotiation process, counter-productively, to vent their emotions. If ODR can work in a domain as fraught as divorce law, then applying these techniques in other parts of the legal system should be as easy as walking out of a law library.

If it is surprising that ODR is thought to be workable in handling divorces, it may be even more shocking, given that I am rather downbeat in much of this chapter about the government's investment in IT for the English courts, that one of the most successful, operational ODR systems was developed and is made available by the Court Service in England and Wales. This is Money Claim Online, an award-winning system that was launched in 2002. It enables users, with no prior legal knowledge, to recover money owed to them without handling complex forms or setting foot in a County Court. The service covers claims, such as unpaid debts and rent arrears, up to the value of £100,000 and enables a claimant to request a claim online, monitor the status of the claim and, where appropriate, request entry of judgment and enforcement. Payment of the court fee can be either by credit or debit card. Defendants can also use the online system to reply to and check the status of their cases. My understanding is that Money Claim Online handles more than 60,000 claims each year and so is busier than any single County Court

---

[48] <http://www.themediationroom.com>.

[49] AR Lodder and J Zeleznikoff, 'Developing an Online Dispute Resolution Environment: Dialogue Tools and Negotiation Support Systems in a Three-Step Model' (Spring 2005) 10 *Harvard Negotiation Law Review*, 287.

in the country. This is a remarkable achievement and the Court Service is to be commended for its innovation.[50]

Along similar lines, although it has suffered from some teething problems, has been the more ambitious system known as Possession Claims Online. This is another ODR application delivered by the Court Service, and again it is for use by both claimants and defendants. It offers a straightforward way of making claims for possession of residential property for non-payment of rent or mortgage. Status tracking and payment is handled in a similar way to Money Claims Online. Additionally, court diaries for claims issued within Possessions Claims Online can be viewed online.[51]

These two systems exhibit electronic public service as it surely should be—reaching out to large numbers of citizens (around two-thirds of UK homes now have Internet access) and providing a modern and streamlined alternative to an often cumbersome paper-based service. More, these systems should also help those who might previously have been deterred, by the forbidding nature of the process, from pursuing their entitlements at all. I am enthused.

Yet, I also recognize that I may still be applying yesterday's thinking to tomorrow's world. In the US, the iCourthouse initiative may point to a very different, allegedly more democratic model. The iCourthouse is an online hearing room to which Internet users can present their cases. In turn, they are heard and decided upon by lay, volunteer jurors. The court is 'always in session' and many of the procedures echo traditional court practice.[52] This set-up is remarkably similar to various proposals put to me when I made some draft parts of Chapter 1 of this book available for discussion on *Times Online*. The basic idea presented to me was to recruit millions of volunteers who are willing to play the role of juror-cum-judge in relation to disputes put before them. If a disagreement arises, each party would submit written pleadings via some Internet-based system to a panel of, say, 1,000 lay people, drawn randomly from the pool of volunteers. The Solomonic 'wisdom of crowds'[53] would no doubt then click in, delivering a common sense judgment, untrammelled by legal niceties. In a sense this would be a type of mass collaboration or open-sourcing in relation to dispute resolution. Who knows if this might work? But it certainly challenges some fundamental assumptions.

---

[50] <http://www.moneyclaim.gov.uk>.
[51] <http://www.possessionclaim.gov.uk>.
[52] <http://www.i-courthouse.com>.
[53] J Surowiecki, *The Wisdom of Crowds* (London: Abacus, 2004).

ODR is potentially disruptive for lawyers *and* for judges, arbitrators, and mediators. If clients are going online and sorting out some of their difficulties on their own, this is time and money not spent on lawyers. And if differences are being settled without the direct involvement of independent human decision-makers, this might severely impinge on those who make a living from sitting in the middle of warring parties and resolving their disputes. Alternatively, if judges, arbitrators, and mediators end up exercising their responsibilities from their dining rooms at home, this is a disconcertingly far cry from the traditional litigation or ADR that most are trained to oversee.

Predictably, as ODR gathers force, so too will its opponents. The law is not short of conservatives and reactionaries who will raise countless, plausible objections. I welcome debate and I want ODR to be put under the micro-scope. At the same time, we should not look uncritically at our age-old tradi-tions. Let me illustrate my point with one example. Sceptics of ODR have often pointed out to me the importance of taking oral evidence from wit-nesses in physical hearings, a process that cannot be simulated, they say, through ODR. Indeed, without this process, it is claimed that the basic facts of cases cannot be determined or assessed reliably. To this I say that we should also be open to possible faults in today's methods. The critics seem to regard witnesses as though these individuals have super-human recall. To get a sense of just how imperfect a human being's perceptions can be, however, we need look no further than a celebrated experiment by psychiatrists. Participants are asked to look at a video recording of basketball players pass-ing a ball to one another. They are also asked to count the number of passes. Unbelievable though this may sound, most viewers fail to notice that a man in a gorilla suit carrying an umbrella is walking in their midst.[54] Witnesses can easily be distracted and are far from infallible when in the courtroom. More generally, we cannot assume that current legal processes cannot be improved upon.

Nonetheless, I concede that it is still early days for ODR. And today there is as much if not more cynicism about its potential as there was in the early 1990s about its distant cousin, ADR. What, then, does the future have in store? Of two developments I am quite confident and of a third I have high hopes. I am confident that ODR-like techniques will, in due course, be embraced as a way of settling high volumes of fairly low-value disputes. In part, this will displace conventional court work; but it will also liberate a latent market— people and organizations, who have not felt able to take action in the past,

---

[54] See <http://viscog.beckman.uiuc.edu/djs_lab/>.

will have an unfussy and yet quasi-authoritative way of sorting out their conflicts. The great social benefit of ODR, in other words, will be in offering access to the inexpensive and simple resolution of disputes that parties would otherwise not feel able to take to the courts.

I am also confident that the Net Generation will often prefer ODR to conventional mechanisms of resolving disputes. Following the thinking of Section 3.5, clicks will often be preferable to mortals.

I have high hopes for ODR in relation to the resolution of commercial disputes, although I cannot yet see how this might play out. Perhaps an entrepreneur or a private equity house or an organizational psychologist will bring this idea to fruition. But I suppose the market first has to recognize that wildly excessive and disproportionate amounts of time, energy, and cash are dispensed on dispute resolution. And this will have to coincide with a dawning realization—and this is my game theory point again—that litigation, in the long run, may not be in the commercial interests of any party, other than in exceptional circumstances.

6.7 Dispute avoidance

In Section 5.3, I tell the tale of the power drill manufacturer that claims it sells holes in walls rather than drills. And I ask, 'what is the hole in the wall in the context of legal services?' What is it that clients of law firms really want? What value do lawyers bring to the markets they serve? I say that I know of only two satisfactory responses to these questions. In Section 5.3, I focus on one of these—on the many ways in which clients, when instructing lawyers, are actually wanting the application of lawyers' *knowledge* in their specific circumstances. The second answer I delay until this part of the book. Based on countless discussions, interviews, and research projects with clients of law firms, this second answer runs as follows: what clients actually want is lawyers who can help them to *avoid* legal problems, difficulties, and disputes. Clients prefer to have a fence at the top of a cliff rather than an ambulance at the bottom.

The avoidance of legal problems has been a running theme of my work since I wrote an article on the subject in the *Financial Times* in 1992.[55]

---

[55] 'Why lawyers should consider consultancy' *Financial Times*, 13 October 1992.

I argued then for the development of a discipline known as legal risk management. The column generated considerable interest, not least from a government department that called upon my services and those of colleagues at Masons (now Pinsent Masons) for several years. The piece also seemed to resonate with many in-house lawyers who complained that their work was dominated by firefighting rather than the strategic management of legal risk. Since that time, lawyers and their clients have continued to talk with some enthusiasm, if a little vaguely, about this idea of legal risk management. However, although conferences and seminars on this subject have proliferated, no distinct discipline has yet to crystallize. I have in mind here an approach which enables the job of lawyers to be genuinely proactive. Although many firms say they already are proactive, clients tell me that most are not. Nor can they be, I argued in 1992 and continue to do so today, until they overhaul their working practices. Proactive legal risk management requires more than bright lawyers shooting from the hip when clients suspect they face a difficulty. It requires the development and use of structured and formal techniques and processes that are already used by strategy consultants, professional risk managers, and tax specialists too. Lawyers indeed have much to learn from the world of tax—I have seen, while advising the tax practice of Deloitte, their evolution of a selection of tools for helping clients to identify, evaluate, and control tax risk.

In stark contrast, very few legal risk tools have been crafted for the legal profession.[56] When I wrote in 1992, I had fully expected the rapid emergence of a wide range of tools for *legal risk review*. I thought these would include audits, risk reviews, and health checks to help clients to assess, for example, their exposure to various categories of liability, their processes for managing their regulatory compliance, their preparedness for litigation (now including e-disclosure), the threats to the reputations of their organizations, the soundness of their standard form documentation, and the adequacy of their escalation procedures when serious problems arise. I wondered if economists might be engaged to help with some models for quantifying some of the legal risks. I had also expected a corresponding set of services devoted to *legal risk control*, so that the legal risks, once identified, could be kept at bay. Under this heading, I had anticipated some nifty techniques ranging from new-look insurance products to novel forms of standard form documentation; from

---

[56] One notable exception through the years has been the Australian firm, Blake Dawson—<http://www.blakedawson.com>. See eg their online legal compliance system—<http://www.compliance.blakedawson.com>.

standardized working practices and procedures to legal risk awareness raising programmes; from embedding legal content into the standard project and business life cycles of client organizations to proposals for entirely novel ways of structuring and prioritizing the work of in-house legal departments.

In the event, but a handful of law firms around the world have actually invested seriously on behalf of their clients in legal risk management. The lack of investment and imagination by law firms in this area astounds me. In all the studies that I undertake on behalf of law firms, when I am asked to interview and later summarize the views of General Counsel, I invariably hear from these top in-house lawyers that legal risk management is the main focus of their job. General Counsel are highly concerned, for instance, about compliance risks—the global regulatory environment is regarded as increasingly complicated and subject to ever more aggressive attitudes by regulators to enforcement. Major international financial institutions have to submit thousands of reports each year to dozens of different regulators and will only be able to carry on doing so efficiently if they are supported by advanced systems and processes. And yet, these tools—legal risk management tools—do not exist. There is an unparalleled opportunity here for innovative law firms to extend their range of services beyond traditional reactive work to a fundamentally different, proactive suite of services. These services will not be a variant of one-to-one consultative advisory service delivered on an hourly billing basis. Instead they will be a blend of facilities, methods, systems, and services which together will focus on helping clients to identify the legal risks they face, evaluate the severity of these risks, and, where necessary, take appropriate precautionary measures.

In controlling legal risk, we will need to move away from the idea that the best and only technique for managing legal risk is to throw lawyers at the job. Another method is to increase awareness of legal risk across an organization, so that non-lawyers are able to avoid legal pitfalls without the direct intervention of legal advisers. Pursuing this course, an entrepreneurial US company, LRN, has pioneered the use of e-learning to enable entire workforces to recognize compliance and liability risks for themselves.[57] In a similar vein, the UK legal publisher company, PLC, offers a legal risk service to assist in-house legal departments in educating business people about legal risk[58] The service includes a portal to a range of legal risk resources, hosted and maintained by PLC but tailored for subscribing companies. It also includes a series

[57] <http://www.lrn.com>.
[58] <http://www.practicallaw.com/marketing/legalRisk/legalRisk.html>.

of legal risk modules, on thorny legal issues, containing e-learning courses and practical briefings for those not of legal background. It is noteworthy that both of these offerings have been developed not by law firms but by entrepreneurial and nimble new-wave legal publishers.

Another way of increasing legal awareness is to embed legal knowledge into organizations, in the ways I envisage in Section 4.9—using tools such as document assembly, workflow, and personalized alerting. There is no shortage of techniques.

The difficulty for law firms in all of this is that it is notoriously tricky to encourage clients to pay for the development of legal risk management tools. With fees for conventional legal work already gargantuan and under scrutiny from on high, it is hard to make a business case for spending money on legal problems that have not yet arisen. This dilemma of the aspiring legal risk manager is neatly reflected in the tale of the chief fire officer. In this anecdote, we hear of a large manufacturing company that is suffering from regular fires in its various factories. The chief executive calls for action and demands the recruitment of an individual to sort out the problem. A chief fire officer is duly brought on board and, with the assistance of a team that he builds, the fire problem is brought comfortably under control. In due course, the chief executive leaves the company and his successor, on arrival, makes it one of his priorities to trim excess costs. On examining the company's figures, his eyes alight upon the not insignificant expense of the chief fire officer and his team. He expresses surprise at the scale of this cost and asks his finance director when the company last suffered from a factory fire. He is told that there have been no fires for over a year. His immediate response is to fire the chief fire officer and scrap his department.

Whether in law or in relation to fires, it is hard to quantify the benefits of disasters averted. And so, irrational though it may appear, it is much harder to sell legal risk management services than litigation services. When a dispute arises, the budgets often seem to be without limit. A tiny fraction of that budget is rarely released to avoid litigation in the first place.

I can imagine that this is an area where external investors might work with law firms. Whereas lawyers might be unwilling to sink their own profits speculatively into new tools and techniques, private equity houses or major legal publishers may regard legal risk management as a wonderful investment opportunity.

More generally, though, law firms' lack of enthusiasm for legal risk management services may reflect the deeper, structural defect in the relationship between firms and clients that I identify in Section 5.1. I refer there to the asymmetry of commercial interests between lawyers and those they advise.

Most law firms, if we are honest, would prefer to advise on a mammoth dispute than have helped to avoid it. I return to the all-important case study of Cisco—only when that company's external law firm took on their commercial litigation on a fixed price basis did the lawyer and client come to share the same point of view. Both then had a very strong interest in reducing Cisco's legal risks.

In the long run, perhaps law firms will only take legal dispute avoidance seriously when they are sharing legal risks with their clients.

7

Access to Law and to Justice

Much of this book is devoted to the transformation of legal services that are delivered to a particular type of client—the substantial enterprise that is of sufficient scale and complexity to merit its own in-house legal department. But what about citizens, individuals, voters, consumers, regular people, who have no special access today to lawyers and legal services? Forget, for a while, the General Counsel with his or her team of perhaps hundreds of in-house lawyers. We may sympathize with their everyday workload and their growing legal risk burden. The challenge for these organizations is how best to allocate their often very considerable but nonetheless finite legal resources. In contrast, the challenge for citizens who are not lawyers is often more daunting, because these lay people have no legal resources whatsoever and, unless they are uncommonly wealthy or sufficiently impecunious to qualify for state funding, they seldom have the wherewithal to engage lawyers. Franz Kafka, in a haunting short story, 'Before the Law', sets the scene for us: 'Before the law stands a gatekeeper. A man from the country comes to this gatekeeper and requests admittance into the law. But the gatekeeper says that he cannot grant him admittance right now . . . The man from the country had not expected such difficulties; after all, he thinks, the law should be accessible to everyone at all times.'[1]

---

[1] F Kafka, *A Country Doctor* (Prague: Twisted Spoon Press, 1997), 29–33. This story is analysed at length by the prison chaplain and Joseph K, in F Kafka, *The Trial* (Harmondsworth: Penguin, 1983), 235–43.

It should indeed. But is it? To grasp the scale of the 'difficulties' in England and Wales, consider various observations made by the formidably credentialled Public Legal Education and Support (PLEAS)Task Force, in the opening pages of an important report published in July 2007:

One-third of the population has experienced a civil justice problem, but many do nothing about it – often because they think, wrongly, that there is nothing they can do or that there is no local legal advice provider who might help . . . around one million civil justice problems go unresolved every year. This is legal exclusion on a massive scale . . . the cost of managing legal problems is staggering. Ministry of Justice economists estimate that over a three-and-a-half year research period, unresolved law-related problems cost individuals and the public purse £13 billion.[2]

This alarming snapshot succinctly captures the problem of 'inaccess' to justice in England and Wales. And this problem is the subject matter of the current chapter.

7.1 Redefining access to justice

It has been fashionable for some time now, amongst policy-makers, law reformers, and commentators, to speak of increasing 'access to justice'. While everyone seems to agree that access to justice is a fine thing, there is less unanimity over what this actually involves in practice. As a term of art, 'access to justice' perhaps peaked in popularity in the mid-1990s, when Lord Woolf's seminal reports bore the phrase as their title.[3] His emphasis was consistent with much theorizing and policy-making that has followed—on providing easier access to improved, cheaper, and fairer means of resolving legal disputes. While I emphatically welcome any initiatives that improve the accessibility and efficiency of our courts and of other methods of resolving disputes, and I remain a strong supporter of Lord Woolf's work, I do not think we should be satisfied that improving dispute resolution will be sufficient to achieve justice under the law. To be wholly or even largely focused on disputes

---

[2] 'Developing capable citizens: the role of public legal education' (July 2007) 7–8, at <http://www.pleas.org.uk>. These conclusions are drawn in large part from H Genn, *Paths to Justice* (Oxford: Hart, 1999) and P Pleasence, N Balmer, and A Buck, *Causes of Action: Civil Law and Social Justice*, LSRC Research Paper No 14 (Norwich: The Stationery Office, 2nd edn, 2006), available at <http://www.lsrc.org.uk>.

[3] See Section 6.1 and notes 4 and 5 to Ch 6.

in our pursuit of justice is, I submit, to miss much that we should expect of our legal systems.

A richer analysis is needed. I could turn here, as I have done in the past, to a fairly philosophical approach to justice and look in turn at categories such as formal justice, substantive justice, and distributive justice.[4] But I do not think these are the right tools for the job. Much as I enjoy legal theory, the discussion would run the risk of being too abstract. Instead, I prefer to draw a simple analogy—from the world of health care. In law, as in medicine, I believe that prevention is better than cure. Most people would surely prefer to avoid legal problems altogether than to have them well resolved. As I say in relation to clients in Section 6.7, most people would surely prefer a fence at the top of the cliff rather than an ambulance at the bottom (no matter how swift or well-equipped). If this is so, then access to justice is as much about *dispute avoidance* as it is about dispute resolution. Just as lawyers are themselves able, because of their training and experience, to recognize and avoid legal pitfalls, in a just society (one in which legal insight is an evenly distributed resource) we should want non-lawyers to be similarly forewarned. In large part, this will involve introducing novel ways of putting legal insight at everyone's fingertips; and to an extent that has not been possible in the past. This readier, cheaper, and more widespread access to legal guidance should give rise to a more just society in the same way that immunization leads to a healthier community. Another effect is also likely—more widespread understanding of the law and access to legal remedies may deter unscrupulous individuals (such as some landlords) from pursuing unlawful or exploitative courses of action. In the past, they may have behaved as they wished regardless of the law, secure in the knowledge that those to whom they were causing suffering were deterred from taking action precisely because of the complexity or inaccessibility of the law and the courts.

The medical analogy also helps identify a third sense of access to justice. I am thinking here of relatively recent work on health promotion—we are advised today to exercise aerobically for at least 20 minutes, three times a week, not just because this will reduce our chances of, for example, coronary heart disease but because it will make us a feel a whole lot better. The idea is not only to prevent ill-health but to promote our physical and mental well-being. Similarly, the law can also provide us with ways in which we can improve our general well-being; and not simply by helping to resolve or

---

[4] R Susskind, *Transforming the Law* (Oxford: Oxford University Press, 2000; paperback edition, 2003) ix–x.

avoid problems. Instead, there are many benefits, improvements, and advantages that the law can confer, even when there is no perceived problem or difficulty. And yet, many people are lamentably unaware of the full range of facilities available today—from welfare benefits through tax planning to making a will. In contrast, I look forward to the day when we will be committed to *legal health promotion* underpinned by community legal services that are akin perhaps to community medicine programmes. Providing access to justice, in this third sense, will mean offering access to the opportunities that the law creates. This underlies one of the themes of *The Future of Law*—that in legal systems of tomorrow, the law will come to be seen as empowering and not simply restrictive.[5]

To summarize this line of argument so far—when I speak of improving access to justice, I mean more than providing access to speedier, cheaper, and less combative mechanisms for resolving disputes. I am also referring to the introduction of techniques that help all members of society to avoid disputes in the first place and, further, to have greater insight into the benefits that the law can confer.

To translate this aspiration into reality, however, we must to go further than simply re-scoping the term, 'access to justice'. We need to assess, more systematically than we have been inclined to in the past, the facilities and techniques that will help to bring about this extended access to justice. My starting point here is a model that I developed some years ago—the Client Service Chain.[6] A simple variant of this is presented in Figure 7.1.

This model proposes that the activity of obtaining legal guidance can be represented along a simple life cycle, made up of three basic processes. The first is *recognition*, which is the process by which citizens or clients recognize, in respect of their particular circumstances, that they would benefit from legal guidance. Second is *selection*, the process by which citizens or clients select the particular source of legal guidance to help them in their given circumstances. And the third is *service*, the process by which legal guidance is received.

Each of these elements raises access to justice issues. The first, the process of recognition, is characterized today by what I call the 'blatant trigger'. By this I mean that the client is urged to seek legal guidance on the occurrence of some event, or in a set of circumstances, that quite patently call for formal legal input. It is at the client's instigation, therefore, that the legal machine

---

[5] R Susskind, *The Future of Law* (Oxford: Oxford University Press, 1996; paperback edition, 1998) 288.
[6] Susskind (n 4 above) Ch 2.

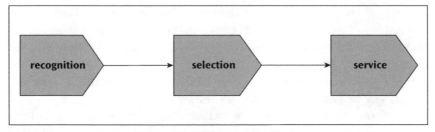

Fig. 7.1 The Client Service Chain

rolls into action. It is in this context, in *The Future of Law*, that I characterize traditional legal service as being 'reactive' in nature.[7] The blatant trigger (perhaps the receipt of a claim, the death of a relative, the commencement of negotiations on some major deal, or some similar such occurrence which clearly demands proper legal help) leads a client of today to instruct his or her lawyer. In other words, the lawyer *reacts* to the client's call for help. All too often, and unhelpfully, the lawyer responds in the first instance (accompanied by an irritating intake of breath) by saying that it would have been better if the client had come along earlier. This is the basis of what I have called the 'paradox of traditional reactive legal service'—you need to know rather a lot about the law to recognize not just that you need legal help but when best to seek such counsel. The net result is that clients are often disadvantaged, either because they look for legal guidance too late or because they miss altogether an opportunity to assert their entitlements. In a society in which there is genuine access to justice, there should be facilities in place to help non-lawyers to recognize, at the most propitious time, that the law impacts on them (whether to empower or inhibit them).

As for the selection process, currently this remains rather hit-and-miss. Traditionally, a variety of factors have brought a lawyer's capability to the attention of potential clients, including advertising, local physical presence, recommendations, and general reputation. Sometimes non-lawyers will instruct a law firm, not with any knowledge that the legal business has relevant skills but simply in the comfort that that same firm has undertaken legal work satisfactorily for them in the past. Even for the most sophisticated users of legal service, like the General Counsel in charge of a substantial in-house legal department, the full range of law firms in practice gives rise to a bewildering selection process, given the diversity, complexity, and sheer numbers

---

[7] Susskind (n 5 above) 23–6.

of apparently qualified legal providers. If we are sensibly to claim that our legal system affords access to justice, we must surely have processes in place that enable clients with no legal knowledge to find appropriately qualified lawyers who will offer a competitively priced legal service. And similar assistance will also soon be needed to help citizens to make sense of what may appear to be a bewildering array of online legal tools.

What about the third element in today's client service chain? This is the service element. Today, the dominant means of imparting legal guidance is through the delivery of advice by lawyers, invariably reduced at some stage to writing, usually after face-to-face consultation, and normally invoiced on an hourly billing basis. More, the advice tendered is packaged for the direct consumption of one particular client; rarely is it intended that that guidance should be re-used by others (even the client themselves). If we are to increase access to justice, I submit that we must continually be exploring and introducing methods of legal service that are less costly, time-consuming, emotionally-draining, and forbidding than the time-honoured consultative, advisory approach. Much that is said in Section 2.5, about the multi-sourcing of legal service, can therefore be applied in the context of the citizen.

Improving access to justice, therefore, will require much improved facilities in place to support clients: to recognize that they need or would benefit from guidance on dispute resolution, dispute avoidance, and legal health promotion; to help them to identify and select the most appropriate source of guidance (under all three headings); and to ensure that a wide range of sources are indeed available.

Improving access to justice, on this more ambitious scale, should also help us to liberate what I call 'the latent legal market'.[8] I am alluding here to the innumerable situations, in the domestic and working lives of all non-lawyers, in which they need and would benefit from legal guidance (or earlier, more timely, or empowering insight) but obtaining that legal input today seems to be too costly, excessively time consuming, too cumbersome and convoluted, or just plain scary. I believe this market will be liberated by the availability of straightforward, no-nonsense, online legal guidance systems and by other methods of sourcing legal service. They will not always replace conventional legal service, but they will provide affordable, easy access to legal guidance where this may have been unaffordable or impractical in the past. I have often been asked if my latent legal market is just a fancy term for

[8] Susskind (n 5 above) 27.

the rather more earthy concept of 'unmet legal need'. In a sense it is, in that they are two sides of the same coin. The underpinning fact here is that specialist legal help is needed today far more extensively that it can be offered and taken. From the point of view of society generally, this is well characterized as unmet legal need; whereas from the lawyers' perspective, I regard this as a large untapped market, happily not an opportunity for exploitation or monopoly but the chance to contribute, at a fair rate of return, to the grave problem of inaccess to justice. In law, as elsewhere, there seems to be a 'long tail' of demand that has not been satisfied by the working practices of the past.[9]

7.2 The building blocks of access to justice

With this analysis of access to justice to hand, we can now pin down the fundamental social challenge. The standard rendition of the problem proceeds along these lines—insofar as lawyers and (sometimes) the courts are involved, solving legal problems and resolving disputes is affordable, in practice, only to the very rich or those who are eligible for some kind of state support. And the standard question that follows this bleak peroration runs something like this—how can we extend the availability of legal services so they are not confined to the poles of the financial spectrum?

If my thesis of the previous section is accepted, this standard analysis understates the dilemma. The broader reality is that it is not just legal problem-solving and dispute resolution that require legal experience and knowledge that most citizens do not possess and cannot afford. Also beyond their ken and wallet are problem recognition, adviser selection, dispute avoidance, and legal health promotion. How on earth, at affordable cost, can we deliver this full range of legal tools and facilities and, in turn, access to justice?

The options are limited. One possibility is to increase state funding of legal services. In most jurisdictions with which I am familiar, this looks very unlikely to happen, not least because justice (especially civil justice) tends to compete poorly with other demands on the public purse, most notably health, defence, education, and transport. We can argue with conviction,

---

[9] See C Anderson, *The Long Tail* (London: Random House, 2006).

along with Lord Neuberger, the Law Lord, that civil justice and the preservation of civil society (through enforceable contracts and property rights, for example) are the foundations upon which nation states are built and so should have a first call on public funding.[10] I fear, however, and for reasons too numerous to itemize, that this line of thought does not resonate with today's policy-makers and politicians. I have seen inside the workings of government for long enough now to hazard instead that there will be less rather than more funding made available to promote access to justice in the foreseeable future.

This situation is in many ways similar to that facing in-house lawyers who are strapped for resources. Like General Counsel, citizens who hanker after greater access to justice want more for less. If this is so, they should pursue the two basic strategies that I put forward in Section 5.7,—the efficiency strategy and the collaboration strategy. Using the former, we can *cut the costs* of providing access to justice—for example radical efficiency gains and cost savings should be achieved within law firms through standardization and computerization, while various other sources of legal counsel can also be brought into play, often using different channels for delivery, such as call centres and video calling. Or, following the latter strategy, we can *share the costs* of providing access to justice amongst the participants involved—for example through legal open-sourcing or closed legal communities that enable the burden to be shared across large communities of those in legal need (see Sections 4.6 and 4.7).

In seeking to meet the grave social and economic challenge of providing greater access to justice at less cost to the public purse and the citizen, I therefore hope we can draw on the thinking and practical suggestions made elsewhere in this book in relation to commercial clients. Even if the legal problems of the citizen are quite different from those of the in-house lawyer, the more general theme—that of providing more for less—is remarkably similar. In the pages that follow, then, I point once again to the wide range of disruptive legal technologies, as discussed in Chapter 4 and Section 6.6. As ever, while these systems may be unattractive and threatening to conventional legal businesses, the changes they bring will often deliver direct benefits (especially cost savings and quality improvements) to the client. And, once again, those legal businesses that choose to embrace disruptive technologies ahead of later adopters, may in so doing secure some kind of advantage in the marketplace. More generally, though, the challenge of increasing access

---

[10] Lord Neuberger, unpublished speech at Property Litigation Association Dinner, 2 October 2007.

to justice can be met, at least in part, by using the techniques of decomposing and multi-sourcing, as introduced in Section 2.5. If we are serious about reducing the costs of legal service, we should be decomposing legal work that has been, or should be undertaken, for citizens, into constituent tasks and allocating these to the least costly sources of service that we can find, so long as this multi-sourcing and mass customization (Section 2.5) does not fail to deliver the requisite quality of guidance that the non-lawyer needs.

We can look at the future in another way—in terms of the evolutionary path that I lay out in Section 2.1. On this model, I am anticipating a move away from an arbitrary few citizens receiving traditional bespoke legal advice to many more members of society benefiting from the efficiencies and savings that can be achieved across the justice system, along my evolutionary path, through standardization and computerization. In a more efficient justice system, when there is mass customization, the unit cost of individual bits of legal service will reduce and, in turn, there should be greater access to legal services and to justice. We will get more punch from our pound.

In practice, assuming that there is no radical change (up or down) to the level of public funding made available for legal services, and in parallel with the improvements to the court system that I recommend in Sections 6.4 and 6.5, I propose that improved access to justice can be achieved in the future by a combination of six building blocks, as follows. First of all, citizens themselves must be appropriately empowered, so that they can take care of some legal affairs on their own and work more productively with those who advise them, if guidance from others is needed. The second building block is a streamlined legal profession with law firms that multi-source, embrace technology, progress towards commoditization, and offer pro bono services that dovetail sensibly with other sources of legal guidance. The third is a healthy third sector; recognizing that many citizens who are in need of legal assistance want a kind, empathetic ear with only a light sprinkling of legal expertise. Fourth, a new wave of imaginative, entrepreneurial, and market-driven alternative providers of legal service are vital to the mix, bringing new ways of making state funding go further, keeping law firms on their toes, and delivering service in a manner with which consumers are comfortable. Penultimately, to support all who need to wade their way through the law, statutory source materials and case law should be easily accessible and digestible through no-cost (to users) legal information systems. In turn and finally, there must be in place and in practice an enlightened set of government policies relating to the availability of public sector information. In the remainder of this chapter, I look at each of the six in turn.

7.3 The empowered citizen

In economic terms, lawyers are a scarce resource; and they are a resource that is distributed unevenly across society. When most private citizens seek legal advice, they cannot afford to retain lawyers for anything but a very few consultations; and those who wish to resolve disputes are often deterred by the prohibitive cost of litigation. However, and I hope I can take all readers with me on this fundamental point, even if lawyers are a scarce resource, we cannot allow justice to be similarly pigeon-holed.

The social challenge here, one of forbidding complexity, is to provide those who lack the funds to engage lawyers in the traditional manner with alternative and complementary sources of legal help. Part of the answer is to blend the work of new-look law firms with contributions from the third sector and from alternative providers. But even this more imaginative sourcing will not be enough. In the end, citizens themselves will need to bear much of the burden. In prosaic terms, we are in the realms of DIY law and legal self-service. In the lexicon of the day, we need to empower citizens to sort out some of their own legal issues.

How do we actually go about empowering citizens? I suggest there are two principal techniques: the first is what I call 'legal awareness raising' and the second is information technology (IT) in various shapes and forms.

With regard to awareness-raising, I draw a distinction between this notion and the apparently broader idea of 'public legal education' (PLE), as defined, for example, by the PLEAS Task Force.[11] My ambition for legal awareness-raising is to enable citizens to be sufficiently familiar with the law and the legal system to *recognize* when they need some kind of legal help. I take the Task Force to be more ambitious. As I interpret their view of PLE, this seems to extend to educating citizens so that they actually know and understand various substantive legal issues.

When I speak of legal awareness, I am reminded of the knack that most lawyers have, of sensing when certain circumstances give rise to a legal concern, even if they are not really familiar with the particular area of law. Just as alarm bells ring in their ears, I want citizens to have sufficient awareness of the law to have the same in-built early warning systems. I do not think we need to take the further educational step of teaching citizens in any depth about their civil rights and duties. All that we need do is equip them with

---

[11] 'Developing capable citizens: the role of public legal education' (July 2007) 9, at <http://www.pleas.org.uk>.

knowledge of where and how to look up the law and so determine these entitlements and obligations. In the same spirit, this is what many professors say
to their students about undergraduate legal studies—that the object is not to
learn the law but to know where and how to find it. Likewise with citizens.
They should be coached so that they know when they need legal assistance
and what resources are available.

In terms of my Client Service Chain (see Section 7.1), I am therefore inclined
to restrict awareness-raising to the *recognition* element, so that citizens can
tell when legal guidance will help them to solve a problem, avoid a difficulty,
or even promote their legal health. I see a much more modest role for
awareness-raising in respect of the *selection* and *service* components, where
guidance from human advisers or smart systems is more practicable than
educating citizens.

As for channels for the delivery of legal awareness-raising, there are many
options. Public bodies, law firms, third sector bodies, and others can produce handy leaflets, magazines, information packs, and websites. Newspaper
articles and TV coverage should also work well. And here, too, is a wonderful
opportunity to unleash e-learning in earnest (see Section 4.4). There can be
little doubt that a web-cast, or even a simple voice-only podcast, presented
by a friendly and articulate person in ordinary language and not legal jargon,
will be easier for many citizens to assimilate than inviting them to plough
through text.

I turn now to the ways in which IT, more widely, can complement legal
awareness-raising. This is the second technique for empowering the citizen.
In the past, most discussions of increasing access to justice through advanced
IT have focused on online self-help facilities that offer guidance on questions of substantive law. In terms of my Client Service Chain, the focus has
therefore been on the *service* component. This has been appropriate but we
can and should go further and give thought to the ways in which citizens can
be supported by IT in *recognizing* when legal help would be beneficial and in
selecting the most appropriate sources of legal help for their purposes
(although, in practice, these two processes often blend into one).

So, what kinds of systems might make it fairly easy for citizens to recognize
that legal assistance would be beneficial? On analysis, it emerges that there
are two problems of *recognition*. The first is where citizens already sense that
legal input of some sort would be useful but need help in understanding
and classifying their situation, so that they then know what kind of help or
solution to pursue. This sense that they have might be the result of some
successful legal awareness-raising or it may be triggered by some self-
evidently legally charged event (an aggressive letter from a solicitor perhaps).

In either case, are there online systems that might offer the navigational help they require?

I think we should again borrow and computerize a technique that seems to work well in health care. The technique is known as 'triage'. When resources are scarce and all patients cannot be treated at once, this is a process for assessing and prioritizing needs according to the seriousness of patients' conditions. The idea is to optimize the deployment of available professionals and facilities, so that more patients can be seen than would be on a 'first come first served' approach. Vitally, top clinicians only see severe or complex cases and the most straightforward conditions are dealt with by the most junior medics or nurses. By analogy, I envisage a form of legal triage and I discuss this in more detail in Section 7.4. For now, though, I propose the idea of online legal triage. This would provide citizens with guidance on the type of legal help they require (a law firm or third sector provider, for example). One version of this could be entirely IT-based; perhaps an interactive, diagnostic expert system that would ask a series of questions and then make recommendations. The system may confirm that it would be wise to secure legal guidance of a particular kind or it may suggest that their problem is not really a legal one. Another online tool could be a facility that invited citizens to explain their circumstances through e-mails; and these messages could be assessed by human lawyers or advice workers who, again, might confirm (or not) that legal guidance would be appropriate or beneficial. An impressive variant of this approach is found in LawHelp, a US-based system that allows citizens to interact with specialists through a type of instant messaging (a real-time chat facility). The specialists do not answer the questions put to them but point the user to promising online resources.[12] This to some extent combines both the recognition and selection elements of the Client Service Chain.

I now see that I had a type of online legal triage lurking in my head when I was an adviser, in 2000 and 2001, to Sir Andrew Leggatt on his *Review of Tribunals*.[13] I suggested then that there was a pressing need for some kind of facility which would help citizens and organizations to identify the most appropriate forums for the resolution of their differences and difficulties. Again, I envisaged a web-based expert diagnostic system—a citizen would answer a series of online questions about his or her grievance and, in turn, the system would identify the court, tribunal, ombudsman, complaints

---

[12] <http://www.lawhelp.org>.
[13] <http://www.tribunals-review.org.uk>.

procedure, or other method of resolution that seemed best suited to the dilemma at hand. This idea remains unimplemented; but I still like it, because I do know that many citizens are bamboozled by the wide range of options that seem to confront them when they seek to solve a problem through official channels.

The second problem of recognition is more challenging—this is when citizens have no sense at all that the law bears directly on their circumstances. More accurately, it is a problem of non-recognition. This most commonly prevails when there is no blatant trigger—such as personal injury or a pugnacious letter from a solicitor—to alert the citizen and set alarm bells ringing. Often, the consequence is an opportunity lost. Without legal insight, a chance is missed, perhaps to take steps to avoid some impending legal problem or to take advantage of some benefit that the law would confer. Aside from legal awareness-raising, whose focal point, I argue, is in widening recognition, how can IT help? Drawing on my arguments of Section 4.9, this is surely a job for what I call embedded legal knowledge. There is scope, for example, for the more widespread introduction of personalized alerting which will result in citizens being notified of new legal developments that affect their lives. Once an individual builds up a profile of his or her activities, or joins communities, whether open or closed, of people with shared interests, then distilled, relevant, and tailored briefings will be sent to them. In this way, citizens may be urged to be proactive. Personalized alerting will function like a lawyer who calls up periodically and suggests, because a client works in a given trade or business, then he or she should take a particular precaution or might like to take advantage of some opportunity. I say more about this in Section 7.7. Document assembly technology (Section 4.1) can also help here—in enabling lay people to create robust legal documents that will protect them in the future. Consider RiskRemedy from NatWest—this online service helps lay people to prepare legal documents (for example employment contracts) without, as it is claimed, 'resorting to expensive solicitors'.[14]

What about the *selection* element of the Client Service Chain? If we assume that a citizen has recognized that he or she would benefit from legal guidance, what kinds of systems might guide that person, for example, to the most appropriate lawyer or advice worker or online service in the circumstances? I have high hopes here for the emergence of the electronic legal marketplace that I discuss in Section 4.3. Using techniques with which citizens will be

---

[14] <http://www.natwestriskremedy.co.uk>.

familiar from their other online activities, I predict there will soon be many websites that will actually help clients to identify suitable lawyers or other sources of help (much as systems can help patients to find appropriate doctors); and they will help clients to secure services at highly competitive prices. Such systems already exist and I provide examples of them in Section 4.3. In due course, citizens will even benefit from online legal auctions, akin to eBay. These sites will drive prices down. And facilities will also be available to offer better insight into what legal fees to expect, and to hear from others about their legal experiences. This will give the comfort of knowing that the lawyers they choose have given satisfaction to others.

Still on the question of selection, citizens should also be able to consult the Web when contemplating whether to pursue formal action in the courts. Online help, perhaps using e-learning techniques, on how to pursue or defend a claim should be readily available, in punchy and graphical form. This could be designed for those who are already involved in a dispute as well as those contemplating action. A basic system could be provided by the court service but feedback, observations, insights, and tips from court users could also be encouraged, thereby helping citizens make informed decisions about how or whether to proceed.

Turning now to the *service* element of the Client Service Chain, I also expect that citizens will increasingly turn to the Web, as their first port of call, whenever they have a legal problem, or they have recognized a risk that needs to be managed, or they are pursuing some way to enhance their legal health (exploring their eligibility for some tax rebate, for example). Whether through primitive FAQs (frequently asked questions) or artificial intelligence-based, diagnostic expert systems, many legal issues on the minds of citizens will be handled through consultation with some online legal service. No longer will it be assumed that the citizen always needs to consult a qualified lawyer or third sector adviser.

Once again, my disruptive legal technologies (Chapter 4) will come into play: automatic document assembly systems will enable citizens to generate (at fixed or no cost) reliable and robust letters and agreements simply by responding to online questionnaires; online legal services will actually provide guidance and answers to legal problems; online communities will burgeon, where useful materials are made available in open source spirit and built up using wiki techniques; citizens will record their legal experiences on blogs, for others to examine; and they will pose and answer questions on discussion forums.

That citizens may come to be guided by unofficial sources rather than authoritative law itself raises interesting issues about the nature of law.

This guidance itself may come to be regarded by many as the law itself and not just a representation of it. This would be a poweful illustration of what the legal sociologist, Eugen Ehrlich, once called the 'living law'—the law which actually reflects and conditions behaviour in society.[15] This new genre of legal help may also introduce a further dimension to what has been called the 'delegalization of law'.[16]

In any event, these new facilities will not be organized under conventional legal headings, such as contract, tort, or agency. Nor will they be subdivided into legislation and case law. Instead, the resources will be presented and categorized as life events that citizens will immediately recognize as matching their position or predicament. Beneath self-evident headings—such as 'I have been fired', 'I want to start my own business', 'I want to write a will', 'I am in dispute with my landlord'—will lie the resources that I describe. This idea of organizing online legal information in terms that non-lawyers will immediately grasp is well illustrated by a fairly simple website that helps motorists who fall foul of the increasingly draconian road traffic laws in the UK.[17] The site provides a wealth of information on road traffic offences, including guidance on speed cameras, motor accidents, mobile phone usage, seat belts, and car insurance. A handy table of driving offences is presented, indicating for each the likely penalties, and whether or not disqualification or fixed penalty options are possible. A free 'road reckoner' is available to answer that age-old query—'what will I get?'

Finally, in relation to online facilities for citizens that may complement or displace conventional service, there is online dispute resolution, as I describe in Section 6.6. Systems such as Money Claim Online allow non-lawyers to prepare their own claims and to pursue legal action without directly involving anyone from the legal profession.

These various suggestions for securing legal service and guidance online will no doubt be frowned upon by technophobes and legal reactionaries alike. In concluding my discussion about the empowerment of citizens, I want to address some likely objections.

One important concern is that not all websites with legal content will be accurate or reliable. This clearly is a legitimate worry. Part of the challenge here will be to raise awareness amongst citizens about which online legal

---

[15] E Ehrlich, *Fundamental Principles of the Sociology of Law* (New York: Arno Press, reprint edition, 1975).

[16] See F Schauer and VJ Wise, 'Nonlegal information and the delegalization of law' (2000) 29(1) *Journal of Legal Studies* 495.

[17] <http://www.road-law.co.uk>.

brands are robust and perhaps officially endorsed. I see this as an important role for government. Once again, there is an interesting analogy to be found in medicine. Some doctors have major misgivings about the volumes of medical information that are now available online. They agitate about the accuracy of the guidance offered and harbour the more general fear that, when it comes to medical health, a little knowledge can be a dangerous, if not fatal, thing. On the other hand, other doctors welcome online medical resources, less perhaps for their accuracy but more for the way in which they encourage patients, as is said, to take greater responsibility for their own illnesses. On this argument, patients come to their doctors if not fully informed then certainly more engaged than has been possible in the past. Similarly, in law, even if the provision of online legal service, whatever its manifestation, may not always definitively resolve or dispose of a legal issue, it may nevertheless engender a greater willingness amongst deserving citizens to seek further help where, in the past, they might have felt deterred.

Another understandable concern that I expect to be voiced is that online service is rarely as good as the real thing. There is no substitute, it will be said, for seeing an experienced lawyer face-to-face. In many (but not all) circumstances, I agree. I return to this question in the following section. For now, though, I want to stress a harsh reality—given the extent to which legal expertise is a scarce resource, one-to-one consultative advisory guidance is a service we cannot always resource or afford. So, I respond, as I have for many years, by saying that the judicious use of IT can sometimes help to provide legal guidance to individuals who would otherwise go without any counsel whatsoever. And those who reject IT-based services because, in an ideal world, human service of a higher standard would be available, are allowing, as Voltaire would have said, the best to be the enemy of the good.

A further well intentioned objection to all of this technology, I know, is that some citizens do not have access to the Internet. This problem is known in the trade as the 'digital divide'. This refers to a new partition in society, between those who have access to the Internet and those who do not. In fact, around two-thirds of households in the UK have Internet access.[18] My guess is that this figure will rise in the next few years but it may well plateau at around three-quarters. Whatever the fraction, the percentage is significant (although not nearly as significant, I cannot resist saying, as the number of homes whose information seeking habits have been transformed by the Internet).

---

[18] See the Oxford Internet Surveys—W Dutton and EJ Helsper, *The Internet in Britain* 2007 (Oxford: Oxford Internet Institute, 2007), available at <http://www.oii.ox.ac.uk>.

To be blunt, I think that the impact of the digital divide on access to justice can be overstated, and sometimes disingenuously so. In the first instance, when we look at the research more closely, we find relatively lower levels of usage amongst the elderly and the less well-off. The cynical might say we should not be too worried, from an access to justice perspective, about the less well-off not having Internet access, because many of those who are least likely to afford technology will, by definition, be eligible for Legal Aid. Whether or not this is convincing, it is unquestionably the case that some Internet-deprived citizens can be described as secondary or proxy users, which means that they do not themselves sit down and put finger to keyboard but have someone else sit in the driving seat on their behalf. They can be said to be indirect beneficiaries of the legal resources on the Web. Many elderly people fall into this category—they delegate Web browsing to their children and grandchildren. Another class of indirect beneficiary, of course, are citizens who are guided by advisers (not least in third sector) who themselves are productive Internet users. All of which is to say that the number of people who are actually disadvantaged by being non-users is appreciably less than at first blush.

In any event, to rehearse another running theme of my work since the 1990s, even if we concede that some individuals do not have direct or indirect access to technology, I maintain that a higher percentage of members of our society have access to the Internet today than have access to justice. In 2000, I wrote, with some regret: 'I would bet that more people (of all social classes) will have access to the Internet (and so to the law, on my theory) in five years' time than have access to justice today.'[19] Sadly, I think I was right.

7.4 Streamlined law firms

With all kinds of Internet-based services available to the citizen, where does that leave lawyers? To pinpoint the role of lawyers and law firms in the new world of consumer legal services, we should return to first principles. In the first chapter of this book, I challenge lawyers to introspect and ask themselves honestly what parts of their current workload might be undertaken differently (more quickly, cheaply, efficiently, or to a higher quality) using

---

[19] Susskind (n 4 above) 158.

different methods of working. I say that the market is increasingly unlikely to tolerate costly lawyers for jobs that can equally or better be undertaken by less expensive workers or through smart systems and processes. This same thinking should be brought to bear in the context of access to justice for the individual citizen.

We should expect, following the arguments of section 3.5, that some tasks (for example those requiring deep expertise or inter-personal communication) will still require the traditional lawyer. But firms that are keen to survive must nevertheless be willing to decompose and multi-source across their practices, in the manner laid out in Section 2.5. Far more internal delegation to more junior lawyers will be needed, as will 'de-lawyering', that is, passing work to paralegals and legal executives, or intelligent lay people; where to use legally qualified individuals would be to over-egg the pudding. Outsourcing, subcontracting, relocating, and the various other means of sourcing that I identify should also be deployed. In this new world, if law firms wish to remain centre stage in the production of legal service, they will also need to develop their project management skills so that they can be responsible for managing a multi-sourced service and delivering it to clients (see Section 2.5).

At the same time, computerization should always at least be an option for consideration. This will involve systematizing, packaging, or commoditizing, as I explain these terms in Chapter 2; and will inevitably require some investment in those technologies that I dub 'disruptive' (see Chapter 4). For instance, the far greater use of automated document assembly (Section 4.1) and workflow systems (Section 4.8) should become standard practice amongst firms that aspire to the efficient disposal of relatively routine work. Another example—the advent of social networking, instant messaging, video conferencing, and telepresence will change the way that lawyers and citizens communicate with one another, removing much of the unnecessary noise and friction that characterizes conventional legal service and gives rise to unnecessary expense (see Section 4.2). And with the emergence of electronic markets, where legal work can be auctioned, details about reputation and performance can be recorded and maintained, and where directories of lawyers are available, citizens will be able to secure legal services at far lower and transparent cost than in the past (see Section 4.3).

In other words, law firms that serve citizens will be as deeply affected by the arguments of this book as their commercial cousins. And the tools and techniques that I have identified for larger firms can and should similarly be put to service in support of smaller practices.

Whether law firms can survive in this market will depend on the extent to which traditional lawyers are genuinely needed, when they are frankly and dispassionately compared with their emerging competition in the broadest sense, which includes a healthy third sector, entrepreneurial alternative providers, online self-help, and the various other sources of legal guidance that are and will become commonplace. Survival will also rest to some degree, therefore, on whether law firms can reinvent themselves, embrace new skills, and so provide newly competitive legal services. My expectation is that law firms will adapt but within limits. I predict that they will be most active in relation to the 'service' component rather than 'recognition' and 'selection' elements of my Client Service Chain (see Section 7.1). And the service itself, I suspect, will be largely dispute resolution and problem solving rather than dispute avoidance or legal health promotion.

Within these limits, lawyers who advise citizens will probably come to think that they have two classes of new 'competitor': lay people who are armed with packaged or commoditized self-help online legal tools, or less costly legal or quasi-legal workers supported by smart systems and often operating from low cost areas. However, following the arguments of Section 4.6, there is another threat; if not a distinct threat, then a development that will bolster the two threats already in play. I have in mind legal open-sourcing. Just as citizens can go online today and obtain punchy and effective help on how to fix their computers and on medical matters, then so too a rich body of open source legal material (standard documents, commentaries, personal experiences, and more) will appear on the Web. These will radically enhance the self-service experience and greatly assist the less costly and quasi-legal workers. As I suggest a little later in this section, lawyers could have a role in contributing to this body of knowledge. More generally, entrepreneurial law firms will not see threats in all of these developments—some will find promise and business in the latent legal market, for example.

Some lawyers will be quick to respond to much that is said above in words of the following sort—most clients, when they are in life-changing or career-threatening circumstances, will want to sit face-to-face with a proper lawyer and will not want to go online or speak to a paralegal. This is an important challenge that must be addressed squarely. I start with a concession—I have little doubt that some people today, as a matter of fact, do indeed prefer to consult a lawyer when a major personal or work-related issue arises. That said, we also know from the research of *Which?* and others that satisfaction levels with lawyers are not compellingly high and many are sympathetic to alternative providers.[20] In any event, aside from what *is* the case today, I am more concerned with how we *ought* to configure and provide legal services

---

[20] The research in question was conducted in 2004—see <http://www.which.co.uk>. Also see the various articles in (2000) 16(6) *Consumer Policy Review*.

in the future. I am focusing here, incidentally, in terms of the Client Service Chain (Section 7.1), on the 'selection' and 'service' elements.

I think it helpful now to introduce a new concept—the idea of 'legal triage'. For a lay person to visit a lawyer directly whenever he or she deems it appropriate may be as wrong-headed as a patient with a mildly grazed knee going directly to an accident and emergency consultant without being reviewed by a nurse. A sensible first step, for clients and patients alike, is an initial appraisal of their circumstances to determine the most sensible course of action. In law, I call this legal triage—whether by human or online triage (see Section 7.3), the citizen's situation can be assessed and the best type and source of guidance can be determined. This assessment need not involve a lawyer. It might be the province of a suitably trained paralegal. The client might be directed to a lawyer in the first instance but, on many occasions, their situation and profile may lead to a different referral—to an advice worker, to a website, or perhaps to an alternative provider. This form of human legal triage can straddle the recognition and the selection elements of the Client Service Chain.

Lawyers should only be engaged when their distinctive skills and expertise are needed. And here is the crux. The lawyer might feel, because of the gravity of the circumstances, that he or she is the person for the job. Legal triage may suggest otherwise—a marriage counsellor or a social psychologist, for example, might be a better first port of call. And even if a lawyer is thought to be necessary in the first instance, this does not mean that this adviser should be personally engaged throughout the life cycle of the client's episode. Triage may suggest, for instance, an initial consultation with a lawyer, but followed thereafter by a supervised, multi-sourced service.

Looking some years into the future, and following what I say in Section 3.4, I do not think we can, in any event, simply assume that our children will find it as natural as their parents to meet face-to-face with those who advise them. Mere assertion today by lawyers that clients like to look them in the eyes will not bind future generations.

The net result of all of this is that, in years to come, legal triage, multi-sourcing, and IT will combine to diminish the direct involvement of lawyers in the legal affairs of citizens. In fact, there are many areas of legal service delivery (for example social welfare law), where lawyers are already much less involved than they were in the past. When lawyers are engaged in the future, they will bring to bear deep expertise or the specific inter-personal skills that are called for; and this service will be underpinned by newly fashioned and more sustainable business models.

For those law firms that continue to trade, pro bono work will continue to be important but it will change in scope. The next generation of pro bono activity will extend beyond volunteer (or volunteered) lawyers sitting in advice centres, dispensing guidance at no cost. Lawyers who are prepared to work on a pro bono basis should be encouraged to contribute in ways that reach beyond conventional advisory service to citizens. One possibility here is for lawyers to participate in well facilitated and orderly online discussions and to offer direct help to citizens through this medium. Another is to become active contributors to the online communities that I recommend (in Section 7.5) should be set up for third sector workers. Yet another option is for lawyers and their firms to provide resources (standard documents or suitably anonymized letters of advice, for example) to the banks of open source legal materials that I predict will evolve on the Web (Section 4.6). Lawyers may indeed have a crucial role in promoting legal open-sourcing. In turn, one way in which law firms may be judged in the future to be fulfilling their social responsibilities will be in relation to their contributions to online communities and resources. The support of professional bodies could be invaluable here, with a view perhaps to committing every firm, in due course, to providing a minimum number of contributions each year.

There is a further dimension to pro bono work that needs more thought. In a multi-sourced environment, pro bono work will be one amongst many components that contribute to legal service. In practice, this might mean that lawyers or legal executives[21] who make themselves available for pro bono work, may be allocated discrete, modular tasks (perhaps some research or drafting) that will be submitted by them and then integrated as part of a multi-sourced service being coordinated by another. This might come about when third sector organizations invite lawyers, in their pro bono capacity, to undertake particular slices of work that require lawyers' skills or expertise but for which no funds are available.

7.5 A healthy third sector

A vital contribution to our justice system today is made by what is increasingly referred to as the 'third sector'. Bodies belonging to the third sector are third in the sense that they belong neither to the public sector nor to the

---

[21] See 'The extent and value of pro bono work provided by legal executives' (Ministry of Justice Research Series 2/08, February 2008), available at <http://www.justice.gov.uk>.

private sector. The term includes charities, voluntary organizations, community bodies, and social enterprises of various sorts. Generally, then, these are non-governmental, not-for-profit entities. According to the UK government: 'Since 1997 the third sector has grown in scale and impact. There are more organizations than ever before. Overall income has increased. More people are volunteering. More people are setting up social enterprises. The sector is playing a greater role in supporting communities and tackling inequalities, in creating opportunity and enterprise, and in designing and supplying public services'.[22] To champion third sector interests across government, an Office of the Third Sector has been set up within the Cabinet Office.

I am afraid it is easy to be rather cynical about the government's support for the third sector, because this 'thriving' sector is, arguably, undertaking tasks and delivering services that might be expected to be the province of government itself and so paid for through our taxes; rather than the responsibility of an army of admirable volunteers and, in effect, paid for out of the pockets of a few. On the other hand, charitable work and social enterprises do of themselves serve important social functions, for example they help to promote coherence and purpose within given communities; and many third sector workers find the work satisfying and fulfilling.

In any event, it is absolutely clear to me that a wide range of third sector bodies, as a matter of fact, do play a pivotal role in helping to achieve access to justice in the UK. A glance at the website of the Advice Services Alliance (ASA, the umbrella body for independent advice services in the UK) lists a formidable collection of not-for-profit organizations that offer advice and help on the law.[23] These include Citizens Advice, Law Centres and Shelter.[24] ASA's main website is impressive, providing information on a wide range of legal issues in England and Wales.[25] The government complements this on an online basis through Community Legal Advice, the website of the Community Legal Service in England and Wales.[26] (This started life, in April 2000, as the ambitious and award-winning website known as 'Just Ask'.)

In combination, the websites and physical centres of the third sector provide citizens with a remarkable service; and, to some extent, in all three components (recognition, selection, and service) of my Client Service Chain

---

[22] 'Third Sector Strategy for Communities and Local Government', Discussion Paper (Department for Communities and Local Government, London, June 2007), see <http://www.communities.gov.uk>.

[23] <http://www.asauk.org.uk>.

[24] <http://www.citizensadvice.org.uk> and <http://www.shelter.co.uk>.

[25] <http://www.advicenow.org.uk>. Also see <http://www.plenet.org.uk>, which was launched as the manuscript of this book was being completed.

[26] <http://www.clsdirect.org.uk>.

(see Section 7.1). On the ground, however, I understand from people who work on legal matters in the third sector that they feel badly under-resourced. Further, my impression is that the advice that is offered today focuses very largely on solving legal problems that have arisen and there is precious little capacity for extending these services to the avoidance of legal problems; still less to the promotion of legal health.

The funding of the third sector in law raises difficult policy issues. I can see, on the one hand, that the government must be wary of requests from the third sector in law, fearing it to be a potentially bottomless pit; and recognizing too that there is stiff competition—analogous calls on cash from, say, the worlds of health and education. On the other hand, my sense is that a modest increase in investment could greatly enhance the efforts of the third sector.

Looking ahead, and following the arguments in this book, I can see that a core challenge for the future of this corner of the justice system is coordination—not simply amongst the many and various third sector bodies that provide legal guidance (in person and online) but also so that the third sector's contributions can be taken as part of the multi-sourced approach to increasing access to justice. On the first point, not least in building know-how and online resources, there is always the danger of duplicating effort. Such duplication happens in relatively well run single-site bodies, and so presents particular challenges for dispersed organizations. On the question of multi-sourcing, again the issue is that legal work should be divided and allocated, in the circumstances, to the most efficient potential provider. Workers in the third sector, as much as lawyers, must continually challenge themselves and check that the work they do justifies their specific skills and talents, and could not be undertaken in different ways. Once again, a wide range of technologies present themselves as possible tools for this trade.

Some of these tools are disruptive (in the sense discussed in Chapter 4) and threaten to disintermediate the adviser (that is, remove them from the process). There is an interesting contrast here, though, between lawyers and third sector advisers. Many lawyers, who make money, after all, from practising law, are unsurprisingly nervous about being disintermediated. Their livelihoods are threatened. Voluntary legal workers, on the other hand, should welcome the introduction of systems that can enhance or replace the work that they conduct manually, so they can be released to undertake more challenging or fulfilling jobs.

What technologies might be relevant for the third sector? Automated document assembly (see Section 4.1) is clearly one—workers in the third sector might have considerable insight into legal issues but not necessarily the legal experience to draft watertight legal documents or letters. If there are certain types of documents or parts of documents that are used very frequently, then with the assistance of lawyers (perhaps acting on a pro bono basis), systems could be built that could reduce time spent on drafting and increase the quality and consistency of the paperwork. Third sector workers will also benefit from the improved systems that I predict will come to be used regularly for identifying and selecting lawyers. It will surely help voluntary workers to be able to pinpoint easily lawyers who have the right experience, of whom past clients speak highly, and whose rates compare favourably (see Section 4.3). There is ample scope also for the use of e-learning systems to keep third sector workers up to date, well briefed, and confident about legal issues (see Section 4.4). While some such systems might be developed specifically for them, it might also be possible to have permission to use and access systems that have been developed commercially by law firms and legal publishers. A further technique that might be welcomed is personalized alerting (see Section 4.9). For advisers who have special interest or involvement in particular areas of law or wish to keep abreast of a range of legal developments, Web alerts and automatic updates will be invaluable.

Of all possible legal technologies that might be embraced by the third sector, I believe the most exciting to be closed legal communities for advisers. I envisage a facility that could be similar in many ways to Sermo, the online community for US medical practitioners. As I explain in Section 4.7, there are over 50,000 doctors now using Sermo. The system is a cross between a social networking system, such as Facebook, and a collaboration environment, like Wikipedia. Doctors can pose questions to one another and answer queries themselves. An impressive body of medical knowledge and experience is quickly building there. At modest expense, a similar resource could be developed by and for third sector workers. They would be able to keep in regular contact with one another, share experiences and insights, build up a collective body of expertise, capture best practice, extend their fields of competence, access standard documents, retrieve useful opinions, and in so doing have more confidence in the advice they dispense and feel part of a coherent team of advisers gathered under the one virtual roof. There could also be links to legal information systems that contain further source materials (see Section 7.7). More, the facility could be extended to practising lawyers, who could make themselves available to advise workers to help them with specialist legal issues.

The development and implementation of an online community need not be costly. And yet its impact, alongside the other technologies I mention, could be profound. It is here, in legal technologies, that government investment in the third sector might most usefully be directed.

7.6 Entrepreneurial alternative providers

Even with streamlined law firms and a well resourced third sector in place, there may also be scope for new businesses to enter the market. In England and Wales, the Legal Services Act 2007 enables, in due course, the establishment of 'alternative business structures' for legal service organizations and for the investment in law firms by individuals and organizations other than lawyers. (It was agreed in May 2008 that analogous arrangements will be introduced in my native Scotland.) In terms of the Client Service Chain (see Section 7.1), like law firms, I expect alternative providers will be most active in relation to the 'service' element rather than 'recognition' and 'selection'. Further, and again like law firms, the emphasis is likely to be on dispute resolution and problem-solving over dispute avoidance and legal health promotion.

The untutored intuition of many lawyers and legal commentators is that so-called 'low-end' legal service, such as consumer law and Legal Aid work, will not be attractive to external investors or entrepreneurs who are thinking about building new-look legal businesses. However, from my recent work as an adviser to a private equity firm, I can now see why this common view may be mistaken. In the first instance, consumer law and Legal Aid work together have a value in England well in excess of £10 billion. If we also take into account the likely 'latent legal market', depending on the elasticity of demand, this figure may be substantially larger when legal services become more easily accessible and affordable. In any event, where value is being counted in billions and the current working practices seem antiquated or inefficient, I have found a clear interest from potential investors. Where some lawyers might dismiss work as uninteresting because it is high volume and low margin, external investors may be attracted precisely because of this profile. If there is a large turnaround of routine legal activity, investors immediately see scope for more rigorous processes and the introduction of systems that can radically overhaul the conventional ways of operating. On one model, then, Legal Aid work would not be undertaken by myriad sole practitioners and small law firms across the land; rather, bulk legal processing capabilities would be built and they may not always be wholly located in England. In fact, the Legal Services Commission has already begun to encourage working practices that achieve economies of scale.

As the legal market is liberated and non-lawyers are able to invest and participate in the provision of legal services, I have little doubt that the entrepreneurially minded will find new and improved ways of delivering conventional services and will create novel markets and opportunities where none had been recognized before. That most lawyers (and I, for that matter) are not sufficiently imaginative to identify exactly how this might unfold in practice does not kill the idea. Indeed, it is precisely when there is an absence of such entrepreneurial insight from the legal fraternity that canny investors find great possibilities. Many lawyers are too risk averse and immersed in practices of the past to make the leap into the next generation of legal solution providers. Just as librarians did not invent Google, lawyers may not create tomorrow's innovations in legal practice.

One likelihood is the establishment of new-look legal businesses that are entirely devoted to the legal market. However, these will bear little resemblance to the pyramidic, hourly billing partnerships of today. Some may bear the brand of well-regarded law firms whose operations, on acquisition, will be overhauled beyond recognition. Others will be entirely new businesses, built from scratch and driven by what is sustainable and profitable for the future rather than what has worked in the past.

Another strong possibility will be the setting up of legal departments or divisions of existing consumer businesses, such as supermarkets, high street banks, and other commercial organizations that are used to dealing directly with the retail market.

Both of these categories of twenty-first century legal service provider will no doubt design and build disruptive legal systems of the sort I discuss in Chapter 4, including, for example, document assembly and workflow systems. And they will implement these alongside other well-tested techniques, such as telephone call centres. At the same time, there will also be those who strive to attract and build human capital—lawyers and law firms will no doubt be recruited and absorbed as part of these organizations, taken on board to undertake specialist legal work, but only when human legal expertise is genuinely required. By analogy, those supermarkets today that sell spectacles have recruited qualified optometrists to test the eyes of customers and to prescribe accordingly. But the selling of frames is undertaken in the spirit and using the techniques of the mainstream business. While many lawyers will shudder at the very prospect of being a mere cog in a consumer service machine, many citizens will find it more convenient and less forbidding to take their legal concerns to the supermarket rather than the law firm. I do appreciate that, culturally, many traditional legal advisers would find it difficult to relocate to a supermarket or a bank, although some will no doubt be attracted by more flexible working arrangements. But it will be a very different working environment. I expect that professional and regulatory bodies around the world will, in any event, soften the blow somewhat, by requiring that lawyers who come to work in retail and other environments will still be governed and supported by well established professional rules and values. These will include regulations that determine whether specific retail outfits are indeed fit to own and run legal businesses.

A further dimension to this scenario that is threatening for conventional law firms is that we may find some retail organizations (banks or building societies, for example) that will offer legal services not to profit from these directly but as a way of building other businesses or enhancing their brands. The result here would be a service that might undercut that of traditional lawyers, both because more efficient processes and systems are used and also because there will be no profit margin built into their pricing. It is hard to compete with businesses that are not trying to make money.

7.7 Accessible legal information systems

I come now to the question of access to the law itself. For lawyers and advice workers at least, ready access to primary legal sources (legislation and case law) and to various secondary sources (commentaries, texts and analysis) is fundamental. These are basic tools of the trade of lawyering. We cannot have access to justice if our lawyers and legal advisers do not have access to the law.

Today, it might seem blindingly obvious that primary sources should be freely available on the Web. But this was a matter of great contention in the mid to late 1990s. And the story surrounding the debate of the time is worth relating. My focus here, incidentally, is very largely on legislation.

Traditionally, which for current purposes can be taken to mean 'before the Web', to gain sight of statutory material, a reader had to visit a library, or purchase a hard copy of the instrument in question, or perhaps buy a textbook in which the law in question had been reproduced (by permission of the Crown). This state of affairs attracted all sorts of criticisms. It was frequently asked—how can citizens be presumed to know all of the law, if its contents are not accessible? And when the Web came along—why is statutory material not available on the 'information superhighway' (as it was then called)? I ranted about this at some length in *The Future of Law*, railing both against the way legislation was published electronically (it was perceived at the time that the government was seeking to make a profit from selling the law) and in opposition to the way in which the law was promulgated or, more accurately, not being promulgated (this term refers to the mechanism for letting the public know when a new law is enacted). I went as far as to say that the State was failing to 'legislate meaningfully'.[27] These were heady days.

But I had to qualify my words almost immediately. At proof stage, I inserted a footnote that ran as follows: 'As this book went to press, however, the government announced (on 9th February 1996) what appears to be a sensible change in policy in relation to the electronic reproduction of legislation, although it is too early to know what the practical effects might be'.[28] The gist of this Ministerial statement seemed to be that the government would be permitting the free re-publication of statutory material on the Internet.

Nonetheless, progress was slow and an active and articulate group of lawyers and legal technologists ran a campaign under the banner, 'Free the Law'. Their aim was to bring about the free availability of legislation *and* case law on the Internet. They pointed to the formidable Australian system, AustLII (the Australasian Legal Information Institute) in support of their claim that it was both possible and desirable for a modern jurisdiction to have all of its primary source materials online.[29] The applicability of the AustLII approach to England became the focal point of what transpired to be a seminal meeting, itself entitled 'Free the Law', held at Chatham House in London, on 8 November 1999.[30] Professor Graham Greenleaf, one of the original developers of AustLII, enthused the assembled audience and helped to galvanize the community in question into further action. I had the good fortune to chair the debate that followed, although I was far less involved in the initiative than Laurie West-Knights (now QC) and Lord Justice Brooke, who were great champions of the cause and spoke so compellingly that evening.

As a direct result of that meeting, a pilot website offering free access to an integrated body of British and Irish legislation and case law was launched in March 2000. Christened BAILII (British and Irish Legal Information Institute) the pilot held 75,000 searchable documents, taken from the five jurisdictions, and was bound together by 2 million hyperlinks. The system was developed with the assistance, along with the software and the methods, of AustLII.

Just eights years later, we now take so many online resources for granted. But, at the time, two features of the BAILII were remarkable, ground-breaking, and even breath-taking for the legal communities of Britain and Ireland.

---

[27] Susskind (n 5 above) 20.

[28] ibid 20, footnote 1.

[29] <http://www.austlii.edu.au>.

[30] The transcript of that meeting is available at <http://www2.warwick.ac.uk/fac/soc/law/elj/jilt/2000_1/free_the_law/transcript>.

The first was the sheer quantity of materials: to have such a rich body of legislation *and* case law at the fingertips of Internet users at no cost to them was invaluable and almost unbelievable. Second, was the usability of the service—many of the documents were connected to one another by hyperlinks, enabling users to jump, for example, from law reports that referred to legislation into the specific sections being cited. This ability to browse around and between the materials was perhaps the cleverest aspect of the AustLII toolkit. When documents are loaded into the system, the software automatically detects citations and references and then inserts the links between materials. A huge network is created, but manual intervention is minimal.

Today, BAILII is thriving. Run as a modestly funded charity, it provides the largest, free-of-charge online collection of British and Irish primary legal materials (legislation and case law). The service now contains approximately seventy-six databases, covering seven jurisdictions and holding 200,000 searchable documents with about fifteen million internal hypertext links. BAILII continues to use the Australian technology, as contributed originally by AustLII.[31] The databases on BAILII are drawn from a variety of sources. Some are taken from existing websites; others are from databases that are on published and unpublished CD-ROMs; and still others are direct or indirect feeds from relevant courts, government bodies, and other organizations. All of the data is converted into a consistent format and a set of search and hypertext facilities are added.

While BAILII has flourished, the government has been far from idle. For example, vast quantities of UK legislation (primary and secondary) are now made available online, at no cost to users. This is now a key public service, provided by Her Majesty's Stationery Office (HMSO) through the much-used website of the Office of Public Sector Information (OPSI).[32] Amongst other materials, the site provides the full text of all UK Parliament Public General Acts from 1988 onwards, of all UK Local Acts from 1991 onwards, and all published Statutory Instruments from 1987 onwards. Usefully, these are available in HTML and PDF formats. HMSO aims to publish these documents on the OPSI website simultaneously or least within twenty-four hours of their publication in printed form. At the same time, Bills that are current before the UK Parliament are also available online, at the website of the UK Parliament.[33]

---

[31] The AustLII team has gone on to champion WorldLII <http://www.worldlii.org>, which provides a single search facility that operates across an international family of legal information institutes. WorldLII embraces 270 databases from 48 jurisdictions in 20 countries.

[32] <http://www.opsi.gov.uk>.

[33] <http://www.parliament.uk>.

In practice and in terms of policy, the progress that has been made since the mid-1990s in 'freeing the law' has been staggering. However, it would be wrong to assume that we now live in some legislative utopia and that access to justice has been secured by putting statutory material online. Daniel Greenberg, Parliamentary Counsel, a legislative draftsman of considerable experience, expresses the current position in the following terms:

for most practical purposes the access afforded by Queen's Printer's copies or the OPSI website is utterly useless. This is because of the fact that an enormous amount of new legislation, both primary and subordinate, operates by referential amendment of old legislation; the result is that the text of an Act as passed ten years ago is of no help at all in telling me the state of the law now . . . Every time I access an Act or an instrument which amends an earlier one I am forced also to obtain the text of the earlier one and to construct a revised version reflecting what will often turn out to be a complicated multilayered set of amendments. Difficult and time-consuming, but arguably not impossible: more problematically, however, I will have no practicable way of knowing that the Act or instrument I am reading has not itself now been amended by a later one.[34]

If an experienced legislative draftsman finds it challenging to use the HMSO/OPSI website to find what law is in force at any given moment, what hope can there be for the citizen? Having all published legislation available in electronic form is a wonderful facility but it is a first step rather than the last word in providing access to justice. Non-lawyers could not hope to determine their legal rights and obligations simply by browsing through archives of legislation.

Interestingly, the government is working towards a more powerful tool that would meet Daniel Greenberg's concerns. It has developed and delivered the UK Statute Law Database (SLD). And when it launched the service in December 2006, the Department for Constitutional Affairs (now the Ministry of Justice) expressly said that this database was a contribution to the Department's aim of improving access to justice.[35]

I first heard that the SLD was in the pipeline in June 1991. Lord Mackay of Clashfern, then the Lord Chancellor, told me about the project when we met at a conference in Oxford. He was rightly enthused. I was too. Now, I concede that you should not rush into major IT projects in the law, but fifteen years

---

[34] 'The Volume and Complexity of United Kingdom Legislation Today' in S Hetherington (ed), *Halsbury's Laws of England Centenary Essays* 2007 (London: LexisNexis, 2007) 58–9.

[35] The system can now be found at <http://www.statutelaw.gov.uk>—it was developed and is maintained by the Statutory Publications Offices in London and Belfast (themselves part of the Ministry of Justice).

for completion was deeply disturbing. The development of the SLD seemed to be fettered by an unholy and endless series of delays and problems. And between conception and birth, a great deal happened—for instance the Web was invented, BAILII was introduced, and HMSO transitioned from selling printed legislation at a profit to providing a powerful database of legislation at no charge for Internet users.

Nonetheless, SLD has brought features that neither BAILII nor HMSO offer and goes some considerable way to meeting Daniel Greenberg's objections. Impressively, and again at no charge, users can view amended legislation as it has changed over time; examine the way in which legislation will be affected by amendments that are not yet in force; see how legislation has been changed for different jurisdictions (say, Scotland as compared with England and Wales); and browse across links between affecting and affected legislation. A key feature of the system is that it can offer a historical view of the legislation that was in force on any specific day.[36]

There is one wrinkle, however, and it is not trivial. The SLD is not yet up to date. When launched, the database held over 30,000 items of primary legislation that were in force at 1 February 1991 and primary and secondary legislation that has been produced since then. Today, according to the SLD website, the service carries most (but not all) types of primary and secondary legislation, most primary legislation is held in 'revised' form but most secondary legislation is not revised, and all legislation that is in revised form has been updated at least to the end of 2001.[37] The truth is, it is not quite finished; although what is there is very promising.

Until the SLD is up to date, for both primary legislation and for statutory instruments (and the latter, as Daniel Greenberg points out, 'account for an increasingly important part of the practical legal burdens on the citizen'),[38]

[36] Other jurisdictions have been even more ambitious. For example, from 2000 to 2005, the Jersey Legal Information Board <http://www.jerseylaw.je>, under the chairmanship of Sir Philip Bailhache, the Bailiff and Chief Justice of Jersey, undertook a project that involved not simply a consolidation of all statutory laws enacted in the Island since 1771 but an entire revision as well. This meant that all legislation in force, together with countless amendments, was gathered together and restated as a new, coherent body of law. This has now been put online at <http://www.jerseylaw.je/law/lawsinforce> as searchable text and in a print version that corresponds to the authorized text. To help further, the revised law is organized intuitively under a series of 26 chapters, covering topics such as family law, crime and sentencing, and financial services. This initiative is part of a broader strategy to make the law more accessible in Jersey.

[37] <http://www.statutelaw.gov.uk> under 'Frequently Asked Questions'.

[38] 'The Volume and Complexity of United Kingdom Legislation Today' (n 34 above) 59. According to research recently conducted by Sweet & Maxwell, 87% of legislation introduced in 2007 was in the form of statutory instruments—<http://www.sweetandmaxwell.thomson.com>.

and until this is integrated with a similarly up-to-date body of case law (perhaps in the manner of BAILII), those who want to undertake up-to-date research still have to rely on the publications and online services of various commercial providers.[39] While these services are powerful and comprehensive and may be affordable for those who are in the business of law, their subscription fees are beyond the pockets of most citizens.

Before I talk about the implications of this current state of affairs, I feel impelled to throw down a gauntlet for those who aspire to developing the next generation of legal information systems. I would like to see the evolution of a Wikipedia-like service covering the UK legal systems. This online resource could be established and maintained collectively by the legal profession; by practitioners, judges, academics, and voluntary workers. If current leaders in the UK legal world are serious about promoting our jurisdictions as world class, here is a genuine opportunity to pioneer, to excel, to provide a wonderful social service, and to leave a substantial legacy. The initiative would evolve a corpus of UK law like no other: a resource readily available to lawyers and lay people; a free web of inter-linked materials; packed with scholarly analysis and commentary, supplemented by useful guidance and procedure; rendered intensely practical by the addition of action points and standard documents; and underpinned by direct access to legislation and case law, made available by the government, perhaps through BAILII. And we should not stop at text. We should add video and audio clips as well— perhaps of seminal lectures of the day or even of our senior judges delivering judgments (how marvellous would it be if we could watch and listen to, say, Lord Atkin read his judgment in *Donoghue v Stevenson*?). A Wikipedia of UK law could be an evolving, interactive, multi-media legal resource of unprecedented scale and utility.

Let me turn back now to the problem of the day—that we do not have an easily accessible, authoritative, no-charge, comprehensive, fully up-to-date and maintained legal information system. I do see this is a cause for concern and I know that many commentators believe this lack of free access to all law in force as an outrage. But I think, in relation to citizens, there is a far larger worry that should exercise us more. I have no doubt that lawyers and legal advice workers, alongside law students, legal academics, many professional service providers and public sector workers, need easy access to primary sources of law (legislation and case law). And I can see that the readier is this access, then the greater is the likelihood of improving the quality and reducing

---

[39] eg <http://www.lexisnexis.co.uk> and <http://www.westlaw.co.uk>.

the cost of services provided to citizens. In other words, accessible legal information systems that hold primary sources will directly benefit lawyers and those who work with the law but will only indirectly benefit the citizen.[40]

I simply cannot see and never have seen the attraction or the wisdom of citizens ploughing their way through, say, a fifty-page statutory instrument. Even if he or she had ready access to such a document, the average citizen would (a) be bored senseless reading it and (b) not be sufficiently familiar with the legal jargon and the broader legal context to figure out its full implications. If one of my children has a disease of some sort, I do not want to read some paper in medical-speak about the epidemiology or the pathology of the disorder. I want to know what to do. I want advice. I want to take practical steps. If I have a problem with my computer, I do not wish to subject myself to some learned treatise on the shortcomings or idiosyncrasies of the underlying programming language. I want it fixed. I want it not to happen again. I want to be told what to do next. So too in law. As I have said for years, citizens have little interest in the canons of statutory interpretation or in determining the *ratio decidendi* of binding precedents. Instead, they want quick, cheap, punchy, practical, and jargon-free guidance. Citizens who have legal issues also want to be told what to do.

This, for me, helps us to define the next generation of legal information systems for citizens (as opposed to those for law workers). The challenge of having accessible legal information systems in place will not be met when SLD is up to date and integrated with a similar system for case law. No. This battle will only have been won when citizens can go online and, through a second generation of legal information system, secure digestible and actionable guidance that helps them in their own precise circumstances. Databases of statutes and cases will not do this job for citizens. Instead, we will need different tools, ones that actually give help rather than point to potentially relevant legal sources. Some of these are identified in Chapter 4 and are discussed in Section 7.3: automatic document assembly, online legal services, legal open-sourcing and online communities. Simpler aids will also be effective—decision trees, flowcharts, and FAQs (frequently asked questions), for example.

In the broader context of my analysis of the access to justice (in Section 7.1), these second generation legal information systems should help not just

---

[40] For an extended and more sophisticated discussion of the needs of different categories of user of legal information systems, see Philip Leith and Karen McCullagh, 'Developing European Legal Information Markets based on Government Information' (2004) 12(3) *International Journal of Law and Information Technology*.

in solving legal problems but in avoiding problems and even also in promoting the legal health of users. However, in relation to my Client Service Chain (also in Section 7.1), these systems will tend to contribute much more to the service element (providing affordable and accessible help) than to the selection and recognition elements. They will be less useful, that is, in helping citizens to select the best source of guidance and to recognize the optimum point at which they would benefit from legal guidance.

If legal information systems are of comparatively little help to citizens in helping them recognize if and when they need legal guidance, does this then scupper any hopes that IT can crack the problem of promulgation? This problem, to recap, is that we do not have systematic and effective techniques for bringing to citizens' attention when there are new developments in the law, or changes in old law. As many commentators and scholars have pointed out, it is bizarre at best that citizens are presumed to know the content of the law and yet the State takes no responsibility for actually informing the general public about new or changed law. Jeremy Bentham, the great nineteenth-century legal theorist and social reformer, put it more forcefully when he said that: 'The notoriety of every law ought to be as extensive as its binding force. It ought indeed to be much more extensive . . . No axiom could be more self-evident: none more important: none more universally disregarded'.[41] Some legal philosophers have gone further and argued that laws that are not promulgated are not laws at all.[42] Even if we stop short of this position, it is hard to see how genuine access to justice can be achieved without effective promulgation.

Contrast today with the past. In years gone by, all Acts of the Scottish Parliament (the previous one) were published at the market cross of Edinburgh, while sheriffs in England were once required to proclaim all new statutes throughout their bailiwicks. The people of the land could scrutinize the law when it came down from on high. Today, however, new laws come into force and old laws are repealed, and no-one has any clue what is going on. Even lawyers. Part of the problem here is that we are suffering from hyper-regulation, the term I use to bemoan the reality that we are all governed today by rules and laws that are so complex and so extensive that no-one can pretend to have mastery of them all. Recent research by the legal information providers, Sweet & Maxwell, suggested that 3,071 new laws were

---

[41] HLA Hart (ed), *Of Laws In General* (London: The Athlone Press, 1970) 71.
[42] See L Fuller, *The Morality of Law* (New Haven, Conn: Yale University Press, revised edn, 1964).

introduced in 2007 (as compared with 2,702 in 2006).[43] We are running, therefore, at about eight new laws every day. Who on earth could hope to cope with that influx?

Yet, in larger part, the problem of promulgation is about defects in communication. As the statute book and common law have grown, we have not had workable channels through which to keep people up to date with new and changing law. However, I can see a new type of service emerging that might just provide the mechanisms we need to overcome this age-old shortcoming in modern justice systems. I am thinking here of personalized alerting—as I explain in Section 4.9, this is an Internet-based technique for delivering legal updates, briefings, and alerts automatically and proactively to the desktops of citizens. Whether supported by the government or delivered by some intermediary, this would allow citizens to register topics in which they are interested (supplemented perhaps by profiles of their interests that could be derived automatically from their click-streams and online movements) and they would be notified of every new regulation, every rule, and every judgment that affects them directly; or impacts on members of online communities of which they are members. If supplemented by the gloss that Web 2.0 methods can provide—blogs, personal commentaries, guidance through discussion forums, all built up in wiki-like manner—then we can begin to imagine a world where citizens are informed in a digestible way when there is a new law that directly affects them. This can be anyone, from a chiropractor to a carpenter; from a brain surgeon to a tree surgeon.

In the future, on the strength of such techniques, we may come to regard as entirely antiquated the notion that the law-making process ends with the published articulation of legal provisions. An indispensable component of law-making will be that of bringing new law to the attention of the people.

7.8 Enlightened public information policy

If we are serious about radically increasing access to justice, I believe there is a broader challenge than making legislation, case law, and other quasi-legal resources available through online legal information systems. I am thinking

---

[43] <http://www.sweetandmaxwell.thomson.com>.

here about the role and responsibility of public bodies in promoting understanding of legal and regulatory issues. The rules and laws that govern us all are invariably originated, administered, or enforced by public bodies, in central government, local government, and beyond. In total, in the UK, there are over 100,000 public bodies. Although most are intimately involved with the law, very few regard it as part of their public task to raise public awareness of legal matters, to educate on or clarify issues of law, or to alert citizens to legal developments that might affect them. This is a huge opportunity missed. Enlightened public information policy would encourage or even require public bodies to take on the job of drawing attention to the laws, regulations, and rules that are so central to their daily work and ensuring they are made more accessible and digestible to the citizenry.

To grasp the scale of the challenge here requires my final detour of the book; this time into the fairly arcane world of public information policy. Governments and public bodies have, of course, always been in the business of managing information—as creators, controllers, distributors, and more. Looking back, though, as a holder of information, until a decade ago, the State really had only two main roles in relation to information. First, there was the responsibility to ensure that information on matters of national security was held securely and beyond the reach of potential miscreants. Second, there was the job of ensuring that full records of public affairs were maintained, archived, and accessible to authorized persons.

Over the past decade, there has been a clear shift in UK government policy in relation to information generated from within or on behalf of the public sector. In summary, the UK government has shown a commitment to making official information more easily accessible. There are two main strands of thinking here. One is that government should be more open: this has given rise to the freedom of information (FOI) regime. This is about providing *access* to information. The other strand is that public sector information (PSI) can and should be *re-used* where benefits can accrue. FOI and PSI re-use together are the fundamental building blocks of what many call 'information age government'. This is not merely about making formal government publications available online. It is about capturing, nurturing, and maintaining much of the information generated by public sector bodies as a common and easily accessible good for all of society. At a policy level, these developments will combine to bring about an entirely new landscape for the management and control of information in the public sector. It is far from clear, however, that most senior officials and politicians are yet alive to the cumulative shift in policy and practice. Nor is there evidence of analysis of the long-term implications of these changes.

That said, the last decade has undeniably witnessed enormous change, to a large extent catalysed by the advent of the Internet which is steadily, fundamentally, and globally changing the relationship between the individual and the State. Before the 1990s, most government was closed government—official information was made available largely on a need-to-know basis. Restricting the flow of information was clearly central to totalitarian rule, for example. But benevolent democracies also held back, adopting a paternalist posture, releasing information sparingly. Perhaps it was not in people's interests to know too much. Anti-paternalists claim the problem was, rather, that there were no effective channels for fuller information flows between citizen and government. But this changed in the 1990s with the coming of the Internet. Suddenly, information could be shared widely and cheaply. And, in 1996 and 1997, the Conservative and Labour governments stated their commitment to providing official information on the Web. Why? Was it that the Internet made it all but impossible for government to resist greater openness? Or was there, coincidentally, some new political will to make public affairs more transparent? Either way, open government arrived.[44]

I argue that there are two types of open government. A reactive open government, when faced with a request for access to official information, will respond favourably. Request leads to access. In contrast, a proactive open government believes that an integral part of the job is to make all information created in the process of governing available to the people. Proactive open government is much more than meeting, more or less willingly, a request for access. Instead, it is regarding the provision, usually online, of all official information as part of the very business of government. Withholding information is looked upon as exceptional and requiring justification. The UK government is currently moving from being reactively to proactively open. One sign of this is the drive to provide more useful and better stocked websites. Another is that, under freedom of information legislation, all public authorities must maintain publication schemes which indicate what information will be made available proactively. However, full-scale proactivity will require a positive effort on the part of public authorities actually to maximize the value of their information, not just in terms of financial return but in terms also of social utility. A vital step in this direction was the adoption, at the end of 2003, of the EU Directive on the Re-use of Public Sector Information.[44] After extensive consultation, the government decided to implement this Directive through the Re-use of Public Sector Information

---

[44] (2003/98).

Regulations 2005, which came into force on 1 July 2005. It was also decided that there was a need for a dedicated body to be the principal focal point for advising on and regulating the operation of public sector information re-use. The Office of Public Sector Information was established for that purpose,[45] a body that is itself assisted by the Advisory Panel on Public Sector Information (APPSI), of which I was Chair from 2003 until 2008.[46] The Panel is a Non-Departmental Public Body, established by the Cabinet Office in April 2003 and now attached to the Ministry of Justice. Informally, its strap-line is 'realising the value of public sector information'. This intentionally trades on two different meanings of 'realising'. The Panel's focus is on identifying, articulating, and raising awareness of the value of PSI as well as on encouraging its exploitation.

APPSI has found, in relation to the re-use of PSI, that there are two broad challenges. The first is to ensure that core public sector information is made available, under appropriate conditions, to intermediaries who can add value to it. The second challenge is more radical—it is about information management and knowledge management on a grand scale. It is about making sure that the valuable collective knowledge and experience (the intellectual capital) of public sector workers is captured and re-used. Today it is barely managed and is under-exploited. In a sense, knowledge has become disposable. I submit that systematic recycling is instead required.

There are vital lessons here for those who are committed to promoting greater access to justice. Swilling around our public sector, substantially unmanaged, are legal resources and other data that could be invaluable for intermediaries (academics, charities, businesses, and others) who are trying to repurpose this raw material and develop systems that provide legal information and guidance. There seem to be no limits to the ingenuity of people who work with the Web. My strong intuition, from years in the field, and this is the first lesson, is that if we make legal and regulatory information readily available and easily accessible, then exciting developments will follow. BAILII is one clear illustration of this. BAILII indeed is an early and fine example of the re-use of PSI. The raw material, in the form of statutes and law reports, was brought together and subjected to remarkable technology that was developed by Australian academics. A new, extremely valuable information resource was thereby created and is now available to all. More than this, where BAILII has been of immense significance, the service has actually

---

[45] <http://www.opsi.gov.uk>.
[46] <http://www.appsi.gov.uk>.

brought about a shift in the government's approach to statutory material and law reports—a shift from being reactive to being proactive. Source materials for inclusion in BAILII, whether legislation or law reports, are now provided *as a matter of course*; it is part of the process of government (of the Ministry of Justice and OPSI). BAILII is not just about making legal information available to lawyers and citizens, which in itself is of great note. More than this, it is a very early example of a fundamental shift in the nature of government, a shift towards thoroughgoing proactivity.

In the spirit of BAILII, and following the discussion of the previous section, I can easily imagine a wide range of wiki-like, open source services sprouting across the Web, each underpinned by the core legal data that have been released and organized not according to the traditional categories of the legal textbook but built around the life events of citizens (job loss, house moving, borrowing money, setting up pensions, divorce, and so forth).

The second lesson we can learn from experience in the world of PSI relates to knowledge management. And the opportunity here may be even greater. In their everyday work, public sector workers deal with legal and regulatory matters all the time. In so doing, invaluable insight, analysis, and research are produced. If we could capture just a fraction of this collective knowledge and make it available to citizens in a digestible form, then we might contribute immensely to the promotion of access to justice. In terms of my Client Service Chain (see Section 7.1), I can see that this knowledge, if made available via the Web, could be of particular help to citizens in helping them to recognize that they need or would benefit from legal guidance and in sorting out their own legal challenges on an online self-service basis.

Gathering and providing this public sector knowledge would be a huge step towards proactive open government. But it would require a seismic shift in culture in the public sector workplace. Officials and civil servants, amongst many others, would now be asked to view their work in a new way. Beyond the discharge of their daily work in the normal manner, we would be asking them, as a by-product of this work, to identify, capture, and nurture knowledge that they think could be of use to the citizen. I am not sure whether this is too much to ask. I am suggesting that it should be incumbent on all public bodies to promote greater understanding of the legal and regulatory issues with which they deal, to explain and shed light on complex issues and, vitally, to strive to alert citizens to developments in the law that might be relevant for them.

Legal knowledge and experience, as generated in the course of public work, should not be secreted and locked in heads, filing cabinets, or databases; instead, it should be shared with tax-payers; with the citizens in whose interests the law is created in the first place. The purpose of this sharing is not simply to give citizens sight of more documents. Rather, in the spirit of Web 2.0, it is to make public information available as a raw material that citizens, entrepreneurs, charitable bodies and many others can fashion, re-organize, and supplement for their own purposes. Public bodies will be providing the raw information upon which communities of interest and citizen-generated content will be built.

8

Conclusion—the Future of Lawyers

The future for lawyers could be prosperous or disastrous. The arguments and findings of this book can support either end game. I predict that lawyers who are unwilling to change their working practices and extend their range of services will, in the coming decade, struggle to survive. Meanwhile, those who embrace new technologies and novel ways of sourcing legal work are likely to trade successfully for many years yet, even if they are not occupied with the law jobs that most law schools currently anticipate for their graduates.

I believe that lawyers, in order to survive and prosper, must respond creatively and forcefully to the shifting demands of what is a rapidly evolving legal marketplace. In this chapter, I revisit some of the market forces that are at play and suggest what this means for various branches of the legal profession. I then go on to identify what types of legal businesses and lawyers will thrive in the new order.

I make no attempt at this stage to précis the entire book. My main emphasis instead is on questions that flow from its title, *The End of Lawyers?*[1] Will the changes I identify bring about the end of lawyers? Or will a new and reinvigorated legal profession emerge?

---

[1] I reiterate that the question mark in the title is intended to confirm that this book is an inquiry into whether lawyers have a future rather than a prediction of their demise. Contrast N Postman, *The End of Education* (New York: Vintage, 1995) and A Kessler, *The End of Medicine* (New York: Collins, 2006).

8.1 The prognosis

My starting point for this final analysis is clients, especially in-house lawyers. Invariably, General Counsel tell me that they are now under three pressures: to reduce the size of their in-house legal teams; to spend less on external law firms; and to find ways of coping with more and riskier legal and compliance work than they have had in the past. Both internally and externally, clients are requiring *more for less*. From 2004 to 2007, I found this to be a running, background theme in my discussions with in-house lawyers. In 2008, in the slipstream of the economic downturn, it has become not so much a theme as an overriding imperative.

For law firms, these pressures on clients and the imperative that follows have disturbing implications. Increasingly, for example, firms are being called upon to reduce their fees, to undertake work on a fixed fee rather than an hourly billing basis, and to be far more transparent in their dealings with clients. Also they are coming to be selected, more than occasionally, on the advice of hard-nosed, in-house procurement specialists in client organizations rather than by old friends and colleagues. The legal market looks set to be a buyer's market for the foreseeable future.

At the same time, new competitors are emerging, such as outsourcers and entrepreneurial publishers; while liberalization of the legal market will bring external funding and a new wave of professional managers and investors who have no nostalgic commitment to traditional business models for law firms, including hourly billing and gearing obtained through the deployment of armies of hard-working young lawyers.

To cap it all, a number of disruptive legal technologies are emerging (such as document assembly, closed communities, legal open-sourcing, and embedded legal knowledge—see Chapter 4) which will directly challenge and sometimes even replace the traditional work of lawyers.

For many lawyers, therefore, it looks as if the party may soon be over.

I anticipate that the market is likely to respond in two ways to the changes just noted. First, new methods, systems, and processes will emerge to reduce the cost of undertaking routine legal work. This will extend well beyond the back-offices of legal businesses into the very heart of legal work. As I explain in Chapter 2, I expect there to be a strong pull by the market away from the delivery of legal advice on a bespoke basis. To achieve the efficiencies needed, I say that legal services will evolve from bespoke services at one end of a spectrum along a path, passing through the following stages: standardization, systematization, packaging, and commoditization. Many new ways of sourcing will emerge and these will often be combined in the conduct of individual pieces of legal work. I call this multi-sourcing. These changes will affect not just high volume, low value work but also the routine elements of high value work.

The second response by the market will be for clients, in various ways, to share the costs of legal services. Again, this will affect the entire market. In-house lawyers, I suggest, will frequently work together, often as part of online closed communities (see Section 4.7), and find ways of recycling legal work amongst themselves. In areas where their duplication of effort and expense is considerable, such as regulatory compliance, they will collaborate intensively and so spread the legal expense amongst their number. At the other end of the spectrum, citizens will have ready access to online legal guidance and to growing bodies of legal materials that are available on an open source basis (see Sections 4.6 and 7.3). More, they will be able to share legal experiences with one another.

With clients cutting costs and finding alternative ways of sourcing work or sharing costs and collaborating regularly with one another, what does this mean for lawyers? On the strength of the arguments and findings of this book, I predict that there will be five types of lawyer in the future.

The first will be the 'expert trusted adviser'. This is the purveyor of bespoke legal service. The arguments of this book suggest that market pressures will generally discourage lawyers from handling matters in a bespoke manner wherever this is possible. Instead, standardized or computerized service will be preferred. However, on some occasions bespoke work will be unavoidable. For the foreseeable future, intelligent creative lawyers will be needed in certain circumstances—to fashion new solutions for clients who have novel, complex, or high value challenges (the expert element) and to communicate guidance in a highly personalized way (the trusted component) where this is wanted. The end of the expert trusted adviser is not therefore in sight. The danger facing many lawyers, however, is to assume that their clients' work always requires this expert or trusted treatment. Lawyers who handcraft while their competitors introduce new efficiencies (computerizing or outsourcing, for example) will not be practising in ten years' time, because bespoke service is a luxury that clients will not generally be able to afford.

My second category of lawyer for the future will be the 'enhanced practitioner'. This is the individual whose legal skills and knowledge are required not to deliver a bespoke service but, enhanced by modern techniques, to work further to the right-hand side of the evolutionary path that I introduce in Section 2.1. This lawyer will be supporting the delivery of standardized, systematized, and (when in-house) packaged legal service. The crucial point here, though, is that the market will only tolerate this lawyer's involvement where legal experience is genuinely needed. Otherwise, other less costly sources of support will be favoured, such as paralegals, legal executives, and legal process outsourcing service providers. Today, clients frequently pay lawyers to do work that intelligent and trained non-lawyers could undertake. This will stop in years to come and the need for lawyers who perform routine work will diminish accordingly.

In contrast, there will be a much greater need for my third category of lawyer—the 'legal knowledge engineer'. If I am right and legal service will increasingly be standardized and (in various ways) computerized, then people with great talent are going to be needed, in droves, to organize the large quantities of complex legal content and processes that will need to be analysed, distilled, and then embodied in standard working practices and computer systems. This new line of work will need highly skilled lawyers. The development of standard documents or procedures and the organization and representation of legal knowledge in computer systems is, fundamentally, a job of legal research and analysis; and often this knowledge engineering will be more intellectually demanding than conventional work (working out a system that can solve many problems is generally more taxing than finding an answer to one problem). It is entirely misconceived to think, as many lawyers do, that work on standards and systems can be delegated to junior research or support lawyers. If a legal business is going to trade on the strength of outstanding standards and systems, then it will need outstanding lawyers involved in their design and development. These legal knowledge engineers will also be needed to undertake another central task—the basic analysis and decomposition of legal work that I claim will be required if legal work is to be multi-sourced effectively and responsibly. Legal knowledge engineering, in the twenty-first century, will not be a fringe show at the edge of the legal market. It will be a central occupation for tomorrow's lawyers.

Fourth will be the 'legal risk manager'. This category of lawyer is sorely needed and is long overdue. Senior in-house lawyers around the world insist that they are in the business of legal risk management—clients prefer avoiding legal problems rather than resolving them. And yet, as I say in Section 6.7, hardly a lawyer or law firm on the planet has chosen to develop methods, tools, techniques, or systems to help their clients review, identify, quantify, and control the legal risks that they face. I expect this to change. Urgent demand from the market will lead lawyers (perhaps bolstered and emboldened by external funding) to offer a wide range of proactive legal services whose focus will be on anticipating and pre-empting legal problems. This will be quite different from legal work that concentrates on addressing specific deals or disputes. In some ways more like a form of strategy consulting, this legal work will be wider ranging and more generic, helping clients to prepare more responsibly for the future. Again, this is not a peripheral job for the legal fraternity. This could fundamentally change the way in which the law is practised and administered.

My final category of future lawyer is the 'legal hybrid'. My premise here is that successful lawyers of the future, wherever they sit on my evolutionary path, will be increasingly multi-disciplinary. Many already claim that they are deeply steeped in neighbouring disciplines, as project managers, strategy and management consultants, market experts, deal-brokers, and more. In truth, though, these forays into other fields are not strategically conceived, formally planned, or supported by rigorous training. They are rather ad hoc and piecemeal initiatives. In contrast, legal hybrids of the future will be superbly schooled and genuinely expert in these related disciplines and will be able to extend the range of the services they provide in a way that adds value for their clients.

Taking these five categories together, it is clear that there will be work for lawyers to do in the future. What is much less obvious is whether today's lawyers will be equipped to take on the jobs I envisage. While the expert trusted adviser and the enhanced practitioner look much like contemporary lawyers, I predict that their number will be greatly reduced. The range of work of the expert trusted adviser will be reduced by standardization and computerization, while the enhanced practitioner's domain will be diminished by the emergence of alternative, lower cost individuals who can work responsibly with standards and systems. In some areas of law, lawyers will be less dominant, while in others (where there are, for example, online legal services or there is legal open-sourcing), they will no longer have a role. If the demand for conventional lawyers is reduced, I wonder how easily those whose jobs are threatened will be able to re-skill and become legal knowledge engineers, legal risk managers, or legal hybrids. The transition may not be easy.

In general terms, and to answer the question posed in the title of this book, I do not therefore anticipate (in the next twenty or thirty years at least) that there will be no lawyers. I expect instead that there will be significantly fewer lawyers providing traditional consultative advisory service; and I predict the emergence of new legal professionals with quite different roles in society. We will witness the end of many lawyers as we know and recognize them today and the birth of a new streamlined and technology-based generation of practising lawyers who are fit for purpose in the twenty-first century.

In very broad terms, it seems to me that solicitors and in-house lawyers whose work is largely routine are those most threatened by the future I am predicting. There will soon be less costly and more convenient ways of delivering the service that today is their preserve. Of course, there are many solicitors and in-house lawyers who are highly specialized or are retained because of their special insight or their closeness to the business. For these advisers, the outlook is rather rosier but lawyers must be honest with themselves and recognize frankly when their work might be sourced differently.

The future of the work that is currently undertaken by barristers is generally encouraging. Most of this activity is highly bespoke and it is hard to see how oral advocacy and the dispensing of expert advice can be standardized or computerized. Dispute avoidance and online dispute resolution will chip away at some of this domain but I do not see these as eliminating advocacy entirely. Of greater concern to barristers in chambers should be major law firms who decide to resist the move to the right on my evolutionary path (Section 2.1) and instead build a far greater bespoke capability. This may involve amassing teams of high-powered legal solicitors with skills and expertise that rival those of barristers or it may entail the recruitment of barristers to these firms (which raises questions about the best business vehicles for the delivery of legal services—see Section 8.2).

A common response to much that I say, by cynics, sceptics, and doubters, runs simply and as follows—*computers cannot replace legal work*. Full stop. I will leave to one side the fact that this really is a gross oversimplification of my thesis, in that it ignores what I say about standardization, commoditization, and the transfer of many legal tasks from lawyers to non-lawyers. But even as a claim only about the impact of technology on lawyers, it is weak. I respond in two parts.

First of all, my interest is manifestly not in some wholesale, monolithic substitution of legal advisers by information technology(IT). Instead my focus, as far as IT is concerned, is on the extent to which some, much, or all of what lawyers do can be undertaken more quickly, less expensively, more conveniently, and in a less forbidding way by systems than by conventional work.

The question I therefore prefer to ask in this context is—from the clients' point of view, what tasks of lawyers will be better undertaken in the future by systems? It is a foolhardy lawyer indeed who unreflectively and dogmatically replies to this question by asserting 'none whatsoever'. Open-minded lawyers, and ones who genuinely care about the interests of their clients should, in the Internet age, continually be looking at ways in which IT can play a more prominent role in their services. And all of my experience, of working with innumerable law firms and in-house legal departments, leads me to claim that there is remarkable scope for greater deployment of technology. More radically, though, I do contend that for some lawyers, there are existing and emerging technologies whose widespread adoption will effectively render them redundant. (Much the same has happened in many other sectors; lawyers are not immune from the destructive effects of the Internet and IT revolutions.)

I call technologies that threaten the work of today's lawyers and law firms 'disruptive legal technologies' (see Chapter 4). They do not support or complement current legal practices. They challenge and replace them, in whole or in part. This leads to the second part of my response to the non-believers. Most of the disruptive technologies that I identify (such as document assembly, personalized alerting, online dispute resolution, and open-sourcing) are phenomena of which most practising lawyers are only dimly aware. Also bear in mind that my predictions, in this book and in *The Future of Law*, are long-term predictions, stretching to 2016 and beyond. If lawyers are barely conversant with today's technologies, they have even less sense of how much progress in legal technology is likely in the coming ten years. Politely, it puzzles me profoundly that lawyers who know little about current and future technologies can be so confident about their inapplicability. To be able to claim responsibly that IT will have no or minimal effect on lawyers, as many do, surely requires some considerable depth of insight into what disruptive technologies do and will do in years to come. My purpose in writing my book is precisely to provide that insight.

I mention open-mindedness on the part of lawyers. I can honestly say that I know of no lawyer who has devoted serious time to exploring the impact of IT on the legal profession who has later abandoned legal technology and resumed normal business. On the contrary, lawyers who take the time to delve deeply into the possibilities invariably become committed advocates and practitioners. The commitment does not come, generally, in a matter of days or weeks. It takes, I find, months of study and exposure to practical case studies for the conversion to take place.

Just as research by the Oxford Internet Institute suggests that people who have the least experience of the Web are those who are generally most distrustful of it,[2] I find a similar situation amongst lawyers. Often, the most vociferous opponents of the Internet, those who see no possible application for emerging technologies in their firms, are precisely those who have near zero exposure to the systems in question. Just as in law, however, ignorance here should be no defence. There really is no merit whatsoever in blindly rejecting a set of new developments whose nature and scope are simply not understood.

---

[2] W Dutton and E Helsper, *The Internet in Britain* 2007 (Oxford: Oxford Internet Institute, 2007).

Moving away now from practising lawyers, sceptical or otherwise, no analysis of the future of lawyers would be complete without some reflection on academic lawyers. In the first instance, it is clear that legal research has been transformed through technology. Whether as a top-notch scholar or a research student, the tools and facilities now available are wildly different from those of the past. An unparalleled range of resources are now to hand, delivered largely across the Internet. It is hard to imagine now the hassle involved in legal research two decades ago and more. We were largely constrained by the materials available in the libraries on the campuses in which we worked, with cumbersome and time-consuming processes to invoke if we wished to secure publications from elsewhere.

For many legal scholars engaged in serious legal research, however, electronic mail and virtual communities are even more significant than the greatly extended volumes and resources that are available. When I worked on my doctorate in the 1980s, there was a lady at Stanford University in California who was beavering away on a thesis along similar lines. During the three years, we met once, and exchanged a few letters and, I for one, was frustrated that we could not interact more regularly. If we were working on our theses today, I suspect we would be in almost daily contact by e-mail and participating together, no doubt, in various groups on a social network or two. Scholars need no longer be isolated islands of solitary reflection; they can join or engage in far more cooperative and communal discussions and debates—through social networks and blogs, for example. At the same time, academics think differently about publishing. In the 1980s, for example, it was common to wait over a year before a submitted manuscript appeared in print. Today, while conventional journals remain important, the legal blogosphere is a more immediate mechanism for rapidly sharing ideas. At the same time, we are able to use the Internet as a way of pre-publishing materials, so that ideas, theories, and findings can be publicized electronically prior to formal publication.

I am greatly enthused by the extent of the take-up of technology by academics involved with legal research. I am much less confident that our law professors are sufficiently exploiting emerging technologies (such as e-learning—see Section 4.4) in the teaching of our law students. More worrying still, I fear that few law schools are preparing our future lawyers for the very different legal workplace that I and others are predicting. Few law students have any sense of the likely impact or relevance of, for example, the commoditization of legal services, multi-sourcing, or disruptive legal technologies. Law firms should encourage law schools to expose their students to likely trends and to think deeply about the new skills that will be needed in practice.[3]

A discussion of the future of lawyers would also be incomplete without another quick detour that looks at the key tool of their trade—the law book. I am often asked whether law books will survive. As a bibliophile and a gadget collector, I am torn. On the one hand, one of my favourite gadgets is a digital book by Sony, known as the Reader. It is lightweight, the size of a DVD box, with a print and paper-like display and it can hold hundreds of books. It can connect to the Internet and can handle sound and image. So why bother with legal tomes? Perhaps, many years from now, we will not. Many lawyers already prefer online law reports to conventional volumes, while the business of producing books has become secondary to online services for many legal publishers. Researching electronically is becoming natural and when lawyers do want paper, they can print important pages. However, the old counter-arguments remain: we like the touch, odour, and aura of books and libraries; books are pleasant to own and collect; reading a book seems easier and less prone to error than viewing on screen; and it is convenient to have many books open at once. So, nostalgia, tradition, and some plausible practicalities may keep law books on the go for some time yet. There is another reason that the printed page may not die for some time—unlike online resources, traditional articles and books are reassuringly finite. You know where you stand with print. The end is always in sight and in hand. Contents and index pages provide clear signposts and, although footnotes and bibliographies may send you scurrying for more, at least the original source is clearly bounded. Browsing the Web, even in authoritative and well conceived sites, is generally a more open-ended business. The innumerable links and the essential interconnectedness often give users a sense of a job never finished.[4] It is not unusual to feel lost in cyberspace. After all, there are countless billions of pages out there.

On balance, though, my prediction is that, over the next twenty years, sales of substantive law books will greatly reduce. As display technology, storage, and search improve, it will become increasingly quaint and inefficient to reach for the book shelf. For readers who think this unlikely, think for a moment how few people of today consult traditional print-based encyclopaedias.

---

[3] On new skills see Gene Koo, 'New Skills, New Learning: Legal Education & the Promise of Technology', The Berkman Center for Internet & Society at Harvard Law School (March 2007).

[4] This is so despite the witty end-of-Internet page at <http:www.shibumi.org/eoti.htm>.

8.2 The implications

What are the implications, for the business of law, of the predictions that I make about the future work of lawyers? Three issues spring immediately to mind. The first concerns the structure and size of legal businesses, the second relates to innovation, and the third is about the type of people who will be lawyers in the future. I deal with each in turn.

In relation to the structure of legal businesses, the traditional model for most law firms has been that of a pyramid—with equity partners (owners of the business) employing and running teams of junior lawyers. This provides leverage for the partners—they benefit financially not only from their own efforts but from the surplus profit that is created through the work of their junior lawyers. A highly geared firm will have more junior lawyers per equity partner than a lowly geared firm and, all other things being equal, will be correspondingly more profitable. In accordance with this prevailing business model, law firms can only retain their profitability if this pyramidic structure is kept in place and the broader the base, the better. However, in this book I am suggesting that there are alternative ways of sourcing the work that is currently performed by junior lawyers—for example by outsourcing or computerizing. In other words, many of the tasks currently undertaken by these junior lawyers, often in costly buildings in leading financial centres, can more efficiently (cheaply) be done elsewhere or differently. More, the pyramidic structure is often also recognized as a source of unhappiness within law firms—the work that is parcelled up and delegated to junior staff is often tedious drudgery, even if its discharge in quantity can be profitable. On the face of it, if the grunt work is outsourced or computerized, then the cost goes down and the sum of human happiness increases. A win-win? Perhaps it is for the client and the disgruntled employee but it is not for many law firms. What is involved here is rather fundamental—subcontracting or computerizing work will result in a different shape of business model underpinning law firms. In summary, legal businesses make much of their money today from leveraging their junior people; if that leverage is displaced, then the profits will dip.

Of course, not all areas of work can be outsourced or computerized or sourced in other ways, and so the threat is not generic. But, I maintain, much can and will. This will not finish law firms but will necessitate major structural change in the long run. For example, it may lead very large firms to give up routine work (or multi-source it) and to build instead a much narrower pyramid with a lower proportion of junior lawyers to partners. Profitability might be retained by seeking to charge more for the genuinely expert lawyers who are perched atop the pyramid dispensing bespoke advice. I can envisage various medium-sized firms merging to achieve a critical mass of experts, while divesting themselves of some of the junior lawyers who previously had been central to their business model. On this philosophy, though, I also expect that some very expert and experienced lawyers will leave large firms and set up niche practices, characterized by strong market reputation and track record, outstanding people, modest gearing, and very high hourly rates or fixed fees.

I fear for the future of very small firms whose work in not highly specialized—those with a handful of partners or even sole practitioners who are general practitioners. Unless their clients want to retain them for a highly personalized service, I cannot see how they will be able to compete with alternative methods of sourcing, whether by much larger law firms or by alternative providers.

The business model that supports the work of barristers may also be subject to change. While these trusted expert advisers will still be in demand (according to my thinking at least), there may be other commercial structures from which they can operate. The current model at the Bar—the self-employed, sole practitioner, who shares various services with fellow barristers—assumes no gearing, little capacity to multi-source, and few mechanisms for hedging against the risks of being a one person band. There is probably scope here for running the shared services more effectively through various forms of alternative sourcing. But some barristers might find it more comfortable to move to the highly niche expert firms that I am predicting or even, as has already happened, to very large firms.

Whether or not the age-old split of the profession, between barristers and solicitors, makes sense in the legal world I foresee, I defer for discussion on another day. The premise for any such debate, however, should be open-mindedness and not a reactionary preference for the status quo.

As for innovation, it is apparent that lawyers are heading for a time of great change and so we should ask whether and how lawyers, firms, and the profession might be the authors of this transformation. Should lawyers be innovating? Or setting up research and development programmes to cope in the new world?

For the law firm, there are three broad ways in which it can innovate: in the way in which it delivers its services (perhaps through some ground-breaking online system); in the actual advice it offers (for instance, a novel form of contractual arrangement); or in the way the business is run (for example in the way in which graduates are recruited). In the context of this book, innovation in the first and second senses are relevant—I discuss the need to meet market demands by introducing new ways of sourcing legal work and note also that if lawyers want to live by bespoke work alone then they will need continually to develop imaginative new solutions.

I know from my work on legal technology, however, that lawyers do not find it easy to innovate, especially in the way in which they deliver their services. Historically, UK law firms have a stronger track record than US practices in technological innovation that benefits clients. The local market in the UK has been more competitive and there has been much stronger demand from clients. But how has innovation been achieved here? Management textbooks might suggest that these innovations will have flowed elegantly from the insights of management consultants, from lengthy strategy documents, from market research, and from away-days devoted to blue-sky, out-of-the-box, and lateral thinking. Not a bit of it. The reality is that the overwhelming number of innovations have evolved from the efforts of mavericks within law firms—energetic, often eccentric, frequently marginalized, invariably demanding, single-minded individuals who pursue ideas that are regarded in the early days as peripheral, irrelevant, and even wasteful. But the mavericks persevere and in their dining rooms or studies at home they beaver away, creating new forms of service for clients. Gradually, their innovations come to be recognized as significant and even client-winning. And soon, everyone claims that the mavericks had the firm's full support from the outset. A new discipline thus emerges—maverick management. This is the art of nurturing and encouraging mavericks, giving them space to innovate and wrapping some strategy and structure around their innovations only once their ideas have fully gestated. Mavericks are the research and development departments of many law firms.

Why have US firms exhibited an apparent indifference towards IT that directly helps clients? Generally, I have found that the major American firms have resisted serious investment beyond their own back-offices. They have often rejected knowledge systems and document assembly systems, for example, even though these can actually enhance or simplify client service. I believe they have done so because there has been little incentive to do otherwise. It is not easy to convince a group of millionaires within clear sight of retirement that their business model is wrong and that they should change direction and embrace new technologies. The top US law firms have been massively and satisfyingly profitable. Accordingly, they seem to be moved to change more by the threat of competitive disadvantage than by the promise of competitive advantage. Without hunger for change, without the worry of being left behind by the competition and, vitally, without clients clamouring for new forms of service, it will be business as usual for the US legal behemoths for many years yet unless the credit crunch hits hard. They will wring every last cent out of the increasingly unsustainable practice of hourly billing and will steer well clear of innovative IT. Unless, of course, clients demand otherwise.

Should lawyers be technology pioneers? When they hear, say, about the great promise of wikis and blogs, or of the likely impact of e-learning and automated document assembly, should legal practitioners reach enthusiastically for their cheque books or more reflectively for a stiff, single malt? Broadly, when new technologies loom, a law firm can embrace one of three strategies. The first is to resist. Whether grounded in fear, ignorance, conservatism or insight, the purpose of resistance is to delay investment, often in expectation that the technology has been over-hyped. Alternatively, many senior partners hope they can hold out until retirement before the latest systems engulf them. Either way, Ned Ludd would have been proud. The second strategy is to prepare. This may be a grudging preparation—for the fateful day when clients or competitors leave the firm with no option but to invest. Or it may be part of a master plan, according to which the firm is like a finely tuned track athlete, poised at the final bend to pass and surge away from the early pace-makers. The third strategy is indeed to pioneer, to lead the way, and in so doing to try to achieve first-mover advantage.

Successful pioneering in IT is not temporary pace-making. It is about continually striving to keep ahead of the pack and reaping substantial rewards as a result. In the world of IT, however, there is much debate about its benefits. The whimsical sceptics often say you can recognize the pioneers by the arrows in their backs. The pioneers, it is jested, work at the bleeding edge rather than the leading edge. Flippancies aside, a more profound challenge to pioneers was recently laid down by Constantinos Markides and Paul Geroski, of London Business School. They argue in their book, *Fast Second*, that pioneering thinkers of radically new business ideas do not necessarily excel in commercially exploiting them.[5] The idea of online bookselling came from an Ohio-based bookseller and not from Amazon. What about law? In truth, it is not yet clear whether it pays for lawyers to innovate and pioneer in IT. Did great benefits accrue to firms that led the way, for instance, in advanced financial systems, document management systems, or in human resource systems? Was the investment in the early bespoke systems worth it or might it have been better to wait for off-the-shelf solutions?

The systems just noted, no matter how trail-blazing, were for internal use within law firms. In contrast, competitive advantage will be achieved by firms

---

[5] C Markides and P Geroski, *Fast Second* (San Francisco: Jossey-Bass, 2004).

when the technologies in question touch the lives of their clients—by providing new ways of working together or in packaging legal advice as online or embedded offerings. If technology can help to deliver cheaper or better service, many clients will sign up. That said, client-facing pioneering is not sufficient to sustain advantage. The trick here is not just to deploy the first workable system but to make it impossible or unattractive for competitors to imitate, and inconvenient or undesirable for clients to switch allegiance.

Although this book anticipates a veritable revolution in the nature of legal services, the changes I predict and advocate will not come about in one big bang. Rather, through a process of what I like to call 'incremental revolution', lawyers and their clients will change their ways in significant steps rather than huge leaps, but collectively these steps will add up to a very different legal world.

What about the types of people who will be our best lawyers in the future? It follows from what I say in this book that tomorrow's lawyers can and should be far more efficient and business-like in the running of their practices; that they can and should be far more transparent in communicating with those that they advise and in exposing their working methods; and that large latent markets of unmet need can be realized and satisfied by delivering professional guidance as commoditized online service. The arguments and findings in this book call not only for a de-skilling and re-skilling of lawyers and for some fairly fundamental reconfiguration of legal businesses but, perhaps more fundamentally, for very different kinds of people working in the legal profession. I have been heavily influenced in my thinking in this context by an exceptionally thought-provoking book by Daniel Pink, *A Whole New Mind*.[6] Published in 2005, Pink argues that:

> The last few decades have belonged to a certain kind of person with a certain kind of mind – computer programmers who could crack code, lawyers who could craft contracts, MBAs who could crunch numbers. But the keys to the kingdom are changing hands. The future belongs to a very different kind of person with a very different kind of mind—creators and empathizers, pattern recognizers and meaning makers. These people—artists, inventors, designers, storytellers, caregivers, consolers, big picture thinkers—will now reap society's richest rewards and share its greatest joys.[7]

In themes that resonate with some of the central messages of this book, Pink imagines a world where automation and outsourcing are commonplace;

---

[6] D Pink, *A Whole New Mind* (London: Cyan, 2005).
[7] ibid 1.

and when goods and services are in such abundance that design rather than functionality distinguishes one from another. Applying Pink's thinking to the legal world, the keys to the kingdom, as he puts it, will pass from the traditional, analytical, logical legal mind to a more creative and imaginative cadre of lawyers. His thesis applied to law would suggest that much legal work will either be outsourced or automated, and that which remains will be distinguishable on grounds of packaging and presentation more than on expertise. This certainly reflects an observation frequently made by in-house lawyers—that most good law firms are indistinguishable in terms of their legal expertise. This knowledge is taken for granted. At beauty parades and in bids for work, it is the flair, style, and presentation that often distinguishes one from another. Looking forward, I expect this to continue to be the case in relation to what I call 'enhanced practitioners', although it may hold less with respect to the finest legal experts, operating at their rarefied heights of the largest deals and disputes in the kingdom.

Pink also argues his case by suggesting that there will be a shift away from the dominance of 'left brain' thinkers to those of greater 'right brain' capacity. There is some interesting overlap here with the set of observations I made in Section 5.1 in relation to lawyers' inability to empathize with their clients. If Pink's analysis is right, the legal world today is dominated by 'left brain' thinkers who will not find it easy to empathize. And, of course, there is an interesting correlation here between the 'male brain' and the 'female brain'. Following the analysis of Simon Baron-Cohen, in his first rate book, *The Essential Difference*, the typical male brain systematizes while the female brain empathizes.[8] Pulling all of these strands together, if my analysis in this book is sound, and the twin forces of commoditization and IT do indeed combine to create a legal environment in which much legal work is standardized and computerized, then we can well imagine that those individuals who are in future responsible for innovating, designing, marketing, and selling a multi-sourced legal service, will not be traditional, left brain males, but far more creative, innovative, artistic, and often female lawyers.

These individuals will inhabit a very different legal world, different not simply because lawyers will be drawn from a wider gene pool. The more fundamental difference—and we should not be deterred from noting this by dwelling too much on major law firms—is that a new interface will emerge between the non-lawyer and the law, between the citizen and the State. This is a central theme of the book. Traditionally, in a print-based industrial society

---

[8] S Baron-Cohen, *The Essential Difference* (Harmondsworth: Penguin, paperback edition, 2004).

with an advanced legal system, much of the law (legislation, case law, and standard practice) is inaccessible to most lay people. There is too much law, it is too complex, and its impact is often not at all obvious to the non-lawyer. The legal profession has evolved to help to manage, interpret, and apply the law. This body of lawyers has become the principal interface between the law and the people. However, I am suggesting that possible new interfaces are emerging, so that lawyers will not, in the long run, be the only means of securing access to legal understanding and justice. Indeed, it will transpire, for the ordinary affairs of most citizens, that lawyers are not even the dominant interface.

For many lawyers, the idea of new legal interfaces may seem anathema to the very nature of professional service. Some will argue that a truly professional service is an irreducibly human service. But what do clients think? From my various research and consulting projects, I have discerned two broad views of the legal professional. The first might be called the 'trust model', according to which clients put trust in legal professionals largely because of who they are perceived to be. Lawyers are considered to be experts with competence and state-of-the-art knowledge not possessed by lay people and, on this view, they are regarded as the benevolent custodians of the law and legal institutions, ideally qualified to guide non-lawyers in relevant legal intricacies. But there is a second view and this I call the 'George Bernard Shaw model'. In accordance with this, as Shaw famously noted, 'all professions are conspiracies against the laity'. This view regards legal professionals not as benevolent custodians, but as jealous guards, who have for too long hindered access to the law and legal processes.

On balance, I think it is unhelpful to generalize about the motives of lawyers across the profession. I have little doubt that, within the legal population, there are both benevolent custodians and jealous guards. Either way, I do feel passionately that if IT-based services or other forms of sourcing can give rise to a quicker, better, more widely available, or cheaper service than that offered today, then I support these innovations wholeheartedly, even if their effect is financially disadvantageous to some lawyers.

Bibliography

This bibliography is divided into two parts. The first is brief and can be regarded as identifying some essential reading materials, while the second is a longer listing which should serve as a more general reference resource.

Section 1

The books listed in this section have very greatly influenced my thinking over the past 12 years, since the publication in 1996 of *The Future of Law*. I regard them as required reading for anyone who is taking the future seriously.

Benkler, Y, *The Wealth of Networks* (New Haven: Yale University Press, 2006).

Christensen, C, *The Innovator's Dilemma* (Boston: Harvard Business School Press, 1997).

Friedman, TL, *The World is Flat* (London: Penguin, updated and expanded edn, 2006).

Katsh, E and Rifkin, J, *Online Dispute Resolution* (San Francisco: Jossey-Bass, 2001).

Kurzweil, R, *The Singularity is Near* (New York: Viking, 2005).

Levy, F and Murnane, RJ, *The New Division of Labour* (New York: Russell Sage Foundation, 2004).

Pink, D, *A Whole New Mind* (London: Cyan, 2005).

Shapiro, C and Varian, H, *Information Rules* (Boston: Harvard Business School Press, 1999).

Section 2

This section of the bibliography presents the full references for all books, reports, and articles referred to in the body of the text that are published conventionally in print or on the Web.

Amis, M, *The Second Plane* (London: Jonathan Cape, 2008).

Anderson, C, *The Long Tail* (London: Random House, 2006).

Aristotle, *Nicomachean Ethics* (trans, Irwin, T) (Indianapolis: Hackett, 2nd edn, 1999).

Baron-Cohen, S, *The Essential Difference* (Harmondsworth: Penguin, paperback edn, 2004).

Battelle, J, *The Search* (London: Nicholas Brealey, 2005).

Benkler, Y, *The Wealth of Networks* (New Haven: Yale University Press, 2006).

Bentham, J, *Of Laws In General*, Hart, HLA (ed) (London: The Athlone Press, 1970).

Bray, DA *et al*, 'Sermo: A Community-Based, Knowledge Ecosystem', Oxford Internet Institute, Distributed Problem-Solving Networks Conference (February 2008), available at <http://ssrn.com/abstract=1016483>.

Cabinet Office, *Crown Copyright in the Information Age* (Cm 3819, 1998).

Cabinet Office, *Future Management of Crown Copyright* (Cm 4300, 1999).

Capper, PN and Susskind, RE, *Latent Damage Law—The Expert System* (London: Butterworths, 1988).

Chandler, M, 'State of Technology in the Law', address at Northwestern University 34th Annual Securities Regulation Institute, January 2007, available at <http://blogs.cisco.com/news/comments/cisco_general_counsel_on_state_of_technology_in_the_law>.

Chandler, M and Lippe, P, 'Five Ways In-house Counsel Can Talk to Law Firms' *ACC Docket* No 10 (November/December 2005) 74.

Christensen, C, *The Innovator's Dilemma* (Boston: Harvard Business School Press, 1997).

Christensen, C and Raynor, ME, *The Innovator's Solution* (Boston: Harvard Business School Press, 2003).

Clementi, D, *Report of the Review of the Regulatory Framework for Legal Services in England and Wales* (Final Report, December 2004), available at <http://www.legal-services-review.org.uk>.

Cooper, A, *The Inmates are Running the Asylum* (Indianapolis: SAMS, 1999).

Cresswell, P *et al*, 'Modernising the Civil Courts—The Judges' Requirements' (2001), available at <http://www.courtservice.gov.uk>.

Deloitte, 'Information Risk Benchmarking Survey' (October 2007), available at <http://www.deloitte.co.uk>.

Department for Communities and Local Government, 'Third Sector Strategy for Communities and Local Government', Discussion Paper (London, June 2007), available at <http://www.communities.gov.uk>.

Dreyfus, HL and Dreyfus, SE, *Mind over Machine* (New York: The Free Press, 1986).

Dutton, W and Helsper, EJ, *The Internet in Britain* 2007 (Oxford: Oxford Internet Institute, 2007).

Ehrlich, E, *Fundamental Principles of the Sociology of Law* (New York: Arno Press, reprint edn, 1975).

Eversheds, *Law firm of the 21st Century* (2008), available at <http://www.eversheds.com>.

Friedman, TL, *The World is Flat* (London: Penguin, updated and expanded edn, 2006).

Fuller, L, *The Morality of Law* (New Haven: Yale University Press, revised edn, 1964).

Garreau, J, *Radical Evolution* (New York: Doubleday, 2004).

Genn, H, *Paths to Justice* (Oxford: Hart, 1999).

Gilmore, JH and Pine, BJ (eds), *Markets of One* (Boston: Harvard Business School Press, 2000).

Gladwell, M, *The Tipping Point* (London: Abacus, 2000).

Gray, J, *Men are from Mars, Women are from Venus* (London: Thorsons, 1992).

Greenberg, D, 'The Volume and Complexity of United Kingdom Legislation Today' in Hetherington, S (ed), *Halsbury's Laws of England Centenary Essays 2007* (London: LexisNexis, 2007).

Hart, HLA, *The Concept of Law* (Oxford: Oxford University Press, 2nd edn, 1994).

HM Government, *Modernising Justice: The Government's Plans for Reforming Legal Services and the Courts* (Cm 4155, 1998), available at <http://www.justice.gov.uk>.

HM Government, *Your Right to Know: the Government's proposals for a Freedom of Information Act* (Cm 3818, 1997), available at <http:// www.justice.gov.uk>.

Hodkinson, P, 'E-auctions: reviewing the review' *Legal Week*, 9 June 2005.

House of Commons Committee of Public Accounts, *Government on the Internet: Progress in delivering information and services online* (Sixteenth Report of Session 2007–08, 29 April 2008, HC 143).

Joy, B, 'Why the Future Doesn't Need Us' *Wired*, April 2000.

Kafka, F, *The Trial* (Harmondsworth: Penguin, 1983).

Kafka, F, 'Before the Law' in *A Country Doctor* (Prague: Twisted Spoon Press, 1997).

Katsh, E, and Rifkin, J, *Online Dispute Resolution* (San Francisco: Jossey-Bass, 2001).

Kay, J, *The Truth About Markets* (London: Penguin, 2003).

Keen, A, *The Cult of the Amateur* (London: Nicholas Brealey, 2007).

Kelly, K, 'We are the Web' *Wired*, August 1995, 96.

Kessler, A, *The End of Medicine* (New York: Collins, 2006).

Kim, WC, and Mauborgne, R, *Blue Ocean Strategy* (Boston: Harvard Business School Press, 2005).

Koo, G, 'New Skills, New Learning: Legal Education & the Promise of Technology', The Berkman Center for Internet & Society at Harvard Law School (March 2007).

Kurzweil, R, *The Singularity is Near* (New York: Viking, 2005).

Leadbetter, C, *We-Think* (London: Profile, 2008).

Leblebici, H, 'Your Income' in Laura Empson (ed), *Managing the Modern Law Firm* (Oxford: Oxford University Press, 2007).

Leith, P and McCullagh, K, 'Developing European Legal Information Markets based on Government Information' (2004) 12(3) *International Journal of Law and Information Technology* 247.

Lessig, L, *Code: Version 2.0* (New York: Basic Books, 2006).

Levett, T, 'Production-line Approach to Service' (September-October 1972) *Harvard Business Review* 41.

Levy, F and Murnane, RJ, *The New Division of Labour* (New York: Russell Sage Foundation, 2004).

LexisNexis Martindale-Hubbell, 'European Study 2006: How mid-sized companies in Europe select and review their legal service providers' (LexisNexis Martindale-Hubbell, 2006).

Lord Chancellor's Department, *civil.justice: resolving and avoiding disputes in the information age* (Consultation Paper, September 1998).

Lord Chancellor's Department, *civil.justice.2000: a vision of the civil justice system in the information age* (Strategy Paper, June 2000).

Lloyd, R, 'In-house Lawyer: The Power of One' *Legal Week*, 29 May 2008.

Lodder, AR and Zeleznikoff, J, 'Developing an Online Dispute Resolution Environment: Dialogue Tools and Negotiation Support Systems in a Three-Step Model' (Spring 2005) 10 *Harvard Negotiation Law Review* 287.

Maharg, P, *Transforming Legal Education* (Aldershot: Ashgate, 2007).

Markides, C and Geroski, P, *Fast Second* (San Franciso: Jossey-Bass, 2004).

Mayson, S, 'Legal Services Reforms: Catalyst, Cataclysm or Catastrophe', Legal Services Policy Institute (21 March 2007).

Ministry of Justice, 'The extent and value of pro bono work provided by legal executives' (Ministry of Justice Research Series 2/08, February 2008), available at <http://www.justice.gov.uk>.

Moore, G, 'Cramming More Components onto Integrated Circuits' (1965) 38(8) *Electronics* 114.

Mountain, DR, 'Disrupting Conventional Law Firm Business Models Using Document Assembly' (Summer 2007) 15(2) *International Journal of Law and Information Technology* 170.

National Audit Office, *Government on the internet: progress in delivering information and services online* (13 July 2007, HC 529 Session 2006–07).

Negroponte, N, *Being Digital* (London: Hodder & Stoughton, 1995).

Niblett, B (ed), *Computer Science and Law* (Cambridge: Cambridge University Press, 1980).

Parsons, M, *Effective Knowledge Management for Law Firms* (New York: Oxford University Press, 2004).

Peltu, M and Wilks, Y, 'Close Engagements with Artificial Companions: Key Social, Psychological, Ethical and Design Issues', OII/e-Horizons Discussion Paper, No 14 (Oxford Internet Institute, January 2008).

Phillips, Lord, 'Alternative Dispute Resolution: an English Viewpoint', a speech given in India (29 March 2008), available at <http://www.judiciary.gov.uk>.

Pink, D, *A Whole New Mind* (London: Cyan, 2005).

PLEAS Task Force, 'Developing capable citizens: the role of public legal education' (July 2007), available at <http://www.pleas.org.uk>.

Pleasence, P, Balmer, N, and Buck, A, 'Causes of Action: Civil Law and Social Justice', LSRC Research Paper No 14 (Norwich: The Stationery Office, 2nd edn, 2006).

Postman, N, *The End of Education* (New York: Vintage, 1996).

Plotnikoff, J and Woolfson, R, 'Replacing the Judge's Pen? Evaluation of a Real-time Transcription System' (1993) 90 *International Journal of Law and Information Technology* 1.

Polanyi, M, 'The Logic of Tacit Inference' (1996) 41 *Philosophy* 1.

Popper, K, *Objective Knowledge* (Oxford: Oxford University Press, 1972).

Practical Lawyer Company, 'Technology: a ten-year view', a special report of PLC Law Department Quarterly (October–December 2007) 3(4), available at <http://www.practicallaw.com/lawdepartment>.

Pullman, P, *His Dark Materials* (London: Scholastic Press, 2001).

Quinn, BC and Adams, KA, 'Transitioning your Contract Process from the Artistic to the Industrial' *ACC Docket* (December 2007) 60.

Reed, RC (ed), *Beyond the Billable Hour: An Anthology of Alternative Billing Methods* (Chicago: American Bar Association, 1989).

Rheingold, H, *The Virtual Community* (Reading, Mass: Addison-Wesley, 1993).

Rheingold, H, *Smart Mobs* (Cambridge, Mass: Perseus, 2003).

Saville, Lord, 'Information and a public inquiry' in Saville, M and Susskind, R (eds), *Essays in Honour of Sir Brian Neill: The Quintessential Judge* (London: LexisNexis, 2003).

Saxby, S, 'Crown Copyright Regulation in the UK—Is the Debate Still Alive' (2005) 13(3) *International Journal of Law and Information Technology* 299.

Schank, RC, *Designing World-Class e-Learning* (New York, McGraw-Hill, 2002).

Schauer, F and Wise, VJ, 'Nonlegal Information and the Delegalization of Law' (2000) 29(1) *Journal of Legal Studies* 495.

Seidl, J *et al* (eds), *Legal Transformation Study: Your* 2020 *Vision of the Future* (Minneapolis: DSI and LRC, 2008).

Seidman, D, *HOW* (New Jersey: Wiley, 2007).

Shadbolt, N, Hall, W, and Berners-Lee, T, 'The Semantic Web Revisited' (May/June 2006) *IEEE Intelligent Systems* 96.

Shapiro, C and Varian, H, *Information Rules* (Boston: Harvard Business School Press, 1999).

Shapiro, C and Varian, H, 'Versioning: The Smart Way to Sell Information' in Gilmore, JH, and Pine, BJ (eds), *Markets of One* (Boston: Harvard Business School Press, 2000).

Siemer, DC, *Tangible Evidence* (Notre Dame, Indiana: National Institute for Trial Advocacy, 1996).

Siemer, DC and Land, DS, *Wilmer, Cutler & Pickering Manual on Litigation Support Databases* (New York: John Wiley, 2nd edn, 1989).

Siemer, DC, Rothschild, FD, Stein, ER, and Solomon, SH, *PowerPoint for Litigators* (Notre Dame, Indiana: National Institute for Trial Advocacy, 2000).

Sinniger, K, 'Low cost of going high-tech' *ACC Docket*, October 2003.

Spence, AM, 'Signaling in Retrospect and the Informational Structure of Markets', Nobel Prize Lecture, 8 December 2001.

Sprowl, JA, 'Automating the Legal Reasoning Process: A Computer that Uses Regulations and Statutes to Draft Legal Documents' (1979) 1 *American Bar Foundation Research Journal* 1.

Sunstein, CR, *Infotopia* (New York: Oxford University Press, 2006).

Surowiecki, J, *The Wisdom of Crowds* (London: Abacus, 2004).

Susskind, RE, *Expert Systems in Law* (Oxford: Oxford University Press, 1987; paperback edn, 1989).

Susskind, RE, 'Why lawyers should consider consultancy' *Financial Times*, 13 October 1992.

Susskind, RE, *The Future of Law* (Oxford: Oxford University Press, 1996; paperback edn, 1998).

Susskind, RE, *Transforming the Law* (Oxford: Oxford University Press, 2000; paperback edn, 2003).

Susskind, RE, 'Information technology and the criminal justice system' in Mirfield, P and Smith, R (eds), *Essays for Colin Tapper* (London: LexisNexis, 2003).

Susskind, RE (ed), *The Susskind Interviews: Legal Experts in Changing Times* (London: Thomson, 2005).

Susskind, RE, 'From Bespoke to Commodity' (2006) 1 *Legal Technology Journal* 4.

Tapscott D, and Williams, AD, *Wikinomics* (New York: Portfolio, 2006).

Varian, H, 'Competition and Market Power' in Varian, H, Farrell, J, and Shapiro, C (eds), *Economics of Information Technology* (New York: Cambridge University Press, 2004) 9.

Weber, S, *The Success of Open Source* (Cambridge, Mass: Harvard University Press, 2004).

Weizenbaum, J, *Computer Power and Human Reason* (Harmondsworth: Penguin, edition with new preface, 1984).

Welch, J, *Jack* (London: Headline, 2001).

Wilks, Y, 'What is the Semantic Web and what will it do for eScience', Research Report No 12, Oxford Internet Institute (October 2006).

Withers, W and Sheldon, R, 'Behind the Screen: the hidden life of youth online' (London, Institute for Public Policy Research, 2008).

Woolf, Lord, *Access to Justice—Interim Report*, Woolf Inquiry Team (June 2005), available at <http://www.justice.gov.uk>.

Woolf, Lord, *Access to Justice—Final Report*, Woolf Inquiry Team (July 2006), available at <http://www.justice.gov.uk>.

Index